W9-AYC-825

THE ILLUSTRATED HISTORY OF
FIREARMS
IN ASSOCIATION WITH THE NRA NATIONAL FIREARMS MUSEUM

JIM SUPICA • DOUG WICKLUND • PHILIP SCHREIER

Photography by
TERRY POPKIN

CHARTWELL
BOOKS

This edition published in 2011 by

Chartwell Books
an imprint of Book Sales
a division of Quarto Publishing Group USA
276 Fifth Avenue Suite 206
New York, New York 10001
USA
Reprinted 2012 (Three times), 2013 (Twice), 2014

Produced by TAJ Books International LLC
5501 Kincross Lane, Charlotte NC, 28277, USA
www.tajbooks.com

You can join the NRA by contacting them at:
The National Rifle Association of America
11250 Waples Mill Road Fairfax, VA 22030
or by visiting their Web site, www.nra.org
And you can view the treasures of the NRA National Firearms Museum at www.nramuseum.com.
The museum is open every day of the week, except major holidays, at NRA Headquarters in Fairfax VA, near Washington DC. There is no admission charge.

All notations of errors or omissions should be addressed to TAJ Books, 5501 Kincross Lane, Charlotte NC, 28277, USA, info@tajbooks.com.

ISBN-13: 978-0-7858-2738-2
ISBN-10: 0-7858-2738-2

Library of Congress Cataloging-in-Publication Data available on request.

Printed in China.

7 8 9 15 14

CONTENTS

The guns in this volume are from the 6,000 gun collection of the NRA National Firearms Museum located at NRA Headquarters at 11250 Waples Mill Rd. in Fairfax VA. The museum is open to the public every day of the week, and for 76 years has been free with no admission charge.

All guns on display can also be viewed at NRAmuseum.com, with zoomable detail photos and over 200 videos on historic firearms.

Where did these guns come from?

The Museum Collection has been built over three-quarters of a century through the support of millions of NRA members, and the generosity of donors who share the vision of preserving our nation's firearms treasures, and educating future generations on the true story of Americans and their guns.

Over 99% of the guns in the Museum Collection have been donated. Guns come in one or two at a time, or in quantity, including donations of large historically significant collections. They range from common specimens to pieces of great historic significance. Mamie Eisenhower brought in Ike's Winchester shotgun. Cornelius V.S. Roosevelt brought in his grandfather Theodore's engraved pistol (still loaded with a round in the chamber!).

Recently, the estate of well-known publisher Robert E. Petersen made the largest donation in NRA history with the gift of 400 exceptional firearms, now displayed in The Petersen Gallery, which features the finest examples of engraved sporting arms and the largest collection of Gatling Guns on public display anywhere. A few years earlier, Dr. William L. and Colette N. Roberts' donation of their collection of hundreds of historical firearms made the museum a leading institution for the study and advancement of knowledge of firearms and their development and use.

Your guns and the National Firearms Museum

Substantial funding of the Museum comes from The NRA Foundation, which is a 501(c)(3) charitable nonprofit organization, which means qualifying donations are tax deductible. Through the new NRA Firearms For Freedom program, individuals can donate their firearms to benefit the foundation or other NRA programs. These can be current gifts, or estate gifts from far-sighted individuals who would like to see their guns provide firearms education, support the shooting sports, or protect Second Amendment rights for future generations. All donated guns are reviewed for possible display in the National Firearms Museum.

Interested parties may call (877) NRA-GIVE, or email nrafff@nrahq.org. Guns or collections with historical significance may be directed to the Museum Curator's attention by emailing nfmstaff@nrahq.org.

The history of the National Firearms Museum

In 1876, D. Barclay of the NRA won a L.

The NRA Staff, from left to right: Philip Schreier, Caroline Simms, Jim Supica, Sylvia Scneider, Ben Van Scoyoc, Matt Sharpe, Doug Wicklund, Amber Lammers and Wayne Wilson.

National Firearms Museum Staff:

Jim Supica – *Director*

Doug Wicklund and Philip Schreier – *Senior Curators*

Benjamin Van Scoyoc – *Museum Store Manager*

Sylvia Schneider – *Administrative Assistant*

Caroline Simms – *Senior Special Projects Coordinator*

Matt Sharpe – *Curator Programs*

Amber Lammers *Curator Collections*

Wayne Wilson *Sales Associate*

Bill Trible and Jerry Keathley – *Curatorial Assistants*

D. Nimschke engraved Remington Rolling Block rifle during the international long-range rifle matches. This gun was the first of the NRA collection that eventually became the National Firearms Museum. The museum was formally started in 1935 when the Remington was put on exhibit in Washington DC's Barr Building, then the national headquarters of the NRA. It was displayed with many other firearms donated by firearms industry friends who sent them into the editorial offices of *American Rifleman* magazine (est. 1923) for testing and evaluation.

In 1954, the NRA headquarters moved a few blocks up 16th Street to the venerable

1600 Rhode Island Avenue address. The NRA museum continued to grow with exhibits on the fourth floor and eventually on the first two floors off the main lobby. In 1981, the NRA museum was christened the National Firearms Museum and by 1993, when the museum closed in preparation for the NRA headquarters move to Fairfax, Virginia, the collection had grown to 3,000 firearms.

In May 1998, the new National Firearms Museum opened at the Fairfax location with a bold new look and design. In an effort to showcase the historic and valuable arms in the collection, museum staff designed 85 exhibit cases in 15 galleries that told the

comprehensive story of firearms, freedom, and the American experience. With arms dating from 1350 to the present day, the collection traced in chronological order the history and development of firearms and their use in securing American liberty and in maintaining it ever since.

October 2010 was the opening of the Robert E. Petersen Gallery, which has been called "the finest single room of guns on display anywhere." Today the museum houses the largest and most historically significant collection of firearms and related material on exhibit in the United States.

Photography by **Terry Popkin.** Additional photography by **Michael Ives and Philip Schreier.**

Additional text from Museum projects by **Harry Hunter.**

Dedication: This book is dedicated to Kayne Robinson, Executive Director of General Operations of the National Rifle Association, with gratitude for his leadership, vision and support.

To join the NRA: To join the millions of Americans who belong to the National Rifle Association call 877-672-2000 or join online at www.nra.org/museumoffer.

INTRODUCTION

A BRIEF HISTORY OF FIREARMS

Arms were some of the earliest tools. They have been used to provide food and protection since the formation of the earliest social units. From bone and wood through to bronze and iron, humans have made arms for hunting and self-defense—and the longer the accurate range, the better their effectiveness. Few of these arms have proved as effective as the firearm.

For centuries, and continuing through today, men and women have used firearms as the most effective arms individuals can wield. They have been used to implement both the highest and basest goals of humanity—to put food on the table, to provide personal protection, to enforce or defy the law, to defend or acquire territory and treasure, and to liberate or to enslave.

Handguns, rifles, and other firearms have also come to be used for a wide variety of recreational and competitive shooting, and millions of Americans exercise their constitutional right to own firearms simply for the pleasure of shooting in addition to more serious uses.

EARLIEST FIREARMS

The origin of gunpowder is unknown, and probably originated in China where the earliest records are found. The first European references to gunpowder, which described the combination of charcoal, sulphur, and saltpeter to produce a rapidly burning or exploding powder, come from a coded writing by a Franciscan monk, Roger Bacon, shortly before 1250 A.D.

What is certainly true is that gunpowder firearms were in use in the Middle East by the 13th century. The Battle of Ain Jalut in 1260 A.D. between the Arab Mamluks and the Mongols is often cited as the first recorded instance of firearms being used—although it is unclear by which side. It is from the 13th century that the earliest physical example of a gunpowder arm is found: a bronze cannon in China dating to 1288. With a muzzle-bore diameter of an inch, this is almost certainly a hand-held firearm.

Firearms became more common at the end of the 13th and first half of the 14th century. Edward III of England used them against the Scots in the 1320s; they are recorded as being used in sieges in Spain at Alicante in 1331 and Algeciras in 1342. Early cannon—the word comes from the Latin canna, meaning tube—developed as a thick metal tube with a closed end (the breech) and an open end (the muzzle). Loaded first with gunpowder and then with a projectile, the powder was ignited with a torch or smoldering ember through a small hole in the rear (the touchhole). The rapidly expanding gases from the exploding gunpowder threw the projectile from the barrel. This basic principle still applies today.

The effectiveness of early firearms is difficult to assess: initially they certainly scared more people than they killed. There is no doubt, however, that they quickly became an important part of the military inventory. Interesting research by engineers such as Ulrich Bretscher show how effective "hand cannons" or "hand gonnes"— essentially miniature cannons designed to be held by hand or attached to a pole for use by individual soldiers—could be. Using replicas of hand "gonnes" found in Germany—the Tannenberg and Danzig weapons of the late 14th century—Bretscher showed that they could pierce 1.5–2.00 mm. steel and were surprisingly accurate. Larger cannon, often on wheeled carriages, were common on 15th century battlefields and played a significant role in one of the greatest events of the 15th century: the fall of Constantinople to the Turks in 1453—the end of the Eastern Roman Empire that was created in the early years of the 4th century A.D.

A historical interpreter fires a flintlock musket during the Revolutionary War Yorktown Victory Celebration.

FROM MATCHLOCK TO FLINTLOCK

The evolution of firearms from the cannon of the 14th century to the accurate, reliable guns of the 19th makes a fascinating record of the progress of engineering and chemistry in the period. Key to this evolution were the search for more reliable methods of igniting the gunpowder—as well as improvements to the gunpowder itself—and design advances allowing rapid repeat shots and better accuracy.

The term "lock, stock, and barrel" comes from firearms design and represents the three major components of early guns. The barrel is self-explanatory. The stock is the wooden holder in which the barrel is mounted, allowing the gun to be fired from the shoulder or from one hand. The lock is the mechanical contrivance that is used to ignite the charge of gunpowder in the chamber of the barrel.

The first gun to combine all three components was the matchlock, in the early 1400s. Many early hand cannons were ignited with a slow match—a length of slender rope or cord that had been chemically treated so that an end could be ignited and would continue to burn or smolder, much like a 4th of July punk used to shoot fireworks. Obviously it was awkward to hold both gun and slow match while trying to dip the match to the touch hole of the hand cannon.

The matchlock solved this problem by using an arm called a serpentine on the gun to hold the slow match. By mechanical linkage, a trigger mounted on the bottom of the lock could be pressed to lower the match to the touch hole, which now included a small pan of fine gunpowder that would be ignited first, transmitting the fire through the hole to fire the main charge in the barrel.

This increased firing—and, therefore, aiming—efficiency, but lighted matches were not the best accompaniment to powder-fired weapons. Keeping the match lit in poor weather—and keeping it away from the powder at all times—was a continuous problem and an accident waiting to happen.

This simple system was followed by a much safer—but more complicated—approach: the wheellock first seen in the early 1500s. It was the first ignition system to take advantage of the fact that sparks could be produced by striking flint or other substances against steel. The lock contained a wheel with a serrated edge, attached to a spring that could be wound with a separate key called a spanner, much like early clocks, and held under tension. A hammer-like piece called the dog or dogshead held a piece of pyrite rock. To fire a wheellock, the dogshead was lowered onto the edge of the wheel, which was released by a pull of the trigger causing a shower of sparks to fall into the pan igniting the charge. The principle is much the same as a cigarette lighter.

This was an improvement in reliability over the matchlock, primarily because the shooter did not have to constantly attend to the smoldering slow match to ensure that it remained lit. It also avoided the problem of an enemy seeing or of game smelling the smoke of the match before the gun was fired. It took highly skilled craftsmen to build the

clock-like mechanism of the wheellock, making it an extremely expensive piece, primarily available to royalty and the like for hunting. Although wheellocks saw some military use, the matchlock remained the most common military firearm during the wheellock era.

Improvements using flint against steel to provide the igniting spark continued in the second half of the 16th century, with two early examples being the snaphaunce, the first flintlock-type gun, circa 1560, and the Miquelet, which followed a couple of decades later.

The snaphaunce held a piece of flint in the hammer-like cock, with a pan of priming powder mounted on the outside of the barrel over the touchhole as with the matchlock system. When ready to fire, a steel striking plate ("battery") would be manually swiveled into place above the pan, and the cock pulled back until it was caught by a sear. Pulling the trigger would release the cock to swing rapidly forward striking the battery, and showering sparks into the pan, hopefully firing the gun.

As with all flintlock-type systems, sometimes the priming powder in the pan would ignite but fail to transmit the fire

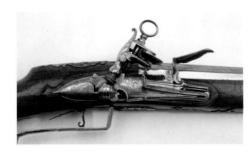

Firing mechanism of a Spanish Miquelet

to the powder in the barrel, resulting in a failure to fire and giving us a colorful phrase still used today—"a flash in the pan."

Of course, it as also vital to "keep your powder dry," and accordingly, many early firearms of this era had a sliding pan cover to hold the powder in place and give it some protection against the elements. The pan cover would have to be manually swiveled out of the way before firing.

Around 1580, the Miquelet system improved on and simplified the snaphaunce by combining the battery and pan cover into a single piece called the frizzen. This L-shaped spring-loaded piece would be pivoted down to cover the pan after it had been primed with powder. When the cock was released by the trigger, it would swing forward striking the frizzen, producing sparks at the same time it pushed the frizzen up and forward to expose the powder in the pan to the igniting sparks.

In the early 1600s, the basic design of the flintlock, originally known as the French lock, was perfected. The major improvement over the Miquelet consisted of moving the mechanical components for the lock mechanism from their previous position on the outside of the lockplate, where they were exposed to elements and damage, to the interior of the lock.

At around the time flintlock systems were first being developed, two improvements were introduced that dramatically increased the accuracy of firearms.

Archers had found that if the fletching feathers on the rear of their arrow were at a slight angle, causing the arrow to rotate in flight, their ability to hit the target was

improved. This concept was applied to gun barrels by cutting slowly twisting grooves down the interior length of the barrel, imparting a spin to the bullet as it left the muzzle. These grooves were called rifling, and "rifled muskets" or "rifles" so equipped were found to be much better at hitting their mark over further distances than "smoothbore" muskets.

With the improved accuracy offered by rifled firearms, a system of aiming them other than pointing became more important, and early forms of sights became more widely used. A common system, still used in many guns today, was a notch of some type at the rear of the barrel and a post on the front. With this type of open sight, the top of the front sight post is aligned with the target, and the post is centered by eye between the edges of the rear sight notch, with the top of the post level with the tops of the sides of the notch. When the sights themselves are properly physically aligned with the axis of the bore, this system still provides all the accuracy required for most practical shooting needs

EARLY GUNS IN AMERICA

Despite imaginative pictures of Pilgrims bearing flared-muzzle flintlock blunderbuses, the earliest firearms in American were doubtless matchlocks and the occasional wheellock.

However, during the colonial years, a distinctly American type of gun would be developed, by first dozens and then hundreds of gunsmiths scattered through the new land. In the late 17th and 18th

INTRODUCTION

centuries, colonists coming to America brought their indigenous European firearms and gun design concepts with them. The gun was a necessary and treasured tool when pioneering a frontier wilderness far from civilization, and gun makers were valued and essential members of the small settlements.

The American long rifle, variously known as the Kentucky, Pennsylvania, or Ohio rifle, is most likely the descendant of the German Jaeger (translated "hunter")-type flintlock, a practical classic European hunting rifle. In the New World, it slowly evolved into a longer-barreled firearm with wooden stock extending the full length of the barrel, while the rear of stock developed a graceful downward curve. Eventually, deluxe versions would come to be decorated with colorful brass or pewter inlays in the stock, with stars, hearts, and simple animal silhouettes being popular motifs. The brass-covered patchbox in the rear of the stock would become more elaborate and decorative over time.

This is a gun that fed and defended early pioneer families. Marksmanship was a valued, necessary, and common skill.

European military doctrine of the time called for the use of smoothbore muskets as the primary martial firearm. Although less accurate than rifled arms, the smoothbore allowed for faster reloading, because a lead ball slightly smaller than bore diameter could be rammed down the barrel with wadding quite quickly, even as the barrel became fouled from gunpowder residue from previous shots. By contrast, to be effective, the lead bullet for a rifled arm must fit the bore tightly to engage the rifling, and takes more time and effort to ram home.

European armies would meet on a field

The Delaware Regiment at the Battle of Long Island

Two unidentified soldiers in nonregulation Confederate uniforms with a single-shot pistol and a Colt revolver

of battle in massed formations and exchange volleys of fire from their smoothbore muskets, more pointing the weapons at the clustered line of enemies across the field than precisely aiming, and relying on volleys of multiple lead balls to strike down some opponents before closing for combat with saber and bayonet. The classic British Brown Bess and French Charleville Musket were sturdy smoothbore flintlock designs, well suited for this type of combat.

The ways and rules were changing, however, and in the French and Indian War, the Revolutionary War, and the War of 1812, American marksmen used their rifled "squirrel guns" and well-honed shooting skills to good effect on selected targets from longer distances and from behind cover in wilderness areas.

After securing independence, the new country rapidly sought its own means of mass-producing military arms, establishing government arsenals in 1794 with the manufacture of firearms beginning at Springfield in 1795 and Harper's Ferry in 1800. Many of their early products were indeed smoothbore muskets, still a useful military arm. But the age of the rifle as an essential arm for the marksman in combat had arrived. In addition to arsenal-made firearms, the federal government and some states contracted with numerous small individual gun-making firms to produce military firearms or parts based on sample patterns provided by the government. America's oldest continuing gunmaker traces its lineage to this era, with Eliphalet Remington producing barrels as early as 1826. The Remington firm remains one of America's premier gun manufacturers today. The famous Henry Deringer, whose name later would become synonymous with small concealable handguns, produced flintlock rifles for the U.S. government as early as 1810, as did Eli Whitney's Whitney Arms nearly a decade earlier.

THE PERCUSSION SYSTEM

Although the flintlock had dominated firearm production for nearly two centuries, it still had major defects as an ignition system. To begin with, a shooter often had to carry two types of powder—fine grained for priming and coarse for the main charge—which complicated reloading and kept down shots per minutes. Second, the system was unreliable in wet weather, and it was difficult to store a gun loaded ready for use.

Eliphalet Remington

In 1807, a Scottish clergyman, Rev. Forsyth, is credited with developing an ignition system based on the principle that certain chemicals would ignite with a spark when struck a sharp blow, a concept which can be observed in toy cap pistols or "pop rock"-type fireworks today. Various methods to utilize this approach were tried, and in 1822 the percussion cap was invented.

The percussion cap contains a small charge of chemical in a small copper cup-like holder which can be quickly pressed onto a nipple mounted in the rear of a gun barrel. When the trigger is pulled, the hammer strikes the cap and ignites the chemical, which sparks through a hole in the nipple into the main charge in the barrel, and fires the gun. This system offered such obvious advantages to the flintlock method that gunmakers around the world rapidly adapted their existing designs to percussion ignition.

The introduction of the percussion system marks the beginning of a dramatically rapid era of firearm advancements, coinciding with the Industrial Revolution and including the era of the American Civil War, through the turn of the century. During this relatively brief time, guns would go from primitive flintlocks to the basic systems that still dominate firearm designs today—and the percussion cap would be obsolete within 50 years of its introduction.

Development of effective breechloading systems was another significant step. From the matchlock through the early percussion era, the vast majority of guns had been "muzzle-loaders;" that is, the powder and projectile had to be dropped down the muzzle at the front of the barrel and rammed to the rear before firing. This made reloading awkward, especially when shooting a long gun from a prone position or behind cover or concealment and, as noted earlier, it became more difficult after a few shots when barrel fouling made the job more strenuous. This led to many attempts to develop a gun that loaded from the rear of the barrel, although most early efforts were not effective due to weakness of materials and the leakage of hot gases from the breech seal when the gun was fired.

In the early 19th century, various breechloading designs were finally produced in quantity. A notable example is the U.S. military Hall North system, which in 1833 marked both the first U.S. percussion arm, and the Army's first breechloader. In 1841, the breechloading Dreyse needle gun,

COLONEL COLT.

Samuel Colt

which packed the projectile and powder together in a combustible cartridge, was adopted in Germany as the first military bolt-action gun.

The Civil War saw the adoption of a wide variety of breechloading systems, including those made by Sharps, Maynard, Burnside, and many others.

BIRTH OF THE REVOLVER

From the start, firearms manufacturers tried to address the problem of slow-repeat shots and reloading. Multiple barrels (and usually multiple locks) loaded onto the same stock was a sensible basic concept and—in the form of double-barrel shotguns—this type of gun is still produced by some of the finest gun makers in the world today, including firms such as Browning, Franchi, Beretta, Remington, Ruger, and Charles Daly, and is a system preferred by many discriminating hunters and competitive shooters.

But with more than two barrels, the system begins to become heavy and cumbersome. Other systems were tried, including manually rotated groups of barrels mounted to a single lock, multiple superposed charges within a single barrel, and cylindrical or rectangular clusters of chambers that could be manually repositioned to align with a firing mechanism and barrel.

The most successful solution was invented by one of the great names of gun manufacturing, Samuel Colt. He developed a handgun design with a rotating cylinder and multiple chambers, each of which could contain a charge of powder topped by the bullet, loaded from the front of the cylinder. The rear of the cylinder was closed, with a nipple for a percussion cap installed at the back of each chamber. When the hammer is cocked, a fresh chamber rotates into alignment with the rear of the barrel, and when the trigger is pulled, the hammer drops, firing the load in that chamber. This is the basis of the mechanical system still used in all revolvers today.

Colt's first manufacturing venture was based in Paterson, NJ, and produced percussion revolvers with folding triggers and revolving shotguns and rifles. These are called Colt Paterson models by modern collectors. Few were produced, and the firm folded, having been in business only from 1837 to 1841. In 1847, however, Colt was back with a new, heavier, and more powerful revolver, this time with a traditional bow-type trigger guard. Prompted by an initial order from Captain Samuel Walker to equip

INTRODUCTION

Capt. Samuel Walker

his troops in the Mexican war, the new model tipped the scales at nearly five pounds, and remained the most powerful repeating handgun until the introduction of the .357 magnum nearly 90 years later. Called the Walker Model after the young captain, Colt's revolvers were initially manufactured by Eli Whitney, but Colt soon had his own plant in Hartford, CT.

Colt had patented his revolving cylinder design, and therefore held a monopoly on revolver manufacture for a number of years. The only serious competition for a repeating handgun was the pepperbox design, in which a cluster of barrels, each with a percussion nipple on the rear, rotated around an axis by the pull of a ring trigger, which also cocked the hammer and released it to fire the chamber that had rotated into position. Pepperboxes were made by a number of European and American firms, the foremost

probably being the succession of companies founded by Ethan Allen, including Allen & Thurber and Allen & Wheelock.

The Colt pattern cap-and-ball revolver rapidly came to dominate the repeating firearms market. Colt also offered revolving shotguns and rifles as well as handguns. Among his most successful designs were the little 1849 Pocket Model in .31 caliber, the mid-sized 1851 Navy Model in .36 caliber, and the 1860 Army Model, offering .44 caliber chambering in a much smaller and handier package than his earlier Walker and Dragoon models. After the expiration of Colt's patent in the mid-1850s, other firms jumped into the revolver business, with major manufacturers being Remington, Starr, Whitney, and Manhattan. Manufactured by these and other makers, the percussion revolver became the major sidearm of the Civil War.

Oliver Winchester

THE SELF-CONTAINED CARTRIDGE

The cap-and-ball revolver offered an effective repeating firearm, with five or six shots available as fast as the hammer could be cocked and the trigger pulled. After the gun was shot dry, however, reloading was a slow and cumbersome process that involved loading each chamber with loose gun powder and a lead bullet, ramming the loads home, and placing a percussion cap on the nipple of each chamber. What was needed was a self-contained cartridge with the primer, powder, and bullet all in one neat and weatherproof unit.

An early attempt at this was the pinfire system, first introduced around 1846, in which a firing pin was mounted on each copper-cased cartridge, igniting an internal primer when struck by the gun's hammer. Although it gained a good deal of popularity in Europe, it never caught on much in the U.S. because the external pin on each round was cumbersome and hazardous.

Among the firms eagerly waiting for the expiration of the Colt revolver patent was the partnership of an inventor named Daniel Wesson and an older businessman, Horace Smith. A few years earlier, in a previous partnership, they had entered the race for an effective repeating firearm that shot self-contained cartridges with a lever-action pistol. This pistol had a tubular magazine mounted under and parallel to the barrel, and shot "rocket balls"—hollow-based lead bullets, with the powder and primer mounted in the base of the projectile itself.

Wesson and Smith pursued production

Annie Oakley

of their lever-action pistols only a few years, and the design was acquired by a shirt manufacturer, who carried it further. His name was Oliver Winchester, and his famous lever-action rifles, based in large part on the design of the first Smith & Wesson partnership, eventually became the most popular repeating rifles of the second half of the 19th century.

The second Smith & Wesson partnership had designed a tiny .22 revolver. Perhaps more important than the revolver was the cartridge it fired. It consisted of a copper casing, with a hollow rim at the bottom that held a priming compound. The case was then filled with gunpowder and capped with a lead bullet mounted in its mouth. When the firing pin of the revolver's hammer struck the rim of the cartridge, the priming ignited the powder, firing the bullet, leaving the empty copper casing in the chamber.

The cartridge was essentially identical to the modern .22 Short rimfire, and was the grand-daddy of all our traditional ammunition today.

Colt had patented his revolver, so Smith & Wesson acquired the patent to their innovation of the revolver, and held a fairly complete monopoly on the production of effective cartridge revolvers through the patent's expiration in 1869. There were a number of infringements and evasions of the patent as the market rapidly recognized the superiority of metallic cartridge ammunition.

THE AMERICAN WEST

The military has sometimes been slow to embrace firearms innovation, preferring tried and true technology over the new and untested. This was certainly true during the Civil War and Indian Wars eras. Winchester had abandoned the rocket ball system in favor of a .44 rimfire cartridge in its famous brass-framed Henry rifle in 1860, but only a few were purchased and used during the Civil War. The Spencer Repeating Rifle Company had also patented an effective lever-action repeater that fired metallic cartridges by the beginning of the Civil War, but its adoption by the U.S. Army was resisted until it was demonstrated to President Lincoln, who promptly personally championed its purchase.

Although the Spencer was the most widely used repeating long gun of the Civil War, and breechloading single-shot Sharps rifles in the hands of expert "Sharps-shooter"

marksmen took a toll, the vast majority of the soldiers on both sides were armed with muzzle-loading percussion muskets.

With the post-war westward expansion, the civilian demand was for the new repeating metallic cartridge firearms. Winchester responded, first with an improved brass frame rimfire Model 1866 lever action, followed by a centerfire Model 1873, and then by Models 1876 and 1886, made strong enough to handle true big-game cartridges in the .45-70 class. Marlin was Winchester's strongest competitor in the field, with Whitney Kennedy and Evans also producing lever-action repeaters. Despite the development of repeaters, single-shot rifles remained a popular option, and in the early years of metallic cartridges, they could handle stronger rounds than the more

Sitting Bull and Buffalo Bill, Montreal, QC, 1885

John Wesley Hardin

complicated repeaters.

The tradition of powerful, big-bore rifles for the large game of the American West, such as bison, wapiti, and grizzly bear, certainly pre-dates the Civil War. As trappers and mountain men and then settlers and farmers pushed into the Great Plains and Rocky Mountain west, a new type of American rifle was developed to meet their needs.

The percussion "Plains Rifle" tended to be shorter than its long, slender Kentucky rifle predecessor and to be handled easier on horseback and in brush. It took a heavier, larger-diameter ball appropriate to the larger game, which necessitated a heavier barrel, the weight of which was another factor that dictated a shorter length. The Plains Rifle tended to have a half-stock, with the wood only cradling the rear half of the barrel, contrasted to the full-stock Kentuckies. As

befits a working gun, decoration tended to be minimal or non-existent.

In the years preceding the Civil War, Plains Rifles by prominent makers such as Hawken and Gemmer, both of St. Louis, were eagerly sought after by long hunters and pilgrims heeding Horace Greeley's advice of "Go West, young man."

After the war, Sharps began producing its well-respected breechloading single shots for centerfire metallic cartridges, and with a half-inch diameter projectile, the Sharps "Big 50" was perhaps the quintessential buffalo rifle. Other popular single shots included the Winchester Model 1885 High Wall and Low Wall rifles, Stevens Ideal rifles, and the sturdy Remington Rolling Block rifles. Most were offered in a variety of frame sizes, barrel lengths and weights, and calibers ranging from .22 rimfire to the .40 to .50 caliber rounds favored by commercial hunters. Various types of sights were available, from simple through elaborate, and various stocking options could be had, from fairly straightforward through the ornate buttplates and trigger guard configuration favored for Scheutzen-style target competitions. The single shot was generally considered to be more accurate than early repeaters, and thus was favored for target competition and other precision work.

The American West of 1865 to 1900 is perhaps one of the most romanticized eras of American history, with the lore of cowboy and Indian, lawman and outlaw, figuring large in our collective imagination. The handguns of this era also have a special fascination.

INTRODUCTION

The most famous handgun is undoubtedly the Colt Single-Action Army, introduced in 1873, and also known as the Peacemaker. Its sturdy reliable design and effective cartridges made it a favorite with Westerners on both sides of the law.

It is little recognized, however, that Smith & Wesson large frame top-break revolvers and their foreign copies represented the most prolific full size handgun pattern of the early cartridge era. All variations on the Model Three frame, the first was the American model in 1870, followed rapidly by the Russian model. The Schofield model was made for the American military in the 1870s, followed by the New Model Number Three and Double Action models.

The S&W design was much faster to load and unload than the Colt. When a latch in front of the hammer was released, the S&W barrel and cylinder pivoted forward, automatically ejecting empties and exposing all six chambers for reloading. To reload the Colt, each individual chamber had to be aligned with a barrel-mounted ejector rod, and the single empty brass case punched out and replaced with a fresh cartridge before rotating the cylinder to the next chamber, repeating the operation a total of six times to fully load the revolver. Smiths were also generally held to have an edge in accuracy, although the Colts were simpler, sturdier, and less liable to malfunction in extreme environments. A large portion of S&W's early production went to foreign military contracts.

Other revolvers of the era included the Remington 1875, similar to the Colt pattern, and the unusual but exceptionally well made twist-open Merwin Hulbert revolvers.

Col. Roosevelt and his Rough Riders photographed at the top of the hill that they captured in the Battle of San Juan. Rough Rider arms would have included the Colt Single-Action Army revolver and the Krag rifle. Roosevelt carried and used a Colt .38 Double-Action revolver.

Jesse James

The military's resistance to new concepts continued into the Indian War years of the late 19th century. As a good example, when repeating rifles with sixteen or more rounds available as fast as you could work the lever were on the market, the U.S. Army chose to stay with a single shot as its primary issue long arm. One concern cited was that soldiers armed with repeaters might expend ammunition too rapidly in the heat of battle.

Economic factors also undoubtedly influenced the decision. Vast quantities of now-obsolete muzzle-loaders remained in inventory from the Civil War. A method was developed to convert these to breechloading cartridge rifles by cutting open the rear of the barrel and installing a breechblock that could be flipped open to load cartridges and remove empty brass like a trapdoor. When manufacture of new rifles resumed, they were based on the same system, and the "Trapdoor Springfield" single shot became the standard military rifle from 1873 through the beginning of the Spanish American War in the late 1890s. In defense of the Army's decision, the trapdoor's .45-70 cartridge was significantly more powerful, with longer effective range, than anything available in a repeater in the early 1870s.

A similar thought process led the military to initially select a Remington single-shot in 50 caliber as its first cartridge handgun. By the mid-1870s, however, the Colt Single Action Army and the Smith and Wesson Schofield six-shot revolvers became the Army's primary sidearms for the Indian Wars era.

After the Custer rout at Little Bighorn, there was a vigorous debate over the military's choice of weapons. Some of the Indian victors had been using repeating rifles. One school of thought contended that if Custer's men had been armed with lever-action rifles instead of trapdoors, and fast-loading Schofields instead of the slower Single-Action Army, the outcome might have been different, although that conclusion is hard to support in light of the vastly outnumbered

George Armstrong Custer

7th Cavalry's forces and strategic choices.

Although the big six guns of the Old West are those that capture the public's fancy, their production quantities were significantly less than smaller-frame revolvers. S&W offered tip-up spur-triggers and top breaks in single or double action; Colt produced a series of single-shot derringers and spur-trigger revolvers; and Remington offered spur-trigger revolvers and its famous double derringers, in addition to other designs.

The late 19th century saw a proliferation of small manufacturers churning out cheap, small single-action spur-trigger revolvers, sometimes derisively referred to as "Suicide Specials." Other firms such as Harrington and Richardson, Iver Johnson, and Hopkins and Allen produced millions of inexpensive, but generally serviceable small top-break and solid-frame double-action revolvers. These companies have been referred to as the "armorers to the nation's nightstands," accurately reflecting the fact that even persons of moderate means could afford their products as a handy means of home and personal protection.

THE SWING-OUT REVOLVER

Just before the turn of the 20th century, a new type of revolver was developed, first by Colt in 1889, followed by S&W in 1896. This revolver used a solid frame, like the Single-Action Army, but the cylinder swung to the side to load and unload. Empty cases were simultaneously ejected by pushing a plunger-like ejector rod at the front of the open cylinder. S&W called their versions hand ejectors to differentiate the method of

John Moses Browning with his BAR

operation from their top-break automatic ejecting products.

These swing-out cylinder revolvers were also double action (DA), a term describing the ways in which the gun could be fired. Early revolvers were usually single action—the hammer had to be manually cocked before the trigger pull performed the single action of dropping the hammer to fire the round. On the DA revolvers, the gun could be fired in the traditional single-action (SA) mode. Alternatively, the DA could be fired by a longer, heavier pull on the trigger, beginning with the hammer in the down, uncocked position. In this mode, the trigger would perform the double action of first cocking and then dropping the hammer to fire the weapon.

This type of revolver rapidly caught on, and would become the dominant handgun design for most of the 20th century in America.

In its early revolvers of this type, Colt offered revolver frame sizes ranging from its massive New Service to handy compact pocket-sized revolvers with short two-inch "snub nose" barrels. When the New York City Police got a brash new young Commissioner just before the close of the 19th century, he selected the little .32 Colt New Police as the department's first standard-issue handgun. He also instituted the first formal police marksmanship training under the guidance of Sgt. William Petty, who happened to be a national shooting champion. The Commissioner's name was Theodore Roosevelt, and a few years later he carried another swing-out cylinder Colt, a New Army model, when he led the First Volunteer Cavalry up San Juan Hill in1898.

The early S&W hand ejectors ranged from the large N-frame, the first of which was the famous Triple-Lock, which introduced the .44 Special cartridge, through the tiny

INTRODUCTION

.22 Ladysmith, which was far smaller than any swing-out revolver being made today.

Smith & Wesson found the workhorse of their product line in 1899 when it made its first medium-sized K frame "Military & Police" (M&P) revolver, chambered for their new .38 Special cartridge. Although Colt & S&W shared the police market in the first half of the century, the S&W K frame .38 Special was probably carried by a majority of law enforcement officers in America after World War II through the 1970s.

The same cartridge was also popular in the smaller short-barrel five-shot J frame "Chiefs Special," which served both the police backup gun and the civilian concealed carry market. Colt's competing Detective Special packed six rounds in a package that

Theodore Roosevelt

John Garand points out features of the M1 Garand rifle to senior Army officials.

was only slightly larger. The little J frame was also the platform for S&W's "Kit Gun," a handy .22 revolver that would easily fit in a hunter's, camper's, or fisherman's kit.

Continuing to the present day, the .38 Special is a well-made double-action revolver like those made by S&W, Ruger, Colt, and Taurus and is considered by many to be the best choice for a first-time shooter's home defense handgun. The small J frame size is also the first choice of many experienced shooters for their personal concealed carry. In a gun that is small enough to carry easily, yet large enough to be manageable, the combination of safety, reliability, simplicity, and effectiveness is still hard to beat.

EUROPEAN BOLT-ACTION RIFLES

The double-action system for revolvers had caught on faster in Europe than in the U.S. It was used for early pinfires and for military handguns, such as Britain's ugly but reliable and hell-for-stout Webley top-breaks in .455 caliber.

While the U.S. market was well satisfied with lever-action repeating rifles, a different repeating mechanism gained favor with the armies of Europe. When the switch to metallic cartridges began, many of Europe's early single-shot rifles used a

bolt-action breechloading system. In bolt-action rifles, a bolt handle extending from the breechblock is lifted up to unlock the breechblock and pulled to the rear, which slides the block back to allow a cartridge to be loaded into the chamber in the rear of the barrel. The bolt handle is pushed forward and then down, engaging locking lugs to hold the breechblock in place while the rifle is fired. Single-shot bolt-action rifles adopted by European military units included the Chassepot (France 1866), Vetterli (Switzerland 1869), Berdan (Russia 1870), Beaumont (Netherlands 1871), and the Mauser (Germany 1871). Of these, the seeds of greatness lay in the last, in the invention of brothers Peter and Paul Mauser.

The earliest military bolt-action repeating rifles used tubular magazines under the barrel, similar to the system on most American lever actions. The Portuguese Kropatschek in 1878 was among the first of this type. Mauser's tube mag repeater was first produced in 1884 as the German Model 1871/84. Most of these early military cartridge rifles chambered cartridges similar to the U.S. .45-70—a large, heavy, round-nosed bullet in a metallic case filled with a

A World War II Poster

healthy charge of black powder. In 1885, smokeless powder was invented and would lead to dramatic changes in firearms and ammunition design.

SMOKELESS POWDER

Smokeless powder, as the name implies, had the military advantage of not generating a cloud of smoke when fired. Black powder smoke would reveal a shooter's position and, after a few rounds, develop a haze that could begin to obscure his vision. Another advantage was that smokeless powder produced far less fouling after shots than black powder, meaning that more shots could be fired before cleaning, and that powder debris was less likely to clog an action.

Its most important quality, however, was that when ignited, its gases would expand more rapidly, creating higher pressures and driving the bullet to a higher velocity when it left the muzzle. As a bullet approaches 2,000 ft./sec. (about the speed of sound), its wounding capacity increases dramatically, allowing a lighter, smaller-diameter projectile to have the same "stopping power" as a larger, heavier round at a slower speed.

The faster, smaller-diameter bullet also has a further range and a flatter trajectory. A bullet leaving the muzzle of a gun does not fly straight. From the instant it departs the barrel, it is "falling" toward the ground due to the effect of gravity. A gun's sights are adjusted so the barrel is actually pointed very slightly up, giving a slight rainbow-like curve to the bullet's path. A faster, lighter bullet will travel further before gravity pulls it to

earth, and a smaller-diameter bullet has less wind resistance. The flatter trajectory means it will be on target over a longer distance.

In general terms, the caliber of a bullet refers to a rough measurement of its diameter, expressed either in decimal fractions of an inch or millimeters. For example, a .45 caliber cartridge takes a bullet approximately 45/100 inch in diameter, which would also be very roughly 11mm in diameter.

Firearms designers took advantage of the new smokeless powder, using a smaller bullet, closer to 1/3 inch in diameter (8mm is the most popular, but they range from under 7mm to 9mm). Heavy lead was still used to form the core of the bullet, but it was encased in a harder copper or brass metal jacket ,so it would not quickly foul the rifling in the bore with soft lead that rubbed off at the higher velocities.

The first such bolt-action repeating rifle and smokeless smaller-caliber ammunition combination to be adopted by a military was the 8mm French Lebel bolt action in 1886.

The pointed "spitzer" bullet design is much more aerodynamically efficient than a round-nose design, offering better accuracy at longer ranges. But when such cartridges are loaded nose to tail in a tube magazine, there is a danger that the pointed nose of one bullet will ignite the primer of the cartridge in front of it when the rifle recoils. Use of a box-type magazine, in which the cartridges are stacked parallel, one on top of the other, overcomes this obstacle to spitzer bullets. The British Lee Metford bolt action, generally based on the Mauser concept, in .303 caliber used such a box mag in 1888, and in 1889 Mauser produced its own 8mm

British troops in North Africa were equipped with Thompson submachine guns and Lee Enfield rifles.

box magazine rifle.

Another early box-magazine repeater was the Mauser & Mannlicher-influenced German 1888 Commission rifle in 8mm, which rapidly became a staple design. Meanwhile, the Austrians adopted a straight-pull bolt-action Steyr Mannlicher repeater in 8mm the same year. Mid-bore bolt-action box-magazine designs rapidly followed, such as the Danish Krag Jorgensen in

1889 (with the U.S. adopting a Krag-based design in 1892) and the Swiss straight pull Schmidt Rubin in the same year. The year 1891 saw the adoption of the Lebel pattern Mosin Nagant by Russia, the 6.5mm Italian Carcano, and the 8mm French Berthier.

During this period, military bolt actions were often modified to incorporate the new advances, and numerous military rifles from the turn of the century or slightly later are bolt-action single shots converted to magazine-fed repeaters, or had large-bore barrels relined to smaller calibers.

The perfection of the bolt-action design is believed by many to be the Mauser 98, introduced in 1898. Improvements include cocking on opening of the bolt rather than on closing, an added safety lug, and a larger chamber ring. This basic design became the basis of many, if not all, subsequent bolt-action military and sporting rifles, and variations served as primary rifles for many countries through World War II. The tried-and-true U.S. Model 1903, which served with distinction through two world

U.S. troops in World War II armed with M1 Garand rifles

INTRODUCTION

wars, with its "thirty ought six" (.30-06) chambering is basically a modified Mauser 1898 design. Current-production sporting rifles, such as the classic Winchester Model 70 and bolt actions by Remington, Ruger, and others, can trace their lineage to the Gewehr 98.

AUTO-LOADERS

Another firearms design trend in Europe given a boost by the introduction of smokeless powder was the attempt to make automatic-loading firearms. In general, gun designs to this point had relied on some mechanical action by the shooter to load a fresh cartridge into the firing chamber after the initial round had been fired, whether it was swiveling a lever; lifting, pulling, and pushing a bolt; or cocking the hammer or pulling the trigger to advance a revolver cylinder to the next chamber. Inventors sought a method whereby the loading of the next round would be accomplished automatically.

The first auto-loading pistol designs to see limited production were the German-made Schoenberger and Borchardt designs in 1893 and 1894, respectively. A couple of

Mikhail Timofeevich Kalashnikov holding the AK74

years later, in 1896, the Mauser firm began to manufacture the first auto pistol that gained widespread acceptance, the Model 1896, nicknamed the Broomhandle for its slender oval cross-sectioned grip.

Germany continued its dominance in European firearms design when Georg Luger introduced his classic pistol in 1900. Whereas early automatics had used fixed box magazines, the Luger magazine was mounted in the pistol's grip frame, was quickly detachable, and was easily replaced with a fresh magazine for a quick reload. Originally manufactured in 7.63mm (.30 cal.), in 1909 it was adapted to a new, larger-diameter cartridge, and the 9mm Luger (or 9mm Parabellum) round was destined to become possibly the most widely used centerfire pistol ammunition of the 20th century. The Luger was widely adopted as a military pistol by many countries, including Germany where it was designated the "Pistole 08" (P-08) for the year it was first purchased, being used through both World Wars. Its distinctive profile is widely recognized and may be identified as "graceful" or "sinister," depending on the eye of the beholder and how many Grade B war movies he or she has seen.

Probably the greatest of U.S. firearms inventors, John Moses Browning, played a significant role in the development of automatics. One of Browning's earliest designs was the Winchester 1885 single-shot rifle. Others brought the Winchester lever-action repeaters into the smokeless powder era, first with the slim and handy Model 1892; followed by the Model 1894, which with its "thutty-thutty" (.30-30)

German troops armed with Mausers and PanzerFausts

cartridge became America's classic deer rifle; and the Model 1895 whose box magazine allowed the chambering of true high-power smokeless rifle cartridges with spitzer bullets in a lever-action repeater.

Browning was also responsible for some of the first repeating shotguns. Revolver-based shotguns had been around since the Colt Paterson models of the 1840s, but had never caught on (probably because of the tendency of hot gases escaping from the cylinder gap to pepper the supporting hand with powder grains). Spencer Arms (of Civil War lever-action rifle fame) had manufactured a moderately successful repeating pump or slide-action shotgun as early as 1882. As would befit the Winchester legacy, Browning's first design for a repeating shotgun for the firm was a lever-action, the Model 1887. This was followed by a pump-action Model 1893, which would be modified to become highly successful Model 1897.

With a pump or slide-action firearm, the

shooter pulls back on the wooden forearm and then pushes it forward to eject the empty shell and replace it with a loaded one. Browning had earlier applied the principal to a handy little .22 rifle for Winchester, the classic Model 1890, which remained popular for decades, happily employed in shooting galleries, by squirrel and rabbit hunters, and for all around "plinking."

It was in the area of automatic firearms, however, that Browning probably made his greatest advances. Auto-loaders use the part of the force of the firing cartridge to eject the empty casing and load a fresh round into the chamber. This may occur by direct or delayed blowback of the breechblock, by utilizing the recoil of the gun, or by redirecting some of the expanding gases of the burning gunpowder from the barrel to operate the action.

In 1900, the same year the Luger was introduced, Colt first offered a Browning-designed auto-loading pistol, the .38 caliber Model 1900 Automatic. Variations and improvements followed in rapid succession, with a smaller Hammerless .32 Pocket model in 1903, and a tiny "vest pocket"-sized .25 caliber pistol in 1908. Colt introduced the .45 ACP (Automatic Colt Pistol) cartridge in the Browning-designed Model 1905.

This is the cartridge that would be chambered in the famous Model 1911. The 1911 was rapidly adopted by the U.S. military, and, only slightly modified over time, remained the primary U.S. issue sidearm through the Vietnam War. Colt and many other firms continue production of 1911 pattern pistols today, and they still serve military, law enforcement, and personal protection duty on a regular basis. It is the handgun of choice for many shooting sports that seek to simulate combat-type shooting and, in accurized forms, is dominant in many traditional target-shooting sports.

Young German Waffen SS soldier with a MG-42

Its mastery requires effort, training, and practice, but in the right hands many would argue that it is the finest combat handgun of all time.

Whereas the 1911 may have been Browning's finest handgun design, his contributions did not end there. His final pistol design, the Model 1935, took advantage of the Luger's smaller-diameter 9mm cartridge "double-stacked" in two parallel columns in the detachable magazine for a total magazine capacity of 13 rounds (compared to 7 rounds in a 1911 mag). The 1935 is also known as the Browning High Power.

It's worth mentioning that most detachable magazine auto-loading pistols present a potential hazard for untrained individuals. It's easy to check whether most double-action revolvers are loaded simply by swinging open the cylinder and looking. However, a person who is not familiar with firearms may assume that an auto-loading firearm is unloaded once the magazine has been removed. This is a potentially lethal mistake. An auto-loading pistol may still have a live round in the chamber after the magazine has been taken out. In most designs, this round will fire if the trigger is pulled, with the potential for tragic consequences.

Browning's auto-loading designs were not limited to handguns. His "humpback" Auto 5 shotgun was a tremendous success, popular still today, and has been made by Fabrique National, Remington, and Browning. He made many military firearms as well, especially machine guns.

Today, the term "semi-automatic" or "semi-auto" is used to refer to the auto-loading guns that fire only one round for each pull of the trigger. Although Colt originally called the Browning pistols "automatic pistols," in modern usage the term "automatic firearm" is used to describe a gun that fires multiple rounds for a single pull of the trigger.

These "full-auto" firearms, popularly called "machine guns," will usually continue rapidly firing until the trigger is released or the magazine is empty. Those that will fire a set number of rounds, usually three, with a single pull of the trigger are called "burst fire," and those that can be set to fire either a single shot per trigger pull or to fire full-auto are called "select fire."

The concept of a firearm that will "spray" a stream of bullets is hardly a recent one. Most famous of the early rapid-fire guns was the Gatling gun, which fired steadily through a cluster of rotating barrels so long as the gunner was turning its crank and his assistant was feeding ammunition. It was first demonstrated in 1861 and was a successful military design.

The first successful true full-auto machine gun, which would fire continuously while the trigger was held back, was perfected by Hiram Maxim in the 1880s and adopted by several armies in the 1890s. John Moses Browning invented a number of successful machine gun designs, beginning in the 1890s. His most remarkable achievements were probably his water-cooled .30 caliber Model 1917 and the .50 caliber M2 "Ma Deuce," which is still in use today.

The machine guns just briefly described fall into the category of fixed-position, crew-served weapons and their continued evolution is outside the scope of this work. Browning's famous BAR was a traditionally stocked box magazine full-auto rifle in .30-06 caliber. While it served decades as an effective military arm, it was generally fired from a bipod.

SUBMACHINE GUNS, BATTLE RIFLES, and ASSAULT RIFLES

While cartridges in the .30-06 class are readily aimed and controlled in single-shot fire, including semi-automatic fire, they tend to be less controllable and thus less effective when fired full-auto offhand due to the recoil and cumulative muzzle climb with each round to leave the barrel.

This limitation of full-auto fire from

INTRODUCTION

Major Uziel Gal holding an Uzi and MP40

a personal arm was first addressed by the development of "submachine guns." Generally, these are full-auto capable weapons designed to be fired from the shoulder like a rifle, but chambered for a lower-powered pistol cartridge instead of a full-power rifle cartridge. The resulting gun was controllable and could be effectively aimed in short-range full-auto fire. The stubby pistol cartridges used by the gun could efficiently burn all their powder in a shorter barrel than required for a high-powered rifle round, resulting in a lighter gun with a shorter and handier overall length. The trade-off was that their effective range is much shorter than a traditional rifle, and an individual round hits with less power. The sub-gun is considered more effective when encounters are likely to be fast and at short range, such as trench warfare, inside buildings, or in heavy jungle. They are less effective for precision shooting or over long ranges.

Probably the first submachine gun was the Bergmann Schmeisser MP18 of WWI. One of the best, and certainly the most famous, was the Thompson Submachine gun, or "Tommy Gun," introduced at the end of WWI in .45 ACP. Used by both law enforcement and gangsters, it has been called "the gun the made the 20s roar" and the "Chicago typewriter." It went on to serve honorably in WWII and beyond. Other WWII sub-guns included the German MP38 and MP40, the British Sten gun, the Russian PPS series, and the U.S. M3 "grease gun."

A milestone in post-war submachine gun design was the 9mm Uzi, designed by Israeli officer Uziel Gal, first produced in 1951. Although still popular, it has since probably been replaced as the first choice submachine gun for military and law enforcement by the MP-5 in the same caliber, produced by the German firm of Heckler & Koch (H&K).

Most countries entered WWII with a bolt action as their primary battle rifle. Germany had its latest Mauser, the 8 mm Kar 98; Britain, the Short Magazine Lee Enfield (SMLE) in .303 caliber; Japan, the Arisaka; and so forth. The Springfield '03 was still widely issued to American forces, but in the decade preceding the outbreak of hostilities, the U.S. Army had been testing competing designs of semi-auto rifles, then proceeding to manufacture and issue the pattern deemed best.

The U.S. M1 Garand in .30-06 caliber was without question the finest full-power rifle fielded in WWII. Instead of a fixed or detachable box magazine, it was loaded with eight rounds held in a metal clip. When the last round was fired, the clip was automatically ejected with the action remaining open for quick insertion of another loaded clip. It was rugged, reliable, and powerful.

It was also heavy. The Army sought a firearm that was more accurate and powerful, and had a longer range than a pistol, but which was lighter and handier than the full-sized rifle, intended primarily as a secondary weapon for tankers, artillery crews, and personnel who were not in a primary combat role. This role was ably filled by the M1 Carbine, a semi-auto accepting a 15-round detachable box magazine. It fired a new straight-wall cartridge, midway in power between the pistol and the full-sized rifle.

Germany also was developing a mid-range shoulder weapon, but with a different intent. They sought a detachable magazine rifle that would fire a reduced-power cartridge and would be controllable and effective in full-auto firing mode, with more range and power than a submachine gun. The resulting MP-43 filled the bill, but was developed late in the war. The concept was one that would survive the conflict—the Germans called the gun a Sturmgewehr, loosely translated as "assault rifle."

Most military establishments hesitated to "downsize" the power and range of their primary rifles in the early Cold War years. The semi-auto detachable magazine concept was an obvious success, and there was something to be said for full-auto capability. A series of full-power "battle rifles" was introduced to meet this need—the FN-FAL and the Heckler & Koch G3 being two patterns that were widely adopted. The U.S. developed a Garand look-alike with detachable magazine and full-auto capability, the M-14.

But the assault rifle concept wouldn't go away. The Soviet Union accepted the lower-power round idea in its fixed-magazine semi-auto chambered for an intermediate power 7.62 x 39 mm round in 1945, the SKS, which saw wide distribution and production in Soviet client states and enjoys popularity in the post-cold war U.S. as an inexpensive semi-auto military surplus rifle.

They followed two years later with what would become probably the most widely produced military long arm design in history, and the quintessential assault rifle—the Kalashnikov-designed AK-47 in the same caliber.

The AK-47 is a select fire (semi-auto or full-auto) carbine-size weapon with a detachable 30-round box magazine. It has a well-deserved reputation for relatively cheap production and for reliability, even in the most adverse environments or when used by undertrained indigenous forces who may neglect maintenance. It makes extensive use of sheet metal stampings in its construction, with a simple wooden buttstock with pistol grip.

The U.S. version of the assault-weapon configuration was introduced in 1963, originally known as the AR-15 and XM-16 designed by Eugene Stoner. It was ultimately adopted as the M-16 manufactured by Colt. It is chambered for the 5.56 mm Nato round, a military twin of the .223 Remington cartridge, and takes a detachable box magazine of 20 or 30 rounds. The rear sight is mounted on a distinctive integral carrying handle, and the stock and handguard are made of black synthetic material.

Initial reviews of the M-16 were mixed. A combination of an improper type of powder used in the manufacture of the cartridge and a mistaken belief that maintenance could be neglected resulted in some early failures in the field. Some in the military establishment resisted a .22 caliber round for combat, dismissing it as a "poodle shooter."

This concern may be understood by reviewing a statistic commonly used to summarize a cartridge's power level—the muzzle energy. Muzzle energy is a product of the weight of the bullet and the velocity at the moment it leaves the barrel, expressed in foot pounds (ft. lb.). The WWII and early post-war battle rifles chambered for .30-06 and 8 mm Mauser-class cartridges typically develop 2,000 to 2,600 ft./lb. of muzzle energy. By contrast, the .45 ACP and 9 mm Luger rounds, commonly used in military pistols and submachine guns, run in the 300 to 400 ft./lb. range. That's nothing to sneeze at by the way…. the common .22 Long Rifle cartridge, which can certainly be lethal, runs in the 90 to 125 ft./lb. range.

The intermediate "assault rifle" cartridges, such as the 7.62x39 mm and 5.56 mm Nato, average in the 1,200 to 1,600 ft./lb. range. The designers of these were effective in "splitting the difference" between the high-power rifle and pistol-cartridge-power ranges, but many old soldiers were not sold on the compromise.

Yet, both M-16 rifle and ammunition were significantly lighter than either the old battle rifles or the AK system, allowing an infantryman to carry more ammunition or other load. With tuning and evolution, the M-16 pattern proved to be highly accurate out to distances reached by the earlier full-sized battle rifles.

The evolutionary descendants of the AK-47 and M-16 have become the dominant

Georg Johann Luger

military rifle patterns as the world enters the 21st century. Both have proven to be effective in combat.

Semi-automatic versions of both designs have become highly popular with civilian shooters in recent decades, with the AR-15 (semi-auto version of the M-16) coming to dominate many types of target competition.

In the 1970s, anti-gun forces incorrectly applied the "assault rifle" terminology to these semi-auto sporting versions. The function of the sporters is identical to other semi-auto sporting guns—it takes a separate pull of the trigger to fire each round. They lack the full-auto capability that originally

defined "assault rifles."

The terminology redefinition stuck, however, leading to ill-conceived legislation that temporarily banned the production of certain types of guns, based solely on cosmetic appearances. Fortunately, the Clinton semi-auto ban has since sunset, so that these popular semi-auto rifles are again available in their original configuration at affordable prices.

MODERN GUN MILESTONES

Recent decades have witnessed the continuing evolution and development

of other types of sporting firearms, with several recurring trends.

Handguns, and revolvers in particular, have seen the development of more and more powerful ammunition. In 1935, Smith & Wesson rocked the handgun world with the introduction of the .357 Magnum cartridge and their prestigious Registered Magnum revolver to fire it. At a time when full power "big bore" handgun rounds ran in the 300 to 350 ft./lb. muzzle energy range, S&W upped the ante to over 500 ft./lb. Results of actual law enforcement shootings suggest that the .357 magnum round, with 125 grain hollowpoint loads, may be the most effective "stopper" still today. The fact that revolvers chambered for the .357 Magnum can also shoot the milder .38 Special has contributed to their continuing popularity.

S&W followed this with the .44 Magnum in 1955. With muzzle energy approaching 1,000 ft./lb., the .44 Mag changed handgun big game hunting from a "stunt" to a serious and common sporting pursuit. When the Dirty Harry movies hit the theaters, lots of folks with more imagination than experience decided they needed "the world's most powerful handgun," not understanding how to manage the considerable recoil. It was not uncommon to find a S&W .44 Magnum advertised for sale in "as new" condition, with 6 cartridges missing from the 50-round box. Once around the cylinder was enough for many would-be Harry Callahans!

Just recently, Smith & Wesson raised the bar to a previously unimaginable level with the introduction of their X-frame .500 Magnum revolver. Developing an incredible 2,500 ft./lb. of muzzle energy, the 500 readily surpasses the power level of many high-power rifles.

Auto-pistol evolution took a leap forward in 1971 when the Smith & Wesson Model 59 was the first weapon to combine the high-capacity double-stack magazine of the Browning High Power with the double-action mechanism of the German WWII era Walther P-38. A number of firms followed suit, and the genre, known as "wonder nines" for their usual 9 mm chambering, began to make inroads into a police market that previously had been dominated by double-action revolvers. The Swiss-based firm of SIG Sauer developed a strong reputation for quality and reliability in this type of pistol, and the Beretta Model 92 in the wonder nine configuration replaced the old warhorse 1911A1 pistol as the U.S. Army standard issue.

In 1982, the semi-auto pistol market was turned upside-down by a new Austrian manufacturer offering a radically different design--the frame was made from plastic-like polymer--and a funny name. Traditionalists initially scoffed at the 17-round design with no external manual safeties other than a lever on the face of trigger and an operating system that was neither SA nor DA, but was instead called a "safe action" by the maker. Beauty is as beauty does, however, and the Glock did nothing but perform. It combined reliability, simplicity, affordability, and functional accuracy. Today, it is likely that more Glocks ride in police holsters than any other make.

The trend to new materials other than traditional blue steel and wood had begun years before. Smith & Wesson used lightweight alloys to make lightweight guns easier to carry, beginning with aluminum-frame Airweight Chiefs Specials in 1952 and continuing through Scandium and Titanium alloys today that get .38 revolver weights down to the 10-ounce range.

Smith & Wesson and Charter Arms led the way in using rust-resistant stainless steel for small revolvers likely to be carried in sweaty environments close to the body, beginning in the mid-1960s. Since then, stainless steel has nearly replaced blued carbon steel in revolver designs and has made major inroads in long gun and semi-auto pistol production.

Many major handgun makers have followed Glock's lead in offering synthetic-framed auto-pistols. For long gun stocks, synthetic stocks have been found to be more lightweight and less affected by environmental extremes than wood. Rubber has replaced wood as the most likely handgun grip material.

In the repeating shotgun field, the Winchester Model 12 was probably the standard for pump shotguns in the mid-20th century and was perhaps replaced by the Remington Model 870 in more recent years. Semi-auto shotguns have overcome their reputation for finicky performance, first with Remington 1100, and then with the Benelli Model 90, and have enjoyed an outstanding reputation for reliability in recent years.

Probably the last of the great firearms inventor/entrepreneurs in the tradition of Sam Colt and D.B. Wesson was Bill Ruger. His Sturm Ruger firm developed a reputation for improving classic sporting gun designs, and turning out a broad line of well-made and reasonably priced firearms, from revolvers and rifles through auto-pistols and over/under shotguns.

Other new firms sprang up to challenge the old line makers with improved or cheaper versions of the classic designs. Springfield Armory has become a major maker of military pattern sporting arms based on classic military designs such as the 1911 and the Garand patterns. Taurus began to offer serious competition to S&W in the revolver field. Firms such as Bushmaster and others began to develop a reputation for quality AR-15 semi-auto rifles, a market once belonging to Colt. Other makers such as Uberti and Navy Arms saw the strong nostalgia market for 19th century designs and began to produce quality versions of early percussion revolvers, Single-Action Armies, Winchester lever guns, and other arms appealing to Old West buffs and participants in the fun new sport of Cowboy Action Shooting.

Options for aiming a firearm have expanded dramatically over the past 50 years. Telescopic sights for precision rifle shooting were used as early as the Civil War. It wasn't until after WWII, however, that it became a standard practice to mount a scope on most serious hunting rifles. The technology of these optics has continually evolved and improved. In the 1970s and 1980s, scopes came to be used on hunting handguns. New forms of sighting equipment, such as electronic red dot sights, glow in the dark night sights, ultra-compact laser aiming systems, and even night vision scopes, have come on the market and met with acceptance. They have been incorporated on firearms from concealed-carry handguns to target competition arms and military issue rifles.

William B. Ruger holding the Outstanding American Handgunner Award for 1975

Glock handguns are now widely used by law enforcement and the military.

THE EARLIEST GUNS

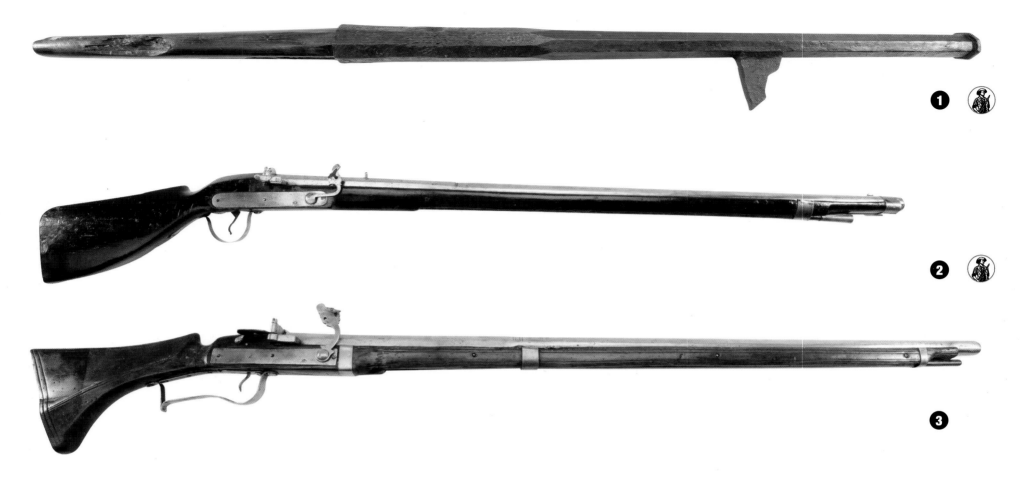

1 European Hand Cannon - 1-inch diameter bore - circa 1350 - This early handcannon was found in a ruined fortress that fell in the mid-14th century, and was once part of the Archduke Eugen collection at Salzburg Castle. It is the oldest gun at the National Firearms Museum and may be the oldest gun on display in America.

2 English Matchlock Musket - .82 caliber - circa 1575-style common to Virginia and Bay Colony Militia units of the 1600s.

3 German Matchlock Musket - .80 caliber - circa 1580-1600.

Hand Cannon

Hand cannon - ca. 1350 A.D. - The earliest and simplest guns are called handcannons, used ca. 1350 into the 1500s. These are essentially metal tubes, closed on one end, with a touch hole for manually lighting the powder charge. Handcannons were the first projectile arms that relied on blackpowder as a propulsive force. Loaded with an assortment of lead shot, nails, small rocks or other material, a handcannon could deliver a devastating blast at close range. Many examples exhibit a protruding flange or spike extending from the barrel to serve as a retaining point against a wall or tree branch during firing.

1 Indian Matchlock Gun - .63 caliber - circa 1760 - This modified Indian pattern gun is decorated with gold damascene.

2 Japanese Matchlock Temple Gun - .60 caliber - circa 1800 - Typical pattern of Japanese matchlocks for centuries.

3 Japanese Matchlock Temple Gun - .50 caliber - circa 1750 - Gold and silver barrel inlays. Temple guns were fired to open religious ceremonies.

Matchlock

Matchlock - ca. 1450 A.D. - The matchlock was the earliest type of lock for firing a gun. The "slow match" was a length of cord treated with chemicals to help it burn slowly, presenting a glowing tip on the end that was mechanically lowered into a pan of gunpowder adjoining the touch hole in the rear of the barrel to ignite the charge in the barrel. The "serpentine" is the device that holds and lowers the slow match. Matchlocks were used in India, Japan, and elsewhere in Asia well into the 19th century.

THE EARLIEST GUNS

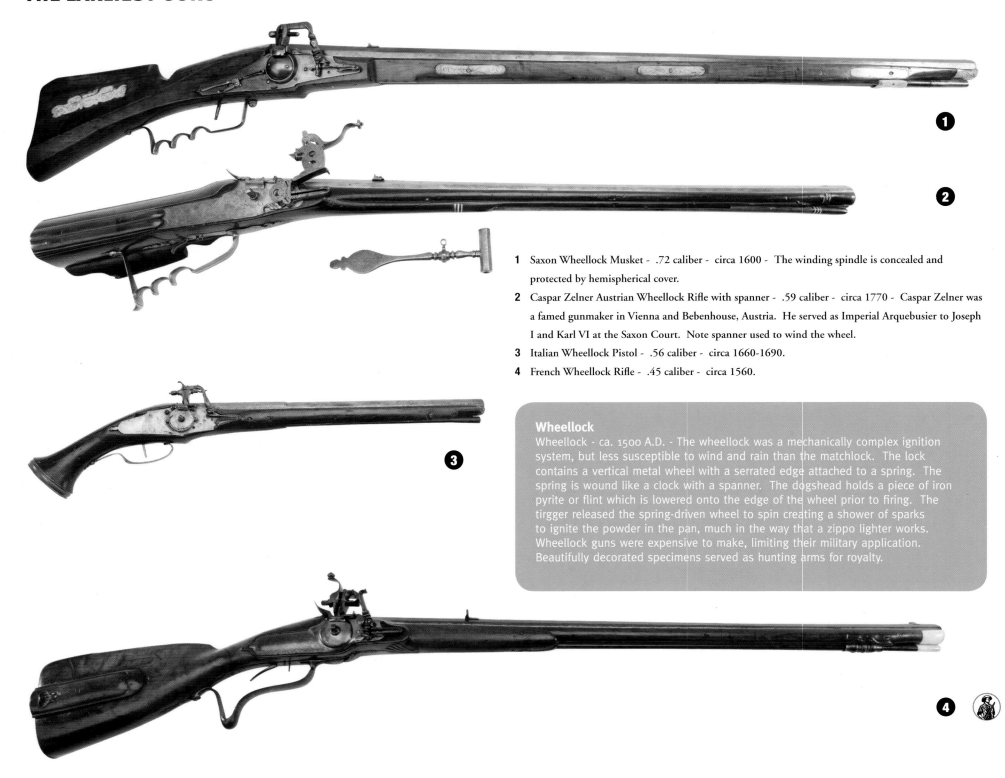

1 Saxon Wheellock Musket - .72 caliber - circa 1600 - The winding spindle is concealed and protected by hemispherical cover.

2 Caspar Zelner Austrian Wheellock Rifle with spanner - .59 caliber - circa 1770 - Caspar Zelner was a famed gunmaker in Vienna and Bebenhouse, Austria. He served as Imperial Arquebusier to Joseph I and Karl VI at the Saxon Court. Note spanner used to wind the wheel.

3 Italian Wheellock Pistol - .56 caliber - circa 1660-1690.

4 French Wheellock Rifle - .45 caliber - circa 1560.

Wheellock
Wheellock - ca. 1500 A.D. - The wheellock was a mechanically complex ignition system, but less susceptible to wind and rain than the matchlock. The lock contains a vertical metal wheel with a serrated edge attached to a spring. The spring is wound like a clock with a spanner. The dogshead holds a piece of iron pyrite or flint which is lowered onto the edge of the wheel prior to firing. The tirgger released the spring-driven wheel to spin creating a shower of sparks to ignite the powder in the pan, much in the way that a zippo lighter works. Wheellock guns were expensive to make, limiting their military application. Beautifully decorated specimens served as hunting arms for royalty.

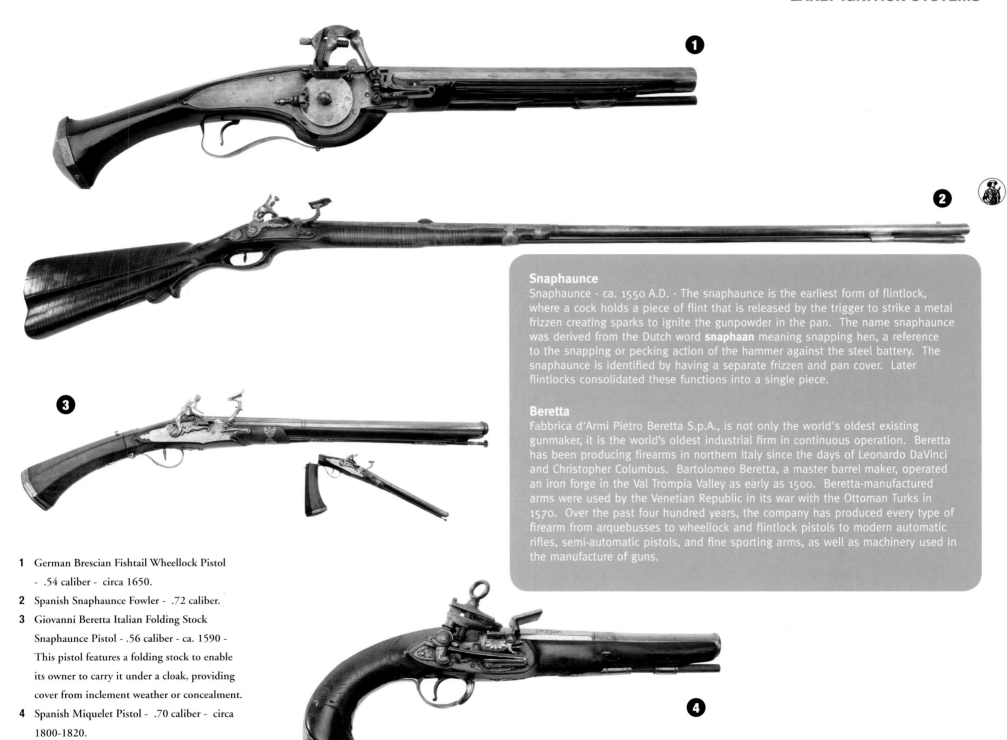

Snaphaunce
Snaphaunce - ca. 1550 A.D. - The snaphaunce is the earliest form of flintlock, where a cock holds a piece of flint that is released by the trigger to strike a metal frizzen creating sparks to ignite the gunpowder in the pan. The name snaphaunce was derived from the Dutch word **snaphaan** meaning snapping hen, a reference to the snapping or pecking action of the hammer against the steel battery. The snaphaunce is identified by having a separate frizzen and pan cover. Later flintlocks consolidated these functions into a single piece.

Beretta
Fabbrica d'Armi Pietro Beretta S.p.A., is not only the world's oldest existing gunmaker, it is the world's oldest industrial firm in continuous operation. Beretta has been producing firearms in northern Italy since the days of Leonardo DaVinci and Christopher Columbus. Bartolomeo Beretta, a master barrel maker, operated an iron forge in the Val Trompia Valley as early as 1500. Beretta-manufactured arms were used by the Venetian Republic in its war with the Ottoman Turks in 1570. Over the past four hundred years, the company has produced every type of firearm from arquebusses to wheellock and flintlock pistols to modern automatic rifles, semi-automatic pistols, and fine sporting arms, as well as machinery used in the manufacture of guns.

1 German Brescian Fishtail Wheellock Pistol - .54 caliber - circa 1650.

2 Spanish Snaphaunce Fowler - .72 caliber.

3 Giovanni Beretta Italian Folding Stock Snaphaunce Pistol - .56 caliber - ca. 1590 - This pistol features a folding stock to enable its owner to carry it under a cloak, providing cover from inclement weather or concealment.

4 Spanish Miquelet Pistol - .70 caliber - circa 1800-1820.

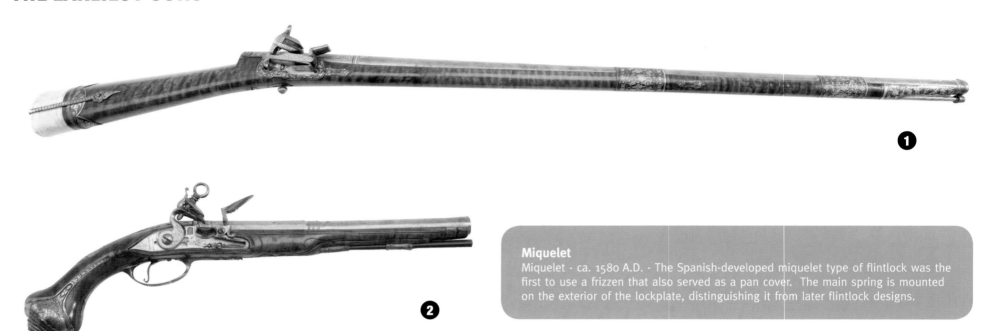

Miquelet
Miquelet - ca. 1580 A.D. - The Spanish-developed miquelet type of flintlock was the first to use a frizzen that also served as a pan cover. The main spring is mounted on the exterior of the lockplate, distinguishing it from later flintlock designs.

1 Persian Miquelet - .58 caliber - circa 1770 - Decorated with gold damascene and an ivory buttplate.

2 Spanish Flintlock Pistol - .66 caliber - circa 1650 - Heavily engraved metal furniture.

3 Spanish Miquelet - 16 gauge - circa 1750 - Gold overlaid brass scrollwork.

1 Thomas Matson English Doglock Musket -
.75 caliber - circa 1650.

2 Samuel Depfer German Cheek-Stock Doglock
Musket - .40 caliber - circa 1670 - Early
flint ignition gun built on an older matchlock
stock. This is an early example of updating an
obsolete firearm. Strassburg proofmarks.

3 Doglock Musket by Thomas Matson
(England) .80 caliber smoothbore flintlock,
circa mid-17th century.

4 Pair of Perkins English Flintlock Pistols - .77
caliber - circa 1790.

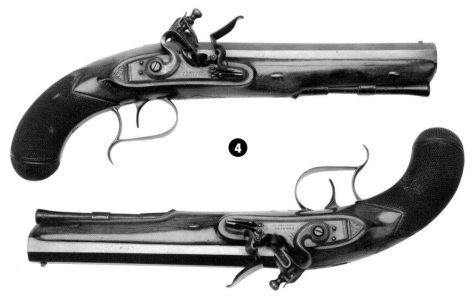

Doglock
Doglock - ca. 1600 A.D. - The
doglock was an early flintlock
with one of the earliest safety
mechanisms. The dog is a flat-
hook-shaped catch mounted
behind the cocking piece and can
be swiveled forward to lock the
mechanism until ready for firing.

THE EARLIEST GUNS

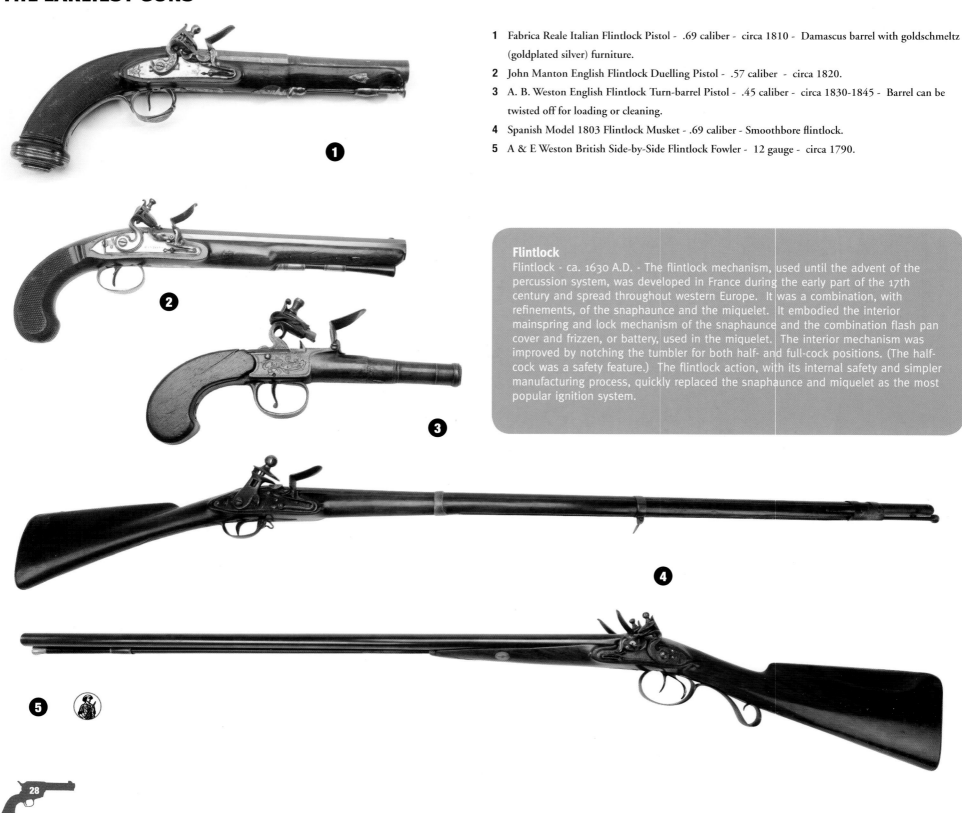

1 Fabrica Reale Italian Flintlock Pistol - .69 caliber - circa 1810 - Damascus barrel with goldschmeltz (goldplated silver) furniture.

2 John Manton English Flintlock Duelling Pistol - .57 caliber - circa 1820.

3 A. B. Weston English Flintlock Turn-barrel Pistol - .45 caliber - circa 1830-1845 - Barrel can be twisted off for loading or cleaning.

4 Spanish Model 1803 Flintlock Musket - .69 caliber - Smoothbore flintlock.

5 A & E Weston British Side-by-Side Flintlock Fowler - 12 gauge - circa 1790.

Flintlock

Flintlock - ca. 1630 A.D. - The flintlock mechanism, used until the advent of the percussion system, was developed in France during the early part of the 17th century and spread throughout western Europe. It was a combination, with refinements, of the snaphaunce and the miquelet. It embodied the interior mainspring and lock mechanism of the snaphaunce and the combination flash pan cover and frizzen, or battery, used in the miquelet. The interior mechanism was improved by notching the tumbler for both half- and full-cock positions. (The half-cock was a safety feature.) The flintlock action, with its internal safety and simpler manufacturing process, quickly replaced the snaphaunce and miquelet as the most popular ignition system.

1 German Ball-Butt Dag Wheellock Pistol - .51 caliber - circa 1620-1650 - An early combination arm, this wheellock pistol could be wielded as a club after firing.

2 Turkish/Balkan Rat-Tail Flintlock Pistol Pair - .62 caliber - circa 1800 - Ornate cast silver stocks.

3 German "Tschinke" Muzzleloading Wheellock Rifle - .34 caliber - circa 1675 - Manufactured in eastern Prussia, this Tschinke, or hinds-foot-stocked sporting rifle was elaborately inlaid with bone, ivory, and mother-of-pearl. The short stock on many early longarms was intended to be supported against the cheek in firing position, rather than further back against the shoulder.

Early Firearms Decoration
The early gunsmiths of Europe were responsible for the basic form and function of the arms that they created. The fine and elaborate decoration often found on early arms, however, was usually created by artisans who also used their skills on furniture, mounts, and caskets. With the contemporary development of firearms, the upper classes adopted richly decorated pieces as an indication of their social status.

THE EARLIEST GUNS

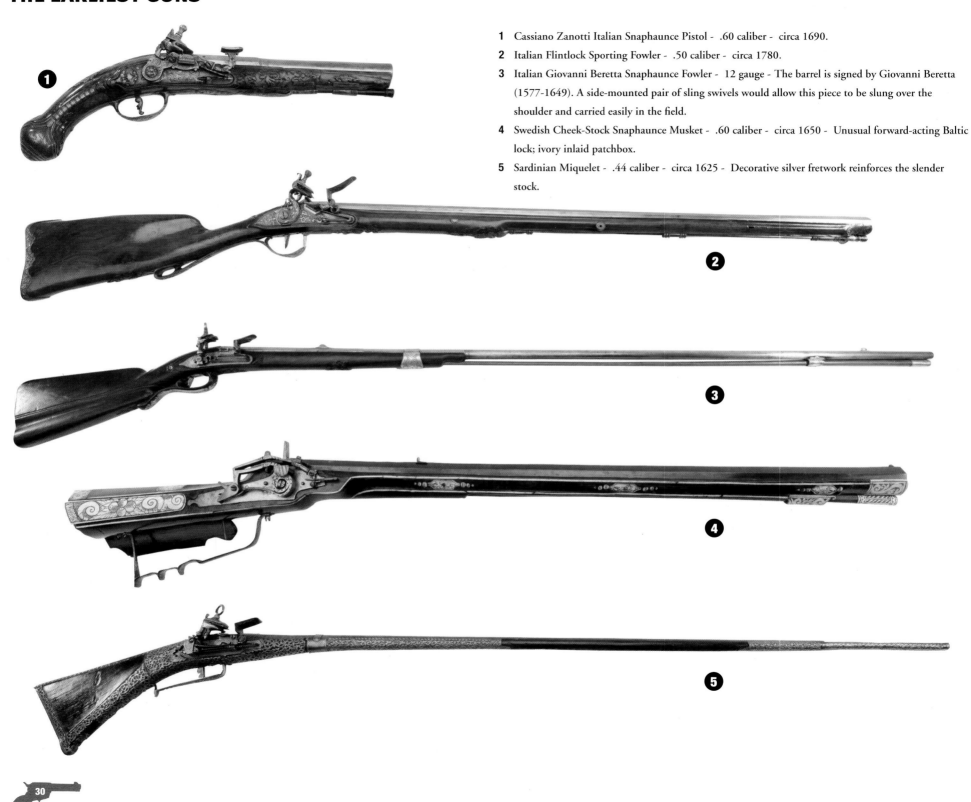

1 Cassiano Zanotti Italian Snaphaunce Pistol - .60 caliber - circa 1690.

2 Italian Flintlock Sporting Fowler - .50 caliber - circa 1780.

3 Italian Giovanni Beretta Snaphaunce Fowler - 12 gauge - The barrel is signed by Giovanni Beretta (1577-1649). A side-mounted pair of sling swivels would allow this piece to be slung over the shoulder and carried easily in the field.

4 Swedish Cheek-Stock Snaphaunce Musket - .60 caliber - circa 1650 - Unusual forward-acting Baltic lock; ivory inlaid patchbox.

5 Sardinian Miquelet - .44 caliber - circa 1625 - Decorative silver fretwork reinforces the slender stock.

1 Napoleon Bonaparte's Flintlock Double Fowler - 20 gauge - circa 1804-1815 - Crafted by Fatou of Paris, this double flintlock fowler, inlaid with gold, silver, and platinum and fitted with a purple velvet cheekpiece, was presented by Napoleon Bonaparte to Marquis Faulte de Vanteaux of Limoges, a general in Napoleon's army.

2 The Duke of York's Flintlock Fowler by John Manton - 16 gauge - circa 1795-1800 - This John Manton flintlock fowler was once owned by Frederick Augustus, Duke of York and son of King George III of England.

3 King James II's Flintlock Fowler by John Cosens - 10 gauge - circa 1688 - A well-worn flintlock fowler bearing the crest of King James II, the last of the Stuart line to hold the throne of Great Britain, Ireland, and Scotland. This piece was reportedly taken from the royal baggage train after James fled England in 1688.

THE EARLIEST GUNS

1   The Mayflower Gun - Italian Wheellock Carbine - .66 caliber - circa 1600 - In 1620, the Pilgrims aboard the ship Mayflower sailed from Portsmouth, England, and landed at Plymouth Rock in Massachusetts. Prior to leaving the ship, the free men on board drafted and signed a Bill of Rights and Governance which become known as the Mayflower Compact. One of the colony members was John Alden who established a home and raised a family despite the harsh winters and disease that thinned the ranks of the first settlers. This is believed to be the carbine he brought with him. It was originally a .50 caliber rifle, but extensive usage has removed almost all traces of rifling. Discovered during the restoration of Alden's home in Duxbury, Massachusetts, in 1924, this short-barreled piece is typical of many European arms possessed by the early New England settlers. Alden's home was occupied by members of his family from 1653 through 1896. When found in this home, the carbine was secured in a concealed compartment and may have been set aside close at hand to serve as personal protection in the event of an attack. Alden, a cooper, is believed to have purchased this carbine as part of outfitting himself for the New World before setting forth on the Mayflower.

❶

The brave and strong settlers who endured the raging ocean voyage to the New World brought firearms that had been crafted in their Old World. These early firearms protected the explorers and colonists against man and beast, and aided them in their unending quest for food.

Relationships between the European settlers and the Native Americans were tenuous at best. English, French, and Spanish colonists, although friendly and peaceful at times to the Native Americans, showed little hesitation in attacking them for economic gain. As tobacco, gold, and other spoils of the New World gained demand in Europe, the competition and greed for land and resources often resulted in war.

As settlements in America were established, protection from attack became a primary concern. Although the colonists' firearms were inaccurate, heavy, and slow to load and fire, these arms had a tremendous effect on the American Indian. James Rosier reported that when the native inhabitants of the Maine coast witnessed in 1605 the firing of the English musket, they were most fearful and would fall flat down at the sound of them.

European colonists formed an alliance with the American Indian by procuring valuable furs, food, and other goods through trade. Desirous of European trinkets and articles, the Indians traded beaver pelts to the colonists. The beaver skin was in great demand and brought high

prices in Europe.

After witnessing the value of the firearm for hunting, war, and protection, the American Indians wanted to obtain firearms for themselves. However, most colonists regarded the possession of firearms by the native population as a threat to life and security. Proclamations, laws, and ordinances were enacted prohibiting firearms trade with natives. By the end of the 17th century, the illegal trade of guns and munitions became so prevalent that the colonies began to establish a legal arms trade which included licensing and taxation.

1 Spanish Matchlock Musket - .78 caliber - circa 1530-1550 - Matchlocks were favored by many European explorers in the New World because they were cheaper to obtain and easier to maintain than mechanically complex wheellock arms. This musket was likely made in Madrid and was intended to be used with a forked rest.

2 Spanish Miquelet Blunderbuss - 1.25inch caliber - circa 1670 - It is believed that this Spanish arm was reworked and restocked in Mexico in the 17th or 18th century. Spaniards had taught Mestizos in the area around Mexico City to repair and refurbish firearms. The decoration on this gun shows a fascinating mix of European and Meso-American symbols.

3 Francisco Targarona Spanish Miquelet Escopeta - .72 caliber - circa 1775 - Spanish military carbine typical of the arms carried in Mexico and Spanish colonial America.

4 Spanish Model 1803 Flintlock Musket - .69 caliber - circa 1800-1830 - Typical of those used by Spanish soldiers in the New Mexico area.

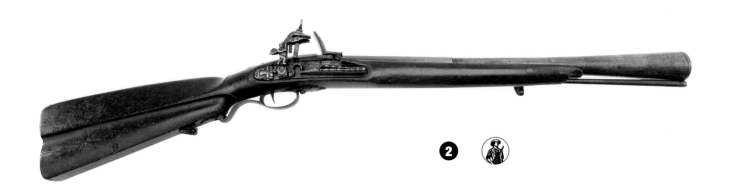

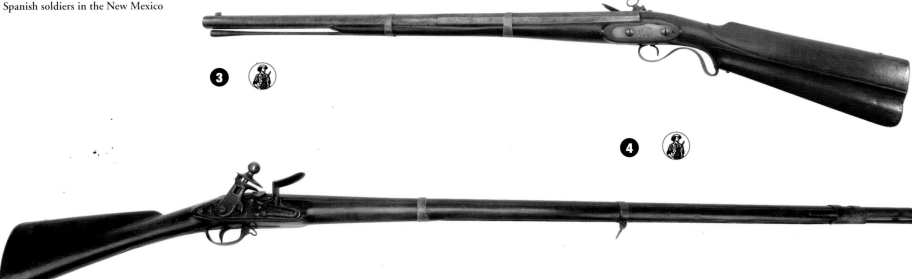

THE EARLIEST GUNS

1. Dutch/English Flintlock Fusil - .65 caliber - circa 1720 - Likely manufactured near Albany, NY, by Dutch settlers.

2. French Flintlock Fusil - .61 caliber - circa 1690 - Type used by French fur traders on the Mississippi and St. Lawrence Rivers and in the Great Lakes region.

3. Ketland & Allport English Flintlock Rifle - .60 caliber - circa 1815 - Type provided to the British to Native American allies during the War of 1812.

4. Dutch/English Flintlock Fowler - .75 caliber - circa 1680 - At the time, longer barrels were believed to provide higher velocity and superior shot patterns.

5. Queen Anne-Style Pocket Flintlock Pistol - .38 caliber - circa 1750 - Typical features of a Queen Anne-style pistol include a screw-off barrel for loading from the breech and a cannon-shaped barrel. Most have the majority of the barrel exposed, with the stock lacking a forend.

Musket, Fusil, Rifle, Fowler.

Musket: From the Spanish word **mosquette**, denoting a heavy military firearm. The earliest muskets were matchlocks weighing as much as 20 pounds and having a bore of nearly 8 gauge. By the colonial period in America, standardization of firearms had begun and the term *musket* was applied to any smoothbore military firearm of large caliber.

Fusil: A lightweight flintlock smooth bore, as distinguished from the heavier military musket.

Rifle: From the German word **riffeln** meaning to cut or groove. The process of rifling a gun barrel was developed by either Gaspar Kollner of Vienna or August Kotter of Nuremberg in the late 15th or early 16th century. In the rifling process, a series of spiral grooves are cut into the inside (or bore) of the barrel. The areas between the grooves are called lands. This rifling imparts a spiral motion to the projectile that aids in accuracy and increases its effective range.

Fowler: By the late 15th century, it had been discovered that when a large number of small lead projectiles (called shot) were loaded into a gun and fired, the projectiles would scatter or spread increasing the chance of success when hunting fowl and small game. The English pioneered the manufacture of shot, and subsequently developed a very long barreled firearm with a large smooth bore, called a fowler, which was designed to kill large quantities of fowl and small game. Often, as much as a pound of shot (200 to 250 pellets) was seated down the long barrel with a significant charge of powder. Any sitting group of fowl or game was an easy target for the resulting hail of projectiles.

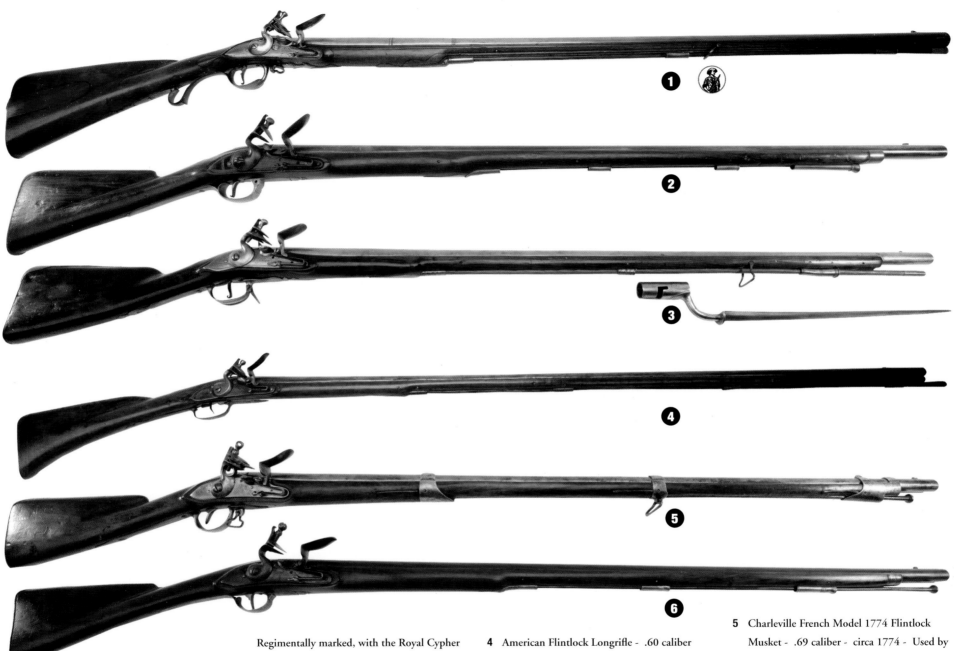

1   Swedish Flintlock Fusil - .63 caliber - circa 1700.

2   British Pattern 1777 Short Land Pattern Flintlock Musket - .76 caliber - circa 1780 - Regimentally marked, with the Royal Cypher of George III.

3   British Long Land Pattern "First Brown Bess" Flintlock Musket with bayonet - .78 caliber - circa 1780 - Contract musket by London gunsmith Willian Predden.

4   American Flintlock Longrifle - .60 caliber - circa 1770-1780 - In the Revolutionary War, many colonists were armed with their traditional hunting arms. Such rifles were slower loading but allowed better accuracy than military muskets.

5   Charleville French Model 1774 Flintlock Musket - .69 caliber - circa 1774 - Used by colonial troops during the Revolutionary War. Later marked "Maryland" for use in the War of 1812.

6   Committee of Safety Flintlock Musket - .80 caliber - circa 1775.

THE EARLIEST GUNS

1 British Pattern 1769 Short Land Pattern
Musket - .80 caliber - circa 1780 - Family
attribution to use in conjunction with the
battles of Lexington and Concord.

2 Committee of Safety Second Model Brown
Bess Flintlock Musket - .80 caliber - circa
1770 - Converted from a British musket

salvaged for issue by a colonial Committee of
Safety.

Shot Heard Round the World

By 1775, relations between England and her American
Colonies had suffered greatly. British military occupation
and rule, and the excesses and abuses inflicted by
the British upon the Americans, greatly angered the
colonists. For example, under the revised Quartering Act
of 1765, an officer of the King's Army could knock on the
door of any private residence and demand lodging for
his men.

Young British officers, spoiling for a fight, regularly took
parties of soldiers on short military exercises through
the Massachusetts towns of Waltham, Dedham, and
Cambridge. The sight of Americans drilling in the fields
greatly amused them. Their superiors, however, saw
these drills as an omen of future armed resistance.
In Cambridge, the British troops seized powder and
arms belonging to the townspeople. Private houses were
entered and arms were seized. In Charlestown, more
arms were seized. These acts sent an alarm throughout
New England. In response, the men of Massachusetts
formed Committees and exercised the right to call out
colonial troops should the occasion arise.

To provide for defense, special groups of men were
established who could answer the call to arms
immediately. These citizen-soldiers were called
Minutemen.

In Boston, British General Thomas Gage commanded
4,000 troops who were called Redcoats by the native
Bostonians. These soldiers had been given the task
of enforcing British ordinances and keeping peace in
the City of Boston. General Gage's exercises through
the countryside and his recent confiscation of civilian
firearms had aggravated the local population to the
point of armed insurrection.

In April of 1775, Gage ordered the confiscation of all
privately owned arms, gun (cannon) powder, and shot
held by the local militia units that dotted the countryside
between Boston, Lexington, and Concord. Hearing of this
plan, residents devised a system of signal lamps hung
in Boston's Old North Church to signal the approach of
British soldiers by land or sea. Paul Revere made his
famous midnight ride to alert the citizenry of the British
approach.

On April 19, 1775, under the direction of Colonel Francis
Smith and Royal Marine Major John Pitcairn, Gage's
troops clashed with the colonial Minutemen and patriot
troops at the North Bridge located between Lexington
and Concord. With the first shot upon the King's troops,
the American Revolution had begun.

As in previous wars, the American Revolution was, for
the most part, fought and won by the infantryman. His
firearm was the flintlock musket with bayonet. This large
bore musket had a maximum effective range between 80
and 100 yards.

The typical inaccuracy of these firearms led to the
development of tactics known as volley firing in which
the massed infantry of one unit fired in unison at
their enemy. Troops were trained to load and fire with
accuracy, three times per minute. Rifles, which provided
excellent accuracy at long ranges, were used by the
Americans in guerilla warfare, but were ineffective on
the battlefield due to their small numbers. The American
rifle, with no provision for a bayonet and a lengthy
loading procedure, gained notoriety only in the hands of
the sharpshooter.

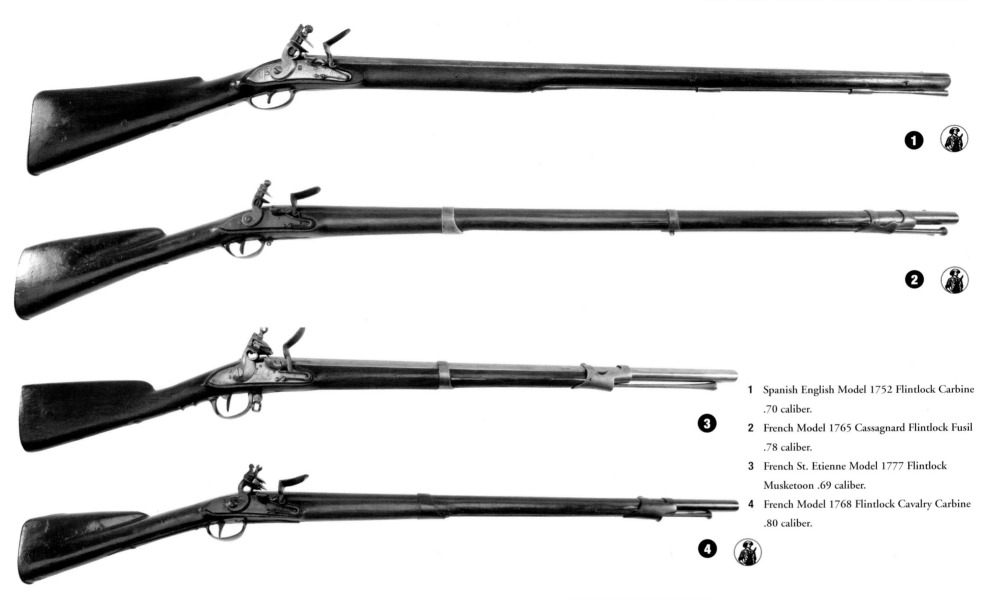

1 Spanish English Model 1752 Flintlock Carbine .70 caliber.

2 French Model 1765 Cassagnard Flintlock Fusil .78 caliber.

3 French St. Etienne Model 1777 Flintlock Musketoon .69 caliber.

4 French Model 1768 Flintlock Cavalry Carbine .80 caliber.

Brown Bess, Charleville, and Committee of Safety

The prevalent long arms of the American Revolution were smoothbore large caliber flintlock muskets of the type used by the British and French military. The British Army Land Pattern musket was nicknamed The Brown Bess. The French pattern muskets were called Charlevilles.

Committees of Safety were established in the thirteen colonies to organize and equip their respective militias for military action against the British. Committee of Safety muskets were produced by local gunsmiths, usually patterned on the British Brown Bess. The muskets did not include any sort of manufacturer's markings lest the makers be charged with treason by British authorities.

THE EARLIEST GUNS

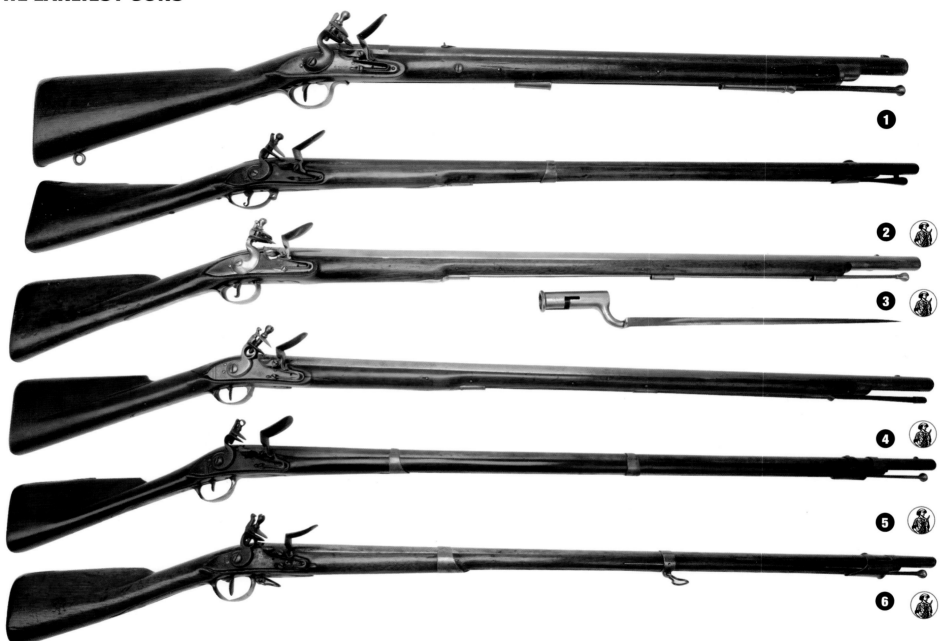

1 Flintlock Yeomanry Carbine by Henry Nock (London, England) - .75 caliber flintlock.

2 Hessian Flintlock Musket - .80 caliber smoothbore flintlock, circa 1770.

3 British Short Land Service Pattern (Second Model Brown Bess) Flintlock Musket - .70 caliber smoothbore flintlock, circa 1775.

4 Committee of Safety Flintlock Musket - .78 caliber smoothbore.

5 French Model 1746 Flintlock Musket - .70 caliber smoothbore flintlock.

6 French Model 1768 Flintlock Musket.

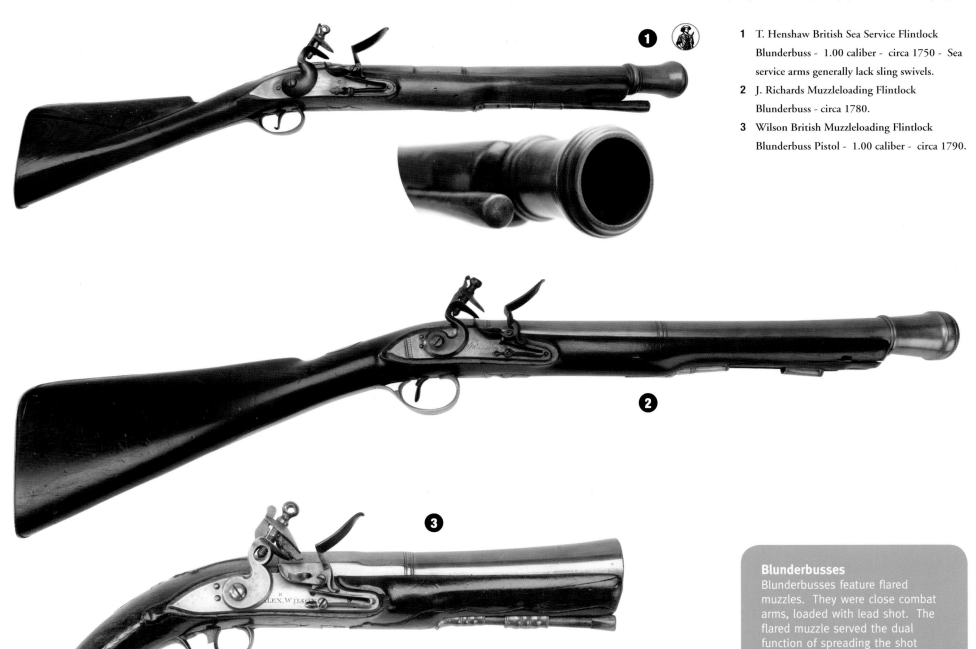

1. T. Henshaw British Sea Service Flintlock Blunderbuss - 1.00 caliber - circa 1750 - Sea service arms generally lack sling swivels.
2. J. Richards Muzzleloading Flintlock Blunderbuss - circa 1780.
3. Wilson British Muzzleloading Flintlock Blunderbuss Pistol - 1.00 caliber - circa 1790.

Blunderbusses

Blunderbusses feature flared muzzles. They were close combat arms, loaded with lead shot. The flared muzzle served the dual function of spreading the shot charge wider than a cylinder bore and of serving as a built-in funnel for reloading. These were used as naval boarding weapons and coach guns, requiring reloading on a pitching ship's deck or a rocking coach.

THE EARLIEST GUNS

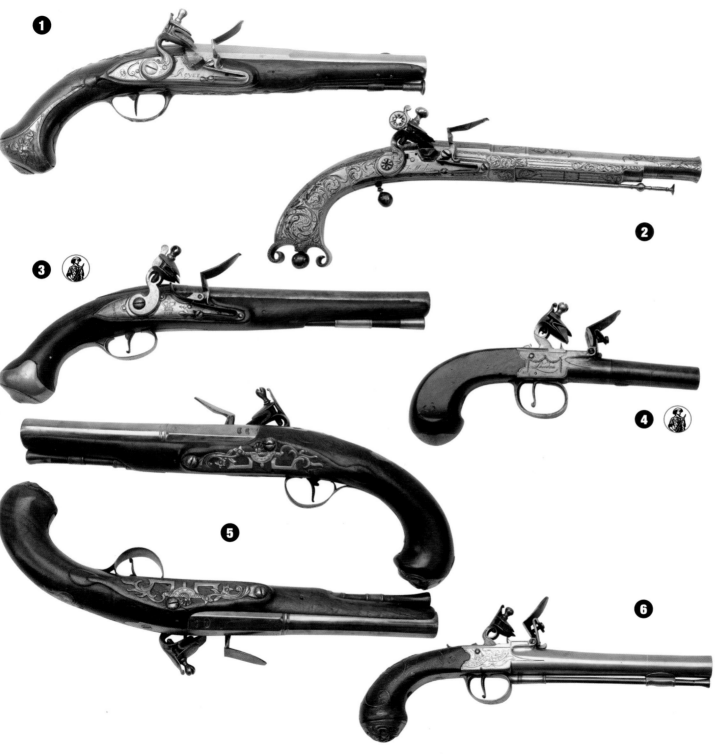

1. Royet French Flintlock Pistol - .59 caliber - circa 1780-1800 - Antique pistol presented to Gen. Solomon Lowe, U.S. Army, by his staff officers after WWII.

2. James Mitchie Scottish Metal Flintlock - .56 caliber - circa 1775 - Made in Doune Scotland. The ball ornament on this pistol's butt unscrews to become a vent pick.

3. Tower English Model 1760 Flintlock Pistol - .69 caliber - circa 1780 - This type was the principal sidearm of the British Army during the Revolution. The Tower of London, where this pistol was made, was a major British arsenal, as well as a royal residence and notorious prison. Many arms of the time were manufactured by gunsmiths according to strict specifications. These were either delivered in final form or as parts that were later assembled at the Tower or other arsenals.

4. Ketland English Flintlock Gentleman's Pistol - .45 caliber - circa 1810.

5. Pair of French Officer's Flintlock Pistols - .64 caliber - circa 1780.

6. I. Richards English Cannon-Barrel Matched Flintlock Pistol - .63 caliber - circa 1780 - Bronze alloy barrel.

Flintlock pistols were popular accoutrements for officers and cavalrymen. Large-bored and short-barreled, they were effective only at very close range. Officers' pistols were seldom used in combat, and were primarily decorative accessories symbolic of status and rank.

1 John Miles Flintlock Rifle - .52 caliber - circa 1790-1808 - Curly maple stock with Leonard Reedy-style relief carving.

2 Mathias Miller Flintlock Longrifle - .50 caliber - circa 1780 - Patriotic engraving on patchbox, unusual on a civilian firearm.

The American Longrifle

The American longrifle, sometimes called the Kentucky or Pennsylvania rifle, was actually made in almost every colony and state from the mid-1700s until shortly before the Civil War.

During the first decades of the 18th century, immigrant German gunsmiths began to redesign the jaeger rifle into a firearm that was better suited to the wilderness of America. During the transition period, the barrel was lengthened to 40 inches or more for greater accuracy. Patchboxes were fitted with sliding wood covers and later with hinged metal covers. Rifles of this early period were relatively plain, although some arms had a few simple embellishments.

Why "Kentucky Rifle"?

At the close of the War of 1812, some 2,000 frontiersmen soldiers under General Andrew Jackson defeated the British at New Orleans in 1815. Carrying longrifles, these pioneers turned the tide of battle and won an American victory. A popular ballad *The Hunters of Kentucky* or *The Battle of New Orleans* memorialized the frontier riflemen, and did much to add the term Kentucky rifle to the common vocabulary:

> **But Jackson he was wide awake,**
> **And was not scared at trifles,**
> **For well he knew what aim we take**
> **With our Kentucky rifles.**

The generic name Kentucky rifle is recognized the world over. It is truly one of the very few indigenous American arms. Their use in the early wilderness, the American Revolution, and the War of 1812, plus their role in opening the American West to settlement, has indelibly linked this gun to many of America's beloved pioneers and frontier heroes.

The longrifle was a practical, graceful, and highly accurate arm that originally was used primarily for hunting and protection. However, it soon became a source of recreation and competition in frontier America. By the late 18th century, the legendary skill of riflemen prompted challenges between competitors for prizes such as livestock, fowl, and purses of money. Offhand shooting was the rule in the early days. Later, the bench rifle would dominate competitive shooting. Competitive shooting often attracted riflemen from long distances, and the sport became a major cultural and social event for many localities.

The Jaeger Rifle

German and Swiss immigrants who settled the Lancaster, Pennsylvania, region brought with them a unique short rifle called the jaeger rifle ("hunter" in German) for use in the heavily wooded areas that resembled their homelands. This rifle was a short, heavy, octagon-barreled gun in large caliber and was used not only for hunting big game, but also for sporting and target competition. In *The Last of the Mohicans*, a classic work of American literature by James Fennimore Cooper, a jaeger rifle is used by the hero Hawkeye.

1 German/English Flintlock Jaeger Rifle - .50 caliber - circa 1730 - Short in barrel, the jaeger offered greatly enhanced accuracy for hunting or military applications at a time when smoothbore muskets were considered "cutting edge" technology. In the closely packed forests of Europe, a short rifle could be carried and quickly brought to bear on a target. But with the arrival of Europeans in the New World, longer hunting distances became common with the open meadows and river valleys of North America. The short-sighted jaeger was updated with a lengthened barrel to provide a better sight radius and higher muzzle velocity, yielding in time the "Kentucky" rifle, a long rifle well suited for frontier hunting.

2 Ambrose Frelig German Flintlock Jaeger Rifle - .52 caliber - circa 1780-1800 - Swamped barrel (thinner in the middle than at breech and muzzle).

3 Dutch English Club Butt Flintlock Musket - .65 caliber - circa 1750 - Late Revolutionary War period. This type made by Dutch gunsmiths who settled in New York.

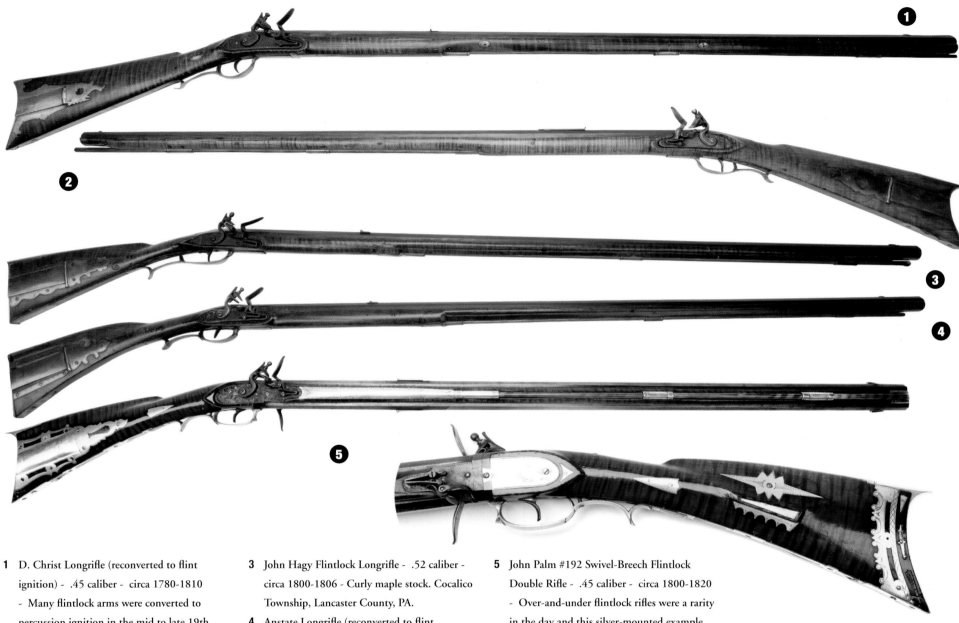

1 D. Christ Longrifle (reconverted to flint ignition) - .45 caliber - circa 1780-1810 - Many flintlock arms were converted to percussion ignition in the mid to late 19th century. Collectors sometimes convert these back to original flintlock, a somewhat controversial modern modification.

2 J. Cooper Left-Handed Flintlock Longrifle - .50 caliber - circa 1795-1815 - Left-handed longrifles are rare. Horsehead patchbox.

3 John Hagy Flintlock Longrifle - .52 caliber - circa 1800-1806 - Curly maple stock. Cocalico Township, Lancaster County, PA.

4 Anstate Longrifle (reconverted to flint ignition) - .45 caliber - circa 1800 - Curly maple stock, Drepperd-marked lockplate, Fordney-style engraving.

5 John Palm #192 Swivel-Breech Flintlock Double Rifle - .45 caliber - circa 1800-1820 - Over-and-under flintlock rifles were a rarity in the day and this silver-mounted example rotates barrels with a squeeze of the trigger guard.

A PROSPERING NEW REPUBLIC

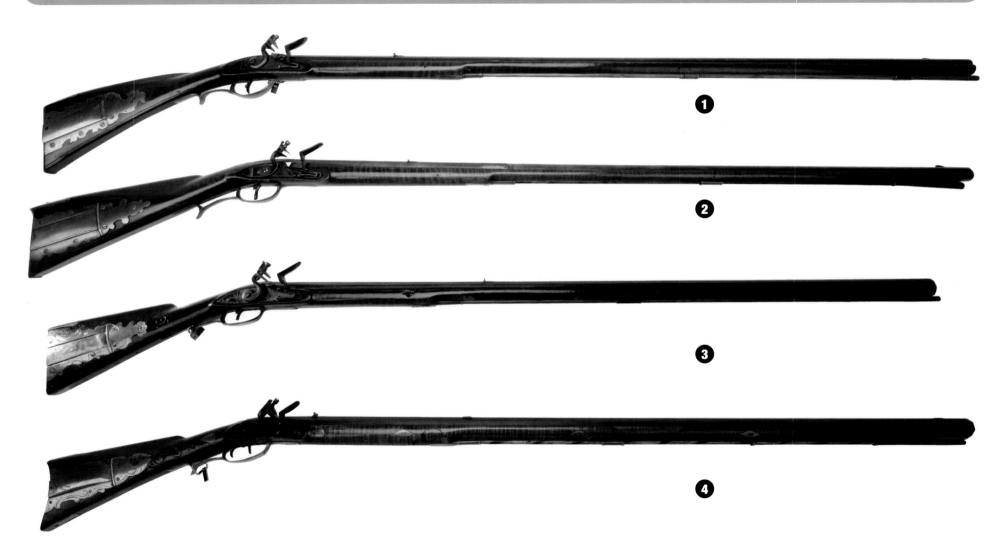

1

2

3

4

1 J.P. Beck Longrifle - .54 caliber - circa 1790-1811 - Incised carved stock, possibly restored.

2 J.P. Beck/Wolfgang Hagy Flintlock Rifle - .58 caliber - circa 1780-1800 - Period restocked in raised carved curly maple, with C. Beck-style engraved patchbox.

3 J. Graeff Flintlock Rifle - .60 caliber - circa 1773-1808 - Lancaster County Fainot-style four-piece daisy-head patchbox.

4 Melchior Fordney Heavy-Barrel Flintlock Rifle with Double-Set Triggers - .54 caliber - circa 1820-1830 - Melchior Fordney crafted this sturdy longrifle in Lancaster, PA, but his gunsmithing career came to a close in 1846 when he was murdered by an axe-wielding neighbor.

1 London-made copy of Lancaster Flintlock Rifle - .60 caliber - circa 1800-1809.

2 P. Quattlebuw Flintlock Rifle - .36 caliber - circa 1800-1820 - Likely made in the Shenandoah Valley of Virginia; two bone inlays; elaborate pierced patchbox.

3 Jacob Albright Longrifle - .50 caliber - circa 1788-1800 - Exceptional rifle. Ketland & Co. lock, relief-carved maple stock, silver star and wire inlays, engraved patchbox.

4 Percussion Longrifle with G. Goulcher lock - .35 caliber - circa 1840 - Goulcher made components, such as locks, that were used by other gunsmiths to build guns. This rifle was likely made in what is now West Virginia.

1 Henry Drepperd Percussion Longrifle
   - .54 caliber - circa 1840-1850 - From the
   Lancaster, PA, area. Converted to percussion
   from flintlock.

2 Elisha Pancost Percussion Longrifle - .40
   caliber - circa 1838.

3 John Border Percussion Longrifle - .28 caliber
   - circa 1851-1860.

4 Tennessee Percussion Mountain Rifle
   - .58 caliber - circa 1840 - This type of
   undecorated but functional rifle is sometimes
   called a "Southern rifle."

5 John Sherry, Jr., Percussion Rifle - .28 caliber
   - circa 1830-1858 - Clarion County, PA.

6 J. & W. H. Moll Percussion Longrifle - .36
   caliber - circa 1840 - Plain maple stock with
   incised wrist.

Percussion Longrifles

In the mid-19th century, the percussion cap and ball rapidly replaced the flintlock as the preferred ignition system for muzzleloading arms. Some longrifles were originally made as percussion arms, while others were converted to the new system.

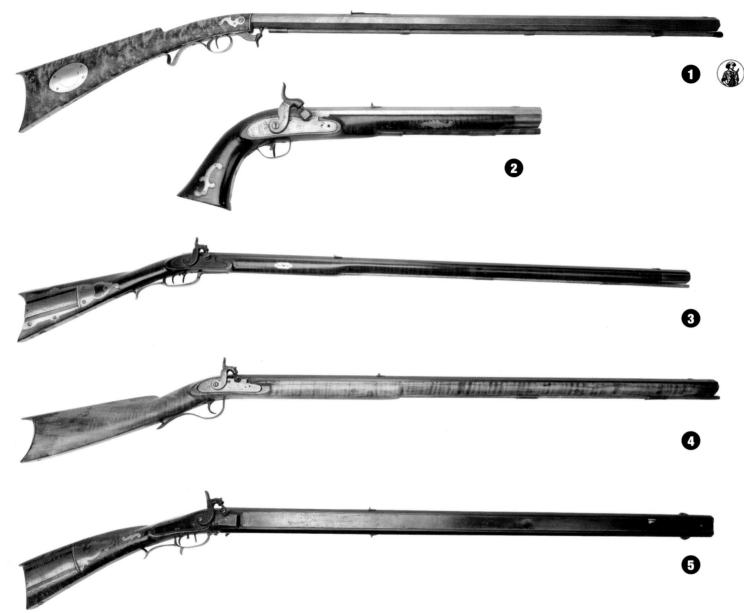

1   Nicanor Kendall Underhammer Percussion Rifle - .50 caliber - circa 1848 - Underhammer guns kept the hammer from interfering with the sight picture along the top of the barrel. It was also believed that the spark from the cap rising from below the powder charge enabled quicker and more reliable ignition.

2   John Domer Percussion Pistol (converted from flint ignition) - .45 caliber - circa 1840 - Flared grip is not typical of "Kentucky pistols."

3   William Hawken percussion rifle - .43 caliber - circa 1850 - The youngest of the Hawken brothers, William Hawken stayed in Hagerstown, MD, and built full-stocked rifles like this example, while Jacob and Samuel Hawken went West and established a St. Louis business that produced the half-stock plain rifles revered by mountain men.

4   Remington Percussion Conversion Rifle - .41 caliber - circa 1816-1830.

5   Pennsylvania Rifle Works Percussion Over/ Under Combination Gun - .45 over .50 caliber - circa 1870 - This two-barrel gun allowed a choice of calibers by simply rotating the barrels.

Remington
Eliphalet Remington II made his first gun in 1816, and promptly began the regular manufacture of gun barrels. In 1828, he established his own forge in Ilion, NY, manufacturing up to 8,000 barrels a year. Other gunsmiths would fit these Remington-marked barrels to lock and stock to produce their wares. In 1848, Remington began to manufacture completed firearms, beginning with a contract for Jenks breechloading carbines for the U.S. military. By the mid-1850s, three sons had joined the firm, and it became E. Remington and Sons.

1. J. Petty Half-stocked Percussion Rifle - .45 caliber - circa 1857-1860.
2. Andrew Wurfflein Percussion Plains Rifle - .50 caliber - circa 1850.
3. Samuel Hawken Percussion Plains Rifle - .50 caliber - circa 1849 - Period replaced stock.
4. J. Henry & Son Percussion Plains Rifle - .36 caliber - circa 1860.
5. Half-Stock Percussion Rifle - .44 caliber - circa 1840-1860.

The Plains Rifle

As America moved West, the old longrifle, with its slender barrel, small caliber, figured wood, and fine ornamentation began to give way to a new type of firearm. Although the longrifle was fit for the forest, the new breed of people who crossed the Appalachians needed to travel vast prairies, ride long distances on horses, and shoot large game such as bison and elk. These activities required a rifle that was shorter, of larger caliber with a heavier barrel, less decorative, and more utilitarian. The development of the short, heavy-barreled, half-stocked plains rifle was the result of these needs.

The Hawken Rifle

The plains rifle was developed in St. Louis, Missouri. Christian Hawken, Sr., a notable riflesmith from Hagerstown, Maryland, taught the skills of gunsmithing to his sons George, John, Jacob, Samuel, and William. Jacob and Samuel Hawken moved to St. Louis in the first decade of the 19th century. The earliest development of the plains rifle and its distinctive form can be traced to these brothers, and their design became known as the Hawken Rifle. Also called a mountain rifle and buffalo rifle, the name Hawken Rifle has become a generic name for the plains rifle style.

The typical form is a short, heavy-barreled rifle with a half-stock and little, if any, decoration. A pair of barrel wedges with oval escutcheons was often used to fasten the barrel to the forestock. A patchbox, if present, was normally of simple design, and was circular or oval in shape. Trigger guards were usually rounded and scrolled in order to avoid snagging on clothing or saddles. Delicacy was not a design consideration, and these rifles were made for hard, rough use. Barrel length was between 36 and 38 inches, and stocks were fashioned of plain maple or walnut.

Other Makers

Plains rifles became so popular that many other riflesmiths began to produce them. Henry Leman of Lancaster and James Henry of Philadelphia joined St. Louis makers, such as H.E. Dimmick, in the production of the plains rifle.

1 U.S. Springfield Model 1795 Flintlock Musket, Type I - .69 caliber circa1805 - The first model produced by an American national armory.

2 U.S. Eli Whitney Model 1798 Contract Flintlock Musket - .69 caliber - circa 1798.

3 British East India Co. Pattern Flintlock Carbine - .67 caliber - circa 1800-1830 - First produced for the United East India Company, this pattern was widely issued to British troops.

4 J. Baker English Flintlock Rifle - .69 caliber - circa 1800-1835 - English military rifle issued to specially trained marksmen.

Eli Whitney Revolutionizes Manufacturing

In 1798, Congress authorized the purchase of muskets from private contractors in order to supplement those firearms being made at the national armories. Eli Whitney of New Haven, Connecticut (who achieved fame at an early age with his invention of the cotton gin), was awarded a government arms contract for 10,000 U.S. Model 1795 muskets on June 14, 1798. Whitney's contract contained a unique idea: "to make the same parts of different guns, as much like each other as the successive impressions of a copper-plate engraving." With this idea, Whitney articulated the industrial concept of parts interchangeability. Whitney devised tools and machines for manufacturing separate components and proved that workmen with little or no experience could operate machinery and turn out large quantities of gun parts with amazing precision. By developing special machinery, jigs, and other devices, Whitney turned a complex manufacturing process into a series of simple operations -- a concept that revolutionized all manufacturing in America!

National Armories

In 1792, Congress authorized two National Arsenals for the storage, maintenance, and repair of military arms. By the end of 1794, Congress also authorized the construction of two National Armories for the manufacture of service arms. President George Washington personally selected the sites of Springfield, Massachusetts, and Harpers Ferry, West Virginia (then part of Virginia), as the locations for the two armories. In 1795, production began at Springfield, and by 1800, arms were being produced at Harpers Ferry.

The new armories at Springfield and Harpers Ferry began production of the U.S. Model 1795 Musket, the first standard pattern arm made for the United States military.

Based on the French Model 1768 Charleville used during the Revolution, the Model 1795 did not have the aesthetic beauty of the British Brown Bess, but it utilized barrel bands with retaining springs instead of pins, a double-bridled lock mechanism, and a reinforced cock, giving it great strength and utility.

The U.S. Model 1795 was produced at Springfield until 1814 and at Harpers Ferry until 1816. Total production at the two National Armories was approximately 168,000 muskets.

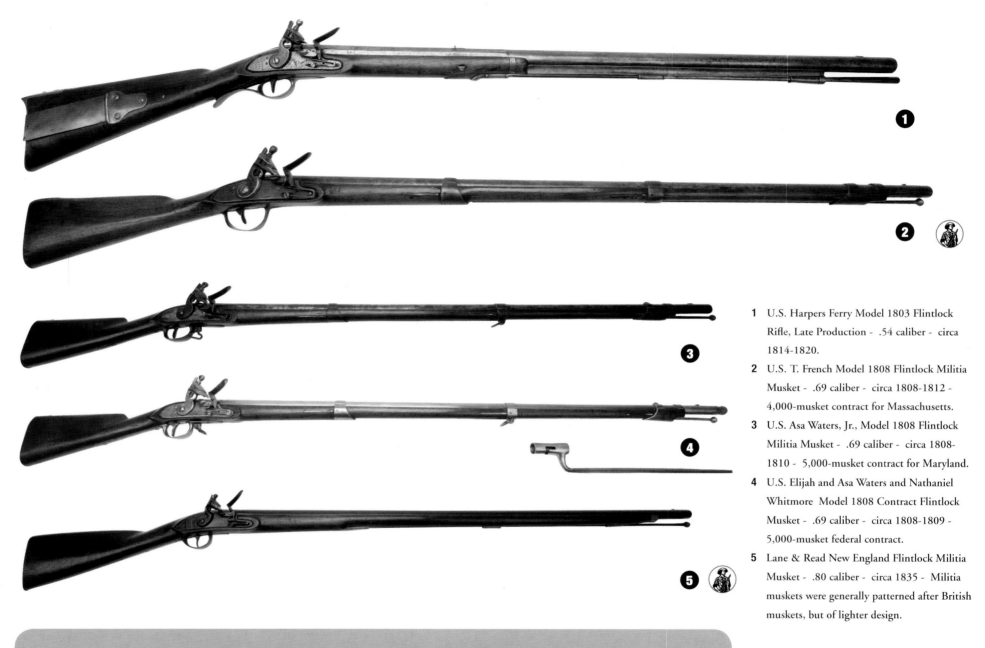

1 U.S. Harpers Ferry Model 1803 Flintlock
   Rifle, Late Production - .54 caliber - circa
   1814-1820.

2 U.S. T. French Model 1808 Flintlock Militia
   Musket - .69 caliber - circa 1808-1812 -
   4,000-musket contract for Massachusetts.

3 U.S. Asa Waters, Jr., Model 1808 Flintlock
   Militia Musket - .69 caliber - circa 1808-
   1810 - 5,000-musket contract for Maryland.

4 U.S. Elijah and Asa Waters and Nathaniel
   Whitmore Model 1808 Contract Flintlock
   Musket - .69 caliber - circa 1808-1809 -
   5,000-musket federal contract.

5 Lane & Read New England Flintlock Militia
   Musket - .80 caliber - circa 1835 - Militia
   muskets were generally patterned after British
   muskets, but of lighter design.

Model 1803 Flintlock Rifle

Patterned after the popular Kentucky rifle, this rifle was an accurate, well-made firearm that was practical for protection and for hunting in the wilderness. Made only at the U.S. Armory at Harpers Ferry, Virginia, it was the first and only muzzleloading flintlock rifle to be produced at a government armory.

A total of 4,015 of these rifles was produced at Harpers Ferry Armory between 1804 and 1807. Additional rifles were needed by the military for the War of 1812, and production of the Model 1803 (Type II) was restarted in 1812. This production run lasted until 1820, resulting in a total of 15,703 Type II rifles.

1 U.S. J. Bishop Model 1812 Flintlock Militia Musket - .60 caliber - circa 1814.

2 U.S. Henry Deringer Model 1814 Flintlock Common Rifle - .65 caliber - circa 1814 - Original production was rifled, but this example was smoothbored for Indian treaty sales.

3 U.S. Harpers Ferry Model 1816 Flintlock Musket, Type II - .69 caliber - circa 1822- 1831 - Originally finished in "National Armory Brown."

4 U.S. Springfield Model 1816 Flintlock Musket - .69 caliber - circa 1818 - Dated 1818; originally finished "National Armory Bright."

5 U.S. Harpers Ferry Model 1816 (Type II) Flintlock Musket - .69 caliber - circa 1816- 1840.

6 U.S. M. T. Wickham Model 1816 Contract Flintlock Musket - .69 caliber - circa 1822- 1837 - In addition to the national armories, Wickham and other contractors produced the Model 1816.

Model 1816 Flintlock Musket

Model 1816 muskets were the first standard U.S. military longarm to be produced at both Springfield and Harpers Ferry Armories. Nearly 700,000 of these muskets were manufactured at Springfield Armory and Harpers Ferry over a 28-year period, making this the largest production total of any U.S. flintlock musket.

A PROSPERING NEW REPUBLIC

1. U.S. Robert & J. D. Johnson Model 1817 "Common" Flintlock Rifle - .54 caliber - circa 1817.

2. U.S. Nathan Starr & Son Model 1817 "Common" Flintlock Rifle - .54 caliber - circa 1823.

3. The Horseshoe Gun. Ramon Zuloaga Spanish Model 1817 Miquelet Fusil - .54 caliber - circa 1820-1830 - Although not a military gun, this fusil is of the same era, with an interesting story. It was made in Spain using steel made from used horse shoes (herraduras). The shoes had been strengthened on the hoof by the constant pounding they received while in use. They were cut up, heated white-hot, folded, and re-pounded over 40 times, making this steel extremely strong. Zuloaga fashioned a light fusil from this steel, dating it in gold, 1817. It is attributed to Juan Manuel De La Sota, who reportedly brought it to the Americas, settling in Monterey, CA.

4. Virginia Manufactory of Arms 2nd Model Flintlock Rifle (reconversion to flint) - .54 caliber - circa 1815 - Similar features to the Harpers Ferry Model 1803. Approx. 1,700 made, 1812 to 1821.

Arming the Militia

On May 8, 1792, Congress passed the Militia Act which provided a general guideline for states to arm and equip militia units. The bill provided that every free, white, able-bodied male between 18 and 45 years could be enrolled in the state militia. The idea was that each state would have a free-standing and independent army that could supplement the regular U.S. Army if needed. Composed entirely of volunteers, the militia units of the 1800s became very social organizations and chose such colorful names as the Fencibles, Washington Greys, Lafayette Troop, Palmetto Guards, and American Highlanders. State governments faced the same problem as the federal government in securing arms for their troops. Some states established contracts with local arms makers. Virginia erected its own arms manufactory and arsenal -- the only state to do so. The General Assembly of Virginia authorized the establishment of the manufactory on January 23, 1798. Over 58,000 muskets, 4,200 pistols, 2,100 rifles, and thousands of swords, bayonets, and accoutrements were produced at the Virginia Manufactory until it ceased operations in 1818.

Model 1817 Common Rifle

The "Common Rifle" designation distinguishes this muzzleloader from the contemporary Hall breechloading rifle. Four contractors made 38,200 between 1823 and the early 1840s.

1 U.S. Hall Model 1819 Breechloading Flintlock Rifle - .52 caliber - circa 1817-1840.

2 U.S. Hall Model 1836 Breechloading Percussion Carbine - .64 caliber - circa 1836 - This model was issued to the 2nd U.S. Dragoons during their service in Florida.

3 U.S. Hall Model 1819 Breechloading Percussion Rifle - .52 caliber - circa 1841-1842 - One of the Hall flintlocks that was later converted to percussion by the military.

Hall's Breechloader

John H. Hall of Portland, Maine, patented a breechloading rifle in 1811 that became a landmark in the arms industry. The breechblock tips up for loading, and the entire lock is easily removed. The rear sight is offset to clear the centrally mounted hammer. Following the War of 1812, Hall successfully petitioned the government to test his breechloader. This firearm was found to be superior to muzzleloaders in every respect, and on March 19, 1819, Hall furnished an additional 1,000 rifles to the government. All of these arms were made at Hall's factory in Harpers Ferry. Hall adopted Whitney's idea of interchangeable parts and installed machinery in his factory to produce standard, interchangeable parts. A series of rifles and carbines utilizing the Hall breechloading system were produced in the United States from 1823 to 1853, both in flintlock and percussion configurations.

A PROSPERING NEW REPUBLIC

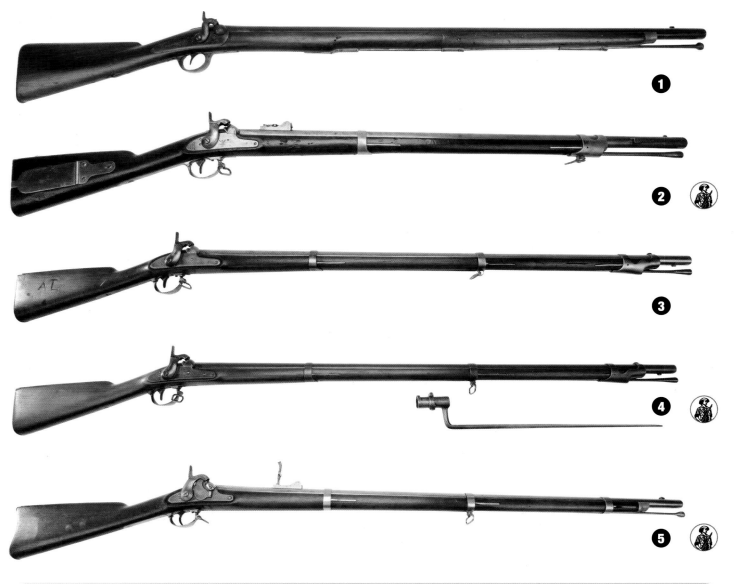

1 British Model 1838 Land Pattern Percussion Musket - .72 caliber - circa 1838-1844 - Typical of the imported arms issued to Mexican forces in the Mexican War.

2 U.S. Harpers Ferry Model 1841 "Mississippi" Percussion Rifle - .58 caliber - circa 1846-1855.

3 U.S. Harpers Ferry Model 1842 Percussion Musket - .69 caliber - circa 1844-1855.

4 U.S. Springfield Model 1842 Percussion Musket - .69 caliber - circa 1844-1855.

5 U.S. Springfield Model 1855 Percussion Rifle-Musket - .58 caliber - circa 1857-1861.

The Mississippi Rifle

This rifle was developed and approved for manufacture by the U.S. government in 1841. An accurate and attractive brass-mounted rifle, it was admired by the men who used it. The U.S. Model 1841 Rifle was first used during the Mexican War at the Battle of Buena Vista in February of 1847. The successful use of this rifle by the First Mississippi Volunteer Infantry, under the command of Colonel Jefferson Davis (later to become president of the Confederate States of America), won the rifle its common name -- the Mississippi rifle.

These rifles were manufactured by the government at Harpers Ferry and by five other contractors (including Remington, Whitney, and Tryon). Over 70,000 of these rifles were produced between 1846 and 1855. On July 5, 1855, the Secretary of War ordered that the standard caliber of U.S. arms be changed from .54 to .58 caliber. Many of the Model 1841 Rifles were altered to .58 caliber prior to and during the Civil War.

Model 1842 Musket

This was the first regulation musket with a percussion lock to be made at both Springfield and Harpers Ferry Armories, and the first with fully interchangeable locks. About 275,000 were made from 1844 to 1855. They were also made by contract makers and South Carolina's Palmetto Armory.

1 Girardoni Repeating Air Rifle, believed to have been used by Lewis and Clark - .46 caliber - circa 1795 - 20-shot repeating air rifle, built by Bartolomeo Girardoni, who originally supplied similar air rifles to the Austrian army around 1790. As originally issued, each Girardoni air rifle had three detachable air reservoirs, each requiring about 1,500 strokes of a separate pump to completely pressurize the reservoir. Once filled to operating pressure (about 800 psi), the air rifle could fire up to 70 shots before the reservoir needed to be replaced. A hollow metal tube on the side of the barrel held up to 20 lead balls that could be fed one at a time to the firing chamber by a simple sideways push of a plunger. At a distance of 50 feet, this rifle is capable of placing 10 shots into a group the size of a quarter, and could penetrate a 1-inch wood plank or bring down an elk.

2 U.S. Harpers Ferry Model 1803 Flintlock Rifle - .54 caliber - circa 1810-1816 - The Model 1803 rifle was once accepted as having been used by members of the Lewis and Clark expedition into the Louisiana Territory.

Lewis and Clark

In 1803, President Thomas Jefferson successfully negotiated the Louisiana Purchase from the Emperor of France, Napoleon Bonaparte. The United States doubled in size with the pen stroke that completed the transaction. An accurate inventory and map of the new territory was urgently needed, and Jefferson chose Meriwether Lewis, his private secretary, to lead an expedition to the Northwest frontier. Lewis chose William Clark, the younger brother of George Rogers Clark (a hero of the Revolution), to assist him. The objectives of the Lewis and Clark expedition were to find the source of the Missouri River, to discover an overland route to the Pacific Ocean, to chart rivers, waterfalls, islands, and rapids, and to notate the weather, animals, and minerals encountered. They also were to document the native populations in the region, secure specimens of strange creatures, and complete the maps of that time. Lewis and Clark left St. Louis with 23 men on May 14, 1804, and reached the Pacific Ocean on November 15, 1805. On a tall pine on the Pacific coast, Clark carved the following notation: **William Clark, December 3, 1805, By Land from the U. States**

After surviving a hard winter on the coast, the expedition began its return. On September 23, 1806, Lewis and Clark finally reached St. Louis, ending their historic expedition. All of Jefferson's tasks, and more, had been fulfilled.

The Air Gun

Lewis and Clark brought a selection of firearms. One the most unusual was a Girandoni air rifle. The principle of the air gun is propulsion of a projectile by compressed air. This type of gun is thought to have been invented in Germany as early as the 15th century. By the 18th century, air guns were used in Europe for hunting, sporting, and military purposes.

In *The Lewis and Clark Expedition Into The American Northwest in 1804-5 and 6* (published in Philadelphia in 1814), the following account is given:

They [the American Indians] **had indeed abundant sources of surprise in all they saw, the appearance of the men, their arms, their clothing, the canoes ... all in turn shared their admiration, which was turned to astonishment by a shot from the air gun; this operation was instantly considered as a great medicine, by which they as well as the other Indians mean something emanating from the Great Spirit, or produced by his invisible and incomprehensible agency.**

The air gun could fire multiple shots without re-priming the air reservoir. Because of the repeating feature, the natives never knew if the expedition had one gun or dozens, and quickly forwarded Lewis and Clark on to their next destimation.

A PROSPERING NEW REPUBLIC

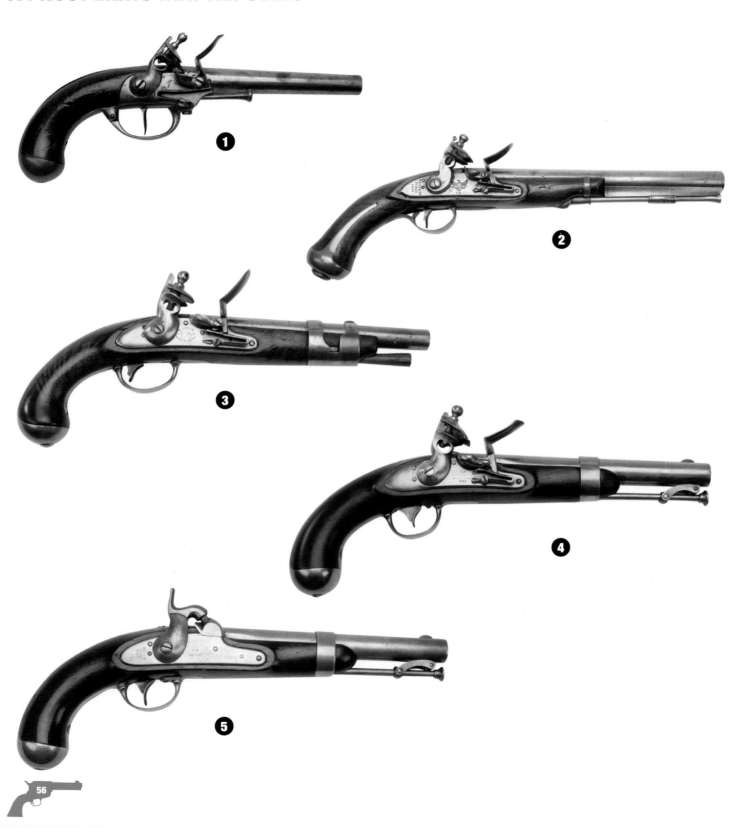

1 French St. Etienne Model 1777 Flintlock
   Pistol - .73 caliber - circa 1790-1800.

2 U.S. Harpers Ferry Model 1805 Flintlock
   Pistol - .54 caliber - circa 1806 - 1808 - The
   first U.S. military pistol to be manufactured
   at a national armory, the Model 1805 was
   later chosen as the symbol of the United States
   Army military police.

3 U.S. Simeon North Model 1816 Flintlock
   Pistol - .54 caliber - circa 1816 - North made
   nearly 20,000 contract pistols for the U.S.
   military.

4 U.S. Robert Johnson Model 1836 Flintlock
   Pistol - .54 caliber - circa 1836 - The last U.S.
   martial flintlock pistol; over 41,000 made
   1836 to 1844.

5 U.S. H. Aston Model 1842 Single-Shot
   Percussion Pistol - .54 caliber - circa 1830s -
   Standard issue during the Mexican War.

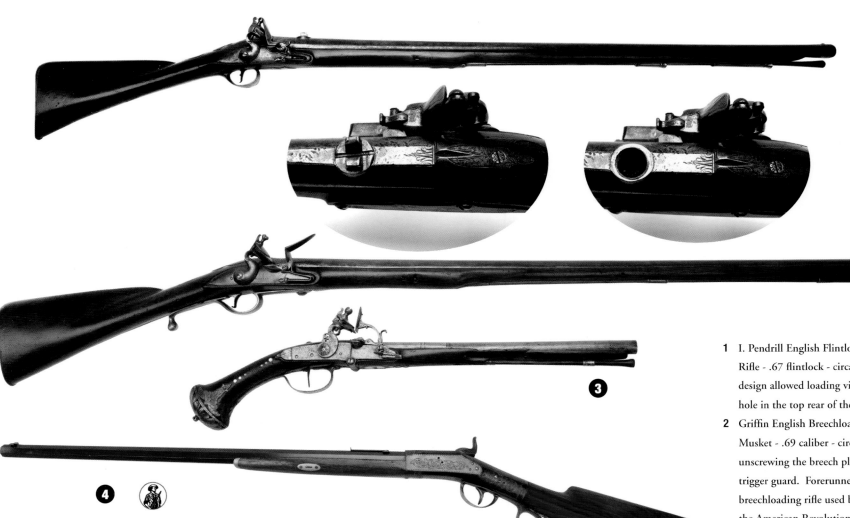

1 I. Pendrill English Flintlock Breechloading Rifle - .67 flintlock - circa 1760 - Pendrill's design allowed loading via a screw-plugged hole in the top rear of the barrel.

2 Griffin English Breechloading Flintlock Musket - .69 caliber - circa 1760 - Loaded by unscrewing the breech plug fastened to the trigger guard. Forerunner of the Ferguson breechloading rifle used by British troops in the American Revolution.

3 Italian Breechloading Snaphaunce Pistol - .60 caliber - circa 1650 - This pistol's break-open design allowed for quick reloading with removable chambers, each fitted with an integral flash pan.

4 Alonzo D. Perry Breechloading Percussion Sporting Rifle - .54 caliber - circa 1856 - 200 of this model in military configuration were purchased by the U.S. in 1855. Unusual automatic percussion cap reservoir in the buttstock feeds a cap into place as the action is operated.

Breechloaders

Traditional early military arms were smoothbore muzzle loaders. This allowed quicker reloads in combat, since a round ball slightly smaller than the bore could be rammed home with little effort, even if the barrel was fouled with residue from previous shots. To be effective, a rifled arm required a bullet that had to fit tightly to the rifling, and took additional effort to ram home, especially as fouling built up. However, a rifled arm that could load from the rear allowed the faster reload with the accuracy and additional effective range afforded by rifling. Breechloading arms also offered the advantage of reloading while in a reclined position behind cover, and the access at the rear of the bore provided for better cleaning capability.

A PROSPERING NEW REPUBLIC

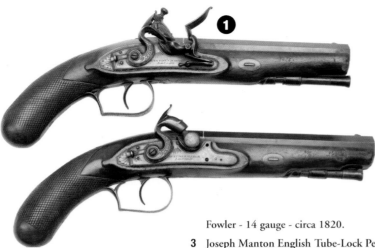

1 S.H. Staudenmeyer English Pistols - .59 caliber - circa 1830 - The upper pistol is an orignal flintlock, circa 1800. The lower pistol is the same model converted from flint to percussion, circa 1830. This was a common modification to adapt old guns to the new system.

2 Joseph Manton English Tube-Lock Percussion Fowler - 14 gauge - circa 1820.

3 Joseph Manton English Tube-Lock Percussion Double-Barrel Fowler - 14 gauge - ca 1820.

4 Ferdi Furwith Austrian Tube-Lock Percussion Rifle - .75 caliber - circa 1835-1840.

5 U.S. Greene Breechloading Underhammer Percussion Rifle - .53 caliber - circa 1859-1860 - Underhammer design with unusual oval-shaped bore. The first U.S. martial bolt action, with 900 purchased by the Army.

The Percussion System

In 1807, Dr. Alexander Forsyth, a Scottish Presbyterian minister, patented a gun lock that eliminated the priming powder charge, flash pan, and frizzen. Forsyth's design instead used a modified hammer to deliver a sharp blow that ignited a small, pill-shaped, impact-sensitive chemical compound placed upon a metal part called a striker. This design, also known as a pill-lock, resulted in the invention of a wide variety of detonating-type locks. Another was the tube-lock, which employed a primer-filled cylinder open at one end, ignited by the force of the hammer. These eventually led to the development of a percussion cap-lock system patented by Joshua Shaw in 1822. The percussion cap was a small, copper cap containing an impact-sensitive chemical compound (usually fulminate). This new percussion system became the principal means of discharging firearms until the perfection of the metallic cartridge used today. The percussion system revolutionized the design and use of firearms. It eliminated the flint and priming pan, and was less susceptible to dampness. But the new system did not immediately replace the old. Although percussion arms were in general use by civilians as early as 1830, the military did not accept them until about 1840. Once the percussion system caught on, both military and civilian flintlock arms were often converted to the more modern system. The Staudenmayer pistols on this page show a flintlock and a percussion conversion of the same model.

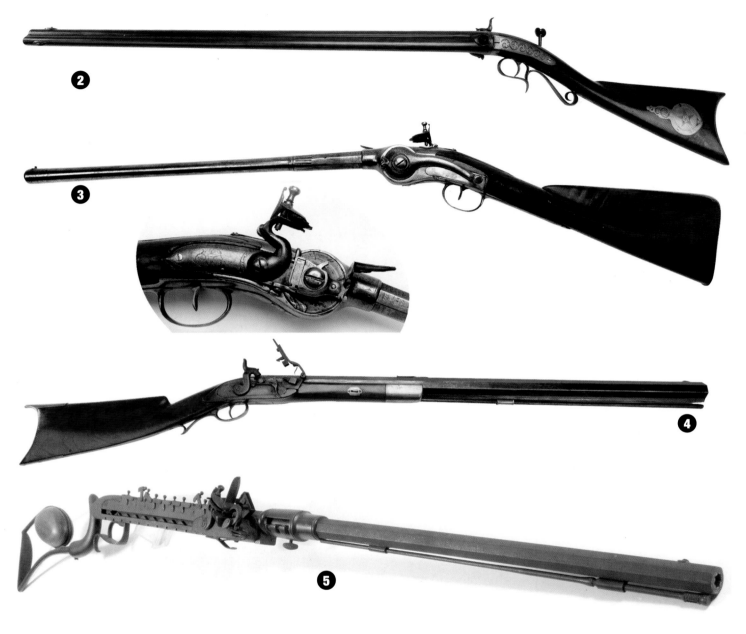

1 Belgian Four-Barrel Percussion Pistol - .32 caliber - circa 1850-1860 - Of course the simplest approach to multiple shots was to add additional barrels.

2 H. V. Perry Three-Barrel Percussion Rifle - .45 caliber - circa 1845-1850 - The multiple-barrel concept begins to become heavy and cumbersome as additional barrels are added. Guns with more than two barrels in this era are scarce.

3 John Shaw Cookson-Type Flintlock Repeating Rifle - .57 caliber - circa 1690-1720 - This Cookson pattern repeater had a powder magazine and a magazine for seven lead balls inside the buttstock. A turn of the crank on the left side of the frame loads the chamber, cocks the hammer, primes the pan, and lowers the frizzen for firing, making for a very early seven-shot repeater. The original concept was by Lorenzoni of Italy about 1680.

4 Superposed Charge Repeating Rifle - .45 caliber - An unknown gunsmith created this rifle which took superposed charges with one loaded on top of the other to give the shooter two shots (assuming they didn't both fire at once!).

5 Isaiah Jennings Multi-shot Flintlock Rifle – circa 1821 - This "Roman candle rifle" took superposed charges to extreme levels, accommodating 12 charges of powder and ball loaded one on top of the other in the barrel breech. A self-priming flintlock was slid back from the front charge to the next behind it as each was fired. Other innovative features include detachable barrel and detachable buttstock.

Repeaters
The muzzleloading system was slow for repeat shots. After a round was fired, a fresh charge of black powder had to be poured down the barrel, a lead projectile rammed down on top of it, and either the priming pan filled with powder on a flintlock or a cap placed on the nipple on a percussion arm. In the early 19th century, experimentation in firearms design was often focused on development of guns that could fire multiple times without reloading.

1 Bennett & Haviland Many-Chambered Revolving Percussion Rifle - .40 caliber - circa 1838-1840 - This rifle has 12 individual chambers that can be rotated into position for successive shots by rotating a wheel on top of the action.   Very rare, estimated that fewer than ten were made.

2 Graham's Patent Horizontal Revolving Turret Percussion Gun - .60 caliber - circa 1856 - Another early revolver concept, instead of a cylinder with parallel chambers, this gun uses a horizontal turret with five chambers pointing outward like the spokes of a wheel. Possibly a one-of-a-kind prototype.

3 French/Persian Repeating Flintlock Musket - .65 caliber - circa 1800 - Rotating chambers allow for multiple shots. An early application of the revolver concept.

4 Ethan Allen Bar-Hammer Pepperbox Revolver - .31 caliber - circa 1842-1847 - In pepperbox firearms, the entire cluster of barrels rotates to allow successive shots, usually with a double action mechanism where a pull of the trigger both rotates the barrel cluster and drops the hammer.

1 Colt Paterson Belt Model No. 2 Revolver - .34 caliber - circa 1837-1840 - Sam Colt's early handguns were frequently presented to influential parties that could further the adoption of Colt firearms by the military. Such revolvers are usually found cased with loading and cleaning accoutrements.

2 Colt Paterson Holster Model No. 5 Revolver - .36 caliber - circa 1838-1840 - Texas Rangers immortalized the fast-shooting Paterson Colt revolver in a series of frontier encounters with Comanche Indians where the five-shot capability of the new handgun provided overwhelming firepower.

3 Colt Walker Revolver - .44 caliber - circa 1847 - A massive revolver weighing nearly five pounds. In total, 1,000 were made for the United States Mounted Rifles and 100 for the civilian market.

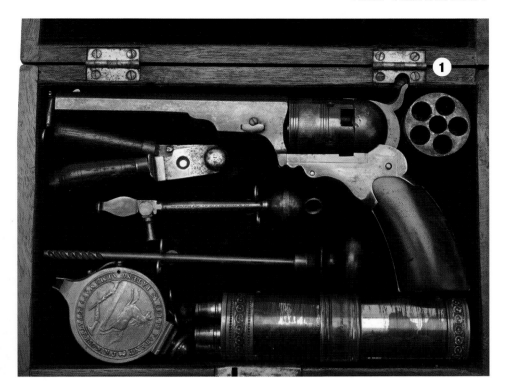

THE COLT SOLUTION: THE REPEATING FIREARM

The best solution for multiple-shot firearms was perfected by Samuel Colt with his revolver. A rotating cylinder brings a fresh loaded chamber in line with the rear of the barrel each time the hammer is cocked, with a new round ready to fire.

His first revolvers are called Colt Patersons after the Paterson, NJ, barrel address marking denoting where they were made. They had folding triggers, and lacked a bit in power and durability, and his first company failed.

However, Texas Ranger Captain Samuel Walker saw the potential of these effective repeaters and contacted Col. Colt about producing a more robust and powerful revolver for use on the frontier. The massive Colt Walker revolver was born in 1847. The new Colt enterprise took root and flourished.

Both Patersons and Walkers are rare, and highly prized by collectors for their pivotal role in firearms history.

1   Smith & Wesson Lever-Action Magazine Pistol - .31 Volcanic - circa 1855.

2   Smith & Wesson No. 1 1st Issue Single-Action Revolver with original gutta percha case - .22 rimfire - circa 1857-1860.

THE SMITH AND WESSON SOLUTION: THE METALLIC CARTRIDGE

Just as Colt was founded on the perfection of the repeating handgun, so Smith & Wesson was established by perfecting the marriage of revolver to self-contained metallic cartridge. And like Colt, the first S&W enterprise failed.

The lever-action S&W Repeating Magazine Pistol, later nicknamed "The Volcanic," used hollow-based bullets with powder packed in the hollow and a primer affixed to the base, carried in a tubular magazine mounted under the barrel. The underpowered design did not flourish, and was eventually sold to a shirt manufacturer named Oliver Winchester who saw promise in the lever-action mechanism and built a firearms empire on the lever-action rifle.

The second S&W partnership introduced a little seven shot .22 revolver, the Model One, that used a self-contained metallic cartridge with priming compound in the rim of the base. This basic cartridge is still made today as the .22 Short.

Smith and Wesson also purchased Rollin White's patent on a revolver cylinder bored through end to end, and thus secured a monopoly on effective cartridge revolver production through 1869. Colt had been offered the Rollin White design, but had passed.

The self-contained metallic cartridge offered tremendous advantages over the percussion system for speed and ease of loading and durability of ammunition, and introduced the modern era of firearms.

THE PINFIRE SYSTEM

One of the earliest self-contained metallic cartridges was the pinfire.

In this system, the firing pin was mounted on the cartridge itself instead of on the face of the gun's hammer. When the pin was struck by the flat face of the hammer, it ignited a priming charge inside the cartridge.

Cardboard pinfire cartridges were introduced in 1835 and metallic cartridges about 10 years later. The pinfire system was much more popular in Europe than in America, although pinfire revolvers did see use during the Civil War.

An unusual 21-shot pinfire revolver is shown on the facing page.

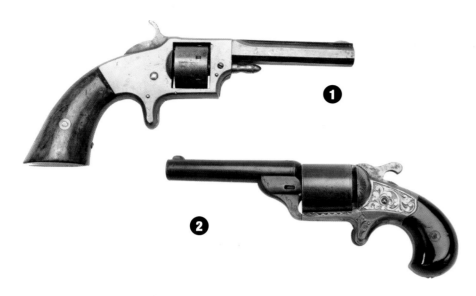

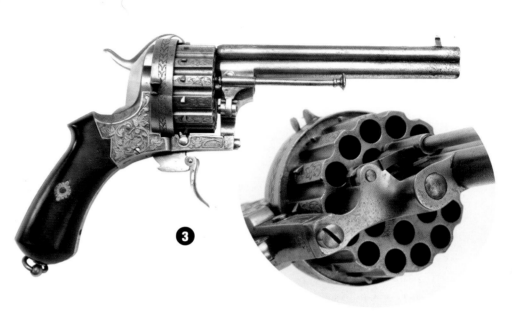

1 Rollin White Arms Co. Single-Action Pocket Revolver - .22 rimfire - circa 1861.

2 Moore's Patent Firearms Co. Front-Loading Single-Action Revolver - .32 teatfire - circa 1864-1870 - S&W's Rollin White patent on a bored-through cylinder resulted in other manufacturers looking for ways to circumvent it. Moore used an unusual proprietary cartridge with a small priming compound-filled teat poking through a small hole in the rear of the cylinder to be struck by the hammer.

3 Belgian Pinfire Revolver - .25 pinfire - circa 1870 - Unusual high-capacity 21-shot revolver.

CARTRIDGE TECHNOLOGY
The Combustible Cartridge
The development of the conical, hollow-based bullet by Francois Minie of France led to experimentation with a variety of cartridge designs. In the combustible cartridge, a percussion cap was combined with a flammable, or combustible, wrapper and a bullet to produce a self-contained cartridge. Heavily nitrated cloth or paper was used to produce highly flammable wrappers. These types of cartridges were used with the Sharps, Starr, and Merrill breechloading carbines.

The Separately Primed Cartridge
The first successful use of a metal cartridge case occurred during the Civil War period. Rubber and cardboard cases were also used for some cartridges. In this type of cartridge, a small hole in the base of the cartridge case allowed sparks from a percussion cap to enter the case and ignite the powder charge contained in the cartridge. The Maynard and Burnside breechloading carbines used metal cases, and the Smith carbine used rubber cases.

The Rimfire Cartridge
Invented by Nicolas Flobert, a noted French gunmaker, this metallic cartridge was developed just prior to the Civil War. It is a self-contained metallic cartridge that consists of four basic components: the case, the primer, the powder charge, and the projectile (or bullet). The primer in a rimfire cartridge is an impact-sensitive chemical compound that is contained in the inside rim of the case's base. When the cartridge is struck on the rim, the primer ignites, and the flame from the primer in turn ignites the powder charge.
Smith & Wesson was the first firearm manufacturer in America to successfully use the rimfire cartridge, and B. Tyler Henry used a .44 caliber rimfire cartridge in his famous Henry Repeating Rifle. Rimfire cartridges have changed little in design over the years and this type of cartridge is widely available today in .22 caliber ammunition that is used in a variety of modern handguns and rifles.

The Center-Fire Cartridge
Great strides in ammunition technology took place between 1860 and 1875 with the development of a cartridge that contained a primer located in the center of the base of the cartridge. The Frankfort Arsenal in Philadelphia had begun experiments based on this idea as early as 1858, and other experimenters continued developing this concept until the cartridge evolved into its present form. Other types of cartridges, such as the pin fire and the teat fire cartridges, offered little competition to this new centerfire concept. Today, the centerfire cartridge is used universally.

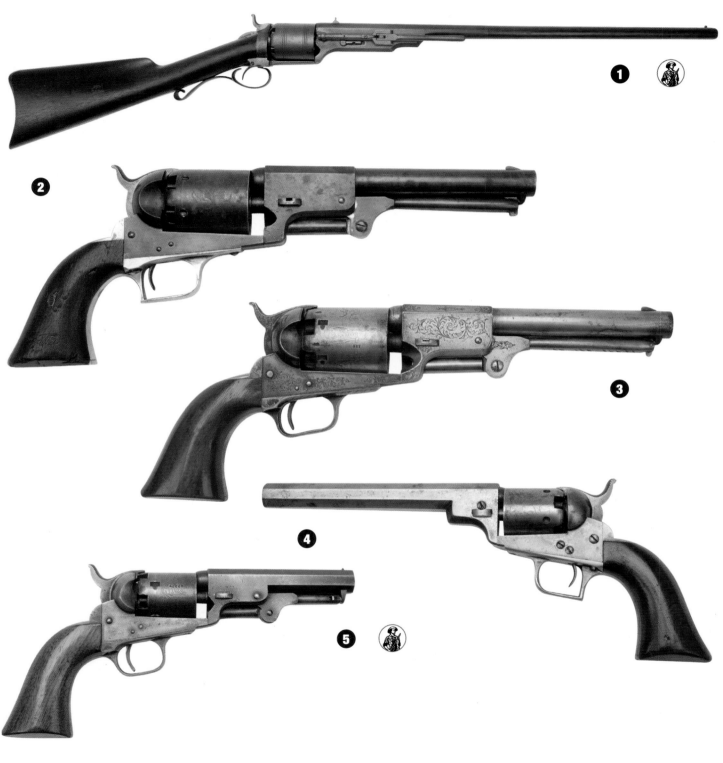

1 U.S. Colt Model 1839 Percussion Revolving Carbine - .52 caliber - circa 1838-1841 - Colt's factory in Hartford, CT, produced both handguns and percussion shoulder arms like this revolving rifle. Due to the potential for injury from accidental multiple chamber discharges, the revolving rifles were not as popular as their shorter counterparts.

2 Colt First Model Dragoon Revolver - .44 caliber - circa 1848-1850.

3 Colt English Dragoon Single-Action Percussion Revolver - .44 caliber - circa 1853-1857.

4 Colt Model 1848 Baby Dragoon Revolver - .31 caliber - circa 1847-1850.

5 Colt Model 1849 Pocket Percussion Revolver - .31 caliber - circa 1850-1873.

Colt

Colt revolving firearms were state of the art in the years leading up to the Civil War. In addition to handguns, Colt also made revolving long guns, both with the first Paterson, New Jersey, company and the later Hartford, Connecticut, company.

The large-frame .44 Walker Model was modified slightly to become the Dragoon Model. In 1848, a small .31 caliber revolver was introduced and was perfected the following year as the Model 1849 Pocket Revolver, destined to become the most widely produced Colt percussion revolver.

1 French Percussion Dueling Pistol - .45 caliber - circa 1850-1870.

2 Henry Deringer Percussion Pocket Pistol - .41 caliber - circa late 1837-1868 - Henry Deringer's small single-shot percussion pistols were popular choices for travelers during the California Gold Rush. Competitors soon produced a myriad copies of the Deringer design and nearly every small pocket pistol soon became known as a derringer.

3 Remington-Beals First Model Pocket Percussion Revolver - .28 caliber - circa 1858.

The Gold Rush

In the wake of the Mexican War, America acquired the former Spanish territory of California. Prior to 1848, California, as a generally undeveloped frontier area, had attracted mountain men and a few enterprising merchants who established trading posts. But the discovery of a few gleaming nuggets in a sawmill's tailrace waters on January 24, 1848, changed California forever. Gold had been found and the world rushed in!

Traveling to California involved a long sea voyage around South America or a faster, but more hazardous, overland route across the Great Plains. Thousands of 49ers seeking their fortunes in California brought an incredible variety of handguns and longarms for personal protection during the arduous trip and at the lawless mining camps.

A PROSPERING NEW REPUBLIC

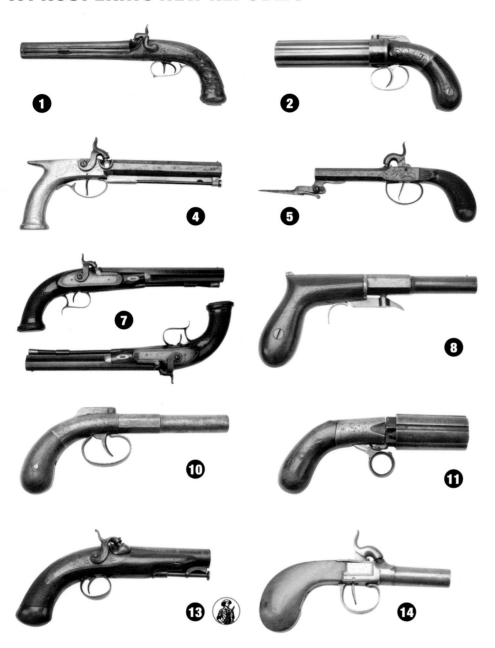

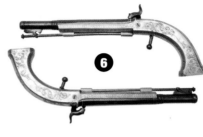

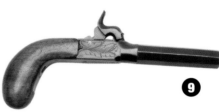

1 Belgian Double-Barrel Percussion Pistol - .58 caliber - circa 1840-1855.

2 Manhattan Pepperbox Revolver - .31 caliber - circa 1855-1860 - The pepperbox was the primary rival of Colt revolvers in the repeating handgun market in the 1850s.

3 Sprague & Marston Double-Action Pepperbox Pistol - .31 caliber - circa 1850-1860.

4 English Saw-Handle Single-Shot Percussion pistol - .52 caliber - circa 1840-1860.

5 Belgian Dagger Pistol - .48 caliber - circa 1850-1860.

6 Pair of C & G Abbott English All-Metal Percussion Pistols - .45 caliber - circa 1850.

7 Pair of William Hollis English Percussion Pistols - .50 caliber - circa 1820.

8 W. Ashton Underhammer Percussion Pistol - .28 caliber - circa 1835-1860.

9 Belgian Screw-barrel Percussion Pistol - .46 caliber - circa 1840-1860.

10 Allen & Wheelock Double-Action Bar Hammer Pistol - .44 caliber - circa 1857-1863.

11 J. P. Cooper's Patent English Pepperbox Pistol - .44 caliber - circa 1840-1860.

12 J. E. Evans Pocket Percussion Pistol - .44 caliber - circa 1850-1860.

13 Turlock English Officer's Pistol - .69 caliber - circa 1850-1870 - Converted to percussion from flintlock.

14 Belgian Percussion Pistol - .44 caliber - circa 1850-1860.

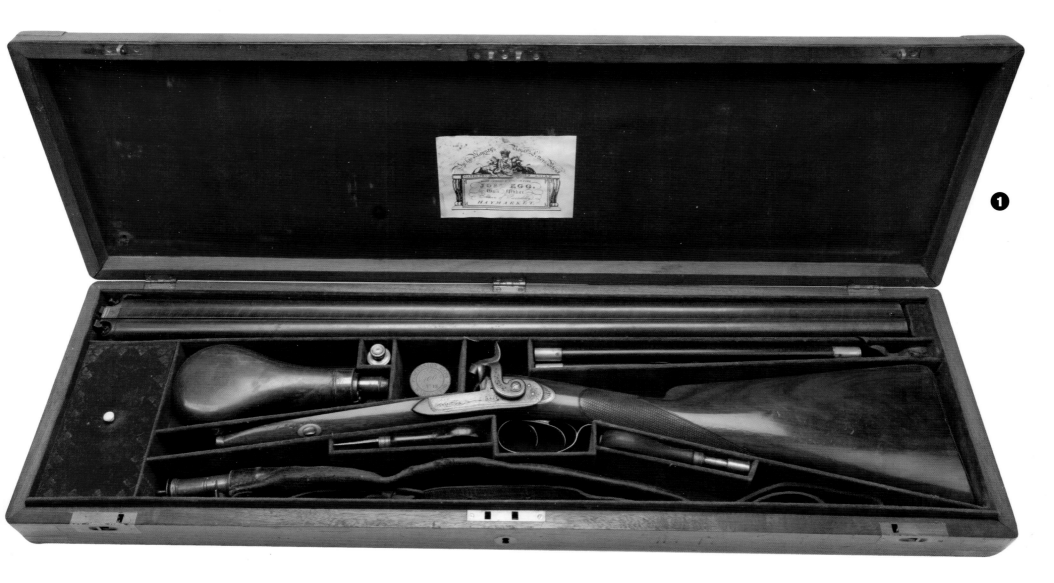

1 Joseph Egg English Percussion Shotgun with
case and accoutrements - 12 gauge - circa
1840-1860 - Englishman Joseph Egg was
known as a maker of high-grade firearms. His
son, Durs, was appointed gunmaker to several
British monarchs and his dueling pistol sets are
among the finest ever produced.

1. Brevete Colt Dragoon Revolving Rifle - .44 caliber - circa 1870 - Copies of Colt revolving arms were produced in Belgium for the European arms market. While many of these were not sanctioned, Colt did license certain firms to officially produce versions of Colt designs under a patent brevette agreement that allowed them to be marketed in regions where Colt products were not well represented.

2. Ann Patrick English Percussion Double Rifle - .70 caliber - circa 1838 - Female gunsmith Ann Patrick regulated the two barrels of this double rifle to shoot to the same point of impact, an exacting task that would have taken nearly three times as long to finish as a single-barreled rifle.

3. Rigby English Percussion Pistol - .54 caliber - circa 1840-1855 - This single-shot pistol incorporates a side-mounted, spring-activated bayonet. Spare percussion caps and lead balls could be stored in the pistol's butt trap. Rigby is one of the more prestigious British makers.

4. Bentley English Percussion Plains Rifle - .44 caliber - circa 1849 - This type of rifle was sold in Canada during the Gold Rush period.

5. A. J. Plate Percussion Side-by-Side Shotgun - 10 gauge - circa 1850 - It was manufactured in San Francisco.

6. Russia America Fur Co. (Tula Arsenal, Russia) Model 1838 Percussion Musket - .70 caliber - circa 1838 - Obsolete military muskets frequently were reissued as trade goods on the California frontier.

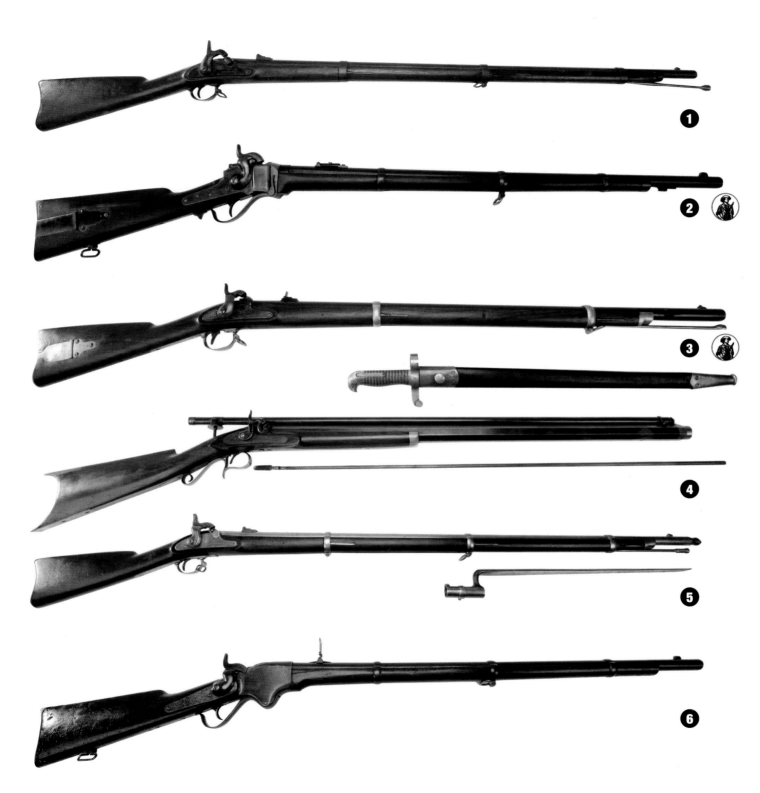

1 U.S. Alfred P. Jenks & Son Model 1861 Percussion Rifle-Musket - .58 caliber - circa 1861-1865 - With total production of over 98,000, Jenks was the largest of 21 private contractors making 1861 Rifle Muskets for the Union.

2 U.S. Sharps New Model 1859 Breechloading Percussion Rifle - .52 caliber - circa 1859-1863 - A falling-block design, Sharps breechloaders were manufactured in great numbers throughout the American Civil War in both rifle and carbine configurations.

3 U.S. Remington Model 1863 Percussion Contract (Zouave) Rifle - .58 caliber - circa 1862-1865.

4 James & Ferris Half-Stock Percussion Target Rifle - .36 caliber - circa 1855-1865 - Both U.S. and Confederate armies employed sharpshooters armed with rifles of this type for long-range shooting, including fire against enemy officers.

5 U.S. Springfield Model 1863 Type II Rifle Musket – .58 caliber – circa 1863-1865. Note the "tampion" barrel plug that was used to provide protection from the elements during carry.

6 U.S. Spencer Model 1860 Army Repeating Rifle - .56 caliber rimfire - circa 1863-1864.

A NATION ASUNDER

UNION LONGARMS

On December 20, 1860, the legislature of the state of South Carolina, exercising the powers granted to it by the 10th Amendment of the Constitution of the United States, passed an ordinance of secession and separated itself from the United States as a free and sovereign government.

Within the next six months, 11 other states adopted similar resolutions and formed the Confederate States of America. After the Battle of Ft. Sumter in April of 1861, the federal government refused to recognize the independence of the Southern states and declared that open rebellion existed, calling 100,000 men to arms to suppress the revolt.

At the beginning of the Civil War, the bulk of the North's longarms were safe in the hands of their regular infantry units or were secured in federal arsenals and armories. Previous U.S. Pattern arms such as the Model 1841 rifle, the Model 1842 musket, and the Model 1855 rifled musket were quickly readied and issued to waiting troops. Changes in the standard service arm resulted in the adoption of the Model 1861 rifled musket, the Colt Contract Model of 1861, and eventually the Model 1863 rifled musket. Over 1.5 million .58 caliber arms were turned out by the Springfield Armory and 32 private contractors during the course of the war.

The age of steam ushered in an industrial revolution, and thousands of advances were made in manufacturing processes. Factories were located to make the best use of water, or hydraulic, power that was sometimes referred to as white coal.

In New England, the Merrimac, Concord, Connecticut, and Chicopee rivers flow through a fertile valley creating a region known as Gun Valley due to the numerous arms manufacturers who set up factories along these valuable water sources.

On April 9,1865, the war ended at a cost of 650,000 lives, the most costly conflict in American history.

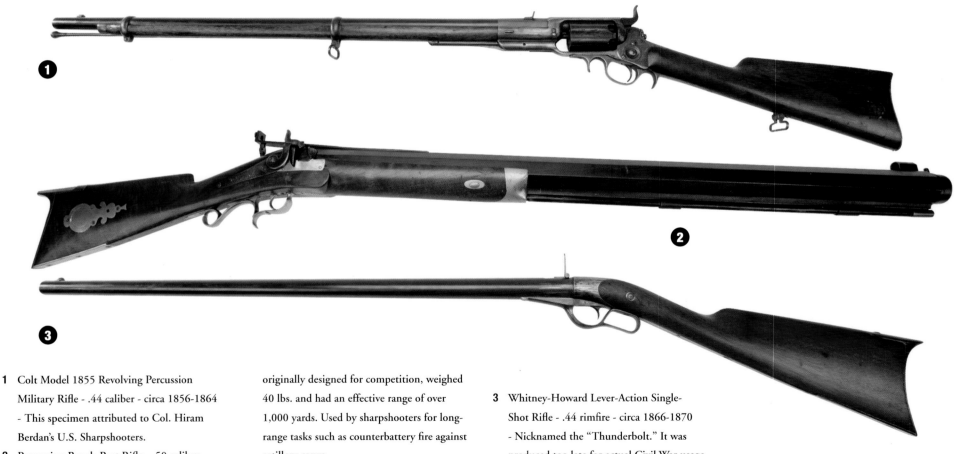

1. Colt Model 1855 Revolving Percussion Military Rifle - .44 caliber - circa 1856-1864 - This specimen attributed to Col. Hiram Berdan's U.S. Sharpshooters.
2. Percussion Bench-Rest Rifle - .50 caliber - circa 1850-1860 - This type of percussion rifle, originally designed for competition, weighed 40 lbs. and had an effective range of over 1,000 yards. Used by sharpshooters for long-range tasks such as counterbattery fire against artillery crews.
3. Whitney-Howard Lever-Action Single-Shot Rifle - .44 rimfire - circa 1866-1870 - Nicknamed the "Thunderbolt." It was produced too late for actual Civil War usage.

1 U.S. Colt Model 1861 Special Musket -- .58 caliber – circa 1861-1865. Approx. 100,000 produced during the war.

2 U.S. Lemuel Pomeroy Model 1840 Contract Percussion Rifle - .69 caliber - circa 1840-1846 - Converted from a flintlock smoothbore.

3 Lindsay Model 1863 U.S. Double Rifle Musket - .58 caliber - circa 1863 - Two-shot capacity was achieved by loading one charge on top of the other in the same barrel, resulting in a superposed charge. 1,000 of these were manufactured in 1863-1864. Their combat usage was unsatisfactory, with reports of simultaneous firing of both charges.

4 U.S. New Haven Arms Co. Henry Lever-Action Repeating Rifle - .44 rimfire - circa 1860-1866 - Although this lever-action 15-round repeater offered a tremendous firepower advantage over the single-shot muzzleloaders commonly fielded at the time, only about 1,700 were actually purchased and saw use during the Civil War.

The Maynard Tape-Priming System

Dr. Edward Maynard, a dental surgeon from Washington, D.C., patented an automatic tape-priming system for percussion firearms in 1845. Dr. Maynard had spent a single semester at West Point. Combining this brief introduction to the military with his knowledge of chemicals, he invented a successful, but short-lived, priming system. Maynard's system used a narrow paper tape that had small quantities of impact-sensitive fulminate placed in a single row down the middle of the tape. The tape was sealed with shellac or varnish and resembled a roll of the paper caps used for modern toy pistols.

During the period 1848-1860, hundreds of thousands of government and contract arms utilized the Maynard Tape-Priming System. In 1861, the government replaced the tape system because the tape failed to hold up to the rigors of foul weather and moisture.

The 1855 Pistol Carbine on the next page is an example of a gun made to use this tape-priming system.

Union Carbines

The war quickly brought about a number of firearm innovations that were heralded as sure-fire ways to end the war quickly. The greatest advances in firearm technology came in breechloading arms, primarily cavalry carbines. A mounted trooper of the war was far more effective as a fighter if his firearm was light, short, and easily reloaded in the saddle. Christian Sharps and the breechloading carbine that he had developed in 1848 opened the door to numerous advances

and dozens of patents. Federal government procurement officers issued contracts for the maximum output of guns from such primary manufacturers as Sharps and Spencer. However, the tremendous demand for arms was still not met, and the government was forced to purchase arms from manufacturers who, although their products were not up to government standards, could make deliveries of shootable firearms on schedule.

1 John Brown Raid Sharps Model 1853 Percussion Carbine - .52 caliber - circa 1854-1857 - This Sharps carbine's serial number falls into the small group of carbines that were used by abolitionist John Brown in his ill-fated raid on Harpers Ferry Armory in 1859.

2 U.S. Springfield Model 1855 Percussion Pistol/Carbine - .58 caliber - circa 1855-1857 - Intended to be used with the shoulder stock in carbine configuration by mounted troops or as a pistol when dismounted; note Maynard tape-priming system.

3 E. G. Lamson & Co. Ball Repeating Carbine - .50 rimfire - circa 1865 - 1,000 ordered during the war, but not received until after it ended.

4 U.S. Richardson & Overman Gallager Percussion Carbine - .50 caliber - circa 1860 - 23,000 made with extensive use by Union cavalry. Made in both metallic cartridge and percussion configurations, this design was subject to extraction problems.

5 U.S. Massachusetts Arms Co. Maynard Second Model Breechloading Carbine - .50 caliber - circa 1863-1865 - 20,000 produced for Union cavalry units.

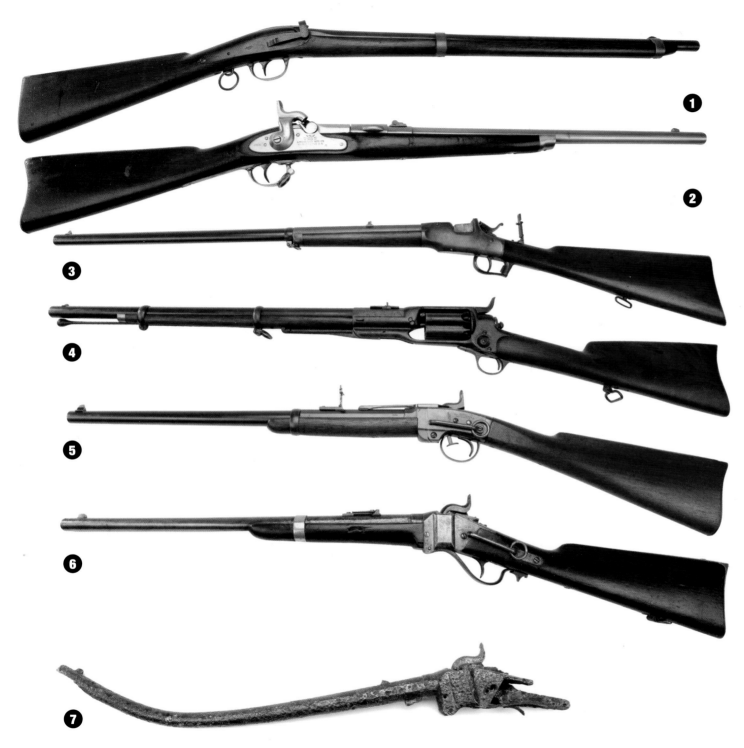

1. U.S. N.P. Ames Jenks Percussion Carbine - .54 caliber - circa 1843-1846 - Unusual side hammer breechloader, nicknamed the Mule Ear carbine. Naval usage.

2. U.S. Amoskeag Mfg. Co. Lindner Percussion Breechloading Carbine, Second Type - .58 caliber - circa 1859 - Some used by 1st Michigan cavalry.

3. Ethan Allen Drop Breech Rifle - .44 rimfire - circa 1860-1870 - Not standard military issue.

4. Colt Model 1855 Percussion Revolving Carbine - .56 caliber - circa 1856-1864.

5. U.S. American Machine Works Smith Breechloading Percussion Carbine - .50 caliber - circa 1861-1865 - 30,000 Smith carbines purchased by federal government.

6. U.S. Sharps New Model 1859 Percussion Carbine - .52 caliber - circa 1859-1866.

7. Sharps New Model 1859 Percussion Carbine (relic condition) - .54 caliber - circa 1859-1866 - Relic, excavated near Appomattox Court House.

1 U.S. Sharps & Hankins Model 1862 Single-Shot Breechloading Percussion Carbine - .52 rimfire - circa 1862 - Leather-covered barrel to protect from salt water for naval usage.

2 U.S. Spencer Lever-Action Repeating Carbine - .52 rimfire - circa 1860-1862 - A seven-shot repeater with magazine in the buttstock, the Spencer was demonstrated to and endorsed by President Abraham Lincoln, and became the dominant cavalry arm by the end of the War.

3 U.S. Burnside Rifle Company 5th Model Breechloading Lever-Action Percussion Carbine - .54 caliber - circa 1862-1865 - The third-most numerous cavalry carbine of the war.

4 U.S. Spencer Lever-Action Repeating Carbine - .56 rimfire - circa 1860-1862.

5 U.S. Whitney Arms Co. Model 1861 Navy Percussion Rifle - .69 caliber - circa 1861-1864 - Nicknamed the "Plymouth Rifle" for service aboard the U.S.S. Plymouth, a test vessel for naval ordnance, where it was developed. 10,000 made during the war, most for naval service.

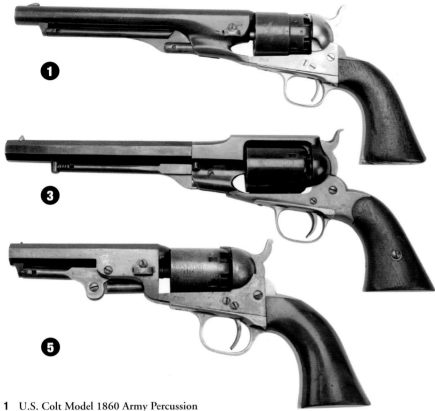

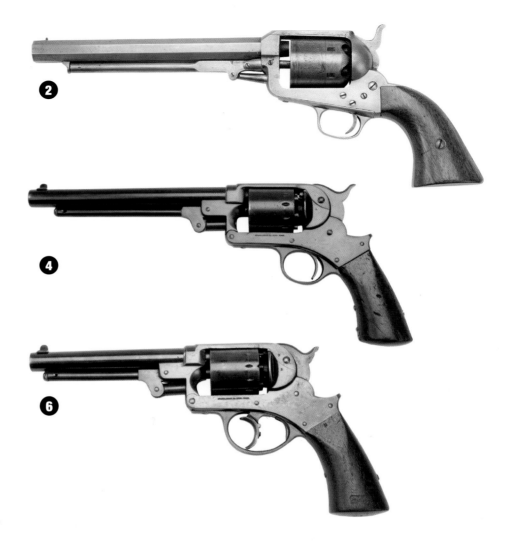

1 U.S. Colt Model 1860 Army Percussion Revolver - .44 caliber - circa 1860-1873 - This .44 revolver weight was only about half of that of its predecessor, the Dragoon; about 200,000 were produced.

2 Whitney Navy & Eagle Co. Percussion Revolver, 1st Model, 2nd Type - .36 caliber - circa 1858-1862 - When Colt's patent on revolving cylinder arms expired in 1857, Whitney introduced the first solid frame percussion revolver and became a significant competitor, producing about 33,000 units. This is a rare 1st Model, 2nd Type, with only about 200 produced.

3 Remington-Beals Navy Model Percussion Revolver - .36 caliber - circa 1861-1863 - About 14,500 produced, with about 1,500 purchased by the U.S. Army and U.S. Navy. As with many Civil War percussion revolvers,

some were later converted to cartridge.

4 U.S. Starr Arms Co. Model 1863 Single Action Army Revolver - .44 caliber - circa 1863-1865 - About 33,000 made, with 25,000 going to the U.S. government. After Colts and Remingtons, Starrs were the Union's third-most widely used handguns.

5 Colt Model 1849 Pocket Percussion Revolver - .31 caliber - circa 1850-1873 - Never issued by the military, but frequently purchased by soldiers as a personal sidearm.

6 U.S. Starr Arms Co. Model 1858 Army Double-Action Percussion Revolver - .44 caliber - circa 1858-1862 - 23,000 manufactured, with most going to the U.S. military. One of the earliest American double action revolvers.

Union Handguns
Federal quartermasters struggled to overcome a severe shortage of firearms that were needed to equip the Union troops. With the age of sword, saber, and lance giving way to the revolver and carbine, pistols were desperately needed by the Union army.

Colt, Remington, and Smith & Wesson made firearms at record levels, but could not produce the quantities that procurement officers needed. As a result, a dozen or more additional revolver companies and manufacturers began supplying their entire production output to the government, even though their arms had not been received favorably by the military or the public prior to the war.

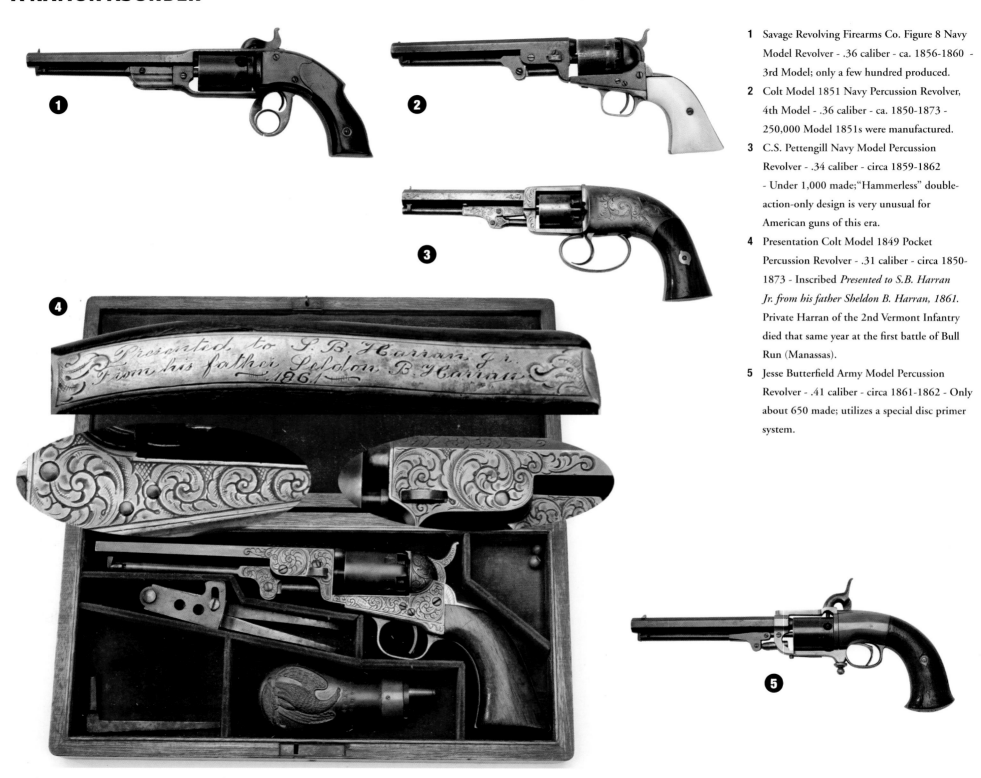

1. Savage Revolving Firearms Co. Figure 8 Navy Model Revolver - .36 caliber - ca. 1856-1860 - 3rd Model; only a few hundred produced.

2. Colt Model 1851 Navy Percussion Revolver, 4th Model - .36 caliber - ca. 1850-1873 - 250,000 Model 1851s were manufactured.

3. C.S. Pettengill Navy Model Percussion Revolver - .34 caliber - circa 1859-1862 - Under 1,000 made; "Hammerless" double-action-only design is very unusual for American guns of this era.

4. Presentation Colt Model 1849 Pocket Percussion Revolver - .31 caliber - circa 1850-1873 - Inscribed *Presented to S.B. Harran Jr. from his father Sheldon B. Harran, 1861.* Private Harran of the 2nd Vermont Infantry died that same year at the first battle of Bull Run (Manassas).

5. Jesse Butterfield Army Model Percussion Revolver - .41 caliber - circa 1861-1862 - Only about 650 made; utilizes a special disc primer system.

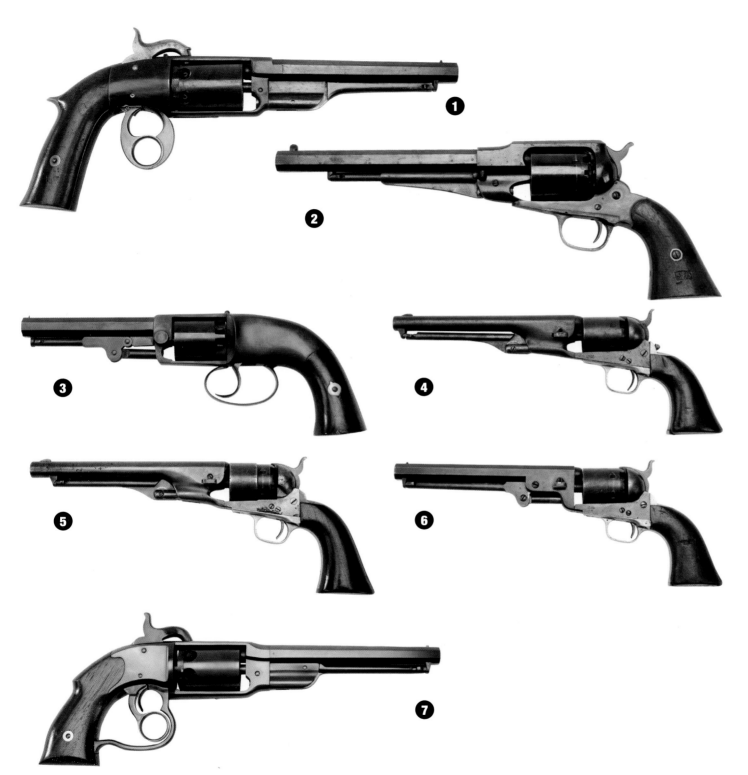

1 Savage & North Figure 8 Percussion Revolver, Second Model - .36 caliber - circa 1858 - Only about 100 2nd Models were made. Unusual two-trigger system in which the lower trigger rotates the cylinder and cocks the hammer, while the upper trigger drops the hammer to fire the gun.

2 Remington New Model Army Percussion Revolver - .44 caliber - circa 1863-1875.

3 C. S. Pettengill Navy Percussion Revolver - .34 caliber - circa 1858-1862 - Pettengills were manufactured by Rogers & Spencer.

4 Colt Model 1861 Navy Percussion Revolver - .36 caliber - circa 1861-1873 - Styled after the larger 1860 Army, with sleek lines and round barrel; otherwise similar to the 1851 Navy Model. Although 40,000 1861s were made, only a few hundred were purchased by the U.S. military.

5 Colt Model 1860 Army Single-Action Percussion Revolver - .44 caliber - circa 1860-1873 - Colt's percussion Army Model revolver was the handgun ordered by the Union in the greatest numbers, with over 120,000 being delivered to Federal authorities before the conclusion of the American Civil War.

6 Colt Model 1851 Navy Single-Action Percussion Revolver - .36 caliber - circa 1850-1873 - This revolver was made in 1856.

7 Savage & North Percussion Revolver - .44 caliber - circa 1856-1859 - Restored. Lower ring trigger operates action; upper trigger fires the gun.

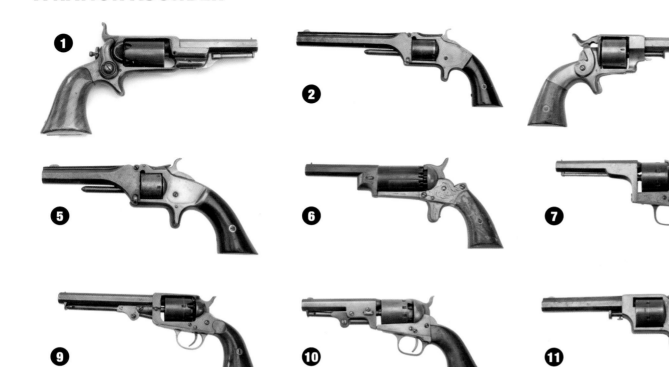

1 Colt Model 1855 Root Sidehammer Pocket Percussion Revolver, Model 2 - .28 caliber - circa 1855-1870 - Although less popular than Colt's conventional center-hammer percussion revolvers, about 40,000 small caliber compact Root sidehammer revolvers were manufactured.

2 Smith & Wesson Model No. 2 Army Single-Action Revolver - .32 rimfire - circa 1861-1874 - Although no S&Ws were purchased by the government, they were a popular personal purchase sidearm for soldiers. The metallic cartridges offered a significant advantage over the prevalent cap-and-ball percussion revolvers. Total production approx. 77,000.

3 Allen & Wheelock Sidehammer Rimfire Single-Action Revolver, 2nd Model - .32 short rimfire - circa 1860 - Only about 1,000 made, with production ordered to cease by a court ruling that this model infringed on the S&W Rollin White patent on a bored-through cylinder.

4 Lucius W. Pond Single-Action Belt Revolver - .32 rimfire - circa 1861-1870 - Another S&W Rollin White patent infringement, with late production marked for Smith & Wesson.

5 Smith & Wesson No. 1 Second Issue Single-Action Revolver - .22 rimfire - circa 1860-1868.

6 John Walch Pocket Model Percussion Revolver - .31 caliber - circa 1860-1862 - John Walch's 10-shot revolver design relied on superposed cylinder charges, with two rounds loaded into each chamber. This unusual handgun was actually manufactured for Walch by Oliver Winchester with the New Haven Arms Company.

7 Moore's Patent Single-Action Belt Revolver - .32 rimfire - circa 1861-1863 - Seven shot. Another S&W patent infringement, later production is marked "**MF'D for Smith and Wesson**" as a result of the lawsuit.

8 Lucius W. Pond Front-Loading Revolver - .32 rimfire - circa 1862-1864 - This Pond model circumvented the S&W patent by using separate removable chambers for each round.

9 W.W. Marston Union Pocket Model Revolver - .31 caliber - circa 1858-1862.

10 Manhattan Pocket Model Percussion Revolver - .31 caliber - circa 1858-1862 - After the expiration of Colt's revolver patent in 1857, Manhattan became a significant competitor, with many of their models closely resembling Colts.

11 Plant's Mfg. Co. Eagle Arms Front Loading Revolver - .30 cup fire - circa 1863-1866 - About 20,000 produced, the cup-primed cartridges circumvented the S&W Rollin White patent.

12 Smith & Wesson No. 1 Second Issue Single-Action Revolver - .22 rimfire - circa 1860-1868 - Donated by the great-grandson of Daniel B. Wesson. The 2nd issue of S&W Model 1 is identified by the flat-sided frame. Over 100,000 made (Springfield, MA) - .22 caliber, circa 1860-1868.

Although not military issue, many small revolvers were privately purchased by Civil War soldiers.

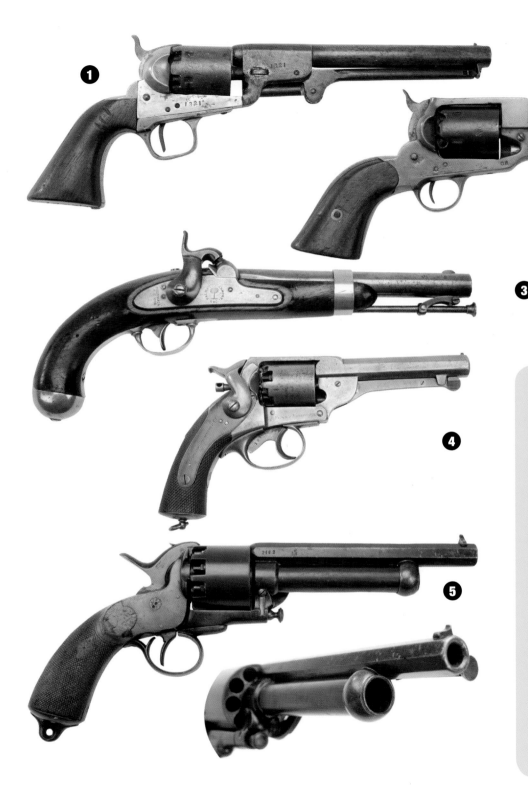

1 **Griswold and Gunnison Navy Model Percussion Revolver** - .36 caliber - circa 1862-1864 - Copied from the Colt Navy with a bronze frame for expediency, manufactured by a transplanted Yankee, Samuel Griswold. The factory in Georgia was destroyed by Union forces in 1864. This had the largest production of any Confederate revolver although only 3,600 were made.

2 **Spiller and Burr Navy Percussion Revolver** - .36 caliber - circa 1862-1864 - Patterned after the Whitney Navy revolver, but manufactured in Richmond, VA, and later Atlanta, GA; about 1,500 were made.

3 **Palmetto Armory Percussion Pistol** - .54 caliber - circa 1852-1853 - Built at the Palmetto Armory in Columbia, SC, by William Glaze and Benjamin Flagg, these copies of the Northern M1842 martial pistol were intended for the South Carolina militia; approx. 1,000 were made.

4 **London Armory Company Kerr Revolver** - .44 caliber - circa 1862 - The sidehammer Kerr revolver, manufactured by the London Armory, was a five-shot handgun imported in limited numbers by the Confederacy.

5 **LeMat French Second Model Percussion Revolver** - .42 caliber cylinder over 20 gauge central barrel - circa 1862-1864 - The "Grapeshot revolver" featured nine rounds in the cylinder, which rotated around a 20-gauge shotgun barrel; favored by Confederate officers such as Gen. J.E.B. Stuart and Gen. Beauregard.

Arms of the Confederacy

The sudden rush by both the North and the South to arm and equip their armies resulted in a boom in the arms industry. The Confederacy had the greatest difficulties to overcome in equipping their troops. Primarily an agrarian society, the South did not possess the manufacturing capabilities of the North.

The Confederacy used arms from a variety of sources, including the former federal arsenals, state militia arms, and personal weapons of individual soldiers. The South was able to augment these arms with imports until the Union navy effectively blockaded Southern ports. For the most part, the Confederacy fought with weapons that had been captured on the battlefields and with a relatively small number of weapons made at armories that were established in the South after the start of the war.

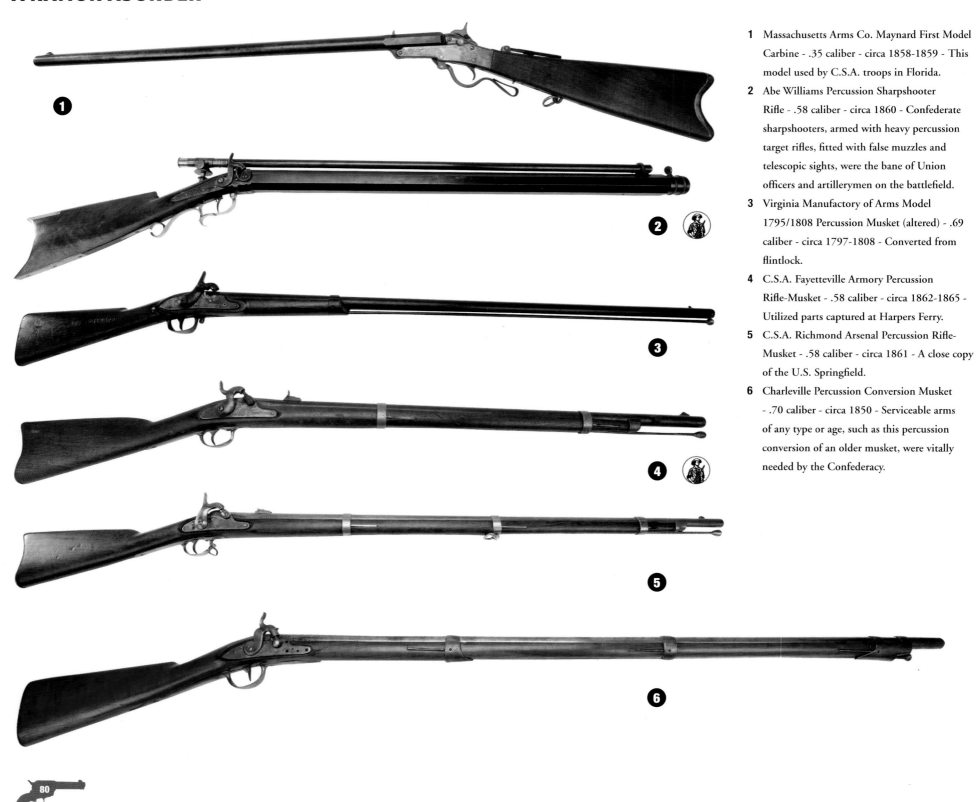

1 Massachusetts Arms Co. Maynard First Model Carbine - .35 caliber - circa 1858-1859 - This model used by C.S.A. troops in Florida.

2 Abe Williams Percussion Sharpshooter Rifle - .58 caliber - circa 1860 - Confederate sharpshooters, armed with heavy percussion target rifles, fitted with false muzzles and telescopic sights, were the bane of Union officers and artillerymen on the battlefield.

3 Virginia Manufactory of Arms Model 1795/1808 Percussion Musket (altered) - .69 caliber - circa 1797-1808 - Converted from flintlock.

4 C.S.A. Fayetteville Armory Percussion Rifle-Musket - .58 caliber - circa 1862-1865 - Utilized parts captured at Harpers Ferry.

5 C.S.A. Richmond Arsenal Percussion Rifle-Musket - .58 caliber - circa 1861 - A close copy of the U.S. Springfield.

6 Charleville Percussion Conversion Musket - .70 caliber - circa 1850 - Serviceable arms of any type or age, such as this percussion conversion of an older musket, were vitally needed by the Confederacy.

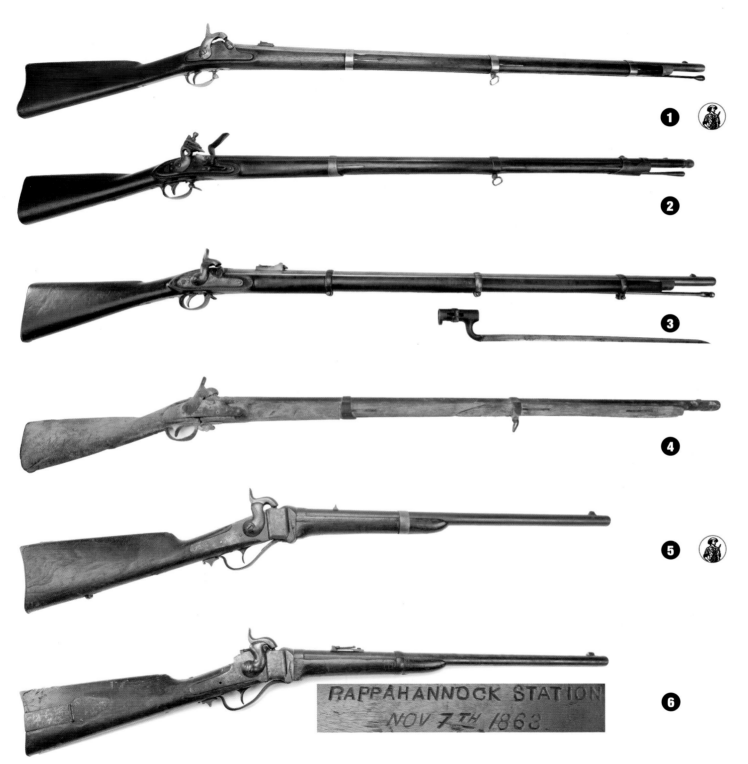

1 C.S.A. Richmond Armory Percussion Rifle-Musket, Type II - .58 caliber - circa 1862 - Carried by James M. Rosser of the 7th Virginia Regiment.

2 U.S. Springfield Model 1816 Flintlock Musket - .69 caliber - circa 1816-1840 - Another older musket of the type that was pressed into service.

3 Barnett English Model 1853 Enfield Percussion Rifle-Musket - .577 caliber - circa 1862 - Britain's Pattern 1853 rifle musket was the percussion longarm smuggled through the Union blockade in great numbers to arm the South. Its .577 bore was a close match to the .58 caliber rifle muskets employed by the North.

4 Model 1816 Percussion Conversion Musket - .69 caliber - Percussion conversion, in battlefield dug-up condition.

5 S.C. Robinson Sharps-Type Breechloading Percussion Carbine - .52 caliber - circa 1862-1865 - Confederate copy of the Union Sharps carbine, made in Richmond, VA, without the Lawrence pellet priming system for simplicity of manufacture.

6 Sharps New Model 1859 Percussion Carbine - .52 caliber - circa 1859-1866 - The buttstock of this carbine is carved "Rappahannock Station Nov. 7 1863" and was captured from Confederate cavalry forces by Union Gen. John Buford's troopers.

RAPPAHANNOCK STATION NOV 7TH 1863

1 Adams Patent Small Arms Company English Army Percussion Revolver - .44 caliber - circa 1857-1861 - Double-action revolvers such as this were more popular in England than in the U.S. The Adams design was made both in England by London Armoury Co. and in America by the Massachusetts Arms Co.

2 David Herman English Double-Action Percussion Revolver - .40 caliber - circa 1860 - One of many copies of the Adams pattern revolver.

3 Tranter/Adams English Patent Percussion Revolver - .458 caliber - circa 1855-1860.

4 Belgian Double-Action Pinfire Revolver - .28 caliber pinfire - circa 1854.

5 Belgian Double-Action Pinfire Revolver - .32 pinfire - circa 1850-1860.

6 Belgian Double-Action Pinfire Revolver - .44 pinfire - circa 1850-1860.

7 LeFaucheux French Single-Action Pinfire Revolver - .32 pinfire - circa 1860-1870 - One of the first metallic cartridge designs, Casimir LeFaucheux's pinfire revolvers were offered in calibers from 5mm to 12mm and were among the many foreign arms imported by both Union and Confederate arms buyers.

8 LeFaucheux Belgian Revolver - .44 pinfire - circa 1860-1870.

9 Austrian Percussion Pistol - .70 caliber - circa 1860-1862.

10 English Double-Action Bar-Hammer Percussion Revolver - .44 caliber - ca. 1845 - This gun was seized by the U.S. Navy from a Confederate blockade runner.

Imported Arms

It soon became apparent from the opening battles of the War Between the States that the conflict would be lengthy. Both the North and the South realized that more guns would be needed quickly, and looked to the armories and arms manufacturing centers of Europe for additional firearms.

On the Union side, General John C. Fremont, Colonel George Schuyler, and Marcellus Hartley (from the private military outfitting firm of Schuyler, Hartley & Graham) worked tirelessly to obtain new arms. Their efforts served not only to equip Union troops, but also to deprive the Confederates of the opportunity to buy these arms.

The Confederates relied primarily on the efforts of Major Caleb Huse, Major Edward C. Anderson, Commander James D. Bullock, and Captain James H. North. Courtney & Tennant of Charleston, South Carolina, S. Isaacs, Campbell & Company of London, and Nelson Clements of Texas also served as arms procurement agents for the South.

The guns obtained from the foreign markets consisted of a variety of small arms whose quality varied from useless to excellent. Many of the firearms were converted smoothbores that were outdated. Calibers ranged from .54 to .71 caliber. Most of the imported arms came from England, Austria, Prussia, Saxony, Bavaria, France, and Belgium.

1 Suhl German Model 1839 Muzzleloading Percussion Musket - .71 caliber - circa 1839.

2 Charles Ingram English Volunteer Pattern Percussion Rifle - .45 Whitworth - circa 1860 - British Rifle Volunteer units were initially established and trained to repulse a potential French invasion in 1858, but their surplus arms were among the munitions offered on the world market as the Confederacy began to equip its forces in 1861 and 1862.

3 Westley Richards English Officer's Model Percussion Musketoon - .50 caliber - circa 1861-1862 - Used by C.S.A. Capt. Matthew West of Mississippi serving in the Army of Northern Virginia.

4 Lorenz Austrian Percussion Musket - .71 caliber - circa 1862-1863.

5 Lorenz Austrian Model 1855 Percussion Rifle - .54 caliber - circa 1862.

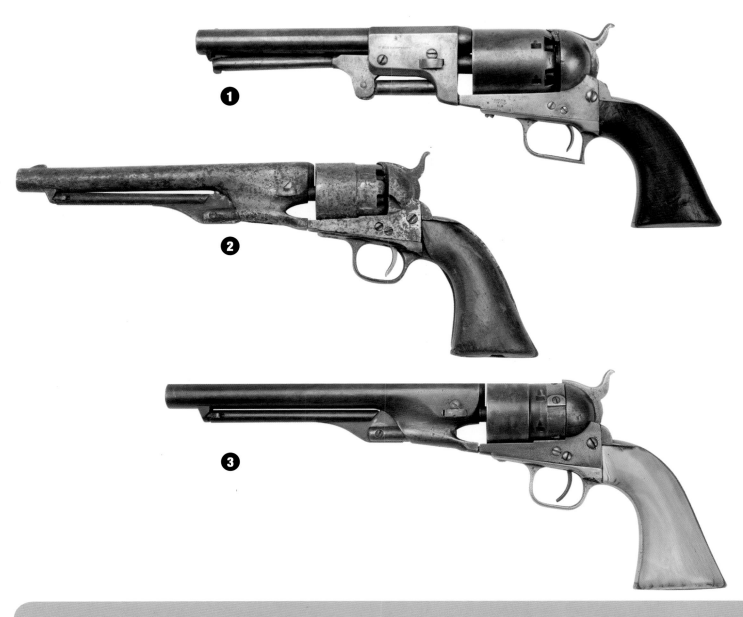

1 Colt Second Model Dragoon Percussion Revolver - .44 caliber - circa 1850-1851 - The heavy Dragoon Model replaced the Walker in 1848, with around 20,000 made through 1861. It weighs 4.25 lbs.

2 U.S. Colt Model 1860 Army Percussion Revolver - .44 caliber - circa 1863 - In 1860 Colt came up with a sleeker, lighter .44, in part by using a rebated cylinder, narrower in diameter at the rear. The popular 1860 weight was about half that of a Dragoon. This relic shows hard use and abuse.

3 Colt Model 1860 Thuer Conversion Army Revolver - .44 Thuer - circa 1869-1872 - The Thuer system was one of the earliest attempts by Colt to convert their percussion revolvers to fire metallic cartridges, with about 5,000 made. Later conversions such as the Richards and Richards Mason were more successful.

Sixguns

Following the Civil War, veterans and other Americans moved west to start a new life. Firearms were important tools for many, used for sustenance hunting, predator and pest control on ranches and farms, personal defense in unsettled areas, and recreation.

The West of this era holds a special spot in America's collective imagination, and certainly the icon of this era is the sixgun.

While cartridge arms were rapidly replacing percussion guns in manufacturer product lines, the older guns were still widely used. Many cap-and-ball revolvers by Colt and other manufacturers served for decades after most production ceased around 1870.

In addition, many revolvers were converted from percussion to cartridge by replacing or modifying the cylinder and hammer.

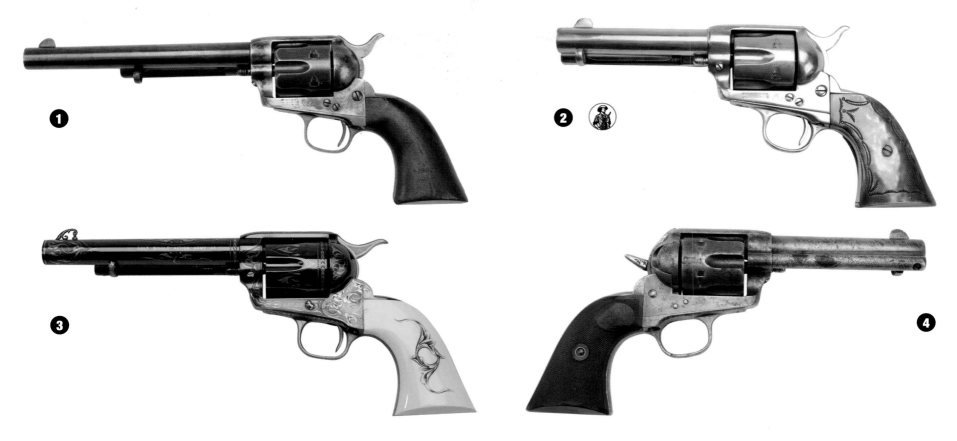

1 Colt Model 1873 Single-Action Army Revolver

2

3

4

The Single-Action Army

The Colt Single-Action Army Model of 1873 is the gun most widely associated with the American West. Also known as the Colt Peacemaker, Colt Single Action, and Colt Frontier Six Shooter (in .44-40 caliber), this revolver incorporated many design innovations and was a vast improvement over the old percussion models.

It used a solid frame with a top strap and screwed-in barrel, similar to the Remington percussion revolvers. One cartridge at a time was loaded through a loading gate on the frame at the rear of the cylinder, and empties were punched out individually using a manual ejector rod mounted on the side of the barrel. A rugged frontier tool that could be used

to provide food or personal protection, The Colt Single-Action Army revolver was to be offered in 36 calibers during its first 50 years of production, with the most common being .45 Colt, .44-40, .38-40, and .32-20. The last three chamberings were orignated for Winchester lever-action rifles. Carrying a handgun in the same caliber as one's rifle minimized the types of ammunition that had to be carried. Standard barrel lengths were 7.5-inch, 5.5-inch, and 4.75-inch.

The U.S. Ordnance Department began field-testing the revolver in November 1872. These tests resulted in the government awarding Colt an initial contract in 1873 for 8,000 revolvers in .45 caliber for use by the U.S. Cavalry. Many famous, as well as infamous,

persons are associated with this revolver: Buffalo Bill Cody, Wyatt Earp, Billy the Kid, Calamity Jane, and Gen. George Armstrong Custer. An unknown wit made the remark: **"God created man, but Samuel Colt made them equal!"**

In addition to the Single Action Army, Colt also produced a myriad of small- and large-frame revolvers in both single-action and double-action models. These Colt revolvers were hugely popular and were used extensively throughout the period of western expansion.

1 Colt Model 1873 Single-Action Army Revolver - .45 Colt - circa 1872-1940 - This revolver was made around 1890 in the classic caliber and 7.5-inch barrel length.

2 Colt Single-Action Army Revolver - .44-40 - circa 1873-1940 - Nickel finish with silver grips and turquoise inlays.

3 Engraved Colt Single-Action Army Revolver - .45 Colt - circa 1990 - Modern production with gold inlays and ivory grips.

4 Colt Single-Action Army Revolver Slip Gun - .45 caliber - circa 1873-1940 - Modified to fire by cocking and releasing the hammer without pulling the trigger, which may have allowed faster firing at the cost of a significant decrease in accuracy.

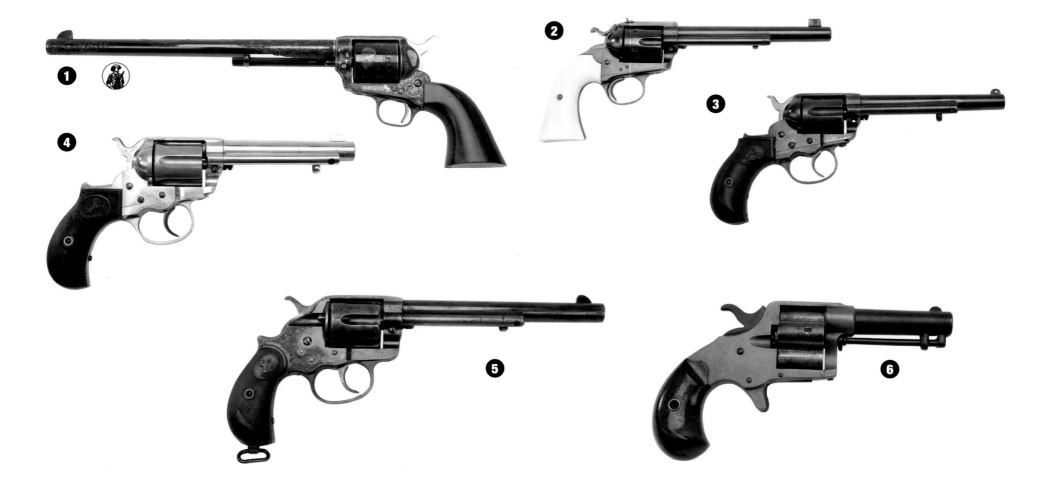

1 Engraved Colt Buntline Special Revolver - .45 Colt - circa 1994 - Although Colt did make some Single-Action Armies with extra long barrels, the Buntline Special story is considered likely to be a myth. This modern-made Buntline is engraved by Ken Hurst in a Wyatt Earp theme, and sports a nonstandard unfluted cylinder.

2 Colt Hartford, CT, Bisley Flat-Top Target Model Single-Action Army Revolver - .44-40 - circa 1894 - 1913 - Colt's Bisley Model, named after the shooting range in Great Britain, was designed with an altered grip frame differing from the plow-handle pattern used with the Single-Action Army. Bisley Colts were offered from 1894 to 1915. Standard Bisleys had fixed sights. The rare ones, such as this one, with adjustable target sights are called "Flat-Top" models due to the flat topstrap of the frame.

3 Colt Model 1877 "Thunderer" Double-Action Revolver - .41 Colt - ca. 1877-1909 - The Model 1877 was Colt's first double-action revolver. Although it was popular in the West and elsewhere, it was a bit mechanically fragile. In .41 caliber, it is nicknamed the "Thunderer." The 1877 was carried by Billy the Kid and John Wesley Hardin, among many others in the Old West.

4 Colt Model 1877 "Lightning" Double-Action Revolver - .38 Colt - circa 1877-1909 - In .38 caliber, the Model 1877 was nicknamed the "Lightning." A rare .32 caliber "Rainmaker" was also produced.

5 Colt Model 1878 Double-Action Frontier Revolver - circa 1878-1905 - Total production over 50,000. The large frame of this model allowed it to accommodate any cartridge chambered in the Single-Action Army revolver.

6 Colt House Model Single-Action Revolver - .41 rimfire - circa 1871-1876 - Fewer than 10,000 made in both four- and five-shot configurations. This scarce four-shot type is nicknamed the "Cloverleaf" model due to the shape of the cylinder when viewed from the end.

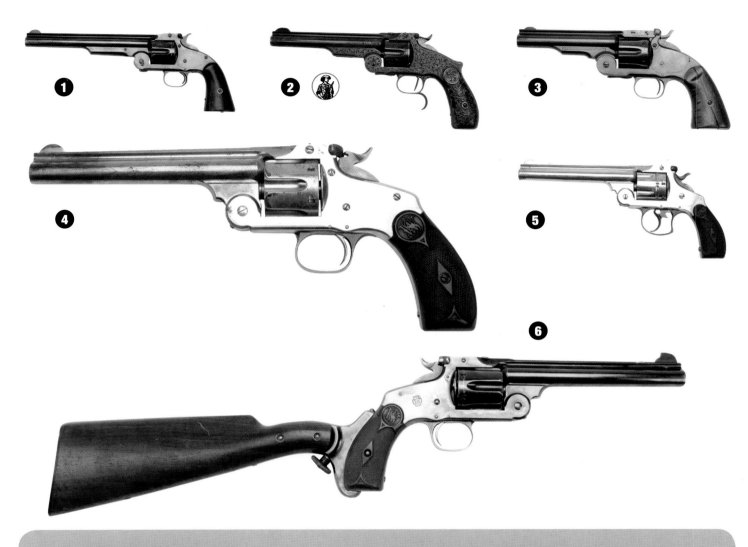

1 Smith & Wesson Second Model American Revolver - .44 American - ca. 1870-1874 - The first Model 3 became known as the American Model to distinguish it from the Russian Model introduced the following year.

2 Smith & Wesson 3rd Model Russian Revolver - .44 Russian - circa 1871-1878 - Large orders of the Model 3 by the Russian military included requested design changes such as the triggerguard spur and extreme knuckle on the back strap. This specimen has nonperiod engraving.

3 Smith & Wesson Second Model Schofield Single-Action Revolver - .45 Schofield - circa 1876-1877 - Most production of the Model 3 Schofield was purchased by the U.S. Army and issued during the Indian Wars era. When sold as surplus, they often were refinished and had their barrels shortened, such as this example. Some were purchased by Wells Fargo to arm their messengers.

4 Smith & Wesson New Model No. 3 Target Model Revolver - .32-44 - circa 1887-1910.

5 Smith & Wesson 44 Double-Action Frontier Revolver - .44-40 - circa 1881-1913 - In .44 Russian, this was known as the .44 DA First Model. The "Frontier Model" designation refers to the .44-40 chambering.

6 Smith & Wesson New Model No. 3 Target Single-Action Revolver with shoulder stock - .38/.44 - circa 1887-1910 - Detachable shoulder stocks were available for most Model 3s, although not widely used. The Australian Colonial Police ordered revolvers in this configuration.

Smith & Wesson Revolvers

Although most think of the Colt as the typical revolver of the post-Civil War 19th century, Smith & Wesson outproduced Colt throughout that time period.

Smith & Wesson's large-frame revolvers were called the Model 3 with specific models including the American, Russian, Schofield, New Model No. 3, and Double Action. Whereas the Colt was more rugged, the S&W had a more advanced top break automatic ejecting design that made it much quicker to load.

The S&W was used by notables such as Frank and Jesse James, Texas Jack Omohundro, Cole Younger, John Wesley Hardin, Pat Garret, Charlie Pitts, Bill Tilghman, Annie Oakley, and Theodore Roosevelt. Military usage included large purchases by Russia and Japan, along with Turkey, Argentina, and the U.S. The pattern was widely copied throughout Europe. In the hands of shooters such as Ira Paine, Walter Winans, Oscar Olson, and Sgt. W.E. Petty, it was used to set most of the revolver target-shooting records of the era.

Model 3 refers to the frame size and includes any large-frame S&W top-break revolver, and is usually omitted from the model name (with the exception of the New Model No. 3). Americans, Russians, Schofields, and Double Actions all have more than one model type, so the terminology can get confusing. For example, guns commonly called "2nd Model Americans," "1st Model Schofields," "1st Model DAs," or "3rd Model Russians" are all Model 3 revolvers.

S&W Small-Frame Revolvers
Smith & Wesson small-frame revolvers can be grouped into four types. The earliest "tip-ups" (1857-1881) were spur-trigger revolvers in .22 or .32 rimfire with barrels that tipped up allowing the cylinder to be removed for loading or unloading.
The single-action small frames (1878-1892) mostly had spur-triggers as well. These were top-break revolvers, where the barrel and cylinder tipped down, and cartridge cases were automatically ejected.
The double-action small frames (1880-1919) were also top breaks but with traditional triggerguards. The Safety Hammerless models (1887-1940) were double-action top breaks as well, but with hammers fully enclosed by the frame so they could be fired double action only, and a grip safety on the backstrap. All the top-break variations were offered in .32 S&W and .38 S&W only.

1 Smith & Wesson Model Two Old Army Revolver - .32 rimfire - circa 1861-1874 - Tip-up revolver. Wild Bill Hickock was known to have carried one in addition to his Colt 1851 Navies. Gen. Custer and Pres. Rutherford Hayes both owned a Model Two.

2 Smith & Wesson Model 1 1/2 Second Issue Single-Action Revolver - .32 rimfire - circa 1868-1875 - This model was introduced after S&W was already making a small .22 caliber Model One and a larger six-shot .32 Model Two. Accordingly, this in-between size five-shot .32 wound up with the ungainly moniker, "Model One and a Half."

3 Smith & Wesson Model One, Third Issue, Single-Action Revolver - .22 short - circa 1868-1881 - Third Issue of the Model One is identified by birdshead butt, fluted cylinder, and round ribbed barrel.

4 Smith & Wesson 38 Single-Action Second Model Revolver - .38 S&W - circa 1877-1891 - Around 160,000 .38 SAs were made; the majority were this Second Model configuration.

5 Smith & Wesson .32 Single Action Revolver - .32 S&W - circa 1878-1892 - Nearly 100,000 were made.

6 Smith & Wesson .38 Single-Action Third Model Revolver - .38 S&W - circa 1891-1911.

7 Gen. Leonard Wood's Smith & Wesson .38 Double-Action revolver - .38 S&W - circa 1880-1911 - Wood was Roosevelt's commander in the Rough Riders and he went on to lead the U.S. Army in the Philippines.

8 Smith & Wesson .32 Safety Hammerless First Model Revolver - .32 S&W - ca. 1888-1902 - Production of the .32 Safety Hammerless continued until 1937 through two more model variations; nearly 250,000 were made.

9 Smith & Wesson .38 Safety Hammerless First Model Revolver - .38 S&W - circa 1887 - Production of five models continued through 1940, with over 250,000 made.

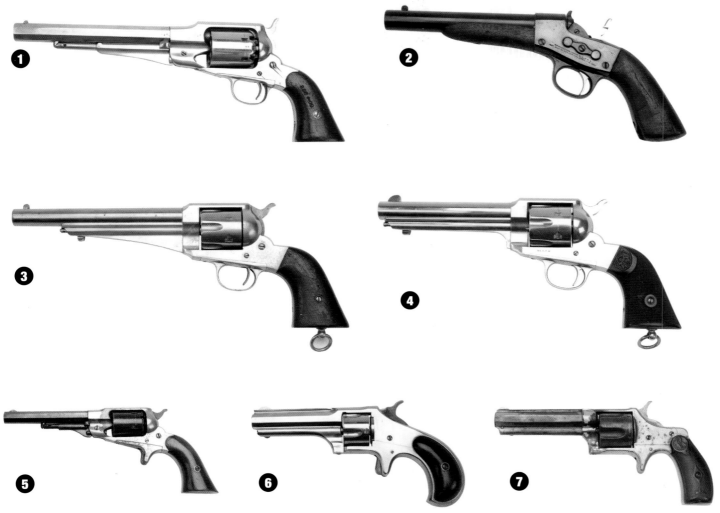

1 Remington Model 1861 Army Single-Action Percussion Revolver - .44 caliber - circa 1862.

2 Remington Model 1867 Rolling Block Single-Shot Pistol - .50 centerfire - circa 1867 - This type of pistol was purchased by the U.S. Army and the U.S. Navy after the Civil War.

3 Remington Model 1875 Single-Action Army Revolver - .44 Remington - circa 1875-1889 - Remington revolvers competed with Colt and S&W. The design is similar to the Colt.

4 Remington Model 1890 Single-Action Army Revolver - .44-40 - circa 1890 - Total production of Remington large-frame cartridge revolvers was around 30,000 from 1875 to 1896.

5 Remington Single-Action New Model Pocket Revolver - .32 rimfire conversion - circa 1878-1888 - As with Colt and others, some Remington percussion revolvers were converted to fire cartridges.

6 Remington-Smoot New Model No. 1 Single-Action Revolver - .30 rimfire short - circa 1875-1877 - Around 64,000 Remington spur-trigger small-frame revolvers were produced from 1875 to 1888.

7 Remington-Smoot New Model No. 3 Single-Action Revolver - .38 rimfire - circa 1878-1888.

Mark Twain on the S&W Model One (pictured on previous page)

Although it was a breakthrough in cartridge firearms evolution and quite popular, the little Model One .22 was neither powerful nor accurate. On a train trip to the West, Mark Twain wrote:

"I was armed to the teeth with a pitiful little Smith & Wessons seven-shooter, which carried a ball like a homeopathic pill, and it took the whole seven to make a dose for an adult. But I thought it was grand. It appeared to me to be a dangerous weapon. It had only one fault - you could not hit anything with it. One of our conductors practiced a while on a cow with it, and as long as she stood still and behaved herself she was safe; but as soon as she went to moving about, and he got to shooting at other things, she came to grief."

The Other Sixguns of the Old West

The solid-frame single-action design of the Colt and Remington and the top-break design of Smith & Wesson were not the only sixguns in the West. Unusual revolvers from the U.S. and abroad found a market west of the Mississippi.

1 Merwin Hulbert & Co. Single-Action Pocket Army Revolver - .44-40 - circa 1876-1883 - Large-frame Merwin revolvers competed with S&W, Colt, and Remington. Production has been estimated low, but based on surviving examples may have actually approached that of Remington. They were exceptionally well made at the Hopkins and Allen plant, to tolerances that are difficult to match today. They featured a unique twist-open design in which barrel and cylinder are rotated 90 degrees clockwise and pulled forward from the frame. This design allows selective extraction of fired cases only.

2 Galand Double-Action Revolver - .38 Galand - circa 1868-1870 - Unusual European design. Pivoting the trigger guard down and forward pushes barrel and cylinder forward for unloading.

3 Galand-Somerville Double-Action Revolver - .450 Eley - circa 1868-1870 - Made in England.

4 Enfield Model 1884 Double-Action Revolver - .476 Enfield - circa 1884 - A heavy hinged-frame revolver, the cumbersome Enfield Mk II revolver relied on an awkward forward-sliding movement for cylinder extraction. Despite these faults, it was selected by the Royal Canadian Mounted Police for issue.

5 VK Belgian Single-Action Revolver - .44 S&W - circa 1880-1890 - The Smith & Wesson top-break design was widely copied in Belgium, Spain, and elsewhere, making it the predominant large-frame revolver design of the late 19th century.

6 Belgian Revolver - .45 caliber - circa 1880-1890.

7 P. Webley & Son British Metropolitan Police Double-Action Revolver - .450 Eley - circa 1890-1900 - Webley in England turned out large numbers of rugged top-break and solid-frame double-action revolvers.

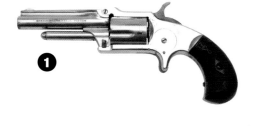

Pocket Pistols

Despite Hollywood and TV westerns, the most popular revolver of this era was not the full-size, big-bore "hogleg" six shooter, but rather more compact medium- and small-frame guns. Most popular calibers were .22 and .32 rimfire, and .32 and .38 centerfire. They cost less and were much handier to carry. Many towns prohibited open carry of handguns, and the smaller models could be easily concealed. They are, in fact. sometimes called "pocket pistols."

1 Marlin No. 32 Standard 1875 Single-Action Pocket Revolver - .32 rimfire - circa 1875-1887.

2 Marlin XX Standard 1873 Pocket Revolver -- .22 rimfire – circa 1873-1887. Approx. 10,000 made.

3 Forehand & Wadsworth Model 1890 Hammerless Top-Break Double-Action Pocket Revolver - .38 S&W - circa 1890.

4 Spanish Single-Action Revolver - 9 mm - circa 1885-1900 - Copy of a British Webley design.

5 Merwin Hulbert & Co. Single-Action Pocket Revolver - .38 S&W - circa 1876-1883.

6 Harrington & Richardson Double-Action Pocket Revolver - .32 S&W - circa 1880-1883.

7 Marlin XXX Standard 1872 Single-Action Pocket Revolver - .30 rimfire - circa 1872-1887.

8 H. Remy Spanish Merwin Hulbert Double-Action Revolver (copy) - .38 S&W - circa 1880-1890 - The Merwin pattern was copied in Spain and elsewhere.

9 Merwin Hulbert & Co. (NewYork, NY) Double-Action Pocket Revolver - .32 S&W - circa 1880-1885.

10 Colt Open-Top Pocket Model Single-Action Revolver - .22 short - circa 1871-1877 - A competitor to the Smith & Wesson No.1 line of revolvers, also seven-shot spurtriggers; over 114,000 were made.

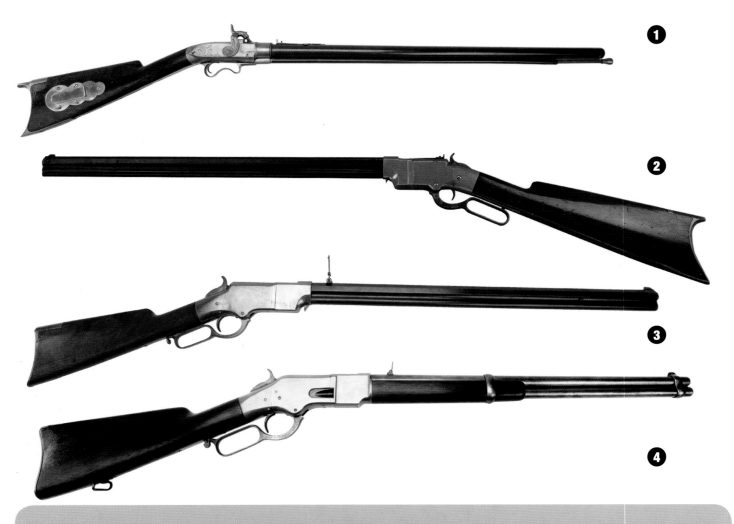

1 Jennings by Robbins & Lawrence Rifle - .54 rocket ball - circa 1848-1853 - The Jennings is considered the great-grandfather of the Winchester. Firearms design titans Tyler Henry, Horace Smith, and Daniel Wesson participated in its development. Although a repeater was made, this example is a single shot and has been "back converted" to percussion. This was to make it usable when the supply of rapidly discontinued proprietary "rocket ball" ammunition dried up.

2 New Haven Arms Company Volcanic Rifle - .41 rocket ball - circa 1857 - Smith & Wesson introduced this lever-action magazine rifle, which was nicknamed "The Volcanic." It was then made by Volcanic Repeating Arms and then by New Haven Arms Company. The rocket-ball ammo had the gun powder loaded in the base of the hollow bullet.

3 Henry Lever-Action Rifle by New Haven Arms Co. - .44 Henry RF - ca. 1860-1866 - Approx. 14,000 were made. It is quickly identified by its brass frame and lack of wooden forend. The tubular magazine under the barrel is loaded from the front. The Henry lacks the loading gate of later Winchester lever actions.

4 Winchester Model 1866 Third Model Lever-Action Carbine - .44 rimfire - circa 1866-1898 - The first true Winchester, known on the Western frontier as the "Yellowboy" for its brass receiver. The first lever action with a loading gate in the frame; over 170,000 were made.

The Lever-Action Rifle

Just as the Colt Single-Action Army is considered the handgun of the Old West, the Winchester lever-action rifle is the iconic Old West long gun. Early predecessors included the Hunt, Jennings, and Volcanic rifles.

The 15-shot Henry was the first truly successful lever-action repeating rifle. It was patented by B. Tyler Henry in 1860, and earned its laurels on the battlefields of the Civil War. It was known to Confederates as **"that Yankee rifle you load on Sunday and shoot all week."**

Oliver F. Winchester purchased Henry's company and the patent rights for this unique firearm. In May 1866, he changed the name of the firm from the New Haven Arms Company to the Winchester Repeating Arms Company, thus beginning a long history of legendary firearms.

The Model 1866 Winchester boasted a number of important improvements, principally in the method of loading and ejecting cartridges and in the adoption of a side-frame loading gate. Attempts to market the gun to the federal government failed, but sales to foreign countries flourished.

Improved models based on this design were developed and offered for sale in 1873, 1876, 1886, 1892, 1894, and 1895. These various models gave the public a wide variety of choices, and Winchester lever-action rifles became legendary throughout the United States and the world. The Model 1873 was immortalized in the Hollywood film Winchester '73 starring James Stewart. The most popular has been the Model 1894, considered America's deer rifle and an iconic presence both in saddle scabbards and pickup truck gun racks well through the mid-20th century, with a total of over six million produced.

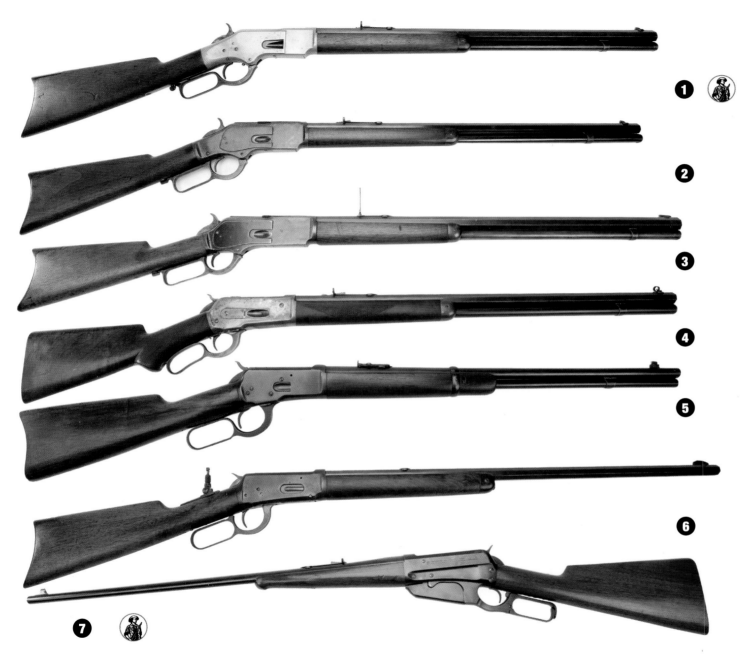

The major models, top to bottom:
MODEL 1866 - 170,000 made 1866-1898. .44 rimfire. Brass frame with loading gate. Yellowboy.
MODEL 1873 - 720,000 made 1873-1919. Relatively low power cartridges, 44-40 (44WCF), 38-40 (38WCF), 32-20 (32WCF). Colt and others made revolvers for the same cartridges. Medium frame with irregularly shaped flat sideplate. The gun that won the West.
MODEL 1876 - 64,000 made 1876-1897. Heavy black powder rifle cartridges 40-60, 45-60, 45-75, and 50-95. Large frame with irregularly shaped flat sideplate.
MODEL 1886 - 160,000 made 1886-1935. Various rifle cartridges from 33 WCF through 50-110 Express. Improved large frame; solid frame (no sideplate) oval loading gate.
MODEL 1892 - Over one million made from 1892 to 1941. Same 44, 38, and 32 WCF calibers as Model 1873, plus .25-20. Light handy solid-frame gun in pistol calibers, identified by distinctive half-oval loading gate with straight front edge. A staple of early Hollywood westerns, even when an anachronism.
MODEL 1894 - Over six million made from 1894 to 2006. The first design made for smokeless powder, in a variety of calibers with the classic being .30-30. Medium solid frame, oval loading port.
MODEL 1895 - 425,000 made 1896-1931. Previous models all had tube magazines. The distinctive box mag of the 1895 allowed it to be chambered for high-powered rifle cartridges with pointed spitzer bullet, in the .30-06 class up to .405 Winchester.

1 Winchester Model 1866 Lever-Action Rifle - .44 Henry RF - circa 1866-1898.

2 Winchester Model 1873 Lever-Action Rifle - .38-40 - circa 1873-1919.

3 Winchester Model 1876 Lever-Action Rifle - .45-60 - circa 1876-1897.

4 Winchester Model 1886 Lever-Action Rifle, Deluxe Grade - .45-90 - circa 1886-1935 - Deluxe grade, special octagonal barrel, and double-set triggers.

5 Winchester Model 1892 Rifle - .32-20 - circa 1892-1941.

6 Winchester Model 1894 Rifle - .30-30 - circa 1894-Present.

7 Winchester Model 1895 Lever-Action Rifle - .30-40 Krag - circa 1896-1931.

1 Winchester Model 1866 Third Model Lever-Action Musket - .44 Henry RF - circa 1866-1898 - The 1866 was offered in carbine (20-inch barrel), rifle (24-inch barrel), and musket (27-inch barrel) configurations. The practice of offering carbine, rifle, and musket lengths continued through most of the Winchester lever-action line.

2 Winchester Model 1873 Lever-Action Carbine - .44-40 - circa 1873-1919.

3 Winchester Model 1873 Lever-Action Rifle - .32-20 - circa 1873-1919 - Deluxe pistol grip stock, made in 1884, British proofs.

4 Winchester Model 1873 Rifle - circa 1873-1919.

5 Winchester Model 1876 Lever-Action Rifle - .40-60 - circa 1876-1897.

1 Winchester Model 1886 Rifle - .38-56 - circa 1886-1935 - Nonstandard short barrel and "button" half mag.

2 Winchester Model 1886 Light Weight Rifle (.33) - circa 1886-1935 - The Light Weight Model features a fast taper 22-inch barrel and half mag.

3 Winchester Model 1886 Deluxe Lever-Action Rifle - .50-110 Express - circa 1886-1935 - High-grade wood, checkering, Three folding leaf express rear sight. Most powerful chambering for an 1886.

4 Winchester Model 1886 Lever-Action Rifle - .45-90 - circa 1886-1935 - Western hunters called this model, in .45-90, the "Grizzly bear rifle,"a rifle for dangerous big game.

5 Winchester Model 1892 Lever-Action Rifle - .25-20 - circa 1892-1941 - Takedown model, can be easily broken into two parts for convenient transport.

6 Winchester Model 1892 Lever-Action Rifle - .44-40 - circa 1892-1941 - Standard model; compare to above.

1. Winchester Model 1894 Lever Action Carbine - .38-55 - circa 1892-1941.

2. Winchester Model 1894 Lever Action Rifle - .25-35 - circa 1894-Present.

3. Winchester Model 1895 Lever Action Carbine - .30-06 - circa 1896-1931.

4. Winchester Model 1895 NRA Lever Action Musket - .30-40 - circa 1903-1906 - Rare variation made for NRA military rifle competition matches.

5. Townsend Whelen's Winchester Model 1895 Lever-Action Rifle - .40-72 Winchester - circa 1902 - Noted arms writer and shooter Colonel Townsend Whelen carried this lever-action Winchester rifle in .40-72 on hunting trips to British Columbia and South Africa.

1   Marlin Model 1881 Lever-Action Rifle, Second
    Style - .45-70 - circa 1881-1892 - 20,000
    made. Competitive with the Winchester
    Model 1876.

2   Marlin Model 1892 Lever-Action Rifle - .32
    centerfire/rimfire - circa 1895-1916 - 45,000
    made. Wide-firing pin allows the use of either
    rimfire or centerfire cartridges.

3   Marlin Model 1893 Lever-Action Rifle - .30-
    30 - circa 1893-1935 - Around one million
    made, in calibers ranging from .25-36 to .38-
    55. This was the first Marlin lever-action rifle
    model to utilize smokeless powder cartridges.

4   Marlin Model 1894 Lever-Action Rifle - .32-
    20 - circa 1894-1935 - 250,000 made, in the
    same "pistol class" cartridges as the Winchester
    1892.

5   Marlin Model 1897 Lever-Action Rifle - .22
    long rifle - circa 1897-1917 - 125,000 made,
    all in takedown configuration.

Marlin Lever-Action Rifles
The Marlin Firearms Company
was founded by former Colt
employee John Mahlon Marlin in
1863. The comapny's first products
were handguns and single-shot
rifles. In 1881, the company
began manufacturing lever-action
repeating rifles. Its product line
grew to become Winchester's
primary competition in that field.

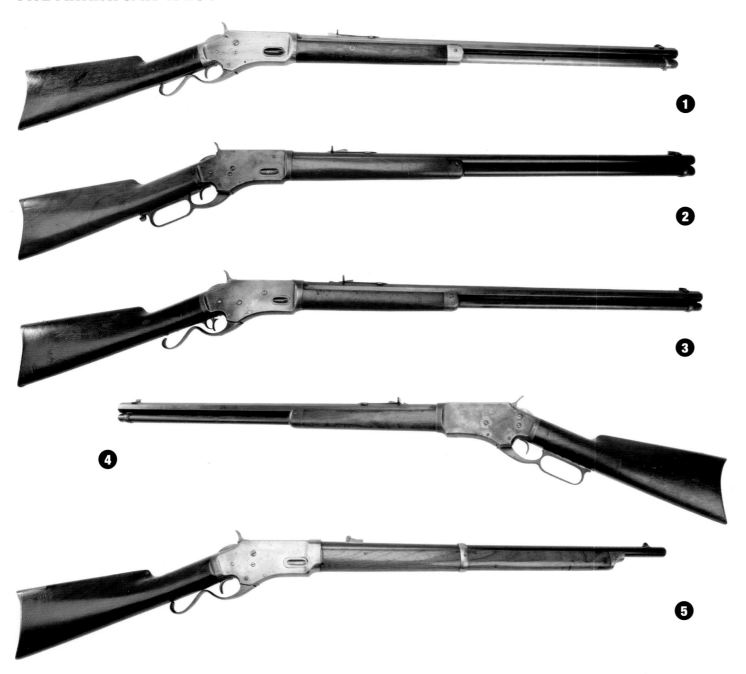

1 Whitney-Burgess-Morse Lever-Action Repeating Rifle - .45-70 - circa 1878-1882 - Approx. 3,000 made.

2 Whitney-Kennedy Lever-Action Repeating Rifle - .40-60 - circa 1879-1886 - Approx. 15,000 made. Most Whitney repeaters featured their distinctive S lever, but some later examples were made with the traditional loop, such as this.

3 Whitney-Kennedy Lever-Action Sporting Rifle - .44-40 - circa 1879-1886 - A smaller frame variation, chambered for the less powerful .44, .38, and .32WCF rounds.

4 Whitney Kennedy Lever-Action Sporting Rifle - .38-40 - circa 1879-1886.

5 Whitney-Burgess-Kennedy Lever-Action Repeating Musket - .45-70 - circa 1878-1882 - Most Whitney repeating muskets went to Central or South America.

Whitney Repeating Rifles
For nearly a century, Whitney was a major force in American firearms manufacturing. Cotton gin inventor Eli Whitney began manufacturing firearms for the U.S. military in 1798, and continued in that role through the Civil War, in addition to civilian arms manufacture. By that time Eli Whitney, Jr., headed the firm.
They entered the lever-action repeater field in 1878, but the firm's fortunes were fading. They were acquired by Winchester in 1888.

1 H. Pieper Mexican Military Revolving Carbine
- 7mm Pieper - circa 1893 - Nine shot.

2 Colt Lightning Slide-Action Rifle, Large Frame
- .38-55 - circa 1887-1894 - Colt-made pump-
action rifles in three frame sizes. The large size
handled full-power black-powder rifle rounds
up to .50-110 Express; 6,500 made.

3 Colt Lightning Slide-Action Rifle, Medium
Frame - .32-20 - circa 1884-1902 - Medium
frames handled the "pistol class" cartridges,
.44, .38, and .32WCF; 84,000 made.

4 Colt Lightning Slide-Action Rifle, Small Frame
- .22 long rifle - circa 1887-1904 - The small
frames were all .22 rimfire; 35,000 made.

5 Evans Lever-Action Repeating Carbine - .44
Evans - circa 1873-1879 - The Evans repeaters
featured a unique helical magazine in the
buttstock that could hold 28 to 34 cartridges;
over 12,000 made.

1 Sharps "Big Fifty" Model 1874 Single-Shot Falling Block Rifle - .50-90 - circa 1871-1881 - Called the "Big Fifty" for its heavy .50 caliber projectile, backed by a powerful 90-grain powder charge. Shipped to Fort Griffin, Texas, for buffalo hunters.

2 Ballard No. 5 Pacific Falling Block Single-Shot Rifle - .45-70 - circa 1876-1891 - The Ballard was among the most popular single-shot rifle designs.

3 Sharps/Freund Bros. Model 1874 Falling Block Rifle - .45-70 - circa 1876-1877 - Frank Freund manufactured Sharps-style rifles, but the Freund Bros. marking on a Sharps often indicates their role as dealers and agents for Sharps.

4 Remington No. 1 Rolling Block Rifle - .32-40 - circa 1867-1888.

5 Remington No. 1 Rolling Block Single-Shot Rifle - .45-70 - circa 1867-1888.

Remington Rolling Blocks
The rolling block action consisted of a hammer and a pivoting breechblock that provided both great strength and ease of operation. To load, the hammer was cocked, and then the breechblock was rolled backward through finger pressure on a lever that projected from the block. This action also ejected the spent cartridge. A new cartridge was then inserted, and the breechblock was rolled forward into its closed position. Sturdy, accurate rolling blocks were popular for hunting and competition, and widely purchased internationally as military rifles.

1. Marlin-Ballard Single-Shot External Extractor Hunter's Rifle - .44 caliber - circa 1875-1876 - Marlin-made Ballards featured a reversible firing pin that could be changed for centerfire or rimfire cartridges.

2. Sharps Model 1874 "Old Reliable" Single-Shot Falling Block Rifle - .45-70 - circa 1871-1881 - This lesser-quality A-marked Sharps rifle was assembled from leftover parts and was sold in 1879.

3. Sharps Model 1874 "Old Reliable" Single-Shot Falling Block Rifle - .45-100 Sharps - circa 1871-1881 - The Sharps trademark "Old Reliable" was added to barrel markings in 1876 and is typically found only on rifles manufactured in Bridgeport, CT.

4. Sharps Model 1874 "Old Reliable" Single-Shot Falling Block Rifle - .45 caliber - circa 1871-1881.

Buffalo Hunting on the Plains

From Canada to Mexico and from the Mississippi to the Rocky Mountains, an incredible herd of 50 to 100 million American bison, popularly called buffalo, roamed the West. For the Plains Indian, this animal was the staff of life, providing meat for food, fur for warmth, and bones for tools. For the commercial hunter who was primarily interested in obtaining hides and meat to sell, the buffalo was regarded only as a source of wealth.

Thousands of hunters traveled west to make their fortune by killing buffalo. The loud noise of a rifle being fired could scare a buffalo herd into a stampede and reduce the number of animals taken by a hunter. For this reason, most hunters armed themselves with rifles capable of scoring a kill at tremendous distances so that the sound of the gunshots would not panic the herd.

Many hunters used Civil War surplus arms that had been fitted with new barrels and converted to fire centerfire cartridges. Manufacturers such as Ballard, Marlin, Sharps, Remington, and Winchester soon began to produce and promote rifles that were specifically designed for hunting buffalo.

By 1883, the unchecked harvesting of the buffalo herds left the American Bison in danger of becoming extinct. Due to the enactment of strong and effective conservation measures, however, some limited numbers of buffalo now exist in our national parks.

THE AMERICAN WEST

1 Remington No. 1 Rolling Block Single-Shot
  Rifle - .40-70 - circa 1868-1888 - Offered in
  over 30 different chamberings.

2 Whitney Phoenix Single-Shot Breechloading
  Rifle - .40-70 - circa 1867-1881 - Hinged
  breechblock lifts up to load.

3 Westley Richards British Monkeytail
  Percussion Carbine - .450 caliber - circa 1865 -
  British military carbine; Whitworth hexagonal
  rifling.

1. Roper Repeating Shotgun - 16 gauge - circa 1867 - One of the earliest repeating shotguns, using a revolver-like mechanism. First shotgun to use detachable choke.

2. Model 1887 Lever-Action Shotgun - 10 gauge - circa 1887-1901 - Six-shot capacity, 65,000 made.

3. Marlin Model 19 Slide-Action Shotgun - circa 1907 - Winchester and Marlin both made exposed hammer pump shotguns. Some of these early Marlin exposed hammer pump shotguns are unsafe to shoot with modern shotshells.

4. Colt Model 1883 Shotgun - 12 gauge - circa 1884 - 7,300 of these high-grade shotguns made.

5. Burgess Slide-Action Folding Gun - 12 gauge - circa 1892-1899 - Unusual folding stock design. The company was purchased by Winchester in 1899.

6. Sawed-Off Double-Barrel Shotgun (deactivated) - 12 gauge - circa 1936 - Short-barrel shotguns held some popularity for close-range defense. Today, possession of shotguns with barrels shorter than 18 inches is highly regulated.

2

1 Colt Derringer Collection - Various -
This collection of Colt derringers was all
manufactured at Colt's London plant. These
handguns were part of the merchandise an
immigrant hoped to sell in America.

2 Remington Double Derringer - .41 rimfire -
circa 1866-1935 - The archetypical derringer,
150,000 were made. The cartridge only
delivered 500 fps muzzle velocity.

Derringers
Compact single-shot or multi-barrel
pistols designed for concealment
and personal defensive use at close
range picked up the designation
"derringer" from the tiny percussion
pistols made by Henry Deringer
of Philadelphia. These served
as hideout guns in gentlemen's
vest pockets, ladies muffs, or up
gambler's sleeves.

1

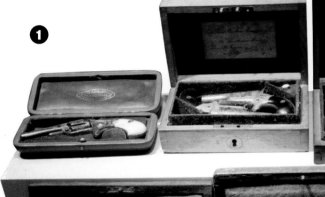

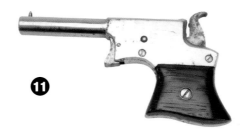

1 Frank Wesson Small-Frame Single-Shot Pistol - .22 short - circa 1859-1885.

2 E. Allen & Co. Vest Pocket Derringer - .22 rimfire - circa 1869-1871.

3 Moore's Patent Firearms Co. No. 1 Derringer - .41 rimfire - circa 1860-1865.

4 Remington Zig-Zag Derringer - .22 rimfire - circa 1861-1862 - Rotating barrel cluster.

5 Eclipse Single-Shot Pistol - .22 rimfire - circa 1870-1887.

6 L. B. Taylor & Co. Single-Shot Pocket Pistol - .32 rimfire - circa 1868-1870.

7 Remington-Elliot Derringer 32RF - .32 rimfire - circa 1863-1875 - Multiple fixed-barrel Remington derringers used a rotating firing pin.

8 Connecticut Arms & Manufacturing Co. Hammond Patent "Bulldog" Single-Shot Derringer - .44 rimfire - circa 1866-1880 - One of the most powerful derringers of this era, heavy at 24 oz.; 7,400 made.

9 Brown Manufacturing Co. Southern Derringer - .41 rimfire - circa 1866-1873 - Bronze frame.

10 Sharps Breechloading Four-Shot Pepperbox Pistol - .22 rimfire - circa 1859-1874 - Stationary barrels with a rotating firing pin on the hammer.

11 Remington Vest Pocket Pistol - .22 rimfire - circa 1865-1888.

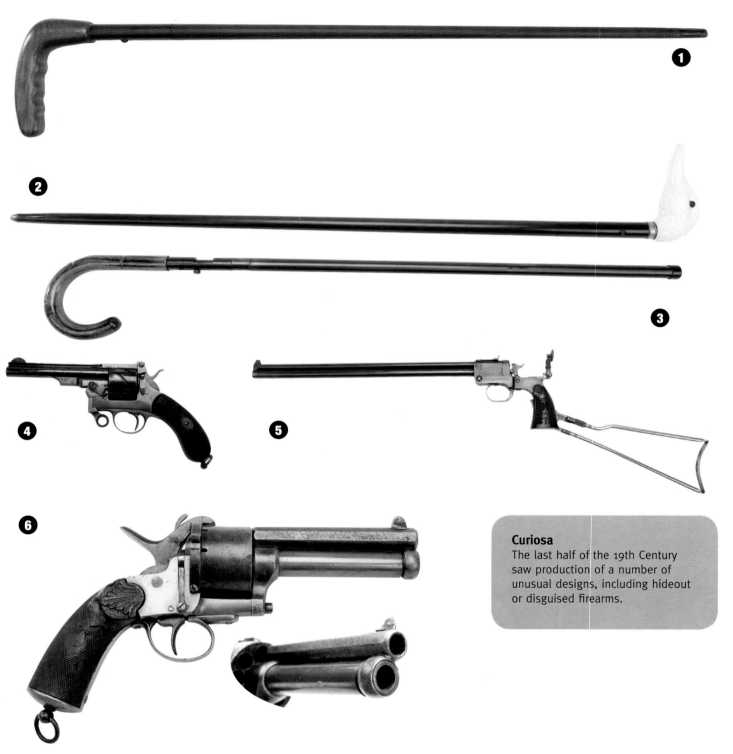

1 Remington Single-Shot Cane Gun - .32 rimfire - circa 1866-1888 - Any finely dressed gentleman that carried a cane might have opted for the capability to use one of Remington's gun canes, designed to fire a single shot when a button on the shaft was depressed. A removable plug at the bottom of the shaft prevented debris from clogging the bore.

2 Remington Percussion Cane Gun - .31 caliber - circa 1858-1866.

3 Percussion Cane Gun - circa 1950.

4 Gebruder Mauser und Cie Model 1878 "Zig-Zag" Single-Action Revolver - .38 Mauser Rimmed - circa 1878-1882 - Named for the alternating grooves that served to index the cylinder in rotation. Both top-break and solid frame versions were manufactured by Mauser.

5 Marble Arms Game Getter Combination Gun with folding shoulder stock - .22 rimfire over .44 smoothbore - circa 1930-1934 - Offered choice of rifle or shotgun barrel. Barrel lengths ranged from 12 to 22 inches. Today, those with smoothbore barrels shorter than 18 inches are illegal to possess in the U.S. unless previously registered.

6 LeMat Belgian Pinfire Revolver - .38 cylinder and .44 caliber smoothbore - circa 1859 - As with the Civil War percussion version, the axis around which the cylinder revolves is a shotgun barrel.

Curiosa
The last half of the 19th Century saw production of a number of unusual designs, including hideout or disguised firearms.

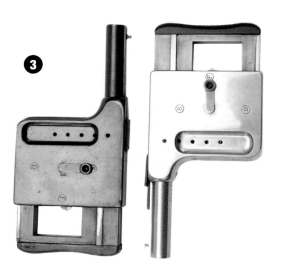

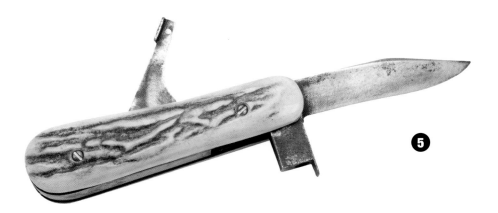

1 William W. Marston Three-Barrel 22 Derringer - .22 rimfire - circa 1858-1864 - Around 1,500 made, most with a sliding dagger blade attached.

2 Chicago Firearms Co. "Protector" Palm Pistol - .32 rimfire - circa 1890s - Seven shot; chambers arranged like the spokes of a wheel in a rotary magazine.

3 Gaulois French No. 1 Palm Pistol - .32 rimfire - circa 1880-1900 - Another palm squeezer design, about the shape and size of a cigarrette pack.

4 James Reid "My Friend" Knuckle Duster Revolver - .22 rimfire - circa 1865-1877 - The grip doubles as impromptu brass knuckles, made in .22, .32, and .41 rimfire chamberings. Most had no barrel and fired directly from the front of the cylinder chambers.

5 Pocket knife/pistol - circa 1900-1920 - Combination guns, in which a pocket knife is combined with a single-shot pistol, offer a concealing aspect such that the firearm characteristic is minimized by being part of another artifact.

1. U.S. Springfield Joslyn Breechloading Rifle - .56-50 rimfire - circa 1865 - First cartridge breechloaders assembled at Springfield Armory.

2. Burnside Rifle Company Model 1865 Spencer Repeating Carbine - .50 rimfire - circa 1865 - Rechambered after the Civil War from .52 to .50 rimfire, and kept in service.

3. Parkers Snow Co. Rifle-Musket; Miller Model 1861 .58 Caliber Conversion - .58 rimfire - circa 1863-1864 - One of 2,000 converted to breechloaders in Meridan, CT, after the Civil War in 1865-1867.

4. English Enfield Snider Rotating Block Conversion Rifle - .577 caliber (conversion) - circa 1866-1870 - The Snider side-swing breechblock conversion was used in the British Empire. It was invented by American Jacob Snider.

5. English Barnett Model 1853 Rifle (altered) - .58 Berdan - circa 1866-1870 - This rifle was used by Colt to develop a prototype tested in 1866 at the U.S. Army Board Trials. This design was rejected.

6. New Model 1859 Percussion Carbine by Sharps .52 Cal.

The Army on the Frontier

Prior to the Civil War, U.S. Army garrisons had been established throughout the American West to protect our frontier. Beyond these military posts lay the great American desert and numerous tribes of American Indians.

U.S. Cavalry troopers stationed throughout the West often found themselves fighting at a disadvantage because the firearms supplied by the government tended to lag behind the most current advances in technology. Troopers engaged in such battles as The Little Bighorn (June 1876) were armed with single-shot breechloaders while their victorious adversaries were armed with the more advanced repeating rifles of the day.

Eventually, as witnessed before during the War Between the States, overwhelming numbers and resources prevailed during the series of battles between the U.S. Cavalry and various Indian tribes that took place over a period of 40 years, culminating with the death of nearly 300 Sioux at the Battle of Wounded Knee on December 29, 1890.

1 U.S. Springfield Model 1868 Single-Shot Breechloading Rifle - .50 centerfire - circa 1869-1872.

2 U.S. Springfield Allin Conversion Model 1866 Single-Shot Breechloading Rifle - .50 centerfire - circa 1866 - The Allin trapdoor system was initially used to convert muzzleloaders to cartridge breechloaders.

3 U.S. Springfield Model 1884 Trapdoor Carbine - .45-70. These Trapdoor arms were to serve throughout the Indian Wars. The initial metallic cartridges issued demonstrated extraction issues, but these .45-70 arms remained in government arsenal through the end of the century.

4 U.S. Springfield Model 1878 Trapdoor Rifle - .45-70.

5 Gen. Wingate's U.S. Springfield Model 1875 Trapdoor Officer's Rifle, Second Type - .45-70 - circa 1877-1881 - Originally owned by NRA founder and president George Wingate. The Officers Model was a unique product of a national armory, in that it was made for private sale to officers for their personal sporting use rather than military issue. It used the action and caliber of the standard military arm, but added deluxe features such as decorative engraving, checkering, target sights, and a detachable pistol grip. Fewer than 500 were made.

The Springfield Trapdoor

At the close of the Civil War, the federal government had an enormous inventory of surplus arms and equipment, including numerous muzzleloading rifled muskets. Rather than destroy these arms, the Chief of Ordnance decided to convert them from their muzzleloading configuration to a breechloading system. E.S. Allin, the Master Armorer at the Springfield Armory, developed a system that converted the old muskets into breechloaders.

The breech of the barrel was cut away and a breech block installed that flipped up and forward to load like a trap door. It was so successful that beginning in 1868, new military arms were manufactured using this system. The cartridge was standardized as the .45-70 in 1873, and trapdoors were manufactured by Springfield Armory well into the 1890s.

At the time the Trapdoor was adopted, there were successful repeaters available, such as the Henry, Winchester 1866, and Spencer.

Military thought of the era was that troopers would waste ammunition if armed with repeating arms. Also, when Trapdoors were first issued, the repeating arms chambered less powerful cartridges with shorter ranges. However, single-shot military arms were still manufactured and issued as full power repeaters were perfected and widely available on the commercial market.

1 U.S. Springfield Model 1875 Lee Vertical-Action Rifle - .45-70 - circa 1875 - 150 made for testing and evaluation. Martini dropping-block action; serial number 2.

2 U.S. Springfield Model 1871 Rolling Block Rifle - .50-70 - circa 1871-1872.

3 U.S. Springfield Model 1870 Rolling Block U.S. Navy Rifle - .50 centerfire - circa 1870-1871 - Made under license from Remington.

4 Joslyn-Tomes Model 1870 Straight-Pull Single-Shot Rifle - .58 Martin (conversion) - circa 1872-1873 - Tested by the Army, but rejected.

5 Sharps Springfield Altered Model 1870 Rifle - .50-70 - circa 1870-1876 - 1,300 made by converting muzzleloaders, but cost of supplemental parts proved prohibitive.

6 Providence Tool Co. Peabody Lever-Action Single-Shot Carbine - .50 centerfire - circa 1866-1871.

1 Little Bighorn U.S. Springfield Model 1868 Trapdoor Rifle (altered) - .50-70 - circa 1868-1876 - Originally an Army-issued rifle, this cut-down piece was once owned by Lakota chief Kicking Bear, who fought against Gen. G.A. Custer at the Battle of the Little Bighorn in 1876. It was donated to the museum collection by a descendant of the commander of the Indian Scouts at Wounded Knee.

2 Cut-down U.S. Springfield M1816 Percussion Conversion Musket - .69 caliber - ca. 1870 - Wet rawhide was stretched over the cracked stock and, as it dried, the shrinking of the rawhide firmly drew the parts together.

3 Percussion Conversion Chief's Trade Musket - .63 caliber - circa 1840-1860 - This type of smoothbore was made for trade to Native Americans.

4 Cut-down Springfield M1861 Musket - .62 caliber - circa 1861-1862 - Shortened firearms such as this are sometimes called "blanket guns" because they could be concealed under a blanket worn as a cloak.

5 Sharps Model 1859 Single-Shot Percussion Carbine - .52 caliber - circa 1859-1866 - Captured by Native Americans and later ornamented with bone and shell inlays. Like many of these arms, the tang of the receiver was broken during its service and crudely repaired.

Native American Arms

Native American used arms often show hard use, rawhide reenforcements of stock, and sometimes distinctive decoration including brass tacks. Metal buttplates are often removed to fashion hide scrapers or other tools. Native American guns are sometimes faked and sold to gullible collectors or Old West enthusiasts. Authentic examples are scarce.

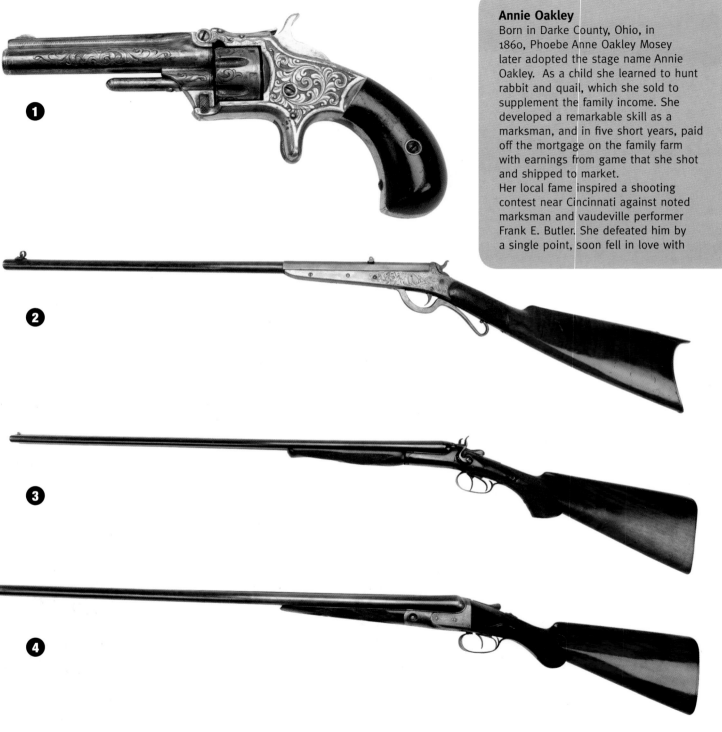

Annie Oakley

Born in Darke County, Ohio, in 1860, Phoebe Anne Oakley Mosey later adopted the stage name Annie Oakley. As a child she learned to hunt rabbit and quail, which she sold to supplement the family income. She developed a remarkable skill as a marksman, and in five short years, paid off the mortgage on the family farm with earnings from game that she shot and shipped to market.

Her local fame inspired a shooting contest near Cincinnati against noted marksman and vaudeville performer Frank E. Butler. She defeated him by a single point, soon fell in love with him, and eventually married him. Butler became Annie's manager and booked her on various show and circus tours. In 1885, she joined Buffalo Bill's Wild West show in Louisville, Kentucky.

Annie's dead-eye accuracy with rifle, pistol, and shotgun brought her worldwide fame. She could hit a dime tossed in the air, shoot a cigarette placed in her husband's lips, and slice in half a playing card that was held edge-on to her at a distance of 30 paces. Perhaps the most famous woman marksman in history, she was further immortalized in the 1946 Broadway musical *Annie, Get Your Gun*.

1   Annie Oakley-attributed Smith & Wesson Number One, Third Issue Revolver - ca. 1868-1881 - Reportedly given by Annie to a young boy after a shooting competition.

2   Annie Oakley's Remington-Beals Single-Shot Rifle - .32 rimfire - circa 1866-1868 - A favorite caliber and model of Annie; sold by one of her relatives in 1940 for $5. Factory engraved.

3   Annie Oakley-attributed Gold Hibbard Side-by-Side Hammer Shotgun - .410 gauge - circa 1880-1929 - Reportedly given by Annie to her close friend, Mary Estell Beavers, during a shooting exhibition in Oklahoma. Trade name used by Hibbard Spencer & Bartlett on imported shotguns.

4   Annie Oakley's Parker Presentation BH-Grade Shotgun - 12 gauge - circa 1901 - Ordered on April 1, 1901, by Annie's husband and fellow exhibition shooter, F.E. Butler, and shipped c/o of Buffalo Bill's Wild West Show, Allegheny City, PA. Inscribed on pistol grip plate: *Annie Oakley April 1901*.

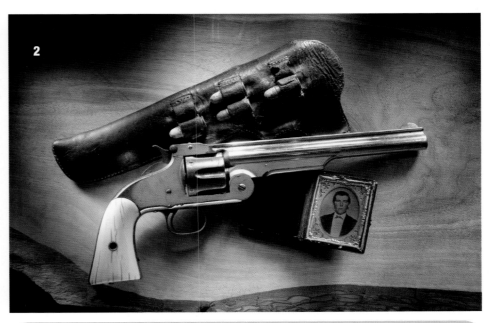

1 Buffalo Bill's Colt Model 1851 Navy, London-marked, percussion revolver. - .36 caliber - Serial number 1 of the London-made Navy Models, engraved and punch-dot inscribed "W.C. CODY." Previous owners include the "poet scout" Capt. Jack Crawford.

2 John Wesley Hardin attributed S&W Model Three Single-Action Revolver and Holster - One of the most notorious outlaws in the Old West, Hardin became a frontier lawyer after serving time in prison. Distinctive holster with three pairs of cartridge loops.

3 Jesse James-attributed S&W Schofield Revolver and Holster - .45 S&W - ca. 1875-1878 - Outlaw-attributed guns are rarely clear cut. This one is attributed to Jesse James by chain of ownership, left-hand holster matching a known James right-hand holster and belt, and gang member A. Ryan's name inscribed under the grips.

William F. "Buffalo Bill" Cody

Born in Scott County, Iowa, in 1846, William F. Cody spent his boyhood in Kansas. For a short period, he was employed as a rider for the Pony Express. During the Civil War, he served with the 7th Kansas Infantry and 9th Kansas Cavalry. From 1867-1868, Cody hunted buffalo to feed workers building the Kansas-Pacific Railroad and earned the nickname of Buffalo Bill. Cody also had a distinguished career as an Army Scout and became Chief Scout for the 5th U.S. Cavalry. He participated in over 16 military engagements and was awarded the Congressional Medal of Honor in 1872.

Buffalo Bill's rise to legendary status began with the writings of E.Z.C. Judson (also known as Ned Buntline). Buntline's dime novels romanticized the heroic life of Buffalo Bill who was encouraged to write his first autobiography in 1879. In 1883, Cody organized an outdoor exhibition that became world famous as "Buffalo Bill's Wild West." Dramatizing life and legend in the American West, the show remained on the road for more than 30 years. Acts in the show included the Pony Express, the Attack on the Deadwood Stagecoach, Rough Riders of the World, and the roping of broncos (wild horses). Attractions such as these were the basis for today's rodeos. Stars of the show included Buck Taylor ("King of the Cowboys"), Annie Oakley ("Little Sure Shot"), Johnny Baker ("The Cowboy Kid"), and, for one season, Custer's nemesis -- Sitting Bull.

William F. Cody died on January 10, 1917. He provided much-needed employment to many people at a time when job opportunities were few, and brought thrills, laughter, and excitement to huge and admiring audiences. His use of buffalo in the show increased public awareness of the animal and its plight, and helped to preserve the animal from extinction. He was truly an American original and the first superstar of the 20th century.

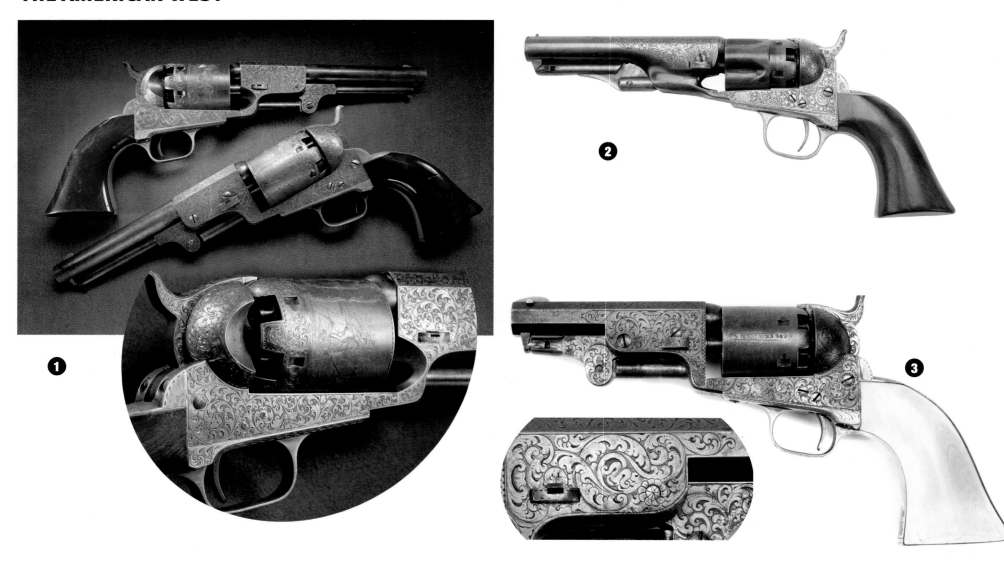

1 Exceptional pair of Colt Engraved Presentation Third Model Dragoon Revolvers - .44 caliber - circa 1851-1861 - Inscribed on backstraps "Prize Shot of Company C, Mounted Riflemen U.S.A." and "George Hess." C was the Texas Ranger Company of Capt. Walker, who greatly influenced the design of the Dragoon's predecessor, the Colt Walker. Probably engraved by Gustave Young.

2 Colt Model 1862 Police Percussion Revolver - .36 caliber - circa 1861-1873 - Scroll engraved with wolf's head motifs.

3 Colt Model 1851 Navy Presentation-Grade Percussion Revolver - .36 caliber - ca. 1854 - Has Colt factory engraving; ivory grips such as these, or mother of pearl grips, were another factory option or might be added after-market. Barrel has been shortened to make the gun handier and more concealable.

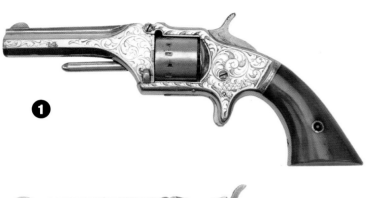

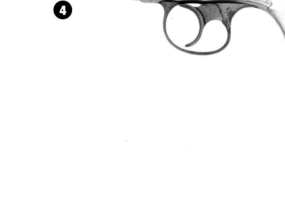

1 American Standard Tool Revolver - .22 rimfire - circa 1868 - 1873 - Although the standard model was plain, engraved specimens are often encountered.

2 Merwin Hulbert & Co. Double-Action Pocket Revolver (manufactured by Hopkins & Allen) - .38 S&W - circa 1880 - Merwin Hulbert offered a distinctive "punch-dot" style of factory engraving.

3 Smith & Wesson Model No. 1 Third Issue Single-Action Revolver - .22 short - circa 1868 - 1881 - Period engraving, possibly factory, and fancy special-order pearl grips.

4 Marlin Model 1887 Top-Break Revolver - .38 S&W - circa 1887 - 1899 - Pearl grips.

5 Merwin & Bray Single-Action Revolver - .28 cup primed - circa 1859 - 1866 - Made for an 1876 centennial display of the firm's products; it has fine engraving, etched cylinder, and carved pearl grips. Pearl grips were especially difficult to carve because of their brittle nature. The dust created in carving was hazardous to inhale.

Engraving

The popularity and quality of American firearms engraving reached a high-water mark in the mid- through late 19th century. German engravers brought their artistry to America and trained successive generations in the demanding craft of sculpting the flat and curved surfaces of iron and steel with hand tools to create works of art.

Engraved arms were signs of prestige and made an impressive presentation piece or gift. In addition to being a firearms design genius, Colt was also a master of marketing and promotion, and had a practice of presenting exquisitely engraved and cased arms to individuals who might exert beneficial influence on behalf of the company's products.

Engraved firearms by independent engravers were commissioned by individuals, distributors, and manufacturers. Manufacturers also hired in-house engravers. A master engraver would often work with apprentices, and multiple artisans might work on the same piece.

Perhaps the two best-known engravers of the era were L.D. Nimschke and Gustave Young. They and other engravers of the era tended to favor ornate floral vine or scroll motifs. Young's style is considered typical of Colt through about 1869, at which time he moved to Springfield and began to do a large number of guns for S&W. The large relief scroll pattern most associated with American arms of the post-Civil War era came to be called Nimschke-style or New York-style engraving, due to the many engravers working in that city. Young's typical tight scroll style was continued by his sons as factory engravers for Smith & Wesson.

1 Forehand & Wadsworth Swamp Angel Single-Action Revolver - .41 rimfire - circa 1870-1880 - Even relatively inexpensive revolvers were offered with simple engraving. Although this revolver is gold plated with ivory grips, it is easy to see this quickly done minimal decoration does not compare to the work of master engravers.

2 Brooklyn Firearms Co. Pocket Revolver - .32 rimfire - circa 1863 - 1864 - Engraving by L.D. Nimschke with scroll and animal motifs including an alligator on the cylinder. Ivory grips. This gun circumvented S&W's Rollin White patent on the bored-through cylinder by having individual removable chambers.

3 Merwin Hulbert & Co. Single-Action Army Revolver - .44 Merwin Hulbert - circa 1876-1883 - The punch-dot factory engraving of Merwin Hulbert is simpler than carved engraving, but colorful. It often includes panel scenes, such as this revolver with a lion on one side of the frame and a Mexican eagle and snake on the other.

4 Colard Belgian Double-Action Pinfire Revolver - 12mm pinfire - circa 1870-1880 - Elegant decoration includes flush gold and silver inlays, sculpted sights, and carved ebony grips.

❶

❷

1 Winchester Model 1866 Engraved Rifle - .44 rimfire - circa 1866-1898 - The brass frames of Henrys and 1866s offer appealing canvases for the engraver, such as this example. Period engraving, likely factory.

2 Berne y Carron Belgian Rolling Block Rifle - 11 mm - circa 1880 - Belgian copy of the Remington action, with elegant sparse European-style vine scroll engraving.

A BRIGHT NEW CENTURY

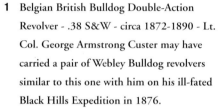

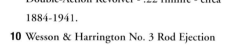

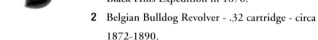

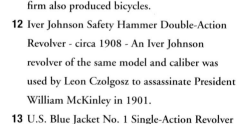

1 Belgian British Bulldog Double-Action Revolver - .38 S&W - circa 1872-1890 - Lt. Col. George Armstrong Custer may have carried a pair of Webley Bulldog revolvers similar to this one with him on his ill-fated Black Hills Expedition in 1876.

2 Belgian Bulldog Revolver - .32 cartridge - circa 1872-1890.

3 German Velo-Dog Double-Action Revolver - 5mm Velo-Dog - circa 1880-1900 - Velo-dog is a term used from a particular pattern of small inexpensive European revolver with folding trigger, is usually hammerless, and often chambered for the 5 mm Velodog centerfire cartridge. Velo is from velocipede, an early term for bicycles. The guns were marketed as ideal for a cyclist's defense against stray canines offended by the new-fangled bicycle.

4 Red Jacket No. 3 Spur-Trigger Revolver - .30 rimfire - circa 1890-1900.

5 American Arms New Safety Hammerless Revolver - circa 1890-1900.

6 Prescott Pistol Co. Crescent Double-Action Revolver - .30 rimfire - circa 1873-1875.

7 C.S. Shattuck Single-Action Revolver - circa 1880-1900.

8 Henry M. Kolb Baby Hammerless Revolver - .22 rimfire - circa 1900.

9 Harrington & Richardson Young America Double-Action Revolver - .22 rimfire - circa 1884-1941.

10 Wesson & Harrington No. 3 Rod Ejection Single-Action Revolver - circa 1874-1879.

11 Iver Johnson Model 1879 Double-Action Revolver - circa 1878-1882 - The Iver Johnson firm also produced bicycles.

12 Iver Johnson Safety Hammer Double-Action Revolver - circa 1908 - An Iver Johnson revolver of the same model and caliber was used by Leon Czolgosz to assassinate President William McKinley in 1901.

13 U.S. Blue Jacket No. 1 Single-Action Revolver - circa 1890-1900.

14 Stevens No. 41 Tip-Up Single-Shot Pocket Pistol - circa 1864-1916.

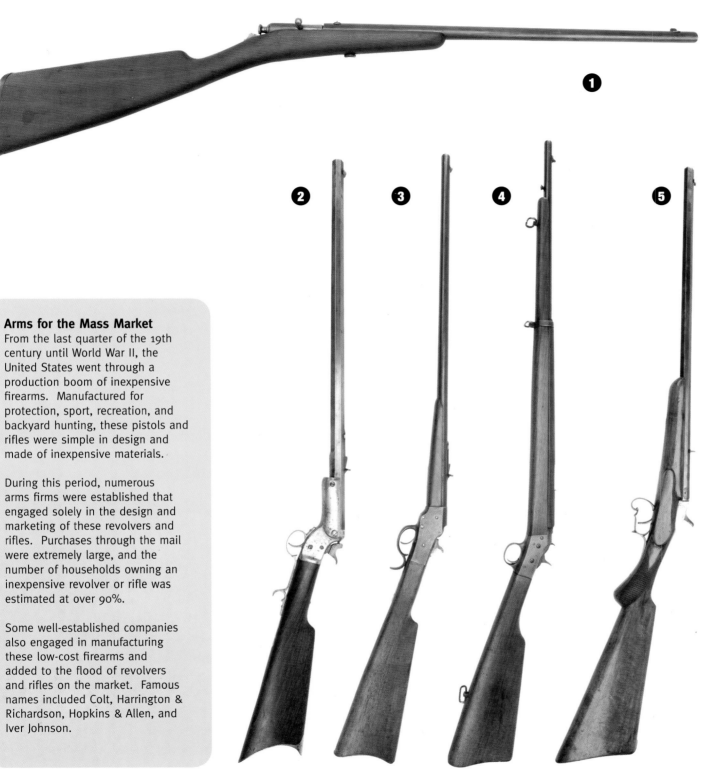

1 Winchester Model 99 Thumb Trigger Rifle - .22 rimfire - circa 1904-1923 - An unusual .22 rimfire rifle intended to be fired by pushing the thumb instead of pulling a trigger with a finger, Winchester's Model 99 had excellent sales abroad in Australia and in the first three years of production (1904-1906) much of the production was exported there.

2 Stevens Single-Shot Rifle Attributed to Johnny Cash - .32 cartridge - circa 1910-1920 - Once owned by singer/songwriter Johnny Cash.

3 Hopkins & Allen Falling Block Rifle - .32 rimfire - circa 1888-1892.

4 Remington Model No. 4S "Military Model" Rolling Block Sporting Rifle - .22 rimfire - circa 1913-1923 - Remington's Model 4S was originally designed for the Boy Scouts of America and stamped "American Boy Scout." But in 1915, the designation was changed to "Military Model" and the majority of the 15,000 rifles produced were so marked until manufacture ceased in 1923.

5 Flobert Belgian Model 5 Rifle - .22 Flobert rimfire - circa 1890-1900 - Low-powered Flobert rifles and pistols were popular for indoor shooting in a parlor.

Arms for the Mass Market

From the last quarter of the 19th century until World War II, the United States went through a production boom of inexpensive firearms. Manufactured for protection, sport, recreation, and backyard hunting, these pistols and rifles were simple in design and made of inexpensive materials.

During this period, numerous arms firms were established that engaged solely in the design and marketing of these revolvers and rifles. Purchases through the mail were extremely large, and the number of households owning an inexpensive revolver or rifle was estimated at over 90%.

Some well-established companies also engaged in manufacturing these low-cost firearms and added to the flood of revolvers and rifles on the market. Famous names included Colt, Harrington & Richardson, Hopkins & Allen, and Iver Johnson.

A BRIGHT NEW CENTURY

An Age of Elegance

Theodore Roosevelt inspired many persons to take up "the strenuous life," a lifestyle that encouraged hard, outdoor work and various types of outdoor recreation that included hunting, hiking, fishing, rowing, and rifle practice. Legions of persons followed his example and began enjoying the numerous positive aspects of hunting. Hunting trips and expeditions, including African safaris, became a popular form of recreation for millions of Americans.
From 1880 to 1930, a period that became known as the Age of Elegance, the world's finest gunmakers produced some of the most exquisite firearms ever created.

1 Deutsche Waffen & Munitions Fabriken Model 1902 Luger Semi-Automatic Carbine with matching serial-numbered shoulder stock. - .30 Luger - circa 1902-1905 - Shoulder-stocked pistol carbines like this Model 1902 commercial example were favored by Kaiser Wilhelm I, who had a withered arm and had difficulty holding a full-sized rifle in firing position.

2 Mauser Model 1896 Broomhandle Semi-Automatic Pistol with matching serial number shoulder stock - 7.63 Mauser - circa 1897-1901 - Mauser marketed shoulder-stocked semi-automatic pistols as detachable carbines, allowing owners to remove the shoulder stock and utilize the pistol alone. The wooden buttstock was hollow and the pistol itself could be stored inside and the stock used as a holster.

3 James Purdey & Sons Side-by-Side Shotgun - 12 gauge - circa 1892 - James Purdey & Sons since 1814, still one of the world's premiere arms makers.

4 Parker AAHE-Grade Side-by-Side Shotgun - 12 gauge - circa 1901 - Parker Brothers of Connecticut is considered one of the finest of American sporting arms manufacturers.

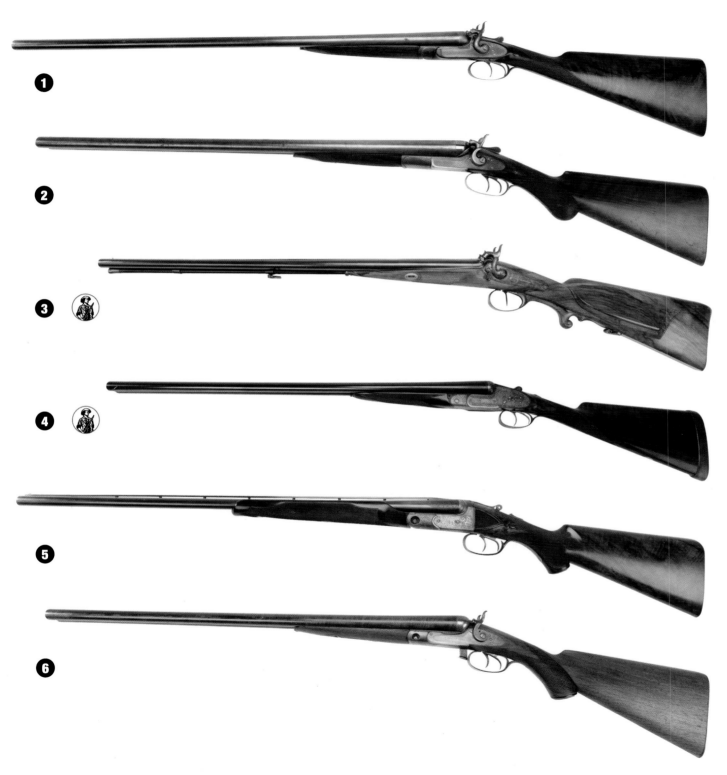

1   James Purdey & Sons Side-by-Side Hammer
    Shotgun - 20 gauge - circa 1877.

2   E. Remington & Sons Side-by-Side Hammer
    Shotgun - 12 gauge - circa 1882-1889.

3   Roos and Sohn Percussion Side-by-Side
    Shotgun - 20 gauge - circa 1855.

4   Cogswell & Harrison British Side-by-Side
    Shotgun - 12 gauge - circa 1937 - Cogswell &
    Harrison was originally established in 1770.

5   Parker A-1 Special Side-by-Side Shotgun - 20
    gauge - circa 1920.

6   Parker Brothers Lifter Action Side-by-Side
    Shotgun - 10 gauge - circa 1882.

1 James Purdey & Sons Ltd. British Best Grade Side-by-Side Shotgun - 12 gauge - circa 1888 - Best Grade meant that there was no finer gun produced by the firm. Boss & Co. and Purdey only sell "Best Grade" guns.

2 President Grover Cleveland's Colt Model 1883 Hammerless Side-by-Side Damascus Shotgun - 8 gauge - circa 1895 - The only 8 gauge shotgun ever to be manufactured by the Colt factory, this side-by-side was presented to U.S. President Grover Cleveland and engraved with his name on the trigger guard.

3 Darne Single-Action Side-by-Side Shotgun - circa 1920-1950 - Incorporating an unusual action, the French Darne shotgun was popular in humid tropical environments because its powerful camming action was able to force moisture-swollen paper shotshells into the chambers and reliably extract them after firing.

The Parker Invincibles

The Parker Company's Invincible line of shotguns were envisioned as the ultimate flagship smoothbore of the day and were priced accordingly at $1,500 each, twice the price of a fine English Purdey shotgun or a Parker A-1 special-order gun. With the onset of the Great Depression, even the most affluent captains of industry could not afford this high pricing and, as a result, only three Parker Invincible shotguns were ever manufactured and sold, all between 1924 and 1929. Two 12-gauge Invincibles and one 16-gauge Invincible are the only three examples ever produced, notable for their gold triggers, full-coverage engraving with gold inlays, and their finely figured wood stocks. The most valuable set of American-made shotguns ever produced.

A BRIGHT NEW CENTURY

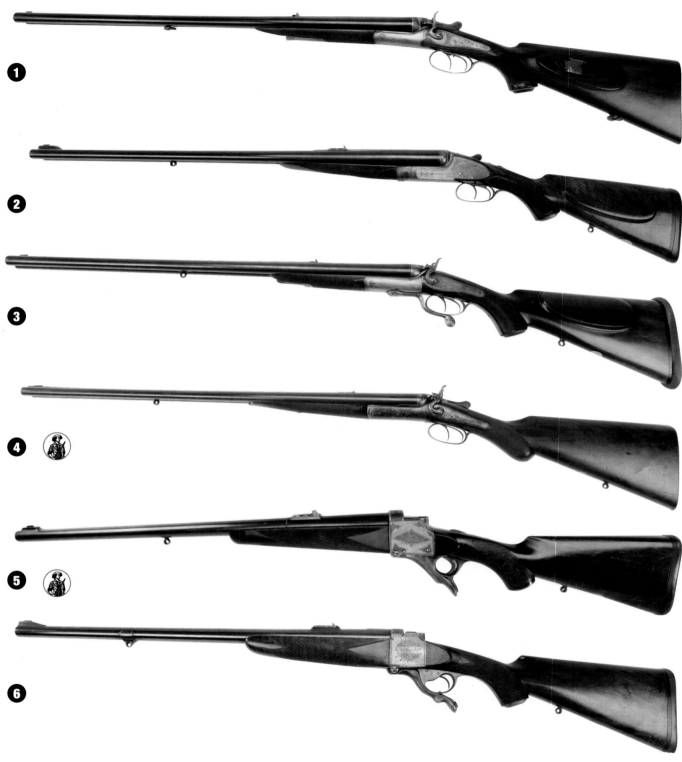

1 Austrian Cape Gun - 16 gauge/6.5mm rimmed - circa 1890-1900.

2 Stephen Grant & Sons Double Rifle - .500/.450-3 1/4inch - circa 1901-1905 - Stephen Grant worked for Charles Lancaster and Boss & Co. before opening his own firm in 1867.

3 Manton & Co. Double Rifle - .500 Express - circa 1885-1890 - Joseph Manton & Co. gun makers to the English royal family since 1781.

4 W. W. Greener Double Rifle - circa 1877 - W.W. Greener began in 1829 and in addition to fine arms also produced many scholarly written works on shooting in the 19th century.

5 Webley & Scott Single-Shot Falling-Block Rifle - .450 caliber - circa 1920 - Webley & Scott began in 1790 and made fine arms in the U.K. for nearly 200 years.

6 Rigby Farquharson Single-Shot Lever-Action Rifle - .470 Nitro Express - circa 1898-1900 – Hammerless falling-block design patented in 1872, in a caliber suited for heavy African game.

African Rifles

The decades immediately preceding and following the turn of the 20th century saw an era of British, European, and American hunting and exploration in Africa. The term "elephant gun" indicated a rifle suitable for harvesting of, or defense against, large dangerous animals such as the "big five" – lion, buffalo, elephant, rhino, and leopard. The classic gun for this application was a double barrel rifle, accommodating a quick and sure second shot, firing a large caliber bullet in the half-inch diameter range over a large charge of powder.

1 Paul Jung Drilling - circa 1890 - Drilling combination guns are popular in European countries where owning more than one firearm can be problematic. A drilling is a three-barrel gun, most often two shotgun barrels and a rifle barrel.

2 G. Knaak GermanVierling Combination Gun - 12 gauge/.22 rimfire/.25-35 Win- circa 1900. A vierling is a four-barrel gun.

3 L. C. Smith Drilling - 12 gauge/.44 - circa 1880-1884 - L.C. Smith began business in 1878 and is considered one of America's finest sporting arms.

4 W. W. Greener Ltd. British Peabody-Martini Single-Shot Rifle - .45 caliber - circa 1910 - This Peabody-Martini action was popular with competition shooters at the turn of the 19th century.

5 Charles Lancaster English Four-Barrel Hammerless Breechloading Rifle - .450 Nitro Express - circa 1900 - Lancaster pioneered the "oval bore" rifling design in the 1800s.

1 Punt Gun - 1.25 inch diameter bore - circa 1883 - Capable of firing a blast of a pound of lead shot, this muzzleloading punt gun was owned by the same family since 1883. Large market guns, capable of harvesting a flock of 100 ducks at one shot, were popular for hunters supplying restaurants in Maryland and Virginia. This massive gun is over six-feet long and traditionally fired from a braced position in a punt – a type of flat-bottom boat.

2 Belgian Four-Bore Rifle attributed to H.M. Stanley - circa 1866-1868 - This single-shot rifle, weighing 22 pounds, was associated with Henry Morton Stanley, an explorer/journalist who traveled through Africa in search of Dr. Livingston.

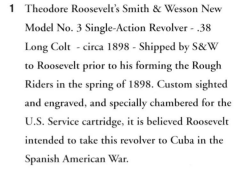

1 Theodore Roosevelt's Smith & Wesson New Model No. 3 Single-Action Revolver - .38 Long Colt - circa 1898 - Shipped by S&W to Roosevelt prior to his forming the Rough Riders in the spring of 1898. Custom sighted and engraved, and specially chambered for the U.S. Service cartridge, it is believed Roosevelt intended to take this revolver to Cuba in the Spanish American War.

2 Theodore Roosevelt's Fabrique Nationale Model 1900 Semi-Automatic Pistol - .32 ACP - circa 1900 - Full-coverage engraving with gold line inlays, it was presented to Pres. Theodore Roosevelt. This pistol was given to the museum by Roosevelt's grandson, Cornelius V.S. Roosevelt.

3 Theodore Roosevelt's Fred R. Adolph Hammerless Double Rifle - .450 Cordite - circa 1909-1911 - Made for Roosevelt following his African Safari of 1909-1910, this gun was displayed in the window of Abercrombie & Fitch in New York City for many years before Roosevelt gave it to an associate.

4 Gen. Roosevelt's Winchester Model 1895 Lever-Action Rifle - .405 Winchester - circa 1923 - Owned by one of Roosevelt's sons, Theodore, Jr., and used on his hunting trips. He rose to the rank of brigadier general and was awarded the Congressional Medal of Honor in WWII.

Theodore Roosevelt

Theodore Roosevelt is an icon of his era. He was a prolific writer, historian, politician, military hero, and loving father and husband. He is also the only person to receive both the Congressional Medal of Honor and the Nobel Peace Prize. Born in 1858, he labored under the ravages of asthma as a child. His father stressed the need for a vigorous personal regimen to combat the asthma, and Theodore (he was never called Teddy by his family) began to thrive in the outdoors.

He earned his spurs as a cowboy during a two-year stint as a rancher in the Badlands of South Dakota, and also became an excellent hunter. Well aware of the fact that he was not a great marksman, he humorously remarked that he **"didn't shoot well, but did shoot often."**

His firearms collection was perhaps the largest ever assembled by any president of the United States. He was known for insisting upon exacting standards for his guns, and favored Winchesters and Colts. He also treasured a pinfire shotgun that was a gift from his father.

An ardent lover of nature and a staunch conservationist, Teddy Roosevelt was responsible for the establishment of the National Forest Service, the conservation and rebuilding of the buffalo herds, the National Conservation and Waterways Commission, the National Monument system within the National Park Service, and the first 51 bird sanctuaries in the United States.

Roosevelt expressed the balance between conservation and sport, saying, **"thus the encouragement of a proper hunting spirit, a proper love of sport, instead of being incompatible with a love of nature and wild things, offers the best guarantee for the preservation of wild things ...."**

Following his years as president, Roosevelt embarked in 1909 upon a year-long African safari. Carrying a sporterized Model 1903 Springfield, a Holland and Holland double rifle, a Fox 12-gauge shotgun, and three Winchester Model 1895s, his adventure acquired 4,897 mammals and more than 4,000 birds, 2,000 reptiles, and 500 fish, all of which were carefully preserved and shipped to the Smithsonian Institution for study and display.

Teddy's Bear

Roosevelt's love for hunting the grizzly bear inspired numerous journalists to compare his squinting eyes and toothy smile to that of a grizzly. The grizzly bear soon became a political symbol for his presidency.

When Roosevelt refused to shoot a motherless bear cub during a hunting expedition, the story of his compassion quickly spread across the country. An enterprising toy merchant labeled all of his stuffed toy bears "Teddy's Bear," and the teddy bear soon became a national sensation that endures to this day as a favorite toy and stuffed companion.

Theodore Roosevelt and the NRA

Theodore Roosevelt was an active proponent of military rifle practice and an ardent supporter of legislation that established the National Rifle and Pistol Matches in 1903. Roosevelt signed Public Law 149 on March 3, 1905, authorizing the sale of surplus military rifles, ammunition, and equipment to National Rifle Association affiliated clubs. Competitions were held for affiliated shooters to qualify as National

Marksman who would be listed by the War Department as members of the National Marksmen's Reserve (called the "Third Line of Defense" for the Army).

On February 16, 1907, the following correspondence was sent to the NRA by President Theodore Roosevelt:

"I am so heartily interested in the success of the National Rifle Association of America and its work done in cooperation with the National Board for the Promotion of Rifle Practice that I take pleasure in sending you herewith my check for $25 for life membership therein."

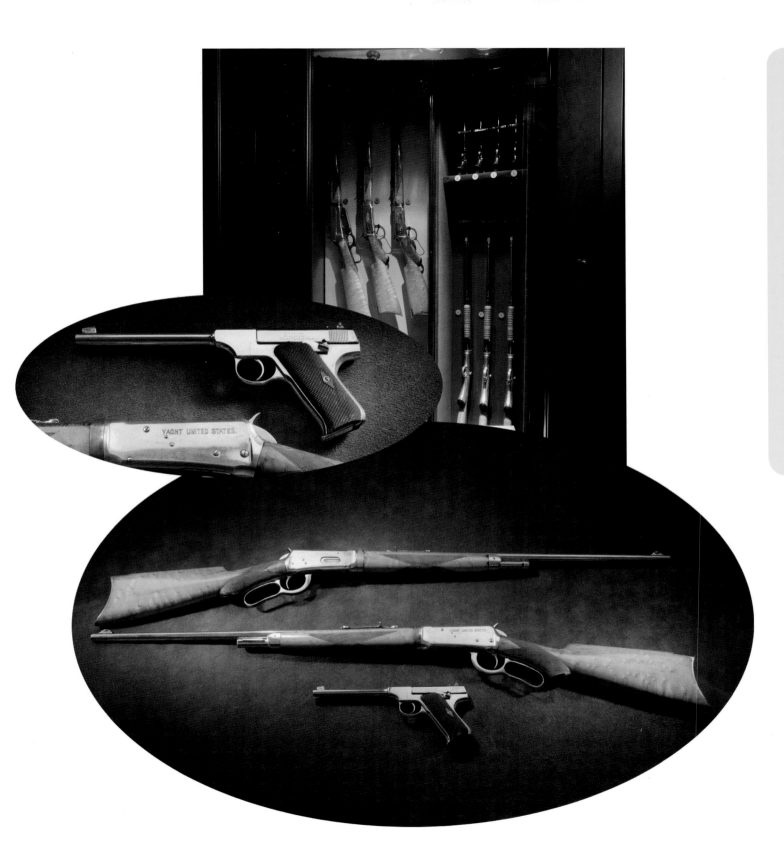

The Golden Guns of the Yacht "United States"

The yacht "United States" was owned by Col. Edward H.R. Green, whose mother Hetty Green was dubbed the "Witch of Wall Street" and was considered the richest woman in America at the time. Green's vessel was the most luxurious American vessel afloat, being twice the length of the presidential yacht and having a stateroom for every state in the Union. As a sea-going arsenal, Green commissioned six Winchester rifles (an 1895 in .30-06, two 1894s in .30-30, and three .22 rimfire Lightnings, all with birdseye maple stocks), along with four Colt semi-automatic .22 pistols. Each gun was gold-plated and engraved "Yacht United States." One pistol was separated from the other arms in this group in the past and was found at auction, where it was purchased by the National Firearms Museum and reunited with the set.

The Rifles of the Brothers Mauser

In the world of firearms, few people have left a greater mark than brothers Wilhelm and Paul Mauser. The genius of the Mausers' first bolt-action design was such that many subsequent Mauser designs were merely adaptations of the original brought about by advances in technology.

The Mauser brothers originally encountered difficulty in attracting the attention of their own government to the possibilities of a bolt-action rifle and sought financial backing in the United States. At one point the Remington Arms Company was approached and seemed interested. But the Ilion, New York, gunmaker backed out of a pending contract just as the German government showed renewed interest.

Eventually the Mausers' designs became the most produced and copied of all firearms innovations. Most sporting and military bolt action rifles (and some shotguns) can trace their development to the efforts of the brothers Mauser.

The four rifles on this page are all prototypes by the Mauser brothers as they perfected the bolt action rifle. When the French Chassepot needle-fire rifle debuted in the Franco-Prussian War, developments in metallic cartridges were already conspiring to make this arm obsolete. Among the individuals that observed the rifle's flaws were Remington's European sales representative, Samuel Norris, and Wilhelm and Paul Mauser. Norris knew that metallic cartridges were the future for military arms and worked with the Mausers to create a

conversion of the French Chassepot rifle that would take metallic cartridges. In 1869, the conversion received a U.S. patent and prototypes were made by the Mauser brothers for use in convincing European military leaders to adopt a new bolt-action rifle system. A number of intermediate prototypes, based on reworked Chassepot rifles, reflected changes in extractors, spring location and self-cocking capabilities. The end result, the Mauser M1871 rifle, utilized an 11mm centerfire cartridge and features a reliable bolt design that cocked on closing. This bolt-action design was the foundation for other designs such as the Mauser Model 1898, which in turn came to influence many other rifle designs including the American Springfield Model 1903 rifle.

1   Mauser prototype: Chassepot French Model 1866 Bolt-Action Rifle with Norris-Mauser Patent Self-Cocking Bolt - 11 mm - circa 1869-1870 - Thought by historians to be the first Mauser ever made, predating any patent models.

2   Mauser prototype: Norris-Mauser Belgian Model 1867/69 Bolt-Action Rifle - 11 mm - circa 1869-1870.

3   Mauser prototype: Chassepot French Model 1873 Bolt-Action Rifle with Kynoch Metallic Centerfire Cartridge Conversion - 11 mm - circa 1875-1879.

4   Mauser prototype: Chassepot French Model 1866 Bolt-Action Rifle with Mauser Experimental Bolt and Hook Cocking Piece - 11 mm - circa 1869-1870.

1 Mauser Belgian Interim Model 1869/70 Bolt-Action Rifle; Model #1 - 11 mm - circa 1869-1870.

2 Mauser Belgian Interim Model 1869/70 Bolt-Action Rifle, Model #2 - 11 mm - circa 1869-1870.

3 Dreyse German M1860 Needle-Fire Rifle - .50 Needlefire - circa 1865 - Used by the Prussian army during the Franco-Prussian War of 1871, the needle gun was rapidly replaced by the Mauser 1871.

4 Mauser German Modified Gewehr 71 Bolt-Action Rifle - 11 mm - circa 1867 - This bolt-action rifle would replace the needle gun as Germany's main service rifle following the Franco-Prussian War of 1871.

5 Societe Industrial Swiss Model 1871 Vetterli Bolt-Action Rifle - 10.35 Vetterli - circa 1871-1887.

6 Brescia Italian Model 1871 Vetterli Bolt-Action Carbine - 10.35 Vetterli - circa 1871-1887.

1 Brescia Italian Model 1871/87 Vetterli-Vitali Bolt-Action Rifle - 10.35 Vetterli - circa 1871-1887.

2 Dutch Beaumont-Vitali Bolt-Action Rifle - 10.35 Vetterli - circa 1870-1887.

3 U.S. Springfield Model 1871 Ward-Burton Single-Shot Bolt-Action Rifle - .50 centerfire - ca. 1871 - Slightly more than 1,000 Ward-Burton rifles were tested in trials, but this early bolt-action was the first bolt-action centerfire rifle brought into American military service. Following a tradition begun after the American Revolution, the front sight of the rifle doubled as a lug point for a socket bayonet.

4 Mauser German Model 1871 Bolt-Action Carbine - 11 mm.

5 Waffenfabrik Steyr Austrian Model 1874 Gras Bolt-Action Rifle - 11mm Gras - circa 1874-1877.

1 Chatelerault French Model 1874 Gras Bolt-Action Carbine - 11mm Gras - circa 1880.

2 French Chassepot Model 1866 rifle - 11 mm - circa 1873 - The standard service rifle of the French Army during the Franco-Prussian War of 1871, this rifle, far superior to the Prussian needle gun, proved that superior firepower cannot make up for bad leadership in combat.

3 Tula Arsenal Russian Model 1879 Berdan II Bolt-Action Rifle - 11 mm - ca. 1879-1881 - Designed by U.S. Civil War General Hiram Berdan, founder of the USSS (United States Sharp Shooters). This model was adopted by the Russian military.

4 Winchester Hotchkiss Model 1879 First Model Bolt-Action Carbine - .45-70 - circa 1880-1881 - This rifle represents Winchester's first significant military contract with the U.S. government.

5 Winchester-Hotchkiss Second Model Bolt-Action Musket - .45-70 - circa 1880-1881.

6 Winchester-Hotchkiss Second Model Bolt-Action Carbine - .45-70 - circa 1880-1881.

A BRIGHT NEW CENTURY

1 U.S. Winchester Hotchkiss Model 1883 Third Model Bolt-Action Musket - .45-70 - circa 1883-1899.

2 Waffenfabrik Bern Swiss Model 1881 Bolt-Action Rifle - 10.35 Vetterli - circa 1881-1883.

3 Remington-Keene Magazine Bolt-Action Rifle - .40-60 - circa 1880-1883 - 500 of these rifles marked "USID" were used by Indian Police on reservations.

4 U.S. Remington-Lee Model 1882 Magazine Bolt-Action Rifle - .45-70 - circa 1882-1886.

5 Remington-Lee Model 1882/1885 Magazine Bolt-Action Rifle - .45-70 - circa 1886-1888.

6 Winchester Civilian Model 3rd Hotchkiss Musket - .45-70 - circa 1879-1889.

1 U.S. Springfield Model 1882 Chaffee-Reese Bolt-Action Magazine Rifle - .45-70 - circa 1884.

2 Amberg Arsenal German Model 71/84 Bolt-Action Rifle - 11mm Mauser - circa 1884.

3 Waffenfabrik Steyr Austrian Gewehr 88 Commission Bolt-Action Rifle - 8mm Mauser - circa 1890 - In the arms race between France and Germany in the 1880s, the Commission 88 bolt-action rifle became the first German military rifle to employ smokeless ammunition. The Commission 88 was also the only German bolt-action rifle design not actually manufactured by Mauser but by other contractors, in part to settle a patent infringement claim by Steyr Mannlicher.

4 Mauser German Model 88 Single-Shot Bolt-Action Target Rifle - 8.15mm x 46R - circa 1928.

5 St. Denis French Daudeteau/Dovitiis Conversion Single-Shot Bolt-Action Carbine - 6.5mm Daudeteau - circa 1877.

6 Carl Gustafs Stads Gevarsfaktori Swedish Model 1894 Mauser Bolt-Action Carbine - 6.5mm Swedish - circa 1904.

A BRIGHT NEW CENTURY

1 Carl Gustafs Stads Gevarsfaktori Swedish Model 1896 Mauser Bolt-Action Rifle - 6.5 x 55mm - circa 1911.

2 Ludwig Loewe Waffenfabrik German Model 1895 Chilean Contract Bolt-Action Rifle - 7mm Mauser - circa 1897-1900.

3 Waffenfabrik Steyr Norwegian Contract Model 1894 Krag Jorgensen Bolt-Action Rifle - 6.5 x 55mm - circa 1897 - This design was the basis for the adoption of the Krag Jorgensen by the U.S. military.

4 Ludwig Loewe & Co. German Argentine Contract Model 1891 Bolt-Action Carbine - 7.65mm Mauser - circa 1891-1907.

5 Gevaerfabriken Kjobenhaven Danish Model 1899 Krag-Jorgensen Bolt-Action Rifle - .30-40 Krag - circa 1892.

6 Danish Model 1889 Krag-Jorgensen Carbine - 8mm - circa 1890.

1   U.S. Springfield Model 1898 Gallery Practice Bolt-Action Rifle - .22 rimfire - circa 1906 - Named for Norwegian inventors Ole Hermann Johannes Krag and Erik Jorgensen, the bolt-action Krag-Jorgensen rifle was the first U.S. Army-adopted rifle that employed smokeless powder ammunition with jacketed projectiles. This example is a .22 caliber training rifle variant.

2   Danzig Arsenal German Gewehr 98 Bolt-Action Rifle - 8mm Mauser - ca. 1916 - The Gewehr 98 or 98 Mauser, as it is known, became the finest bolt-action rifle ever produced. It was, in minor variants, the standard service rifle of Germany from 1898 to 1945.

3   Mauser German Karabiner 98A Bolt-Action Rifle - 8mm Mauser - circa 1918-1920 - This '98 Mauser carbine was popular in the trenches of World War I due to its short and maneuverable length.

4   Blake Bolt Action Repeating Rifle - .30-40 Krag - circa 1892-1910.

5   Steyr Daimler Puch Austrian Mauser Model 98k Bolt-Action Carbine - 8mm Mauser - circa 1944 - This '98 Mauser was the standard service rifle of Germany during World War II.

6   Mukden Arsenal Manchurian Mauser 98 Bolt-Action Rifle - 8mm - ca. 1933-1939 - Built in Mukden Arsenal for the army of Manchukuo during 1933-1939, this bolt-action rifle design incorporates both Arisaka and Mauser elements. The two-piece stock and ovoid bolt handle knob are typical of Arisaka arms, and the barrel bands are thinner than German Mauser counterparts.

A BRIGHT NEW CENTURY

1. Tokyo Arsenal Siamese Contract Mauser Model 1903/Type 45 Bolt-Action Rifle - 8mm - circa 1903-1908.

2. Fabrica Nacional de Arms Mexican Model 1910 Mauser Bolt-Action Rifle - 7mm Mauser - circa 1910-1934.

3. Fabrica Nacional de Arms Mexican Mauser Model 1936 Bolt-Action Rifle - 7mm Mauser - circa 1936-1947.

4. Fabrique Nationale Belgian Mauser Model 1916 Bolt-Action Carbine - 7.65mm Mauser - circa 1916-1918.

5. Fabrique Nationale Venezuelan Contract Model 1924/30 Bolt-Action Rifle - 7mm Mauser circa 1930-1950.

6. Fabrique Nationale Belgian Model 1924/30 Bolt-Action Rifle - 7 mm - circa 1930-1947.

1 Ceskoslovenska Zbrojovka Brno Czech Model 98/29 Persian Contract Bolt-Action Rifle - 8mm Mauser - circa 1930-1938.

2 Ceskoslovenska Zbrojovka Brno Czech Copy of Kar 98K Bolt-Action Rifle - 7mm Mauser - circa 1942-1945.

3 Townsend Whelen's Springfield Sporter Bolt Action Rifle - .30-06 - circa 1920 - Incorporating elements of the Mauser 1898 bolt action design, the 1903 Springfield became a popular sporter.

4 U.S. Springfield Model 1903 Gallery Practice Bolt-Action Rifle - .22 rimfire - circa 1915 - A rare variant of the 1903 Springfield, this .22 was made for training purposes.

5 Weatherby Mark V Bolt-Action Rifle - .300 Weatherby Magnum - circa 1959-1973.

6 Remington Model 700 Left-Hand Bolt-Action Rifle - 7 mm Remington Magnum - circa 1990.

Modern Bolt-Action Sporting Rifles

Since the introduction of the Model 1898 Mauser, most commercial companies have attempted to create similar actions in the sporting arms field. Weatherby, Winchester, Savage, Ruger and Remington have all refined the bolt action to varying degrees.

A BRIGHT NEW CENTURY

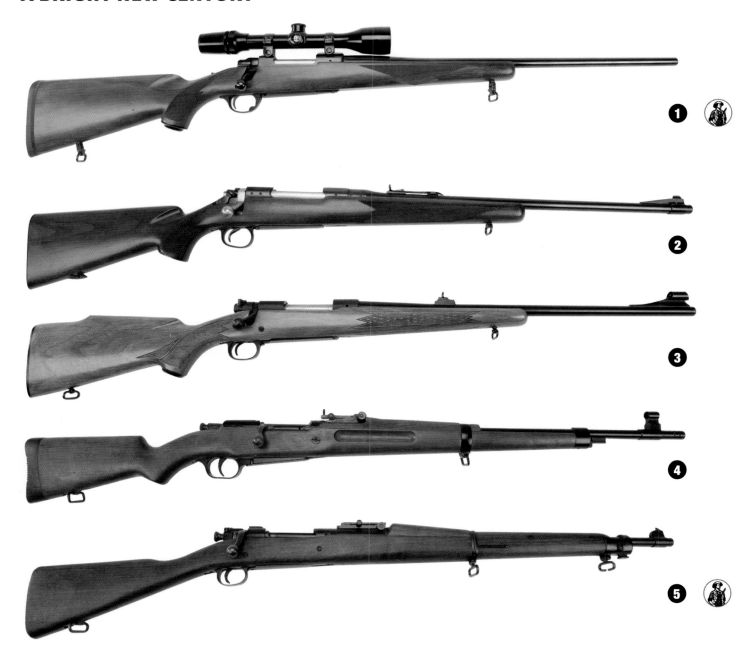

1 Sturm, Ruger & Co. Model 77 Bolt-Action Rifle - 6 mm Remington - circa 1968.

2 Remington Model 720A Bolt-Action Rifle - .30-06 - circa 1942.

3 Winchester Model 70 Bolt-Action Rifle - .30-06 - circa 1966 - Often called the Rifleman's Rifle.

4 Madsen Danish G1A Bolt-Action Rifle - .30-06 - circa 1958 - The Madsen G1A rifle was the last of a long line of military issue bolt-actions. Produced in Denmark for a Columbian military order in 1958, this .30-06 rifle had modern features including an integral muzzle brake and a high comb stock with rubber buttpad.

5 U.S. Springfield Model 1903 Bolt-Action Sporting Rifle - circa 1912 - The Springfield '03 was the American standard service rifle from 1903 to 1936. It first saw service in the Philippines in 1903. Issued in WWI and WWII, it was still in service as a sniper rifle in Korea and Vietnam.

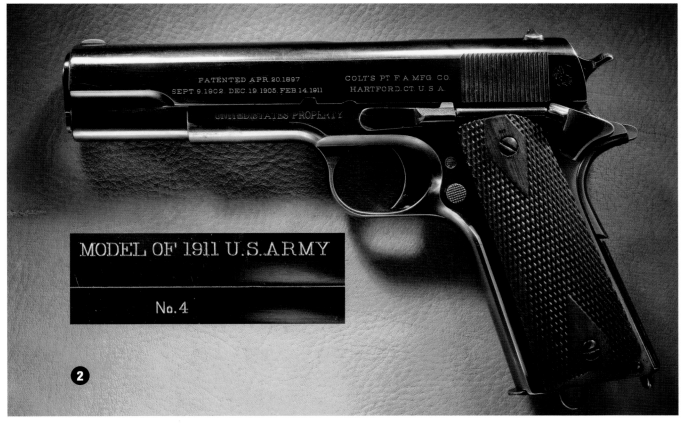

1 Browning Model 1878 Standard Single-Shot Rifle - .45-70 - circa 1878-1882 - An early example of John Browning's single-shot rifle design as built in his Ogden, UT, gunshop. Browning sold the manufacturing rights for this design to Winchester in 1883.

2 Colt 1911, serial number 4 - In near mint condition, this Colt 1911 is considered the finest and earliest 1911 extant. After 100 years, this model is still in production, virtually unchanged, and still considered by many to be the best combat handgun ever made.

THE GENIUS OF JOHN M. BROWNING

The son of a gunsmith, John Moses Browning was born in Ogden, Utah, on January 21, 1855. From his earliest youth, Browning displayed a remarkable talent for invention. By age 13 he had made his first gun – of scrap iron – in his father's gunshop. By age 24 he had been granted his first patent – for a breechloading single-shot rifle. Browning's first firearm patent was bought by the Winchester Repeating Arms Company and marketed as the Model 1885 (the renowned High Wall and Low Wall rifles). Browning's inventive genius produced 128 patents for breechloading rifles, magazine rifles, auto-loading guns, repeating shotguns, gas-operated firearms, semi-automatic firearms, and machine guns. His designs were manufactured by Winchester, Remington, Colt, Stevens, and the Fabrique Nationale d'Armes de Guerre in Herstal, Belgium. Several of his designs were adopted by the U.S. Army, notably the Model 1911 pistol, the Model 1917 Browning water-cooled machine gun, and the Model 1918 Browning automatic rifle. Perhaps the greatest inventor in small arms history, John M. Browning died of a heart attack on November 26, 1926.

1

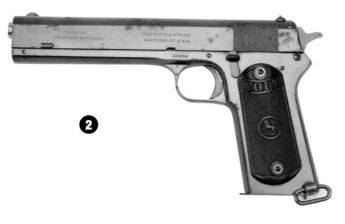

2

3

4

5

6

1 Colt Model 1902 Sporting Semi-Automatic Pistol - .38 Rimless Smokeless - circa 1903.

2 Colt Model 1902 Military Semi-Automatic Pistol - .38 Rimless Smokeless - circa 1916.

3 Colt Model 1903 Pocket Semi-Automatic Pistol - .38 Rimless Smokeless - circa 1927.

4 Colt Model 1903 Hammerless Type III Pocket Semi-Automatic Pistol - .32 ACP - circa 1927.

5 Fabrique Nationale/Browning Model 1910 FN Semi-Automatic Pistol - .32 ACP - circa 1930-1935 - A similar Model 1910 was used by Gavrilo Princip to assassinate Archduke Franz Ferdinand of Austria in Sarajevo on June 28, 1914, an act that ignited the hostilities known now as World War I.

6 Fabrique Nationale/Browning P-35 Hi-Power Semi-Automatic Pistol - 9mm Parabellum - circa 1973 - Considered the last handgun design to be created by John Browning prior to his death in 1926. It was completed by Dieudonné Saive of Fabrique Nationale. The P-35 pistol has been issued to the military of over 50 countries. A single-action semi-automatic pistol with a double-stack magazine holding 13 9mm cartridges, the P-35 or Hi-Power pistol provided significant handgun firepower for the period it was developed.

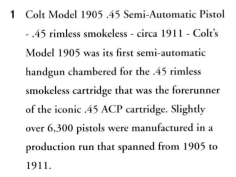

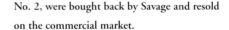

1 Colt Model 1905 .45 Semi-Automatic Pistol - .45 rimless smokeless - circa 1911 - Colt's Model 1905 was its first semi-automatic handgun chambered for the .45 rimless smokeless cartridge that was the forerunner of the iconic .45 ACP cartridge. Slightly over 6,300 pistols were manufactured in a production run that spanned from 1905 to 1911.

2 U.S. Colt Model 1911 Semi-Automatic Pistol - .45 ACP - circa 1917.

3 Savage Military Model 1907 Semi-Automatic Pistol - .45 ACP - circa 1907 - Competing with the John Browning-designed Colt .45 pistol in military trials, Savage's semi-automatic pistol lost and was not adopted. The more than 200 Savage pistols from the trials, including this example which was serial No. 2, were bought back by Savage and resold on the commercial market.

4 Springfield Armory Model 1911A1 Semi-Automatic Pistol (sectionalized) - .45 ACP - circa 1986 - The Model 1911A1 redesign of the orignal M1911 pistol resulted in changes to trigger, hammer, and grip safety length, as well as changing the mainspring housing to a curved profile. This modern cutaway pistol model also shows the frame milling behind the trigger to enhance finger access.

1 Winchester Model 1907 Semi-Automatic Rifle - .351 Winchester - circa 1908.

2 Winchester Winder Single-Shot Musket - .22 short - circa 1918-1919 - Lt. Colonel C.B. Winder of the Ohio National Guard was a competitive shooter who sought to create a single-shot rifle that would combine military rifle lines with a target arm that could be used for both training and competition. Winchester manufactured Winder's musket design in .22 rimfire, based on the Model 1885 falling-block rifle.

3 Browning Belgian Grade 1 Semi-Automatic Takedown Rifle - .22 rimfire - circa 1976.

4 Remington Model 11 Autoloader Shotgun - 12 gauge - circa 1915.

5 Winchester Model 1911 SL Autoloader Shotgun - 12 gauge - circa 1912.

6 Remington Model 17 Slide-Action Shotgun - 20 gauge - circa 1917-1933.

Browning Long Gun Designs
In addition to the guns on this page, Browning designed Winchester lever-action Models 1886, 1892, 1894, and 1895. Many of his designs are still in production today.

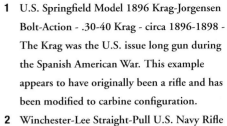

1 U.S. Springfield Model 1896 Krag-Jorgensen Bolt-Action - .30-40 Krag - circa 1896-1898 - The Krag was the U.S. issue long gun during the Spanish American War. This example appears to have originally been a rifle and has been modified to carbine configuration.

2 Winchester-Lee Straight-Pull U.S. Navy Rifle - 6mm Lee Navy - circa 1895-1902 - The first U.S. Navy-adopted military bolt-action rifle that used both smokeless ammunition and jacketed bullets, the straight-pull Winchester Lee had limited issue. U.S. Marine detachments stationed in China during the Boxer rebellion were among the limited units to see combat service with this rifle.

3 U.S. Springfield Model 1884 Trapdoor Rifle - .45-70 - circa 1885-1890 - These obsolete black powder rifles were no match against the smokeless mausers of the Spanish in Cuba.

4 U.S. Springfield Model 1898 Krag-Jorgensen Bolt-Action Rifle - .30-40 Krag - circa 1898-1903.

5 Mauser Spanish Contract M1893 rifle - 7 mm - circa 1893-1898.

A Splendid Little War

On February 15, 1898, the American battleship U.S. Maine exploded in Havana harbor. The United States, believing that Spain was responsible for the loss of the ship and over 200 men, declared war on Spain. The Secretary of State called the conflict "a splendid little war." Victory for the United States came within nine months as America's army troops in Cuba and naval forces in the Philippines dismantled the last vestiges of the once-powerful Spanish Empire.

The Spanish Mauser rifles and the American Krag rifles that were used in the Spanish-American War were evenly matched in effectiveness. Eventually, the Model 1903 Springfield, a licensed copy of the Spanish Mauser, replaced the Krag as the primary service rifle for American troops.

A BRIGHT NEW CENTURY

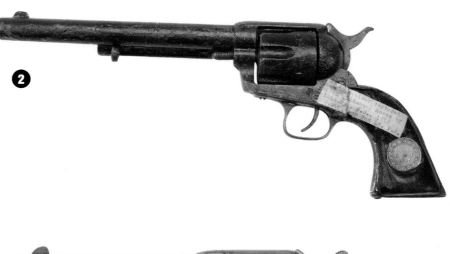

Roosevelt's Rough Riders

Theodore Roosevelt resigned his office as Assistant Secretary of the Navy in 1898 in order to organize a cavalry regiment to fight in the Spanish-American War in Cuba. The regiment was commanded by Colonel Leonard Wood, a Medal of Honor recipient under whom Roosevelt served as a lieutenant colonel.

The response to recruiting advertisements was overwhelming, attracting cowboys, rangers, Indians, and even gentlemen riders from the Harvard, Yale, and Princeton polo clubs!

On the morning of July 1, 1898, near Santiago, Cuba, Roosevelt's Rough Riders, as his regiment was popularly known in the press, attacked the Spanish forces along San Juan ridge and adjoining Kettle Hill. In the mid-afternoon, the Rough Riders overran the Spanish positions and made their heroic way into the history books. Roosevelt's popularity soared upon his return to the United States, resulting in his election as vice president.

1 Colt U.S. Model 1902 Army Double-Action Revolver - .45 Colt - circa 1902-1904. The 1878 DA model was modified with an enlarged triggerguard and issued to fill the need for large-bore revolvers after the failure of .38 revolvers to provide adequate stopping power.

2 Colt Single-Action Army Revolver - .45 Colt - circa 1873-1940 - Colt's Single-Action Army revolver served with, and sometimes against, the U.S. military on a variety of fronts. This near-relic example is attributed as having been captured from Mindanao Moro guerillas by a lieutenant of the Phillipine Scouts in 1912.

3 Colt Model 1892 New Army Revolver - .38 Colt - circa 1892 - Theodore Roosevelt carried serial number 1633 in the fight up Kettle and San Juan Hills, July 1, 1898. His revolver was recovered from the sunken battleship USS Maine. The .38 Colt cartridge was ineffective against suicide attacks by Moro guerillas in the Philippines.

4 Colt Single-Action Army Revolver - .45 Colt - ca. 1873-1940 - Trooper L.G. Bishop carried this Colt revolver up San Juan and Kettle Hills as a member of Troop G, 1st U.S. Volunteer Cavalry ("Rough Riders"). Military SA Revolvers were refurbished by Colt and Springfield Armory, the barrel shortened from 7.5 to 5.5. inches. Reworked revolvers, like this, are called Artillery Model. The original long-barrel version is called the Cavalry Model.

1 Ludwig Loewe Waffenfabrik Model 1895 Spanish Contract Mauser Bolt-Action Rifle - 7mm Mauser - circa 1893-1898.

2 Mauser Model 1896 Spanish Contract Bolt-Action Rifle - 7mm Mauser - circa 1896-1900.

3 U.S. Springfield Model 1896 Krag-Jorgensen Bolt-Action Rifle - .30-40 Krag - circa 1896-1898.

4 Ludwig Loewe Waffenfabrik Spanish Contract Model 1893 Bolt-Action Rifle - 7mm Mauser - circa 1894.

THE WORLD AT WAR

The Great War

The Great War, now commonly referred to as World War I, began after the assassination of Archduke Franz Ferdinand of Austria in June 1914. By mid-August 1914 most of the major European powers were at war. The United States entered on the side of the British and French in April 1917. World War I signaled the end of the age in which conflicts were settled with some semblance of chivalry. It was a war of rapidly changing technology, fought using tactics of the Napoleonic era. Companies, even battalions of soldiers, were thrown against squads of men, each squad manning a single machine gun capable of firing 800 rounds a minute. One General responded to the rapid destruction of his entire Division by telling his men to **"dig, dig, dig, until you are safe."** By Christmas 1914 a trench system wound its way from the Belgian coast on the North Sea to the Swiss border some 1500 kilometers away! For four years, until November 1918, the trenches remained in place, virtually unchanged. The word stalemate entered the dictionary to describe a useless situation with no foreseeable conclusion. The result was 8.5 million dead and 21 million maimed and disabled, plus 12.5 million civilian casualties.

The bolt-action rifle was standard armament among the 30 nations involved in this global conflict, with some members of the Allies – countries at war with Germany – paying licensing fees for their rifles to the German firm of Waffenfabrik Mauser. The dominating firearm of the war was the machine gun. Once thought wasteful and expensive, its use ensured that neither side could advance on the other without incurring horrifying losses. The war was brought to an end on November 11, 1918, by the combination of overwhelming Allied offensive action and the spread of revolution throughout Germany that forced the Kaiser's abdication and the replacement of the monarchy with a civilian government willing to surrender.

1 U.S. Springfield Model 1903 Bolt-Action Rifle - .30-06 - circa 1903-1930.

2 U.S. Colt Model 1911 Semi-Automatic Pistol - .45 ACP - circa 1912-1925.

3 Colt Model 1914 Machine Gun (deactivated) - Manufactured by Marlin - .30-06 - circa 1914-1916 - Sometimes called the potato digger after the reciprocating action of its low-mounted operating rod, this Browning-designed machine gun served in primarily training roles during World War I.

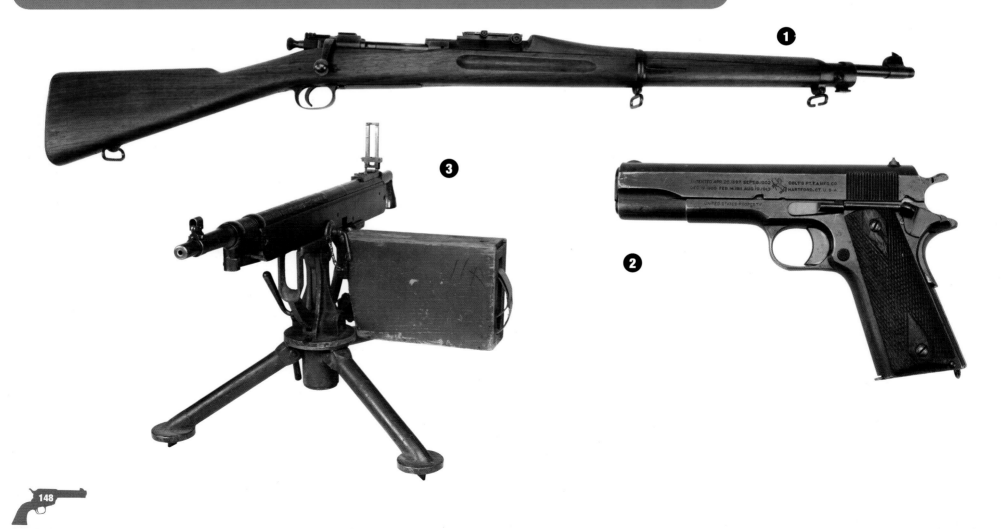

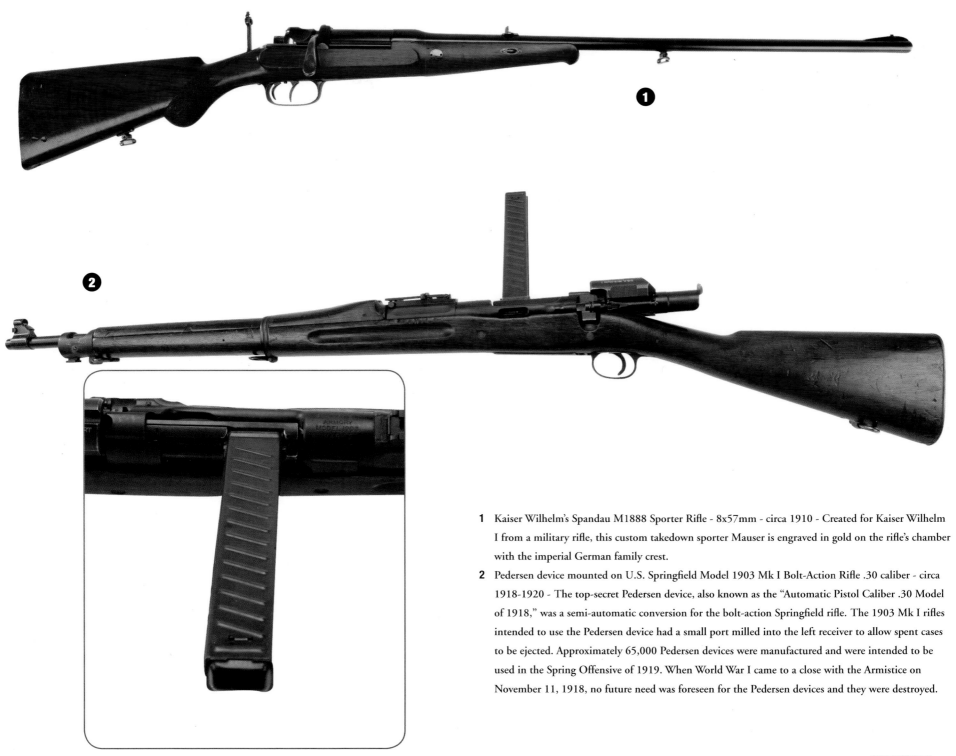

1   Kaiser Wilhelm's Spandau M1888 Sporter Rifle - 8x57mm - circa 1910 - Created for Kaiser Wilhelm
    I from a military rifle, this custom takedown sporter Mauser is engraved in gold on the rifle's chamber
    with the imperial German family crest.

2   Pedersen device mounted on U.S. Springfield Model 1903 Mk I Bolt-Action Rifle .30 caliber - circa
    1918-1920 - The top-secret Pedersen device, also known as the "Automatic Pistol Caliber .30 Model
    of 1918," was a semi-automatic conversion for the bolt-action Springfield rifle. The 1903 Mk I rifles
    intended to use the Pedersen device had a small port milled into the left receiver to allow spent cases
    to be ejected. Approximately 65,000 Pedersen devices were manufactured and were intended to be
    used in the Spring Offensive of 1919. When World War I came to a close with the Armistice on
    November 11, 1918, no future need was foreseen for the Pedersen devices and they were destroyed.

1 U.S. Remington Model 1917 Bolt-Action Rifle
   - .30-06 - circa 1917-1919 - Over two million
   M1917s were manufactured by Eddystone,
   Remington, and Winchester.

2 U.S. Winchester Model 1917 Bolt-Action Rifle
   - .30-06 - circa 1917-1919 - Winchester was
   one of three contractors to produce the M1917
   rifle.

3 U.S. Winchester Model 1897 Slide-Action
   Trench Shotgun - 12 gauge - circa 1918 -
   Winchester's military slide-action shotgun was
   fitted with a barrel hand guard and bayonet
   lug.

4 U.S. Springfield (Springfield, MA) Model
   1903 Bolt-Action Rifle (relic condition) -
   .30-06 - circa 1903-1907 - Buried in a French
   field, this relic M1903 rifle was recovered in
   1963.

5 U.S. Winchester Prototype Model 1917
   Bolt-Action Magazine Rifle - .30-06 - circa
   1917 - This unmarked tool room example
   of a Winchester Model 1917 bolt-action rifle
   was part of a collection assembled by a former
   production line superintendent at Winchester.

1. U.S. Colt Model 1911 Semi-Automatic Pistol - .45 ACP - circa 1912 -1925 - Lanyard loops were added to pistols and magazines prior to WWI for retention purposes. This pistol was carried by an American officer during the 1919 Siberian Expedition in Russia.

2. U.S. Navy Colt Model 1911 Semi-Automatic Pistol - .45 ACP - circa 1912-1925 - Over 31,000 M1911 pistols were produced for U.S. Navy contracts and marked on the slide.

3. North American Arms Model 1911 Semi-Automatic Pistol - .45 ACP - circa 1918 - To provide additional supplies of the Model 1911 semi-automatic pistol, U.S. government contracts were issued to many potential suppliers, including the North American Arms Company of Quebec, Canada. Just over 100 pistols were completed before the end of World War I, but none of these were found to conform to U.S. Ordnance specifications for serial number and model marking.

4. U.S. Remington UMC Model 1911 pistol - .45 ACP - circa 1918-1919 - Less than 22,000 M1911 pistols were made by Remington-UMC.

5. U.S. Springfield Model 1911 .22 Caliber Prototype Semi-Automatic Pistol - .22 long rifle - circa 1914 - Springfield Armory began a .22 rimfire training pistol based on the M1911 platform that was shelved by World War. I Roughly 25 of these semi-automatic .22 pistols were constructed.

1. U.S. Colt Model 1917 Double-Action Revolver - .45 ACP - circa 1917 Over 151,000 double-action Colt M1917 revolvers were produced.

2. U.S. Remington Mk III Flare Pistol - 10 gauge - circa 1917-1918 - The brass barrel of the Mk III was intended to resist corrosion from firing flares.

3. U.S. Smith & Wesson Model 1917 Double-Action Revolver - .45 ACP - circa 1917-1919 - Over 209,000 S&W M1917 revolvers were produced.

4. Colt Model 1909 U.S. Army Double-Action Revolver - .45 Colt - circa 1909 - Colt's M1909 was a military version of the commercial New Service model revolver.

5. Smith & Wesson 2nd Model Hand Ejector Double-Action Revolver - .455 Mk II - circa 1902-1903 - S&W produced almost 70,000 revolvers in .455 caliber for British/Canadian military orders.

6. Farquhar-Hill British Model 1909 Experimental Semi-Automatic Rifle - .303 British - circa 1909 - The long recoil-operated Farquhar-Hill was intended as a squad automatic rifle and was tested by British Ordnance's Small Arms Committee in 1908. A 20-round drum magazine was intended as the standard configuration although other magazine capacities were also tested. This example is one of the rarer semi-automatic-only versions.

7. U.S. Springfield Model 1903 Bolt-Action Sniper Rifle - .30-06 - circa 1907-1919 - The U.S. Warner-Swazey-scoped sniper was the first .30-06 bolt-action sniper rifle fielded.

1 Enfield No. 3 Mk I Bolt-Action Rifle - .303 British - circa 1914.

2 Ross Rifle Co. Model 1910 Straight-Pull Rifle - .280 Ross - circa 1910 - Found to have a potentially dangerous bolt design, Ross rifles were sidelined from active service.

3 Ross Rifle Co. Model 1905 Straight-Pull Rifle - .303 British - circa 1906 - The straight-pull line of Ross rifles had a reputation for being unsafe firearms due to a complicated bolt that could be incorrectly reassembled and would fail to lock the action correctly during firing. During the interwar period and during World War II, the Ross rifles still in inventory were utilized for non-firing training duties.

4 British SMLE Mk III Bolt-Action Rifle - .303 British - circa 1942- 1943 - The fast-firing SMLE could empty its ten-shot magazine in less than 20 seconds with an adept shooter.

5 BSA Sparkbrook Model 1893 Mk II Magazine Lee-Metford Bolt-Action Rifle - .303 British - circa 1893 - In WWI, British forces employed earlier Lee-Enfield models that were updated for issue.

1 Tulle French Model 1886/93 Lebel Bolt-Action Rifle - 8mm Lebel - circa 1900-1918 - The French Lebel was one of the first rifles to employ both jacketed bullets and smokeless powder.

2 French Berthier Model 1916/27 Bolt-Action Carbine - 8mm Lebel - circa 1892-1920 - Shorter carbines were used for cavalry and artillery units.

3 St. Etienne French Model 1917 Semi-Automatic Rifle - 8mm Lebel - circa 1917-1925 - French semi-auto rifle designs did not come into use until late in WWI.

4 Hopkins & Allen Belgian Contract Mauser Model 1889 Bolt-Action Rifle - 7.65mm Mauser - circa 1889-1915 - H&A's contract with Belgian authorities resulted in 180,000 M1889 rifles for WWI.

5 French Lebel Model 1907-15 Bolt-Action Rifle (sectionalized) - 8mm Lebel - circa 1907 - This cutaway of a military firearm illustrates many of its otherwise hidden internal mechanisms.

6 French Berthier Model 1907/15 Bolt-Action Rifle - 8mm Lebel - circa 1917.

1 Norwegian Model 1914 pistol - .45 ACP - circa 1914 - The Model 1911 semi-automatic pistol design proved popular in other nations. Almost 33,000 copies of the M1911 design were built in Norway. This is the last one made.

2 P. Webley & Sons Pryse Double-Action Revolver - .455 Webley - circa mid-1870s - Handguns were indispensable on WWI night trench raids.

3 Webley & Scott Model 1912 Mk I Semi-Automatic Pistol - .455 W&S Self-Loader - circa 1909-1938 - Semi-auto Webley pistols were issued to Horse Artillery units.

4 Webley Mk IV Double-Action Revolver - .455 Webley - circa 1899-1914 - Webley's Mk IV .455 revolver was the last British military blackpowder-proofed model.

5 Webley Mk VI Double-Action Revolver (sectionalized) - .455 Webley - circa 1915-1919 - Sectionalized handguns are created by military armorers as a means of instruction in operating mechanisms. Strategically cut windows in the side of frames, cylinders, and barrels reveal how springs are mounted and the correct alignment or working relationship of parts. Sectionalized or cutaway pieces are often created from condemned pistols no longer suitable for shooting.

6 Webley Mk V Double-Action Revolver - .455 Webley - circa 1914-1915 - Most MARK V Webleys were shipped to former colonies such as Australia or New Zealand.

7 Webley Mk I Double-Action Revolver (sectionalized) - .455 Webley - circa 1894-1897.

8 Belgian Montenegrin Single-Action Revolver - 11.75mm Gasser - circa 1914-1918 - A Montenegrin Air Corps individual reportedly received this revolver in 1914.

9 Webley No.1 Mk 1 Flare Pistol - 26mm - circa 1917-1918 - A strong break-open design, Webley's flare pistols were made of brass to resist corrosion.

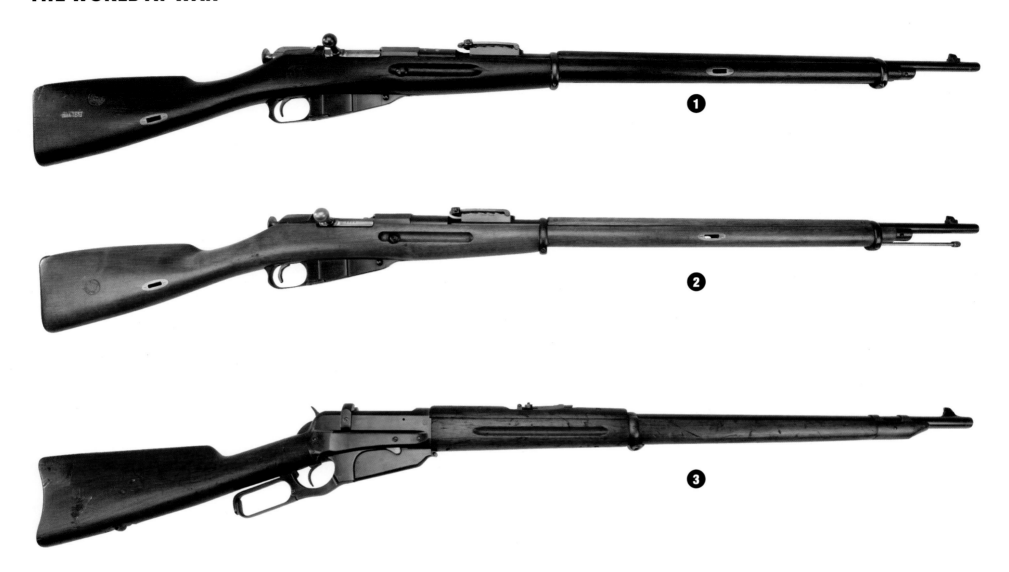

1 Remington Mosin Nagant Model 1891 Bolt-
   Action Rifle - 7.62mm x 54 Russian - circa
   1917 - This Mosin Nagant rifle was tested by
   NRA during the WWI period.

2 Mosin Nagant Model 1891 Bolt-Action Rifle
   - 7.62mm x 54 Russian - circa 1911 - Russia's
   standard service rifle in World War I held five
   cartridges.

3 Winchester Russian Contract Model 1895
   Lever-Action Rifle - 7.62 x 54 Russian - circa
   1915 - 1916 - Winchester made M1895 rifles
   for Russia that used military stripper clips.

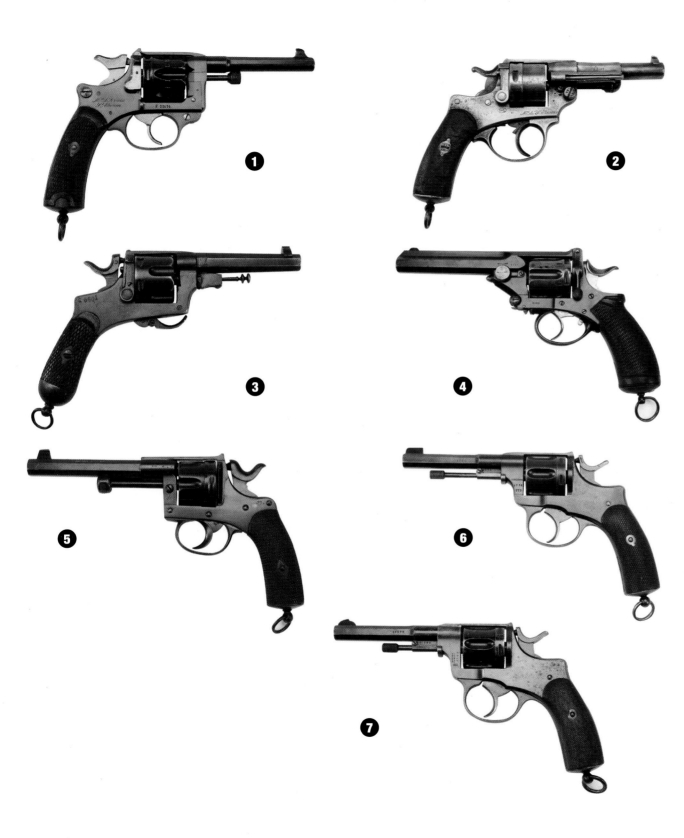

1. St. Etienne French Model 1892 Double-Action Service Revolver - 8mm French Service - circa 1892.
2. Sutterlin Lipmann & Co. French St. Etienne Model 1873 Revolver - 11mm French Service - circa 1873-1885.
3. Castelli G.A. Italian Model 1889 Double-Action Service Revolver - 10.35 Italian Service - circa 1889 - Few military revolvers are designed with folding triggers, but this Italian M1889 example definitely was.
4. Belgian Brevet Counet Double-Action Revolver - 11mm centerfire - circa 1887-1900.
5. Nederlandishe Wapenmagaeijn Haarlem Dutch Double-Action Service Revolver - 9.4mm Dutch - circa 1887-1900.
6. Swedish Nagant Revolver - 7.62mm Nagant - circa 1887-1945 - To gain higher muzzle velocities, Nagant revolvers were designed to seal at the cylinder/barrel gap.
7. Belgian Nagant Brevet Double-Action Revolver - 7.5mm Nagant - circa 1887-1900 Belgian copies of the Nagant revolver were made in several calibers.

1 J.P. Sauer & Sohn Gew98 Sniper Rifle - 8mm - circa 1916-1917 - A limited number of German Gew98 bolt-action rifles were converted to utilize a monocular sight that superimposed a pyramidal aiming point in the field of view. This sniper system was intended for quick target acquisition under low light conditions as this optic proved faster to use than traditional iron sights, but magnification also had to be low to maximize field of view.

2 Deutsche Waffen und Munitionsfabriken German Model 1917 Artillery Luger Semi-Automatic Pistol with holster, shoulder stock, cleaning rod, and loading tool - 9 mm - circa 1917 - Red-painted "9" grip markings refer to the caliber of the pistol to distinguish it from other 7.63mm caliber guns.

3 German Erfurt Luger LP-08 Artillery Semi-Automatic Pistol - 9 mm - circa 1915 - The Luger pistol was manufactured in different barrel-length configurations; the longer Lange Pistole 08 was intended for artillery and ancillary specialty units. A special elevation-adjustable rear sight was mounted at the rear of the barrel and could be adjusted to 800 meters.

4 Waffenwerke Oberspree Kornbusch German Gew98 Bolt-Action Rifle - 8mm Mauser - circa 1917 - The Gew98 featured a Lange-pattern rear sight with a curved range elevator.

5 Mauser German Model 1888 Commission Bolt-Action Rifle - 8mm Mauser - circa 1894 - The Commission 88 rifle featured a barrel jacket and a Mannlicher-style box magazine.

1 **Waffenfabrik Steyr Austrian Model 1895 Bolt-Action Carbine** - 8x57mm - ca. 1895-1940 - The Austrian M1895 rifle was in service in both WWI and WWII.

2 **Austro-Hungarian Model 1867 Werndl Rifle** - 11mm Werndl - circa 1870-1879.

3 **Erfurt Arsenal German Model 1891 Commission Bolt-Action Carbine** - 8mm Mauser - circa 1896 - Recalled Erfurt carbines were upgraded to take new 8mm service ammunition for WWI.

4 **Erfurt Arsenal German Karabiner 98a Bolt-Action Carbine** - 8mm Mauser ca. 1918 - Complete with breech and muzzle covers, this Mauser Karabiner is in original-issue configuration.

Central Powers' Rifles
The bolt action design of the Mauser brothers and the straight pull bolt of the Austrian Mannlicher system accounted for the majority of arms carried by the Central Powers. Most arms accepted a 7.92 mm cartridge, the "8mm," as the Mauser cartridge is also known.

1 Mauser Waffen Munitionsfabrik German Single-Shot Bolt-Action Anti-Tank Rifle - 13 mm - circa 1917 - Heavy with bipod and ammunition, the Mauser anti-tank rifle was the first anti-tank rifle. This massive gun fired a high-velocity tungsten core 13.2 mm projectile, which proved effective against the early Allied tanks.

2 S.I.G. Swiss Mondragon Semi-Automatic Rifle - 7.5mm Mondragon - circa 1914-1916 - The Mexican-designed Mondragon semi-automatic rifle was one of the first semi-automatic rifles. Prior to the usage of machine guns in aerial combat, it was employed by German aviators, offsetting the pistols and rifles brought aloft by their French and British counterparts for aerial combat. The ability to mount a 100-round drum magazine later offered enhanced firepower capability for the Mondragon's selective-fire light machine gun version.

3 Mauser German Gew 98 Bolt-Action Sniper Rifle - 8mm Mauser - circa 1916 - Sniper rifles had both optical and iron sight capability.

1 Ludwig Loewe Waffenfabrik German
Borchardt Model 1893 Semi-Automatic Pistol
- .30 Borchardt - circa 1895 - Borchardt's
semi-auto pistol design derives in part from
the falling-block Sharps rifle action. It is one
of the earliest auto-pistols and the predecessor
of the Luger.

2 CS CGH Suhl German Single-Action Model
1883 Commission Reichsrevolver - 10.6mm
German Service - circa 1890.

3 Gebruder Mauser und Cie (Oberndorf,
Germany) Model 1879 Double-Action
Reichsrevolver - 10.6mm German Service
- circa 1890-1895 - Mauser produced both
revolvers and rifles for German military
contracts.

4 Giessler & Hast German Double-Action
Revolver - 10.6mm German Service - circa
1890-1895.

5 Dreyse German Model 1879 Commission
Double-Action Reichsrevolver - 10.6mm
German Service - circa 1880-1914 -
Reichsrevolvers were issued in both single-
action and double-action versions, with the
cylinder chambers individually numbered.
This example bears unit issue markings from
two artillery units.

6 Mauser German Model 1896 Broomhandle
Semi-Automatic Pistol - .30 Mauser - circa
1920 - Post WWI, many Mauser pistols
received shortened barrels to comply with
Versailles Treaty requirements.

1 Mauser German Model 1896 Broomhandle Export Semi-Automatic Pistol - 9mm Mauser - circa 1914-1918 - The 10-shot Mauser M1896 was widely exported both before and after WWI.

2 Deutsche Waffen und Munitionsfabriken German Model 1914 Artillery Luger Semi-Automatic Pistol with snail drum magazine - 9 mm - circa 1917 - Luger pistol carbines offered better range capability than standard sidearms.

3 Bergmann German Model 1896 Semi-Automatic Pistol - 5mm Bergmann - circa 1896-1910 - Bergmann's compact pistol design utilized a recoil spring within its bolt.

4 Mauser German Model 1896 Broomhandle Semi-Automatic Pistol - 7.63 Mauser - circa 1912-1916 - Mauser's M1896 had an integral magazine that could be quickly reloaded with a 10-shot stripper clip.

5 Charles Clement Belgian Model 1910 Semi-Automatic Pistol - 7.65mm - ca. 1910-1914 Private-purchase pistols were popular officer choices for personal protection.

6 Steyr Daimler Puch A.G. Austrian Model 1907 Roth Steyr Semi-Automatic Pistol - 8mm Roth-Steyr - circa 1909-1920 - Steyr's striker-fired design was later applied to the modern Glock pistol.

7 Steyr Daimler Puch A.G. Austrian Model 1911 Steyr-Hahn Semi-Automatic Pistol - 9mm Steyr - circa 1912-1916 - Steyr's M1911 design had an integral magazine using stripper clips.

8 Mannlicher Argentine Model 1905 Semi-Automatic Pistol - 7.63 Mannlicher - circa 1909-1929 - Mannlicher's M1905 pistol had limited European military acceptance.

9 Werder Austrian Single-Shot Pistol - 11mm Werder - circa 1869-1880 - Single-shot Werders were issued to horse-drawn artillery units.

1908 Bergmann-Bayard Semi-Automatic Pistol - 9mm Bergmann-Bayard - circa 1908-1918 - Bergmann-Bayard's M1908 Spanish military pistols were made in Belgium.

6 Langenhan German FL Selbstlader Semi-Automatic Pistol - 7.65 mm - ca. 1914-1916 A worn Langenhan's breechblock could blow into the shooter's face.

7 Mauser German Model 1896 Broomhandle Semi-Automatic Pistol - 9mm Mauser - circa 1916-1918 - 9mm Mauser M1896 pistols bore special grips marked with a red "9" to show they used a different ammunition.

8 Waffenfabrik Bern Swiss Model 1906 Luger Semi-Automatic Pistol - 7.65 Parabellum - circa 1906-1919 - Swiss Luger pistols continued in secondary military service well into the 1950s.

9 Deutsche Waffen & Munitions Fabriken German P.04 Naval Luger Semi-Automatic Pistol - 9mm Parabellum - circa 1916 - Adopted after a series of trials culminating in 1904 by the Kaiserliche Marine, the Luger P.04 was intend to replace revolvers in the hands of landing parties. This example bears issue markings from the dockyards of Wilhemshaven. Larger German capital ships, such as battleships, received up to 100 pistols.

10 Mauser German Model 1896 Broomhandle Semi-Automatic Pistol with shoulder stock - 7.63 Mauser - circa 1914-1916.

1 Waffenfabrik Steyr Austrian Steyr-Mannlicher Model 1890 Bolt-Action Rifle - 8mm x 50R - circa 1890-1893.

2 Steyr Oester Waffenfabrik Ges. Austrian Model 1909 Semi-Automatic Pistol - 7.65mm - circa 1909-1939 - Steyr's M1909 had a lower barrel axis for lighter apparent recoil.

3 Jager Waffenfabrik German Semi-Automatic Pistol - 7.65 mm - circa 1913-1915 - Jager's stamped construction pistol failed German military review in WWI.

4 Schwarzlose Gmbh German Model 1908 Semi-Automatic Pistol - 7.65 mm - circa 1908-1911 - Austrian Andreas Schwarzlose designed this semi-automatic pistol to function in a unique blow-forward recoil system. The barrel of this pistol moves forward on firing, exposing the expended cartridge casing, which is knocked away by a mechanical ejector. An unusual feature of this pistol is the grip safety that can be locked into the fire position by depressing a frame-mounted button.

5 Anciens Etablissements Pieper Belgian Model

1. U.S. Springfield T3E2 Semi-Automatic Rifle - .276 Pedersen caliber - circa 1931 – Forerunner of the M1 Garand, 20 of these rifles were tested in 1931. Although this general design was chosen, the caliber was changed to .30-06 for military service.

2. Vickers Armstrong Ltd. Vickers-Pederson Semi-Automatic Rifle - .276 Pederson - ca. 1926-1928 The Pedersen was the primary competitor of the Garand for adoption as the U.S. military semi-auto service rifle. It relied on a upward-acting toggle-joint action similar in operation to the Luger pistol, but improved with delayed blowback operation. To work within the special parameters of this design, Vickers-Pedersen rifles were intended to be used with wax-coated ammunition.

3. Harrington & Richardson M1 Semi-Automatic Rifle (sectionalized) - .30-06 - circa 1953 - This cutaway Garand was part of an electronic demonstration exhibit used by the U.S. Army.

4. U.S. Springfield M1 Garand Semi-Automatic Rifle - .30-06 - circa 1941 - This M1 Garand was built in 1941, the year America entered WWII.

5. Liu Chinese Prototype Semi-Automatic Rifle - 7.92 mm - circa 1918 - The innovative Liu was to be the semi-automatic rifle that China planned to arm itself with during the 1930s, but the boat carrying the machinery sunk. China remained at the bolt-action technology level for military rifles through World War II and Korea.

6. Japanese Type 5 Semi-Automatic Rifle - 7.7 mm - circa 1945 - Japanese semi-automatic rifle development during World War II resulted in the Type 5, a direct copy of the American Garand rifle in 7.7mm. A few unissued examples were located in a Japanese naval arsenal at the end of the war.

The Garand

John C. Garand was born in Canada on New Year's Day 1888. Moving to Connecticut at an early age, he developed an interest in firearms while helping his brother operate a shooting gallery. He obtained a position at the Springfield Armory and in 1919 began his work on developing a semi-automatic operating system for a rifle action.

His design, popularly known as the Garand Semi-Automatic Rifle, was ready for testing by 1930. Officially adopted by the U.S. Army in 1936, as the U.S. Rifle, Caliber .30, M1, the Garand is a gas-operated rifle with an 8-round en bloc clip inserted from the top. Ejecting each spent cartridge, the gun automatically loaded a new one with each trigger pull. General George S. Patton, Jr., dubbed the M1 **"the finest battle implement ever devised."** The United States was the only nation in World War II to equip its infantry with a semi-automatic rifle as a standard service arm. As such, arms historians have credited the M1 Garand with an important role in the Allies' victory in World War II.

Over four million M1 Garand rifles were manufactured during World War II. More were built during the Korean War and M1 Rifle serial numbers reach into the six million range. John C. Garand died in Springfield, Massachusetts, on February 16, 1974.

1 U.S. General Motors - Inland Manufacturing Division M1A1 Semi-Automatic Carbine - .30 Carbine - circa 1943.

2 U.S. Remington Model 1903A1 Bolt-Action Rifle - .30-06 - circa 1942 - Rock Island Arsenal machinery was adapted by Remington to produce M1903A1 rifles in WWII.

3 U.S. Smith-Corona Model 1903A3 Bolt-Action Rifle - .30-06 - circa 1944 - Smith-Corona, a former typewriter company, tooled up to make M1903A3 rifles in WWII.

4 U.S. Johnson Automatics Model 1941 Semi-Automatic Rifle - .30-06 - circa 1941 - The Johnson's 10-round magazine could be quickly loaded with stripper clips.

5 U.S. Winchester Model of 1918 Browning Automatic Rifle (BAR) - .30-06 - circa 1944 - The Browning Automatic Rifle was developed to replace unreliable French light machine guns, and although it entered service late in World War I, this firearm was a mainstay of American forces through WWII and Korea. A gas-operated, selective-fire arm intended for squad-level automatic fire, the BAR suffered only from the limited firepower capacity of its 20-round box magazine.

The World at War: World War II
The global conflict, fought between 1939 and 1945, is considered the largest and most destructive war in history. Truly a world war, campaigns were fought in Europe, Asia, Africa, North America (Alaska), and the islands in the Pacific. Total casualties numbered 60-80 million, including the largest number of civilians ever to die as a result of one war. The submachine gun, light machine gun, and semi-automatic sidearms were used in great numbers, further changing the shape and scope of infantry tactics as platoon and squad strength unit actions defined typical combat experiences.

1. U.S. Auto Ordnance Thompson M1A1 Submachine Gun - .45 ACP - circa 1980.

2. U.S. Stevens Model 620 Slide-Action Shotgun - 12 gauge - circa 1944-1945 - Many WWII-era commercial models of slide-action shotguns, such as this Stevens 620, were adapted for military service with the addition of metal handguards that partially covered the barrel and allowed the attachment of a bayonet near the muzzle. These shotguns were used for secondary military roles, freeing up rifles that could be sent to the front lines.

3. U.S. Winchester Model 12 Slide-Action Riot Shotgun - 12 gauge - circa 1943 - Winchester slide-action shotguns were modified to take a rifle bayonet with a barrel handguard.

4. Remington Model 11 Shotgun - 12 gauge - circa 1944 - Semi-auto shotguns were used by Army Air Corps trainees in aerial target shooting simulations.

5. Victory Training Rifle - circa 1941 - Wooden training rifles were utilized in both WWI and WWII eras to allow more drilling and arms handling instruction for soldiers without the need for ammunition.

WWII: U.S.

Products of "The Great Arsenal of Democracy," arms and equipment made in the United States, were directly responsible for the victory of democratic ideals over those of dictators and fascists. The entire country was placed on a war economy in 1942 and all manufacturing and even agricultural resources were turned to the war effort. With men serving on the battlefront, women workers replaced them at their posts in the armories and firearms manufacturing plants throughout the country, becoming competent and skilled contributors to the war effort. Millions of rifles, pistols, tanks, and planes were produced in the greatest manufacturing effort in history. Major gun manufacturers suspended their sporting lines and produced arms for the infantry and Marines. Colt and Winchester produced a dizzying array of arms with Remington and Smith & Wesson supplying a great deal of needed firepower.

Companies that in peacetime produced items such as jukeboxes, sewing machines and typewriters produced rifles and pistols. In just the field of small arms, the list of manufacturers is impressive:

COMPANY -- PEACETIME GOODS -- WAR PRODUCTION

Guide Lamp Division General Motors -- Automotive Components -- OSS Liberator Pistol
National Postal Meter -- Metering Machines -- M1 Carbines
Remington Rand -- Typewriters -- M1911A1 Pistols
IBM -- Business Machines -- M1 Carbines
Smith-Corona -- Typewriters -- M1903A3 Rifles
Quality Hardware -- Sheet Metal Fabricating Machines -- M1 Carbines
Union Switch & Signal -- Railroad Equipment -- M1911A1 Pistols
Rock O La Manufacturing -- Jukeboxes -- M1 Carbines
Singer Manufacturing -- Sewing Machines -- M1911A1 Pistols
Inland Division General Motors -- Automobile Steering Wheels -- M1 Carbines
Standard Products Co. -- Automobile Window -- M1 Carbines

1 Winchester Model 69 Bolt-Action Rifle with sectionalized Maxim suppressor - .22 long rifle - circa 1935-1941 – Reportedly sent to England for training in covert use of suppressed arms.

2 U.S. Auto Ordnance Model 1928 Thompson Submachine Gun (deactivated) - .45 ACP - circa 1940 - Discovered on the Anzio beachhead, this M1928 SMG was reportedly used to eliminate 19 Germans by a British soldier.

3 U.S. Underwood-Elliot-Fisher M1 Semi-Automatic Carbine - .30 Carbine - circa 1944 - Designed to serve as a longer-ranged replacement for handguns and for military personnel who did not require the full-sized M1 Garand, the M1 carbine was a lightweight semi-automatic rifle that was widely issued in both European and Pacific campaigns. Over six-and-a-half million M1 carbines were produced during the WWII years. Underwood-Elliot-Fisher made 19 components for the 62-part M1 carbine that were used by 10 different contractors to assemble guns.

4 U.S. Springfield M1 Garand Semi-Automatic Rifle with Grenade Sight, M7A3 Grenade Launcher - .30-'06 - circa 1945 - Firing rifle grenades from an M1 Garand required a special blank cartridge.

5 U.S. Remington Model 1903A4 Bolt-Action Rifle with telescopic sight - .30-06 - circa 1944 - A quick adaptation for the venerable Springfield M1903 pattern rifle to convert it for sniping service was done by the addition of a modified Weaver 330 telescopic sight. While expedient, the low magnification and low moisture resistance of the optic-challenged long-range shooters of the M1903A4 rifle. Its telescopic mount base prevented reloading via stripper clips.

Thompson
John T. Thompson was born in Kentucky in 1860 and graduated from the U.S. Military Academy at West Point in 1882. He joined the U.S. Army Ordnance Department and retired as a Brigadier General in 1914. He patented numerous devices for automatic small arms. His greatest invention, however, was the Thompson submachine gun. Chambered for the .45 ACP cartridge, this air-cooled selective-fire firearm used a delayed blowback action creating an extremely reliable firearm. The submachine gun, manufactured on contract by Colt and the Auto Ordnance Company, was capable of firing from a two-column box magazine, holding 20 rounds or drum magazines with either a 50- or 100-round capacity.

Thompson's gun was first used in combat by the U.S. Marine Corps in Nicaragua in 1925. Widely purchased by police departments and the U.S. military, the Thompson submachine gun was widely used by both U.S. and allied troops during World War II. The use of this firearm in the hands of legendary lawmen and infamous gangsters alike in the early part of the 20th Century earned it the moniker "the gun that made the '20s roar!"

1 Smith & Wesson 38-100 British Service Revolver -- .38 S&W – ca. 1941 – Identical to the S&W U.S. Victory Model, except for the chambering. Over 500,000 were produced during the war years; replaced grips.

2 Julian Hatcher's S&W Victory Model, serial number V3 -- .38 Special – About 250,000 S&W .38 Hand Ejector revolvers were produced for the U.S. military during WWII, during which time they were known as "Victory Models." When the standard serial number sequence hit 1,000,000 the numbers started over with a "V" for Victory prefix, with serial number V-1 presented to Pres. Franklin Roosevelt. This gun is serial number V-3 and was given a fine commercial finish for presentation to the head of Ordnance, Gen. Julian Hatcher, who later became an editor for the NRA's *American Rifleman* magazine.

3 U.S. Colt Commando Double-Action Revolver - .38 Special - circa 1942-1945 - After WWII, many Victory Models were transferred to law enforcement agencies.

4 U.S. Smith & Wesson Model 1917 Double-Action Revolver - .45 ACP - circa 1935 - Ensign John Wesson (grandson of the S&W founder) received this M1917 when he graduated from the U.S. Naval Academy.

5 U.S. Union Switch & Signal Model 1911A1 Semi-Automatic Pistol - .45 ACP - circa 1943 - Second smallest producer of the M1911A1 pistol in WWII.

6 U.S. Colt Model 1911A1 Semi-Automatic Pistol - .45 ACP - circa 1943 - Finishes on the M1911A1 went from bluing to parkerizing as the war went on.

7 Smith & Wesson 38-100 British Service Revolver -- .38 S&W – ca. 1944 – Note the late war "Black Magic" phosphate-type finish compared to the earlier commercial finishes. After the war, many Victory and 38-100 revolvers were issued to European police forces, and marked accordingly, such as this one.

8 U.S. Smith & Wesson Model 1917 Double-Action Revolver - .22 rimfire (converted) - circa 1943 - This M1917 was used by Norwegian resistance fighters in WWII.

WWII: Allies

In the first years of World War II (Sept. 1939 to June 1941), the British Empire and Commonwealth stood alone, allied against the German-Italian tide. The Soviet Union joined the Allies after Germany invaded Russia in June 1941. The United States maintained a formal stance of neutrality until the Japanese sneak attack at Pearl Harbor on December 7, 1941, brought the nation into the war as an Allied Power. Prior to that time the American public had been generally sympathetic toward the plight of the British. Legislation was passed in Congress allowing for the transfer of arms, ammunition, and vitally needed equipment such as planes, ships, and vehicles to England under the provisions of the Lend-Lease Act. Because British society lacked a heritage of personal firearms ownership, American citizens were encouraged to ship their personal firearms to England in an effort to save a British home. Over 7,000 arms were sent and issued to Home Guard units for local defense.

The Sixguns of World War II

Although the 1911A1 pistol was the standard American issue sidearm of WWII, the demand was such that large numbers of revolvers were produced as well. During WWI, S&W and Colt each adapted their large-frame revolvers to fire the standard-issue rimless .45 ACP cartridges by using sheet metal "moon clips" that held six rounds in position to be fired. These were both named the Model 1917 and contined in use during WWII. The production of the Smith & Wesson factory during WWII went to the war effort, primarily making military versions of their popular six-shot .38 Special Military & Police revolvers. These came to be known as Victory Models, and a V prefix was added to the serial number. The Colt counterpart was the Commando Model. S&W also made the Military & Police in .38 S&W for the British Commonwealth nations, including Britain, Canada, Australia, and New Zealand, with the model designation .38-200 British Service Revolver.

1. Smith & Wesson Model 1940 Semi-Automatic Light Rifle - 9mm Parabellum - circa 1940-1941 – A flawed design, almost all of the S&W Light Rifles were destroyed after WWII.

2. U.S. General Motors Guide Lamp Division FP-45 Liberator Single-Shot Pistol - .45 ACP - circa 1943 - Classified as a flare projector to keep its wartime development a secret, General Motors produced each Liberator pistol for less than $2.40, including 10 rounds of .45 ammunition and a pictorial guide sheet on its usage. Approximately one million Liberators were manufactured at GE's Guide Lamp Division to be dropped to resistance forces behind enemy lines, but most were scrapped after WWII ended.

3. Winchester New Haven, CT, Accuracy Test Fixture - .50 Browning - circa 1942 - Wartime production requirements resulted in faster manufacturing. To test sample lots many companies relied on test fixtures that could be used to chronograph ammunition for velocity and pressure, ensuring that only quality materials were forwarded to the armed forces.

4. Oversized Instructional Cutaway M1 Garand Training Model - circa 1950 – Shown with standard M1 Garand for scale. Constructed of painted wood, this large-scale model of an M1 Garand rifle is cutaway on one side to demonstrate the operating mechanism. Equipped with inert cartridges, the model could be shown in front of an audience as part of a small arms training familiarization.

1. Enfield No. 5 Mk I Bolt-Action Jungle Carbine with No. 5 Mk I Bayonet - .303 British - circa 1945.

2. Savage No. 4 Mk I Bolt-Action Rifle w/ No. 7 Folding Bayonet - .303 British - circa 1941 - Tool room prototype built prior to U.S. entry into WWII at Savage.

3. Enfield SMLE Mk III Bolt-Action Rifle - .303 British - circa 1917 - Older WWI British rifles were recycled for WWII use.

4. MAS French Model 1936 Bolt-Action Rifle - 7.5mm M29 - circa 1937-1940 - The French MAS rifle had a weaker action than the Mauser.

5. French St. Etienne Model 1886/93 (R-35) Bolt-Action Carbine - 8mm Lebel - circa 1939 - Rebuilt with spare parts, older French rifles went into WWII service.

6. French Lebel Model 1907/15 Bolt-Action Rifle - 7.5mm - circa 1917 - Altered for more powerful cartridges, older French rifles were pressed into service.

7. Ross Model 1905 Straight-Pull Bolt-Action Rifle - .303 British - circa 1914 - Many Ross rifles were used only as training arms.

1. Mosin Nagant Finnish Model 27 Bolt-Action Rifle - 7.62mm x 54R - circa 1933 - Captured Russian rifles served Finnish forces in WWII.

2. Russian Mosin Nagant M91-30 Sniper Rifle - 7.62mm x 54R - circa 1940 - Crude in all but accuracy, Russian sniper rifles were built from regular production guns. An actual sniper rifle with a reproduction scope.

3. Russian Mosin Nagant Model 1944 Bolt-Action Carbine - 7.62mm x 54R - circa 1944-1945 - Late-war M/N carbines were fitted with a folding bayonet.

4. Russian Tokarev Model 1938 SVT Semi-Automatic Rifle - 7.62mm x 54R - ca. 1940 Early semi-auto Soviet rifles had operating issues in cold weather.

5. Russian Mosin Nagant Model 1891 Bolt-Action Rifle - 7.62mm x 54R - ca. 1897-1905 Russian-rebuilt rifles for WWII included pre-1900 contract arms.

1

2

3

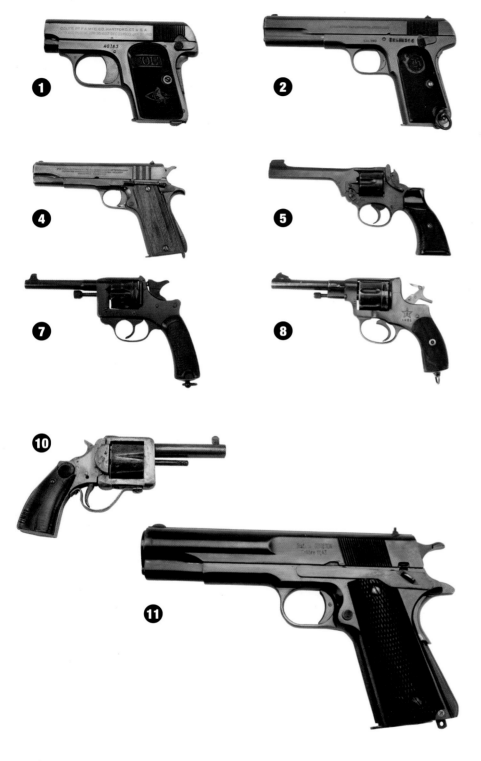

4

5

6

7

8

9

10

11

no grip safety feature.

5 Enfield No. 2 Mk I Double-Action Revolver - .38 S&W (.38-200 British) - circa 1932 Bobbed hammers were done for better maneuvering in tight quarters.

6 Fabrique Nationale/Inglis P-35 Hi-Power Semi-Automatic Pistol - 9mm Parabellum - circa 1944-1945 - Chinese contract copies of the P35 pistol were made by flame pantograph.

7 St. Etienne French Nagant Model 1892 Double-Action Ordnance Revolver - 8mm - circa 1904 - Older obsolete French revolvers continued in WWII service.

8 Russian Nagant Model 1895 Double-Action Service Revolver - 7.62mm Nagant - circa 1931 - Well after military semi-auto pistols were in production, Russia continued to make military revolvers.

9 Russian Tokarev Model 1933 Semi-Automatic Pistol - 7.62 Tokarev - circa 1943 - Copying certain Colt-Browning handgun features, the Tokarev T33 semi-automatic pistol incorporates a modified hammer/sear assembly that can be removed as a unit.

10 Philippine Resistance Revolver - .38 cartridge - circa 1942 - Crudely constructed, this handmade handgun was built by members of the Phillipine resistance using only a file and drill. Reportedly, it claimed the lives of six enemy soldiers and was fired several hundred times without failure.

11 Fabrica de Armas Mexico Obregon Semi-Automatic Pistol - .45 caliber - circa 1930-1936 - Built in Mexico City, the semi-automatic Obregon pistol combines elements of the Steyr-Hahn barrel system with the Colt-Browning M1911 design. Most of the 1,000 pistols made were sold through the Mexican commercial market.

1 Colt Model 1908 Hammerless 25 Caliber Semi-Automatic Pistol - .25 ACP - circa 1933 - Colt's Baby .25 handgun was the company's smallest pocket pistol.

2 Husqvarna Swedish Model 1903 Semi-Automatic Pistol - .380 ACP - circa 1903-1940 - Re-chambered for U.S. post-war importation.

3 Enfield No. 1 Mk VI Double-Action Revolver - .455 Webley - circa 1923 - A between-the-wars Webley pattern .455 revolver.

4 Ballester-Molina British Contract Pistol - .45 ACP - circa 1940 - British military contracts for WWII sidearms included more than 10,000 Ballester-Molina-built copies of Colt's M1911 semi-automatic design. Similar to the Colt M1911A1, Ballester-Molina pistols had

1 Russian SVT Sniper Semi-Automatic Rifle -
7.62mm x 54 Russian - circa 1941 - Russian
semi-automatic service rifles used the same 7.62 x
54mm ammunition employed with Mosin Nagant
bolt-action rifles, but the lighter construction of
the SVT models results in high attrition from parts
failure.

2 B.S.A./Holland & Holland No. 4 Mk I (T)
Bolt-Action Sniper Rifle - .303 British - circa
1944-1945 - Selected No. 4 rifles in World War II,
chosen for accuracy, were forwarded to Holland
& Holland for further accurizing and telescopic
sight fitting. The completed sniper rifles were
placed in transit crates, paired with scout regiment
telescopes.

3 Japanese Nagoya Army Arsenal Type 97 Arisaka
Bolt-Action Sniper Rifle with telescopic sight -
6.5mm - circa 1942 - Japanese sniper rifles were
standard production guns fitted with optics.

4 Japanese Type 99 Bolt-Action Sniper Rifle with
scope - 7.7 mm - circa 1943 - Unlike European
tradition, Japanese sniper rifle optics were aligned
on each rifle to a specific point of aim at a set
distance. There were no external adjustments on
Japanese sniper optics and as the rifle's point of
impact changed due to changes in humidity, their
users learned to compensate.

5 Schmidt-Rubin Swiss K-31/43 Straight-Pull Sniper
Rifle - 7.5mm - circa 1943 - Nearly 2,000 of these
Swiss K-31/43 straight-pull sniper rifles were
manufactured with an integral 2.8X telescopic
sight mounted on a swing-out base that allowed
the iron sights to also be utilized.

1 Mauser (byf) German K98k Sniper Rifle - 8mm Mauser - circa 1941-1945.

2 Mauser German G41 (m) rifle - 8mm - circa 1942 - Issued only in limited numbers in Italy. The Mauser-made G41(m) semi-automatic rifle had the capability to use a rearward bolt handle to continue to function the action if the gas-operated semi-automatic mechanism failed.

3 DWM (Deutsche Waffen und Munitions Fabriken; Karlsruhe, Germany) P.08 Luger Semi-Automatic Pistol - 9 mm - circa 1918 British-captured handguns such as this one required proofing in the U.K. before re-issue.

4 Japanese Type 1 (Folding Stock) Paratrooper rifle - 6.5mm Japanese - circa 1941 - To provide a compact unit while parachuting, Japanese armorers adapted a hinged, folding stock for the Type 1 Paratrooper rifle, constructed from an otherwise standard Arisaka bolt-action rifle.

5 Walther German Gewehr 43 Semi-Automatic Rifle with telescopic sight - 8mm Mauser - circa 1943-1944 - Utilizing roughly cast parts, along with forged and stamped components, Germany's Gewehr 43 provided an expedient semi-automatic service rifle that blended a gas system similar to the Russian Tokarev with a bolt mechanism derived from the earlier G41 rifles made by Walther.

WWII: AXIS

Germany, Italy, and Japan, known as the Axis powers, were the aggressor nations in the global struggle known as World War II. Their primary infantry armament did not differ much from that used in World War I. For these nations, the standard infantry rifle was still a bolt action, although squads and platoon-size units were supplemented with submachine guns and light machine guns on an unprecedented scale, making them very effective.

1. J. G. Anschutz German Wehrsportkarabiner Bolt-Action Carbine - .22 rimfire - circa 1937-1938 - Anschutz's training rifles were part of the Third Reich mobilization for military service; school-age programs featured small arms familiarization with rimfire counterparts resembling the larger-issued 98k rifles.

2. Scotti Italian Model X Semi-Automatic Rifle - 6.5 Italian - circa 1933 - Only 250 of these semi-auto rifles were tested by the Italian military.

3. Waffenfabrik Brunn AG Czech DOT Karabiner 98k Bolt-Action Rifle with grenade launcher - 8mm Mauser - circa 1943-1944 This Czech K98k has a grenade launcher attachment and side-mounted sights.

4. Mauser-Werke German K98k/ZF-41 Bolt-Action Sniper Rifle - 8mm - circa 1941-1944 - WWII German army marksmen employed rifles fitted with the low-power ZF-41 optic.

5. Walther German Volksturm Gewehr (VG-1) Rifle - 8mm Mauser - circa 1945 - Built by Walther as a last-ditch firearm, the VG1 bolt-action was a crudely constructed blend of components from other German military guns that could no longer be produced at the time. VG1s were distinguished by rejected magazines, barrels, and other parts from Gewehr 43 rifles as well as crudely band-sawed wood stocks.

6. Metallwaren Budapest Hungarian Model 98/40 Bolt-Action Rifle - 8mm Mauser - circa 1943 - Hungarian contract M98/40 rifles had expedient two-piece stocks.

7. Waffenfabrik Brunn AG Czech Mauser Model 33/40 Bolt-Action Carbine - 8mm Mauser - circa 1941-1943 - WWII German mountain troops employed the light M33/40 carbine.

1 Walther German Model 41W Semi-Automatic Rifle - 8mm Mauser - circa 1942 - Walther built semi-auto rifles in early WWII to provide firepower for German infantry.

2 Carl Gustafs Stads Gevarsfaktori Swedish Model 96 Sniper Bolt-Action Rifle with telescopic sight - 6.5mm - circa 1917 - Germany seized occupied armaments and reissued these to their own forces.

3 Walther German K43 Semi-Automatic Rifle - 8mm Mauser - circa 1945 - Circa-1945 K43 rifles were crudely assembled.

4 Berliner-Luebecker Maschinenfabrik German Gewehr 41 Semi-Automatic Rifle - 8mm - circa 1942-1943 - The G41 was intended to replace the aging bolt-action rifles that Germany had used in World War I and also to counter Russian semi-auto arms such as the Tokarev rifle. The intricate machining required for manufacture led to production delays, resulting in the design being replaced by the Gewehr 43 rifle.

5 F. B. Radom Polish WZ-29 Bolt-Action Short Rifle with winter trigger - 8mm Mauser - circa 1939.

6 Radom Polish Wz 29 Bolt-Action Rifle - 8mm Mauser - circa 1931.

1   Mannlicher Carcano Italian Model 41 Bolt-Action Rifle - 6.5mm Italian - circa 1942.

2   Brescia Italian Mannlicher Carcano Model 91/24 Bolt-Action Rifle - 6.5mm Italian - circa 1942.

3   R. E. Terni Italian Mannlicher Carcano Model 38 Bolt-Action Rifle with Model 1938 Folding Bayonet - 7.35mm Italian - circa 1939 - This Italian Carcano carbine variant incorporated a permanently affixed folding bayonet. While chambered for the 7.35mm cartridge, many arms were rechambered for the earlier 6.5mm to mitigate ammunition distribution issues later in the war.

4   Brescia Italian Mannlicher Carcano Model 1938 Bolt-Action Rifle - 7.35mm Italian - circa 1938-1942.

5   Terni Arsenal Italian Mannlicher-Carcano Model 91/29 Bolt-Action Carbine with Tromboni Launchi Bombe Grenade Launcher - 6.5 Italian - circa 1930 - Fitted with a side-mounted grenade launcher that required removing the rifle's bolt to fire grenades, the Italian Tromboni Launchi Carabini was reported to generate substantial recoil on firing.

6   Gardone Italian Model 1891 Mannlicher Carcano Bolt-Action Rifle - 6.5mm Italian - circa 1924.

7   Gardone Italian Fascist Youth Bolt-Action Carbine - 6.5mm Italian - circa 1942-1943 - Fascist youth groups received small-scale arms to match the size of their members.

1 Japanese Tokyo Juki Kogyo Type 99 Arisaka Bolt-Action Rifle - 7.7 mm - circa 1942-1943.

2 Japanese Type 38 Arisaka Bolt-Action Rifle - 6.5mm - circa 1939.

3 Japanese Type I Bolt-Action Rifle - 6.5mm - circa 1938-1939 - Italian contractors produced Carcano-based Type I rifles for Japanese military contracts.

4 Japanese Type 44 Bolt-Action Carbine - 6.5mm - circa 1912-1942.

5 Japanese Toyo Kogyo Type 99 Arisaka Bolt-Action Rifle with Nagoya Arsenal Type 30 Bayonet - 7.7 mm - circa 1941 - This Type 99 was captured on Guadalcanal.

6 Japanese Type 20 Murata Bolt-Action Carbine - 8mm - circa 1880-1898 - The Type 20 was the first Japanese-designed magazine bolt-action repeater.

1 Japanese Koishikawa Arsenal Type 30 Arisaka Bolt-Action Rifle - 6.5mm - circa 1897-1905.

2 Japanese Kokura Army Arsenal Type 99 Arisaka Bolt-Action Carbine - 6.5mm - circa 1943-1944 - Two-piece stocks were required because the Japanese mainland did not support large trees.

3 Japanese Koishikawa Arsenal Type 35 Arisaka Bolt-Action Rifle - 6.5mm - circa 1944-1945.

4 Japanese Kokura Army Arsenal Type 38 Arisaka Bolt-Action Rifle - 6.5mm - circa 1905-1938.

5 Japanese Kokura Army Arsenal Type 99 Arisaka Bolt-Action Rifle - 7.7 mm - circa 1942.

6 Japanese Nagoya Army Arsenal Type 2 Arisaka Bolt-Action Rifle - 7.7 mm - circa 1940.

1 Ceskoslovenska Zbrojovka Brno Japanese Contract VZ-24 Bolt-Action Rifle - 8mm Mauser - circa 1937 Czech VZ-24 rifles were ordered for Japanese Special Naval Landing Forces.

2 Japanese Tokyo Arsenal Arisaka Bolt-Action Pressure Test Gun - 6.5mm - circa 1940 - Pressure test guns allowed quality checks on wartime ammunition.

3 Chinese Chiang Kai-Shek Short Model Mauser-Pattern Bolt-Action Rifle - 8mm Mauser - circa 1936-1949 – Also known as the Type 24, this rifle was based on the German K98 and was used by China against Japan.

4 Japanese Model 1922 Light Machine Gun Trainer - circa 1930 - Japanese military training for the invasion of China used an unusual machine gun trainer that required no ammunition. A hose brought carbide gas to a sparking element inside the receiver that detonated the gas as it was cranked. The sound of the detonations emulated actual firing for familiarization purposes.

5 Japanese Nagoya Army Arsenal Type 99 last-ditch Arisaka Bolt-Action Rifle - 7.7 mm - circa 1944-1945 - Throughout World War II, Japan suffered from lack of resources. In the final months of the conflict, marginal-quality bolt-action rifles, missing non-essential features, were the best that could be manufactured. Even these last-ditch rifles were made with chrome-lined bores to protect against corrosive effects of wartime ammunition.

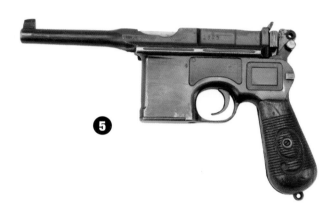

1. Mauser German P.08 Luger Black Widow Semi-Automatic Pistol - 9 mm - circa 1941 These Luger variants were called "Black Widows" by collectors because of the gun's black plastic grips.

2. Kreighoff German P.08 Luger Semi-Automatic Pistol - 9mm Parabellum - circa 1936-1937 - Kreighoff received a contract for 10,000 pistols for the German Luftwaffe in 1935.

3. Mauser/Deutsche Waffen und Munitions Fabriken German P.08 Luger Semi-Automatic Pistol - 9mm Parabellum - circa 1939.

4. Mauser German P-38 Semi-Automatic Pistol - 9mm Parabellum - circa 1942 - To increase military handgun manufacturing in World War II, Germany sought a design that could be mass produced faster than their existing Luger pistol. Walther's double-action HP design, a 9mm semi-automatic that could be made cheaper than the Luger, was adopted as the P-38 and subsequently contracted for production by Mauser and Spreewerke.

5. Mauser German Model 1896 Broomhandle Military Semi-Automatic Pistol - 9mm Parabellum - circa 1913-1914 - Versailles Treaty requirements resulted in shorter-barreled German military handguns.

6. Fabrique Nationale/Browning P-35 Hi-Power Semi-Automatic Pistol - 9mm Parabellum - circa 1942-1944 - FN's P-35 provided 13 shots from its double-stack magazine.

7. Spreewerke GmbH Metallwarenfabrik German P.38 Semi-Automatic Pistol - 9mm Parabellum - circa 1943-1944 - Speerwerke produced the lowest-quality P-38 pistols during WWII.

1. J. P. Sauer & Sohn German Model 38H Double-Action Semi-Automatic Pistol - 7.65mm - circa 1938-1945 - During World War II, German government requirements resulted in most of the production run of the Sauer 38 pistol being taken. This pistol was one of the first modern pistols with a de-cocking capability.

2. CZ Czech Model 1924 Semi-Automatic Pistol - 9mm Kurz (short) - circa 1924-1938.

3. Deutsche Werke A.G. German Ortgies Semi-Automatic Pistol - 7.65mm - circa 1920-1928 Ortgies pistols had a grip safety whose spring also served as the driving force for the striker.

4. Sauer German Model 1930 Berhorden Semi-Automatic Pistol - .32 ACP - circa 1930-1937 Fitted with chamber indicator, trigger also had a security lock to prevent firing.

5. Walther German PPK Semi-Automatic Pistol - 7.65 mm - circa 1942 - This pistol is one of two confiscated from Nazi saboteur teams landed by submarine in 1942. Two four-man teams were set ashore on Long Island and in Florida with explosives.

6. Fegyvergyar Hungarian Model 37 Semi-Automatic Pistol - 7.65mm - circa 1941 - Part of 50,000-gun order in 1941 for Luftwaffe.

7. Walther German Model PP Semi-Automatic Pistol - 7.65mm - circa 1942.

8. Mauser German Model 1934 Semi-Automatic Pistol - 7.65 mm - circa 1942 - Pistol is second seized from Nazi saboteur teams landed in 1942 on Long Island and Florida.

9. Mauser German HSc pistol - .32 ACP - circa 1945 - War trophy brought home by Frank Drummond, 75th Infantry.

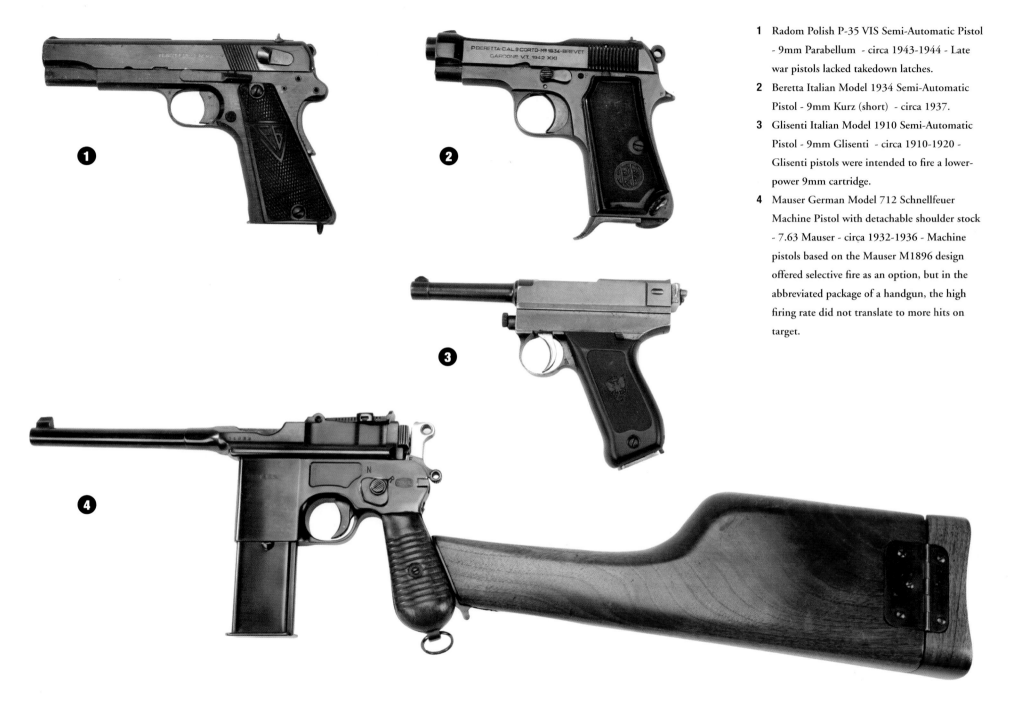

1 Radom Polish P-35 VIS Semi-Automatic Pistol - 9mm Parabellum - circa 1943-1944 - Late war pistols lacked takedown latches.

2 Beretta Italian Model 1934 Semi-Automatic Pistol - 9mm Kurz (short) - circa 1937.

3 Glisenti Italian Model 1910 Semi-Automatic Pistol - 9mm Glisenti - circa 1910-1920 - Glisenti pistols were intended to fire a lower-power 9mm cartridge.

4 Mauser German Model 712 Schnellfeuer Machine Pistol with detachable shoulder stock - 7.63 Mauser - circa 1932-1936 - Machine pistols based on the Mauser M1896 design offered selective fire as an option, but in the abbreviated package of a handgun, the high firing rate did not translate to more hits on target.

1 Unceta y Compania S.A. Astra Model 900 Semi-Automatic Pistol - .30 Mauser - circa 1928-1936 - Astra 900 pistols were used by Spanish Civil Police and National Guard units during WWII.

2 Handmade Japanese copy of Mauser Model 1896 Broomhandle Semi-Automatic Pistol - 8mm Nambu - circa 1944 - This handmade pistol was captured by PFC Edward A. Baldin, USMC, during the invasion of Peleliu.

3 Japanese Nagoya Army Arsenal Type 14 Nambu Semi-Automatic Pistol - 8mm Nambu - circa 1944 - Fitted with both rotating safety

and magazine safety.

4 Japanese Tokyo Artillery Arsenal Type 26 Double-Action Revolver - 9mm - circa 1893-1925 - The 9mm Nambu round used in the Type 26 revolver is used by no other handgun in the world.

5 Japanese Baby Nambu Semi-Automatic Pistol - 7mm Mauser - circa 1909-1929 - Presentation arms were given to graduates of Japanese military schools.

6 Edgar Rice Burroughs' Japanese Nagoya Army Arsenal Type 94 Semi-Automatic Pistol - 8mm Nambu - circa 1944 - Burroughs, creator of

Tarzan, received this pistol while a Pacific war correspondent.

7 Japanese Tokyo Artillery Arsenal Model 1902 Papa Nambu Semi-Automatic Pistol - 8mm Nambu - circa 1909-1926 - The Papa Nambu pistol incorporated a grip safety and could mount a shoulder stock.

8 Japanese Type 14 Nambu pistol - 8mm Nambu - circa 1937 - Pre-war Nambu pistols had rounded, small trigger guards.

9 Japanese Type 90 3-Barrel Flare Pistol - 28 mm - circa 1943 - Japanese naval units with poorly functioning radio systems

communicated though aerial flares and these triple-barrel flare pistols allowed the ability to launch multiple colored signals.

10 Walther SLE Stainless Steel Flare Pistol - 26mm - circa 1941 - Intended for submarine service, a very limited number of flare pistols were constructed of stainless alloys to resist corrosion in marine environments.

11 German Flare Pistol - 26mm - circa 1943-1944 - Stampings were used to build German machine pistols, carbines, as well as flare pistols.

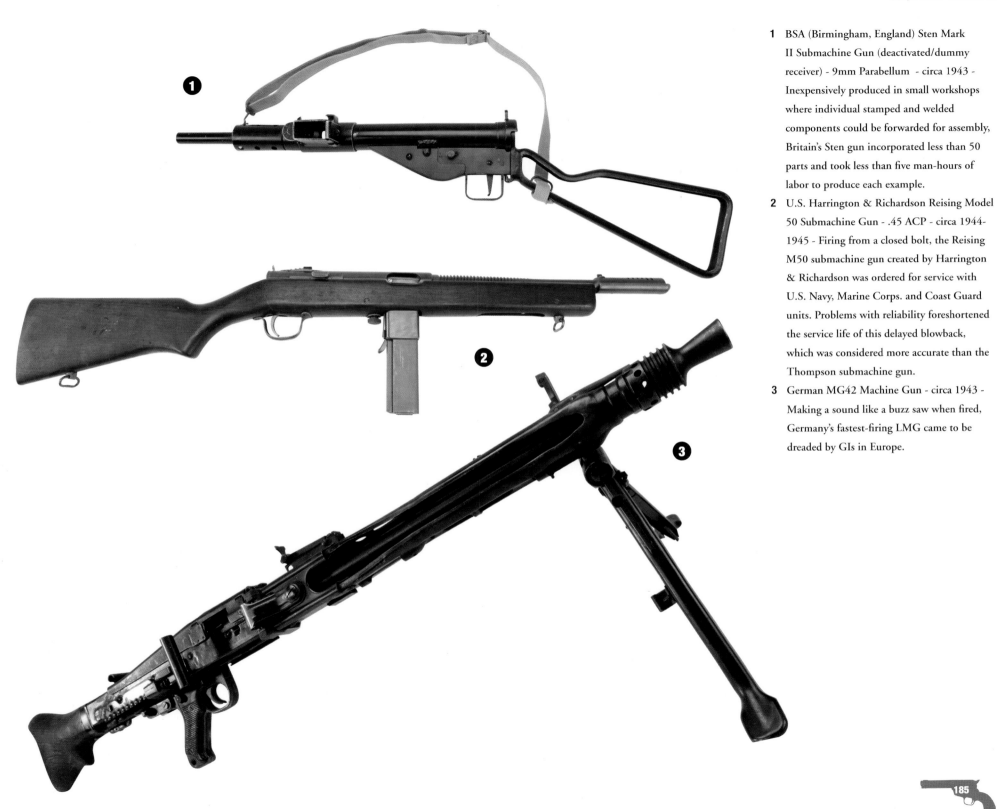

1   BSA (Birmingham, England) Sten Mark
    II Submachine Gun (deactivated/dummy
    receiver) - 9mm Parabellum - circa 1943 -
    Inexpensively produced in small workshops
    where individual stamped and welded
    components could be forwarded for assembly,
    Britain's Sten gun incorporated less than 50
    parts and took less than five man-hours of
    labor to produce each example.

2   U.S. Harrington & Richardson Reising Model
    50 Submachine Gun - .45 ACP - circa 1944-
    1945 - Firing from a closed bolt, the Reising
    M50 submachine gun created by Harrington
    & Richardson was ordered for service with
    U.S. Navy, Marine Corps. and Coast Guard
    units. Problems with reliability foreshortened
    the service life of this delayed blowback,
    which was considered more accurate than the
    Thompson submachine gun.

3   German MG42 Machine Gun - circa 1943 -
    Making a sound like a buzz saw when fired,
    Germany's fastest-firing LMG came to be
    dreaded by GIs in Europe.

1. U.S. Colt Model 1918A2 Browning Automatic Rifle - .30-06 - circa 1942-1945.

2. U.S. M2 Selective Fire Carbine with flash hider - .30 Carbine - circa 1945 - With six million M1 carbines in service, conversion to selective-fire began as an armorer conversion package offered in late 1944. The Korean conflict saw many semi-auto M1 carbines upgraded to M2 (selective-fire) capability.

3. U.S. Ithaca Model 1911A1 Semi-Automatic Pistol - .45 ACP - circa 1943-1945.

4. U.S. General Motors Guide Lamp Division M3 Submachine Gun - .45 ACP - circa 1943-1945 - Approximately 680,000 M3 Grease Guns were manufactured by General Motor's Guide Lamp Division and by the Ithaca Gun Company during WWII and Korea. This inexpensive .45 caliber submachine remained in U.S. military inventory through the Gulf Wars for tanker crews.

5. Russian PTRD Sniper rifle - .50 Browning - circa 1950 - Converted from a Russian PTRD anti-tank rifle by major William Brophy during the Korean War, this single-shot rifle was fitted with a barrel from a U.S. M2 .50 BMG and a Unertl telescopic sight.

Modern Warfare: Korea

The United States entered this conflict – often called a police action – on behalf of the United Nations in June 1950. The war pitted the Democratic People's Republic of Korea (North Korea) – who were backed by the Communist Chinese and the Soviet Union – against the Republic of Korea (South Korea) – backed by the United States and the United Nations. The M1 Rifle remained the standard service rifle of the United States and many of our United Nation allies. Some countries still clung to the effective and powerful, but slow, bolt action rifle. Australian infantry continued to use the same rifle that they had used on the shores of Gallipoli some 40 years before.

1 Fabrique Nationale Egyptian Model FN-49 Semi-Automatic Rifle - 8mm Mauser - circa 1952-1958 - FN-49 rifles were used in the Suez Conflict and in the Korean War.

2 Savage SMLE No. 4 Mk I/3 Bolt-Action Rifle with bayonet - .303 British - circa 1948 - Savage made No. 4 rifles for British/Canadian contracts as well as U.S. training purposes.

3 Ishapore Arsenal SMLE No. 1 Mk III Bolt-Action Rifle (altered) - .303 British - circa 1954 - Indian rifles modified for grenade launching had wire-wrapped forestocks.

4 Czech VZ-52 Semi-Automatic Carbine - 7.62mm x 45 - circa 1953-1954 - VZ-52 carbines utilized a different 7.62mm cartridge than SKS carbines.

5 Springfield Armory M1D Sniper Semi-Automatic Rifle - .30-06 - circa 1942 - Late in WWII, M1D snipers were fielded with offset M84 scopes.

6 Inglis Mk I Semi-Automatic Pistol - 9mm Parabellum - circa 1945 - Canadian copies of FN P35 pistols continued in service with British Commonwealth nations.

MODERN WARFARE

Vietnam

Perhaps the most controversial conflict in modern times, the Viet Nam War began with North Vietnamese communist-led terrorist attacks against the government of the Republic of Viet Nam (South Viet Nam) in the late 1950's. Fought as a jungle guerrilla war, American forces began to be involved in the conflict in 1959 and remained until the fall of Saigon in 1975 suffering 58,000 men and women killed in action. As a guerrilla conflict, the war was fought with a wide variety of arms. U.S. soldiers captured enemy rifles of the type used during the War Between the States 100 years earlier! In the end the North Vietnamese won the conflict not with a combination of ancient surplus arms or conventional communist bloc equipment, but with superior propaganda, extraordinary patience, diplomatic skill, and a crushing military defeat delivered to South Vietnamese forces.

1 U.S. Springfield Model T44 E4 Selective Fire Rifle (deactivated) - .30 T65 - circa 1957 - Forerunner of the M14, T44 prototypes based on a modified Garand receiver in 7.62mm competed successfully against the FN FAL (T48) rifle, with the design being adopted for military service in 1957.

2 Colt AR-15 Automatic Rifle (deactivated) - 5.56 mm NATO (.223) - circa 1964 - Adapted by the U.S. Air Force in selective-fire configuration, Armalite's AR-15 later became the M16A1 for Army issue.

3 Armalite AR-10 Semi-Automatic Rifle (deactivated) - 7.62mm - circa 1956-1957 - Fewer than 10,000 Armalite AR-10 rifles were originally produced as this selective-fire rifle design by Eugene Stoner failed in U.S. military and Nicaraguan army testing. Small quantities of the rifles were sold to military forces in Portugal and the Sudan.

4 Shangshei Arsenal Mauser Model 1896 Broomhandle Semi-Automatic Pistol - .45 ACP - circa 1930-1935 - Chinese M1896 pistol copies were made in .45 ACP.

5 Remington Rand M1911A1 Semi-Automatic Pistol - .45 ACP - circa 1944-1911 pistols were widely distributed in Vietnam, as they had been in previous conflicts.

1 Czech VZ54 Sniper Bolt-Action Rifle - 7.62 x54 Russian - circa 1954 - SHE-marked for the Czech arsenal, this model was built for only three years.

2 Hungarian Mosin Nagant Model 1891/30 Bolt-Action Rifle with telescopic sight - 7.62mm x 54R - circa 1970 - This Hungarian MN rifle was captured from a Vietcong sniper in 1970.

3 Chinese SKS Type 56 Semi-Automatic Carbine - 7.62mm x 39 - circa 1980 - Chinese copies of the SKS carbine had wide distribution in Vietnam.

4 Vietcong Bolt-Action Carbine - 7.62 mm x 39 - circa 1964-1970 - A crude bolt-action fitted to a scavenged US M1 carbine stock, this single-shot rifle is chambered for the same 7.62x39mm cartridge used in SKS and AK-47 arms.

5 Vietcong Slam-Fire Blow-Back Rifle - 7.62mm x 39 - circa 1964-1970 - A spring-loaded bolt is drawn back to load or fire this gun.

6 Vietcong Muzzleloading Thumb-Trigger Rifle - 11/16 caliber - circa 1964-1970 - Crudely built from pipe, this single-shot gun has a sheet metal trigger.

MODERN WARFARE

1. Sterling (Parker Arms import) Semi-Automatic Carbine - 9 mm - circa 1990 - Sterling SMGs utilized a pair of rollers as followers to enhance magazine feeding.

2. MAS French Model 1938 Submachine Gun - 7.65mm MAS - circa 1954-1956 - French MAS SMGs employed a folding trigger as a safety mechanism.

3. Polytech/KFS AK-47S Legend Folding-Stock Rifle - 7.62 mm x 39 - circa 1984 - Modern commercial copies of the AK-47 rifle are manufactured in semi-automatic configuration for sale in markets including the United States by the same manufacturers that produced selective-fire editions for the world's military forces. This Polytech folding-stock rifle utilizes components that also appear in the Chinese Type 56 rifle.

4. Chinese Mosin Nagant Type 53 Bolt-Action Rifle - 7.62mm x 54R - circa 1954-1960 - Chinese copies of Soviet arms included M/N carbines.

5. Chinese Chiang Kai-Shek Short Model Bolt-Action Rifle - 7.92 mm - circa 1936-1949.

6. U.S. Remington Model 1903A4 Bolt-Action Rifle with M82 Telescopic Sight - .30-06 - circa 1945 - M1903A4 snipers utilized low-power scopes adapted from commercial sporting optics.

7. Vietcong Semi-Automatic Pistol - .45 ACP - circa 1965-1968 - Handmade using only sections of railroad track and a file and drill, this .45 caliber semi-automatic pistol is a crude copy of the Model 1911 design, but does fire and extract reliably.

8. Handmade Vietnamese 1911 Pattern Pistol - .45 ACP - circa 1965-1968 - Crudely built from steel rail, Vietcong gunsmiths improvised this copy of a 1911 pistol.

9. MAS French MAS1949 Semi-Automatic Rifle - 7.5mm M29 - circa 1955 - Semi-auto MAS rifles retain the capability to launch grenades using a tilting bolt system.

10. St. Etienne French MAS 1936 Bolt-Action Training Rifle - .22 rimfire - circa 1947-1950 - Former training rifles were pressed into service by Vietcong insurgents.

1

2

3

4

5

6

7

8

1 Colt Model 1903 Semi-Automatic Pistol - .32 ACP - circa 1921 - General Douglas MacArthur received this pistol during his term as superintendent of West Point.

2 U.S. Colt Model 1903 Semi-Automatic General Officer Pistol - .32 ACP - circa 1943 - This Colt Model 1903 semi-automatic pistol was presented to Major General Richard Anthony Bresnahan. Bresnhan received his first set of general's stars in January of 1972.

3 U.S. Colt Model 1903 Semi-Automatic General Officer Pistol - .32 ACP - circa 1943 - In July of 1959, General Bruce Palmer, Jr.,

received this Colt Model 1903 semi-auto pistol in token of his new rank.

4 U.S. Colt Model 1908 Semi-Automatic General Officer Pistol - .380 ACP - circa 1943 - One of the few General Officer pistols to actually see combat, this Colt Model 1908 handgun was with Lieutenant General Ridgely Gaither during Operation Varsity. Gaither jumped with the 17th Airborne to attack German positions held near the Rhine. Using this .380 pistol and his GI issue .45 pistol, Gaither and his men were able to suppress an enemy 20mm gun emplacement.

5 U.S. Colt Model 1903 Semi-Automatic General Officer Pistol - .32 ACP - ca. 1943 Elaborately engraved and fitted with carved wooden grip panels, this Colt Model 1903 pistol was presented to General Frank Thomas Mildren in 1960, then re-presented after his subordinates in Germany borrowed the pistol in 1968 to have it specially embellished to mark Mildren's advancement to lieutenant general.

6 U.S. Colt Model 1903 Semi-Automatic General Officer Pistol - .32 ACP - circa 1943 General Hugh Pate Harris received this Colt

Model 1903 .32 caliber pistol in December 1953, when he served as Deputy Chief of Staff for the 8th Army and was in charge of all military operations in Korea.

7 U.S. Colt Model 1908 Semi-Automatic General Officer Pistol - .380 ACP - circa 1943 Recommended personally for promotion by General George S. Patton, General Issac Davis White received his first general's stars in May 1944, along with this Model 1908 Colt pistol.

8 U.S. Colt Model 1903 Semi-Automatic General Officer Pistol - .32 ACP - circa 1944 Lt. General Richard Meyer received this Colt General Officer pistol.

1 U.S. Smith & Wesson Model 39 U.S. Air Force General Officer Semi-Automatic Pistol - 9mm Parabellum - circa 1969 - The U.S. Air Force was one branch of the armed services that broke with tradition in ordering General Officer pistols. A Smith & Wesson Model 39 9mm pistol was presented to General Bryce Poe in 1969. The grips were later modified by USAF armorers to reflect Poe's rank at retirement.

2 U.S. Colt M15 Semi-Automatic General Officer Pistol - .45 ACP - circa 1973 - Originally receiving a .32 caliber Colt Model 1903 pistol, Maj. Gen. John Carpenter Raaen exchanged that handgun in 1973 for a Rock Island Arsenal-built .45 caliber General Officer pistol, SN GO2. Raaen was the commanding general of Rock Island Arsenal at that time.

3 Beretta M9 Presentation General Officer Pistol - 9 mm - circa 1993 - Former USMC Commandant P.X. Kelley received this presentation Beretta pistol.

1 Beretta Model 1935 Engraved Semi-Automatic Pistol - 7.65mm - circa 1950 - Chuck Yeager received this Beretta pistol from the Cuban Minister of Defense in 1950.

2 U.S. Colt Model 1911A1 Semi-Automatic Pistol - .45 ACP - circa 1943 - General Eisenhower gave this pistol to an aide involved in the 1942 North Africa invasion.

3 Colt Model 1911A1 General Joe Foss Commemorative Semi-Automatic Pistol - .45 ACP - circa 1990 - This is serial number 2 of the Joe Foss commemorative-edition pistol.

4 Chinese M20 Tokarev pistol - 7.62 Tokarev - circa 1969 - Captured in Vietnam, this Tokarev was presented to Major General Pepke.

MODERN WARFARE

Desert Storm and the Global War on Terrorism
Beginning on January 17, 1991, in an unprecedented six-week campaign, United States and Allied forces numbering 450,000 men and commanded by U.S. Army General Norman Schwarzkopf won a sweeping victory against an Iraqi army of nearly 1,000,000 troops. A brilliant two-pronged ground force attack routed the entire Iraqi Army in 100 hours. An estimated 100,000 Iraqi troops were killed and 65,000 captured. The allies suffered only 234 dead, 479 wounded, and 57 missing in action. A variety of selective-fire arms, standard among the coalition forces proved to be more than a match for the communist bloc arms of the Iraqi soldier.

1 Colt CAR-15 Semi-Automatic Carbine - 5.56 mm - circa 1979 - Featuring a collapsible stock that could be compacted down for storage, Colt's CAR-15 model was to be featured in both military and law enforcement contracts; the modern M4 counterpart in current U.S. military service is a direct descendant of the original CAR-15.

2 Beretta XM9 Semi-Automatic Pistol - 9mm Parabellum - circa 1982.

3 Arsenal Inc. AK-74 Semi-automatic rifle - 5.45x39mm Russian - circa 2010 - Given to the National Firearms Museum in 2010, this semi-automatic version of the Russian AK-74 rifle was specially embellished with gold inlays commemorating the illustrious arms-designing career of General Mikhail T. Kalashnikov.

THE AK and THE M-16
In the late 20th and early 21st centuries, assault rifles have come to be the predominant infantry arms. An "assault rifle" is lighter and shorter than a full-size "battle rifle" of the WWI and WWII eras and is capable of either single-shot or full automatic fire. They are chambered for cartridges less powerful than the .30-06 and 8mm Mauser rounds used in the earlier battle rifles. The most common rounds are the 7.62 x 39 and the 5.56 NATO (.223 Remington). The term "assault rifle" has been used incorrectly to apply to semi-automatic sporting rifles that are not capable of full-auto fire, but cosmetically resemble the military rifles.

Two patterns of assault rifle are dominant in the world militaries. The Kalashnikov design, first introduced in 1947, chambered for the 7.62mm cartridge, was used by Soviet bloc forces in the Cold War and has been produced in greater numbers than any other firearm in history. The M16 pattern developed by Eugene Stoner and Armalite in the 1960s in 5.56mm caliber is the pattern that has been adopted by the U.S. and many of its allies.

1. **MAS French FAMAS Bullpup Semi-Automatic Carbine** - 5.56 mm - circa 1989 - Compact and light, the French FAMAS bullpup rifle has its magazine behind the trigger.

2. **Fabrique Nationale FAL Semi-Automatic Rifle** - 7.62mm NATO - circa 1985 - Rejected by the U.S. military, the FN FAL was adopted by other NATO nations.

3. **Harrington & Richardson T48 Selective Fire Rifle** (deactivated) - .30 T65 - circa 1950-1952 - Three firms were contacted to provide FAL pattern rifles for U.S. military testing; this Harrington & Richardson T48 is one of the arms tested for the Light Self-Loading Rifle trials to find the replacement for the M1 Garand rifle.

4. **DPMS M160 Selective-Fire Rifle** - 5.56 mm - circa 2003 - Commercial production M16A2 with three-shot burst capability.

5. **Israeli Military Industries Galil Sniper Semi-Automatic Rifle** - 5.56 mm - circa 1993 - Galil design blends American cartridge with Russian action for desert reliability.

1 U.S. Remington USMC M40A1 Bolt-Action Scout/
Sniper Rifle w/ 10X Scope - 7.62mm NATO - circa 19[?]
- Originally a Vietnam-era Remington M40 rifle, duri[ng]
upgrades by U.S. Marine Corps armorers this rifle was [?]
refitted with a synthetic McMillan stock and re-barrell[ed]
with a heavier-contour 7.62mm barrel. The optic on t[he]
rifle was manufactured by U.S. Optics, a California fir[m]
contracted to replace the original Unertl 10X scopes o[n]
the M40A1 rifles.

2 Russian SVD Dragunov Sniper Semi-Automatic Rifle
- 7.62 x54 Russian - circa 1975 - Designed by Eugenie
Dragunov, a former Russian Olympic competitive
shooter, the SVD Dragunov semi-automatic rifle was
incorporated as a squad sniper arm in 1963. Its optic [?]
be set to detect active infrared night vision sources on [?]
battlefield and includes an illuminated reticle.

3 U.S. Remington USMC M40 Bolt-Action Scout/
Sniper Rifle with Redfield 3 x 9 Variable Range Sight
- .308 Winchester - circa 1968 - U.S. Marine Corps
requirements for a heavy-barrel sniper rifle were fulfille[d]
by Remington Arms of Ilion, NY. The initial 995 rifles
ordered were to be equipped with an auto-ranging retic[le]
optic provided by Redfield.

4 Winchester Model 70 Bolt-Action Sniper Rifle with
Lyman 20X Target Scope - .30-06 - circa 1942 - WWI[I]
era sniper rifles were called back into service for Vietna[m.]

5 U.S. Remington M24 Sniper Bolt-Action Rifle - 7.62m[m]
NATO - circa 1989-1990 - Since 1988, the M24 has be[en]
standard issue for U.S. Air Force and Army snipers.

6 Prototype Remington XM24 Sniper Bolt-Action Rifle
- .300 Winchester Magnum - circa 1987 - Original
prototype rifle made for the M24 sniper project.

1 SIG Sauer M11 Semi-Automatic Pistol - 9mm Parabellum - circa 2009 - Made for the NCIS in Europe. It was a contract overrun sold commercially.

2 Heckler & Koch Mark 23 Offensive Handgun System with Suppressor and Laser Aiming Module - .45 ACP - circa 2000 - H&K's special ops mission pistol was designed to take a suppressor and laser/IR aiming system.

3 U.S. Barrett M82A1 Semi-Automatic Sniper Rifle (deactivated) - .50 Browning - circa 1990 - The first U.S. military orders for the Barrett M82A1 semi-automatic rifle came in 1990 with the first Desert Storm campaign. Initially, 125 rifles were ordered for the U.S. Marine Corps. This example is one of that initial lot. The Barrett "Light .50" is a massive semi-automatic rifle, weighing over 30 lbs. and chambering a round previously used only in heavy machine guns.

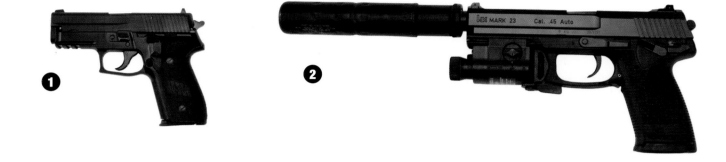

COMPETITION

1

2

3

4

5

6

1 Winchester/Schoyen Model 1885 Falling Block Single-Shot Target Rifle - .32-40 - circa 1885 - Fitted with a George Schoyen heavy target barrel. In competition, often a single cartridge case was reused, again and again, with cast/paper-patched projectile being muzzleloaded down the barrel to rest just outside the chamber.

2 H. Sauer German Percussion Target Rifle - .45 caliber - circa 1870-1890 - European target shooters preferred back-action locks that could be cocked with a forward push from the firing position.

3 S. S. Baird Underhammer Percussion Muzzleloading Target Rifle - .44 caliber - circa 1860 - Underhammer target rifles provided a cleaner line of sight on barrel top as well as faster ignition.

4 Massachusetts Arms Co. Maynard Falling-Block Rifle - .41 caliber - circa 1875 - Maynard rifles could be had with interchangeable barrels in different calibers.

5 Mexican Percussion Target Rifle - .41 caliber - circa 1845 - Percussion target rifles like this Mexican example were used in many countries; competitive shooters followed a variety of activities using targets ranging from paper to longer-range painted metal discs or squares that resounded on impact.

6 Ford Brothers Percussion Target Rifle - .36 caliber - circa 1835-1855 - In the time when turkey shoots offered community entertainment, many gunsmiths produced heavy-barreled rifles to compete in informal competition.

The Era of the Scheutzenfest

Competitive shooting at targets has been a favorite sport among Americans since before the American Revolution. One of the oldest forms of organized shooting in the United States was introduced about 1850 in the Midwest by Swiss and German immigrants, and was known as the Scheutzen match or scheutzenfest. The first competitive shooting club, called a scheutzenbund, was organized in 1865. These competitions were quite stylized in form, and shooters used customized small-caliber rifles equipped with pronged buttplates, hand rests, elaborate sights, and heavy barrels. Shooting took place from a standing position at targets placed at a distance of 150-200 yards. The scheutzenfest was more than just a rifle competition -- it was an important social event. By 1890, nearly all large American communities with a German heritage had large scheutzenbunds.

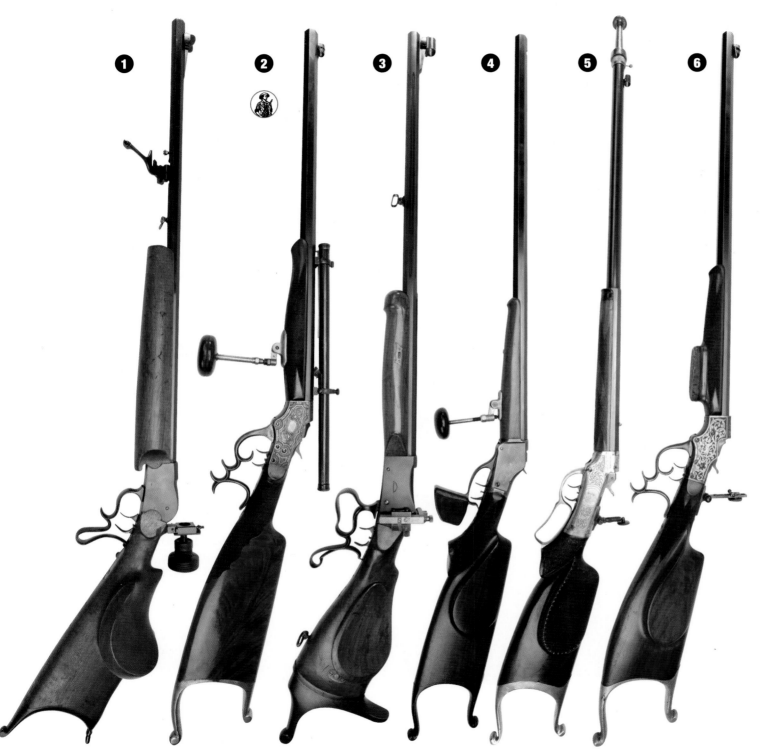

1. German Zimmershutzen Rifle - 4mm rimfire - circa 1900-1920 - Utilized in Europe for indoor competition, the zimmerschuetzen incorporated a port near the muzzle that loaded into the back of a short rifled section of the barrel.

2. Stevens-Pope Single-Shot Schuetzen Rifle - .22 rimfire - circa 1920-1930 - Under the supervision of noted barrel-maker Harry Pope, this Stevens single-shot was fitted with a target barrel.

3. J. Blattman Peabody-Martini Free Rifle - .22 rimfire - circa 1920-1930 - Made for international free rifle competition.

4. Winchester Model 1885 Falling Block Single-Shot Rifle - .32-40 - circa 1885-1920 - Fitted with Harry Pope false muzzle barrel.

5. Marlin-Ballard Lever-Action Schuetzen Rifle - .38-55 - circa 1875-1891 - Re-rifled by Harry Pope and rechambered by Zetler Brothers for sale by dealer Axel Petersen.

6. Stevens-Pope Single-Shot Schuetzen Rifle - circa 1885-1895 - H. M. Pope was renowned as a gunsmith whose attention to detail in rifling barrels was legendary. Pope was hired in 1901 by the Stevens Rifle Company to produce a line of single-shot target rifles and continued to do so until 1905.

COMPETITION

1 Stevens Ideal No. 49 Walnut Hill Single-Shot Rifle - .22 rimfire - circa 1895-1930 - Walnut Hill was the c. 1876 Mass. Rifle Ass'n range in Woburn, MA.

2 Winchester Model 1885 Falling-Block Single-Shot Schuetzen Rifle - .38-55 - circa 1893 - Made for left-handed shooter.

3 Remington-Hepburn No. 3 Mid-Range Creedmoor Rifle - .40-65 - circa 1880 - A shorter vernier tang sight denoted the Mid-Range model.

4 Massachusetts Arms Maynard Model 1873 Single-Shot Rifle - .35 centerfire - circa 1875 - Thick-headed cartridges were used in the Maynard target guns.

5 Redfield Prototype Single-Shot Rifle - .25-20 - circa 1950 - Redfield, a company better known for aperture sights and optics, built a prototype rifle to show what a modern single-shot rifle could represent. Based on the falling-block Ballard action, this rifle never went into full production and only a handful of prototypes exist.

6 Sharps-Borchardt Model 1878 Mid-Range Single-Shot Rifle - .40-90 Sharps - circa 1878-1881 - The hammerless Sharps-Borchardt rifle was manufactured only from 1878 to 1881, at the close of the Sharps Rifle Company's existence, and less than 9,000 were ever made.

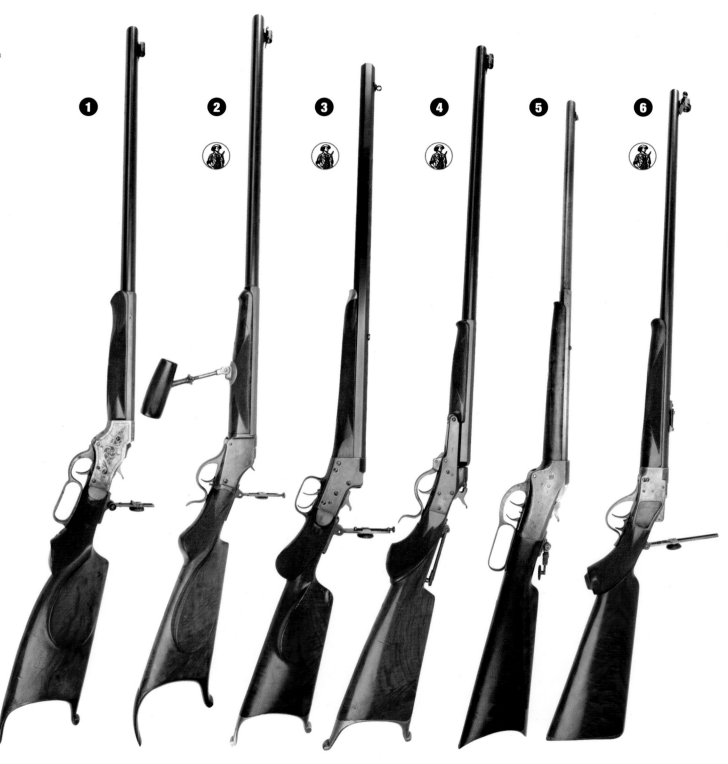

1 Remington Creedmoor Long-Range Rifle - .45-70 Sharps - circa 1880-1907 - Creedmoor, the first NRA range on Long Island, was a facility with specific rifle rules. Rifles like this Remington could be used in competition only with single triggers and had to conform to strict weight limits. Adjustable pistol grip patented by H.H. Handy.

2 Sharps Model 1877 Creedmoor Falling-Block Single-Shot Target Rifle - .45-100 Sharps - circa 1877-1878 - About 100 M1877 rifles were made with Rigby barrels.

3 Frank Wesson No. 2 Mid-Range Underlever Falling-Block Single-Shot Rifle - .44 caliber - circa 1870 - Rifle has rear stock tang mounts to allow reclining shooting position.

4 Marlin-Ballard No. 4 A-1 Mid-Range Single-Shot Target Rifle - .40-65 - circa 1878-1880 - Fitted with best-grade vernier sights by Marlin.

5 Winchester Model 1885 High Wall Falling-Block Single-Shot Rifle - .30-06 - circa 1885-1920 - One of 40 rifles built for U.S. International Match shooting and believed used at Camp Perry in 1913.

The Mists of Creedmoor
In 1872, the Range Committee of the National Rifle Association negotiated with the State of New York to establish a target range for the training of the National Guard and other personnel. The establishment of a range was the principal goal of the NRA at that time. A 70-acre parcel known as Creed's Farm on Long Island was purchased from the Central and Northside Railroad for the new range. Colonel Henry G. Shaw, editor of the *New York Sun*, viewed the property on one misty morning and remarked it was just like the moors of southern England. Perhaps we should call it Creed's Moor, rather than Creed's Farm. The name Creedmoor, now synonymous with firearms and target shooting, was agreed upon as the new name for NRA's target range. The first shots on the new range were fired on April 25, 1873, by George Wingate. The dedication match was held on June 21, 1873, with two individual matches followed by a regimental team competition. Prizes included a purse and a gold-mounted Winchester Model 1866 Rifle. The establishment of the Creedmoor range attracted hundreds of new members to the NRA, as well as inquiries from all over America regarding match competitions. Although urban growth eventually forced the closing of the range at Creedmoor, the name came to imply the highest standard of quality. Arms manufacturers such as Remington, Sharps, and Marlin used the name Creedmoor in their advertising for their top-of-the-line target rifles.

A New Range at Sea Girt
When the Creedmoor range closed, nearly every state in the Union had developed its own rifle teams and private clubs. Many of them had their own ranges based upon NRA rules and patterned after Creedmoor. In 1890, the New Jersey State Rifle Association established a new 148-acre range in the resort community of Sea Girt. In 1892, the National Rifle Association transferred its national and international matches to the new range. The success of these competitions brought national attention to Sea Girt, and the National Rifle Association became internationally recognized as a governing organization.

COMPETITION

1 Wurfflein Single-Shot Pistol - .44 Russian - circa 1890-1910.

2 Stevens No. 41 Tip-Up Single-Shot Pistol - .32 rimfire - circa 1903-1916.

3 Harrington & Richardson Model USRA Single-Shot Target Pistol - .22 rimfire - circa 1928-1941 - Variable front sight could be moved to regulate sight distance.

4 Smith & Wesson Third Model Single-Shot Pistol - .22 rimfire - circa 1909-1923 - Almost 7,000 made.

5 Harrington & Richardson USRA Single-Shot Pistol - .22 rimfire - circa 1928-1941 - About 3,500 made.

6 Julian Hatcher's Harrington & Richardson Model USRA Single-Shot Target Pistol - .22 rimfire - circa 1928-1941 - Famed shooter and writer Julian Hatcher used this

USRA pistol to shoot a 100x100 score at Bisley range in England. Harrington & Richardson's single-shot United States Revolver Association (USRA) pistol was the choice of the U.S. Army's pistol team in 1932, when it established a new national pistol record.

7 Smith & Wesson Straight Line Pistol - .22 long rifle - circa 1925-1936 - Fourth Model in factory casing.

8 Colt Camp Perry Double-Action Single-Shot Target Pistol - .22 rimfire - circa 1929-1941 - Colt changed the round cylinder on an Officer's Model revolver to a flat single-shot chamber insert for their Camp Perry Model.

9 Smith & Wesson Second Model Single-Shot Pistol - .22 rimfire - circa 1905-1909 - About 4,600 were made.

1 Smith & Wesson Model 14 K-38 Target Masterpiece Double-Action Revolver - .38 Special - circa 1955 - Owned by Colonel John Lee, former Director of Civilian Marksmanship.

2 Smith & Wesson Model 41 Semi-Automatic Pistol - .22 rimfire - circa 1947-present.

3 Smith & Wesson Model 52-1 Semi-Automatic Pistol - .38 Special - circa 1963-1970 - Fires rimmed .38 Special ammunition, which is unusual in a semi-auto pistol.

4 Smith & Wesson Model 24 Double-Action Revolver - .44 Special - circa 1954.

5 Colt Presentation Officer's Model Double-Action Target Revolver - .38 Colt - circa 1904-1949 - This presentation Colt Officer's Model double-action revolver was received by noted author Ned Roberts in 1904 during National Guard competition.

6 Crown City/Kart .22 Conversion Semi-Automatic Pistol - .22 rimfire - circa 1975.

7 High Standard Trophy Semi-Automatic Pistol - .22 rimfire - circa 1957.

8 Colt Model 1911 Semi-Automatic Pistol - .38 Special - circa 1911-1925 - Converted from .38 Super to .38 Special by gunsmith A.E. Berdon.

Camp Perry

The range at Sea Girt, New Jersey, served the NRA and the National Matches well in its initial years. But ater 15 years of heavy use, the range began to suffer from overcrowding and outdated camping facilities.

A new site was located by Ammon B. Critchfield, the Adjutant General of Ohio and an NRA vice president. The property was located on a level plain measuring 1 mile long and 1/2 mile deep. It stretched along the shore of Lake Erie just south of Put-in-Bay and was less than 45 miles east of Toledo.

In 1905, the Ohio state legislature appropriated $25,000 toward the purchase and development of a National Guard rifle range and camp, and Critchfield recommended the Lake Erie location. The Ohio State Rifle Association and the Ohio National Guard Association agreed to purchase 30 additional acres to be the site of a clubhouse.

Dedicated in August 1907, this new installation was named Camp Perry in honor of Captain (later Commodore) Oliver Hazard Perry who triumphed over the British during the War of 1812 at the Battle of Lake Erie. The National Matches are currently held each summer at Camp Perry.

COMPETITION

1 U.S. Colt Model 1911A1 National Match Semi-Automatic Pistol - .45 ACP - circa 1959-1964.

2 Colt Model 1911 Semi-Automatic Pistol - .45 ACP - circa 1911-1925 - Accurized by gunsmith James Clark for interservice competition.

3 U.S. Remington Rand Model 1911A1 Semi-Automatic Pistol - .45 ACP - circa 1943-1945 - Accurized by gunsmith A.E. Berdon for target competition.

4 Smith & Wesson Model 46 Semi-Automatic Pistol - .22 rimfire - circa 1957-1966 - Cheaper version of S&W Model 41 pistol.

5 Colt Mark IV Series 70 Gold Cup National Match Semi-Automatic Pistol - .45 ACP - circa 1970-1983 - Originally intended to be a trophy presented at the 1990 National Matches at Camp Perry, OH. Torrential rainshowers resulted in the cancellation of the match where this pistol was to be awarded.

6 Colt Government Model Semi-Automatic Pistol - .45 ACP - circa 1911-1925 - Fitted with Aimpoint sight.

7 Col. McMillan's Colt M1911A1 National Match Semi-Automatic Pistol - .45 ACP - circa 1959-1964 - Later fitted with ornate Mexican silver grip panels, this National Match pistol was awarded in 1963 to Lt. Colonel William McMillan, a Triple Distinguished competitive shooter.

1 Colt Model 1911 Semi-Automatic Pistol - .45 ACP - circa 1911-1925 - Accurized by gunsmith A.E. Berdon for National Match competition.

2 Colt Woodsman Semi-Automatic Pistol - .22 rimfire - circa 1927-1947 - USMC Captain Thurman Barrier won the .22 aggregate championships in 1949 with this pistol. Only one inch of barrel is rifled.

3 High Standard Supermatic pistol (USMC Pistol Team) - .22 rimfire - circa 1954-1957.

4 Smith & Wesson Straight Line Single-Shot Pistol - .22 rimfire - circa 1925-1936 - About 1,800 Straight Lines were made.

5 High Standard Military Model 106 Pistol - .22 rimfire - circa 1969 - Presented to Trudy Schlernitzauer as 1969 Camp Perry Woman's Pistol Champion.

6 Essex Arms M1911 Race Gun - .45 ACP - circa 1998 - Modern competition handguns are often crafted by gunsmiths using match-grade barrels and finely adjustable target sights. This example was rescued from a police department evidence locker where it had been scheduled for destruction after having been taken from its owner.

7 Fabrique Nationale GP Competition pistol - 9 mm - circa 1998 - FN competition model not marketed in the U.S.

COMPETITION

1. Hammerli Single Air Pistol - .177 pellet - circa 1961-1970 - Owned by Stan Mate, recipient of UIT Blue Star.
2. Hammerli Model 208 Standard Semi-Automatic Pistol - .22 rimfire - circa 1966-1968.
3. Feinwerkbau Model 65 Air Pistol - .177 pellet - circa 1961-1971 - Owned by Stan Mate, recipient of UTI Blue Star.
4. Hammerli Model 150 Single-Shot Free Pistol - .22 rimfire - circa 1989.
5. Hammerli Model 103 Free Pistol - .22 long rifle - circa 1959-1960.
6. Sako Finnmaster Pistol - .22 rimfire - circa 1971.
7. H. Stotzer Single-Shot Target Pistol - .22 rimfire - circa 1937-1940.

1 Walther Free Pistol - .22 rimfire - circa 1977.
2 Walther Model LP 2 Air Pistol - .177 pellet - circa 1967-1972.
3 Beretta Tipo Olimpionico Semi-Automatic Pistol - .22 rimfire - circa 1959-1964 - Handmade prototype.
4 Hammerli Master Air Pistol - .177 pellet - circa 1964-1977.
5 Walther OSP Semi-Automatic Target Pistol - .22 rimfire - circa 1961-1970.
6 Hammerli Model 200 Olympia Semi-Automatic Pistol - .22 rimfire - circa 1958-1963.
7 Russian TOZ 8 Bolt-Action Target Rifle - .22 rimfire - circa 1950.
8 Russian MU-55 target pistol - .22 long rifle - circa 1975 - Russian single-shot target pistols, like this MU-55 .22 pistol built by Anschutz, Hammerli, and Walther, compete with other international handguns in free pistol events.

COMPETITION

1. U.S. Springfield Model 1903 Bolt-Action Rifle - .30-06 - circa 1920-1930 - Refitted with Remington match barrel for competition.

2. VMT State Metal Works Finnish Lion Bolt-Action Single-Shot Target Rifle - .22 rimfire - circa 1937-1972.

3. Dunlap Custom Bolt-Action Rifle - .308 Winchester - circa 1950-1960.

4. Winchester Model 70 Bolt-Action Rifle - .30-06 - circa 1942 - Named "Old Yeller," the rifle set a 998-45X National Record in 1968.

5. Champlin Firearms Left-Hand Bolt-Action Rifle - .220 cartridge - circa 1966 - Left-hand action customized by Roy Ivan Baldwin.

6. Anschutz Model 1813 Bolt-Action Rifle - .22 rimfire - circa 1813.

7. Winchester Model 52 Bolt-Action Rifle - .22 rimfire - circa 1929 - Named "Old Bacon Getter" by owner Thurman Randle, a former NRA president, this Winchester Model 52 rifle has a crudely painted stainless barrel to minimize glare when shooting in bright sunlight.

1   U.S. Springfield Model 1903 National Match Bolt-Action Rifle - .30-06 - circa 1921-1928 - Rifle was sold through Director of Civilian Marksmanship to former NRA magazine editor.

2   U.S. Springfield M1 Garand National Match Semi-Automatic Rifle - .30-06 - circa 1953-1963 - About 3,600 National Match Garands were made.

3   U.S. Springfield Model 1903 NRA/NBA President's Match Presentation Bolt-Action Rifle - .30-06 - circa 1932 - During the years of the Great Depression, the National Matches were reduced in scale to small regional competitions held at military bases around the country. This Model 1903 bolt-action rifle was awarded to USMC Corporal W.A. Easterling in 1932 at the Quantico matches that year.

4   Waffenfabrik Steyr Austrian Mannlicher Model 1893 Bolt-Action Rifle - 6.5mm - circa 1901 - Shot in 1901 Sea Girt match between Ireland and NJ teams, rifle was presented to NRA in 1976 after Palma Match competition.

5   U.S. Springfield Krag Jorgensen rifle with Pope barrel - .30-40 Krag - circa 1901 - The rifle was owned by Col. John Caswell, noted sportsman and competitive shooter, who donated in 1923 the Winged Victory statue that is used as the Caswell Trophy.

6   Winchester Model 52 Bolt-Action Rifle - .22 rimfire - circa 1919-1979 - Owned by former NRA President Alonzo Garcelon. Favored in smallbore competition since its inception in 1919, Winchester's Model 52 rifle could be had with standard or heavyweight barrels.

COMPETITION

1 Colt Sporter Target Model AR-15 Semi-Automatic rifle - .223 Remington - circa 1989-1994 - AR-15 based rifles have gradually come to supplant M1 and M14 platforms in Camp Perry service rifle competitions.

2 Tubb 2000 Bolt-Action Rifle - 6 mm - circa 2007 - Chambered in 6mm XC, this Tubb 2000 rifle offers an extended sight radius which can translate to a significant long-range accuracy advantage for an advanced marksman.

3 Ljutic Industries Space Gun - 12 gauge - circa 1980 - Ljutic shotguns, offered in several models, provide competitive shotgunners with unmatched handling characteristics.

1 Anschutz Model 54 Super Match Bolt-Action Rifle - .22 rimfire - circa 1971.

2 Winchester Model 70 Palma Centennial Bolt-Action Rifle - .308 Winchester - circa 1976 - Unfired rifle from 1976 Palma Centennial Match; one of 80.

3 Anschutz Model 220 Air Gun - .177 pellet - circa 1959-1967.

4 Anschutz Model 380 Air Gun - .177 pellet - circa 1971.

5 Anschutz Model 1811 Bolt-Action Rifle - .22 long rifle - circa 1981.

COMPETITION

1 Anschutz Model 1827 Fortner Bolt-Action Biathlon Rifle - .22 long rifle - circa 1990 - The biathlon combines cross-country skiing with rifle target competition.

2 Art Cook's Olympic Gold Remington Model 37 Rangemaster Bolt-Action Rifle - .22 long rifle shot - circa 1947 - In the 1948 Olympic games in London, American Art Cook took gold in the 50-meter smallbore rifle match, firing a 599 (with 43 Xs) score with the Remington Model 37 rifle, fitted with an adjustable barrel bedding system.

3 Morris Fisher's Olympic Gold J. Hartman Hammerli/Martini Free Rifle - .30-06 - circa 1920 - Used by Morris Fisher in 1920 Olympics to win gold in international position shooting.

4 Launi Meili's Olympic Gold Medal Anschutz Model 54 Bolt-Action Rifle - .22 long rifle - circa 1990 - In the 1992 Olympic games in Barcelona, Spain, 29-year-old American smallbore shooter Launi Meili used this Anschutz .22 rifle to win the gold medal in the women's 50 meter, three-position shooting event.

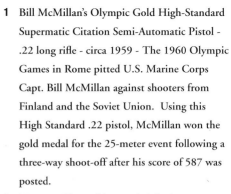

1 Bill McMillan's Olympic Gold High-Standard Supermatic Citation Semi-Automatic Pistol - .22 long rifle - circa 1959 - The 1960 Olympic Games in Rome pitted U.S. Marine Corps Capt. Bill McMillan against shooters from Finland and the Soviet Union. Using this High Standard .22 pistol, McMillan won the gold medal for the 25-meter event following a three-way shoot-off after his score of 587 was posted.

2 T.D. Smith's World Record Colt Government Model Semi-Automatic Pistol - .38 Special - circa 1960-1963 - In the 1963 Pan American Games, Lt. Colonel T.D. Smith used this .38 caliber semi-automatic pistol to set a world record in center-fire pistol competition that remains unbroken. He also shot in the 1964 Olympics.

3 Pistol Wizard A.P. Lane's Olympic Gold Colt Officer's Model Match Double-Action Revolver - .38 Colt - circa 1912 - A.P. Lane, nicknamed "The Pistol Wizard," used this .38 revolver in Olympic competition in the 1912 and 1920 Games, bringing home five Olympic gold medals and a bronze team medal.

4 Colt Olympic National Match Semi-Automatic Pistol - .45 ACP - circa 1933 - This Colt National Match .45 semi-automatic pistol belonged to the coach of the 1936 American Olympic team and was used in training exercises prior to competition in Germany.

COMPETITION

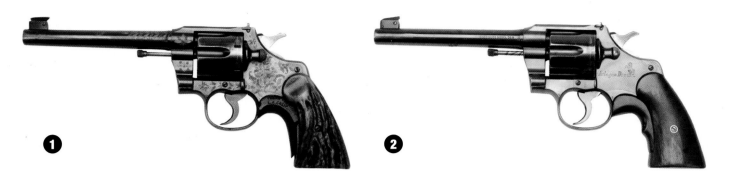

1   Ad Topperwein's Colt Officer's Model Double-Action Revolver - .38 Special - circa 1904-1908 - Ad and Plinky Topperwein, a husband-and-wife shooting team, were renowned for their skills, which included painting pictures with bullet holes. This revolver was owned by Ad Topperwein.

2   Arlayne Brown's Colt Officer's Model Target Double-Action Revolver - .38 Colt - ca. 1929 This custom target revolver was specially ordered from Colt in 1929 by Arlayne Brown, a noted female pistol competitor, for use at the Camp Perry National Matches. She won her first Camp Perry matches at age 13.

3   Herb Parsons' Smith & Wesson Outdoorsman Revolver - .22 long rifle - circa 1931-1940 - Used by noted exhibition shooter Herb Parsons, this .22 caliber S&W Outdoorsman was factory refinished in nickel.

4   Herb Parsons' Smith & Wesson Model 1905 Military & Police 4th Change - .38 Special - circa 1915-1942 - This nickel-finish Smith & Wesson revolver was used in exhibition shooting demonstrations by noted shooter Herb Parsons. Parsons was employed by ammunition companies, including Winchester and Remington, to give presentations showing the capabilities of their products in the hands of an expert.

Elizabeth (Plinky) Topperwein

In 1906, at Sea Girt, at the qualification matches for the NRA National Marksman's Reserve competition, a woman named Elizabeth Topperwein suddenly appeared in the registration lines and signed up as a participant in the match. For the first time in history, a woman competed in an official NRA match against hundreds of male shooters!

Born in San Antonio, Texas, Elizabeth (Plinky) Topperwein may have lacked the fame and showmanship of Annie Oakley, but she was the greatest female marksman of her time. Shattering all previous records, Plinky could handle a pistol, rifle, or shotgun with equal authority. A champion on the tossed target, she could clip coins with a pistol using either hand. Married to marksman Adolph Topperwein, she and her husband were employed as exhibition shooters for the Winchester Repeating Arms Company.

Ed McGivern

Born in Omaha, Nebraska, in 1874, Ed McGivern earned a reputation as the fastest gun in the world. One of this country's most celebrated exhibition shooters, he learned the art of fast shooting with astounding accuracy by pursuing a rigorous path of discipline and self-training in his youth. Ed McGivern became a scientific expert with a handgun. Every spare moment was spent developing championship shooting skills along with a variety of scientific timing devices designed to measure intervals of time as short as 1/20th of a second. At the age of 58 he set a world record for accurate rapid fire shooting – five shots, fired in less than 9/20th of a second into a group that could be covered by a half-dollar coin from a distance of 20 feet.

Some of McGivern's records have been equaled, and in some instances, bested by more modern shooters like Jerry Miculek. However, McGivern's more famous exploits took place as he was in his mid to late 50s and arthritis was threatening his shooting career. Throughout his life, McGivern relied on single-action revolvers for fast-fanning shooting. His Colt Single-Action Army revolvers still retain the original tape wrapped around their triggers. Fitted with custom grip panels, sized and checkered to his specifications

for double-action speed shooting, he favored S&W revolvers. HIs handguns also had special sights fitted, notably a gold bead on black post front sight that came to be known as the "McGivern sight." McGivern's final years were supported by protégé Walter Groff, who brought McGivern east to live in Philadelphia. In gratitude, McGivern's gun collection was given to Groff, whose widow in turn donated 14 of McGivern's handguns to the National Firearms Museum in 1974.

1 McGivern's World Record Smith & Wesson 38-44 Police Target Model Revolver - .38 Special (Heavy) - circa 1931 - The revolver used by Ed McGivern to shoot his five shots in 9/20ths of a second, setting a world record, was commemorated by the brass plaque added to the sideplate. Enlarged trigger guard by gunsmith Sukalle. Gold bead front sight. Ed McGivern's travelling trunk is at right.

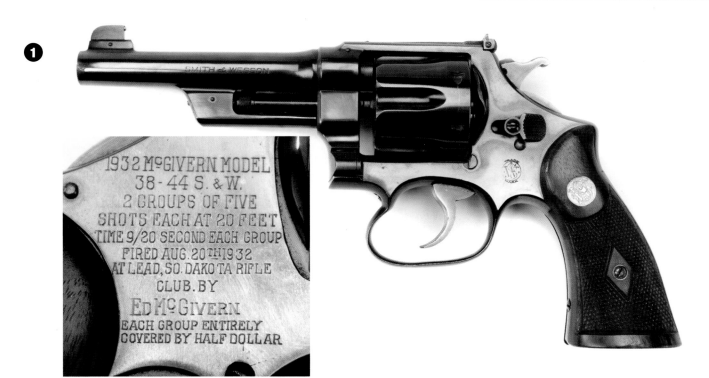

1932 McGIVERN MODEL
38-44 S. & W.
2 GROUPS OF FIVE
SHOTS EACH AT 20 FEET
TIME 9/20 SECOND EACH GROUP
FIRED AUG. 20TH 1932
AT LEAD, SO. DAKOTA RIFLE
CLUB. BY
ED McGIVERN
EACH GROUP ENTIRELY
COVERED BY HALF DOLLAR

Ed McGivern

1 McGivern's Smith & Wesson Model 1917 Double-Action Revolver - .45 ACP - circa 1935 - McGivern gold bead front sight with finger groove grips.

2 McGivern's Smith & Wesson Model 1917 Double-Action Revolver - .45 ACP - circa 1935 - McGivern cut down with modified trigger guard and no hammer spur.

3 McGivern's Smith & Wesson K-38 Double-Action Revolver - .38 Special - circa 1947 - Stock gun with McGivern carved grips.

4 McGivern's Colt Model 1873 Single-Action Army Revolver - .38 Special - circa 1898 - McGivern adjustable-sighted Single-Action Army with checkered grips.

5 McGivern's Smith & Wesson Military & Police Revolver - .38 Special - circa 1915-1942 - McGivern snub-nosed with gold bead front sight; no hammer spur.

1   McGivern's Colt Model 1873 Single-Action Army Revolver - .38 Special - circa 1933 - McGivern slip hammer target sighted SAA with checkered grips.

2   McGivern's Smith & Wesson Military & Police Revolver - .38 Special - circa 1915-1942 - McGivern snub-nosed target sighted with gold bead front sight.

3   McGivern's Smith & Wesson Military & Police Revolver - .38 Special - circa 1917-1940 - McGivern target sights with gold bead front.

4   McGivern's Smith & Wesson Hand Ejector First Model .44 Triple-Lock Revolver - .44 Special - circa 1915-1920 - McGivern target sights with smooth grips.

5   McGivern's Smith & Wesson Military & Police Revolver - .38 Special - circa 1915-1942 - McGivern custom reformed rear trigger guard stop.

6   McGivern's Smith & Wesson First Model Hand Ejector Revolver - .44 Special - circa 1911 - McGivern custom-carved grips.

7   McGivern's Colt Model 1873 Single-Action Army Revolver - .45 Colt - circa 1893 - McGivern fanning gun with taped trigger.

8   McGivern's Smith & Wesson New Model No. 3 Single-Action Revolver - .38-40 - circa 1885-1908 - Engraved "Ed McGivern of Montana 1919."

TO SERVE AND PROTECT

Police Forces

The establishment of police forces can trace its roots to England and to the Magna Carta, agreed to by King John in 1215. This document established the offices of sheriff and constable and provided guidelines for their authority and actions. Local and state militia forces provided protection for cities and townships in the early 19th century, but the political office of sheriff remained the mainstay of the police force. By the early 19th century, larger cities such as Boston and Philadelphia had organized volunteer police forces known as Watch and Ward. By 1850, many cities had police commissioners and forces of officers under them.

Police forces were gradually absorbed into civil service systems. August Vollmer, the police chief of Berkeley, California, in 1910 is generally considered the father of the modern police department. During his term, he introduced motorized patrols and college education for members of the force.

1 Smith & Wesson Model 10 Military & Police Double-Action Revolver with police club extension - .38 Special - circa 1952-1953 - The famous S&W M&P revolver became the standard police officer's sidearm from 1910 to the 1980s. This one is fitted with a rare billy club attachment, which is hollow so the gun can be fired with the club attached.

2 Smith & Wesson Model 14-3 Double-Action Revolver - circa 1974. Beauty is as beauty does. This Wesley Barksdale-modified revolver was used by Alabama State Trooper Sergeant James Collins in recording the first 1500 score in 1978 police revolver competition.

3 Smith & Wesson Model 64-3 Double-Action Revolver (altered) - .38 Special - circa 1988 - This modified Smith & Wesson revolver was used by Lt. Philip Hemphill of the Mississippi Highway Patrol in winning five National Police Shooting Championships,

4 DEA Agent Frank White's Colt Combat Commander Semi-Automatic Pistol - .45 ACP - circa 1971 - The customized Colt pistol was used by Drug Enforcement Administration Agent Frank E. White, including a number of cases involving drug interdiction in Florida. The TV series *Miami Vice* is believed to be modeled in part on events from his career.

5 Championship Springfield Armory 1911-A1 Semi-Automatic Pistol - .45 ACP - circa 1993 - Customized by Alan Tanaka and used by Dwight Van Horn to win the Harry Reeves trophy in police competition.

1 Heckler & Koch MP5A3 Submachine Gun - 9 mm - circa 1980-1985 - The roller-locked blowback operation of the Heckler & Koch MP5 submachine gun allows it to function efficiently with a closed bolt. Widely issued by both law enforcement and military units, this H&K SMG design is among the world's most recognizable firearms.

2 Remington 31R Slide-Action Riot Shotgun - 12 gauge - circa 1938-1940.

3 Remington Model 81 Police Semi-Automatic Rifle - .35 Remington - circa 1940 - Along with the Remington Model 31 shotgun, the Model 81 rifle was the favorite of law enforcement in the field and among prison guards during the mid-20th century.

4 Bill Jordan's Colt Border Patrol Double-Action Revolver - .38 Special - circa 1952 - This Model was designed by famed lawmen Harlon Carter and Bill Jordan. This early production prototype, one of only 400 made in .38 Special, was Jordan's personal sidearm, with his name inscribed on the receiver.

5 Handmade Pistol - .22 rimfire - circa 1989 - This crude .22 zipgun was reportedly hand made in a prison from parts found in the machine shop.

6 High Standard Model 10B Semi-Automatic Tactical Shotgun - 12 gauge - circa 1968 - A compact semi-automatic shotgun, the High Standard Model 10 incorporated a high intensity flashlight whose bulb had a habit of breaking under shotgun slug recoil.

TO SERVE AND PROTECT

1   Colt M1921 Thompson Submachine Gun - .45 ACP - circa 1921-1923 - This Colt-made Tommy gun is in near mint and unfired condition.

2   Sig 550-2SP CounterSniper Semi-Automatic Rifle - 5.56 mm NATO (.223) - circa 2005 - A current favorite of law enforcement SWAT teams.

3   Remington 11-87 Police Semi-Automatic Shotgun - 12 gauge magnum - circa 2004.

4   Winchester Model 1897 Slide-Action Shotgun - 12 gauge - circa 1942 - This cut-stock shotgun was used as an entry weapon by a Florida police department. Winchester's slide-action Model 1897 has been popular with law enforcement since its introduction. Offered in both takedown and solid-frame versions, the 1897 has also been manufactured in riot and trench configurations for the U.S. military.

5   Winchester Model 1907 Police Semi-Automatic Rifle - circa 1955 - Nearly 59,000 Model 1907 Winchester semi-auto rifles were manufactured from 1907 to 1957. The .351 Winchester cartridge used in these rifles was popular with law enforcement; extended magazines were made that offered increased capacity.

6   Colt AR15A3 Tactical Semi-Automatic Carbine - .223 Remington - circa 1994 - Law enforcement carbine with collapsible stock, removable carrying handle, and flash hider.

7   Remington Model 8 Autoloading Rifle - .30 Remington - circa 1930-1936 - Police carbine with extended magazine.

The Texas Rangers

Originally organized in the 1820s as a local militia force to protect settlers from attacks, the Texas Rangers became a full-time, paid corps in 1835. They served the U.S. Army as cavalry and scouts during the Mexican War of 1847 and many individual Rangers served in various Confederate cavalry units during the War Between the States. The Rangers were reconstituted in 1874 as a state-wide law enforcement agency. Active today, the Texas Rangers were placed under the authority of the Texas Department of Public Safety in 1935.

1 Smith & Wesson M&P Semi-Automatic Pistol - 9mm - circa 2006 - Law enforcement agencies transitioned from revolvers to semi-automatics in the mid-1980s. S&W introduced this semi-auto version to follow up on their classic M&P revolver.

2 Glock Model 17 Semi-Automatic pistol - 9mm Parabellum - circa 1990 - Its polymer "plastic" frame and absence of a traditional active safey were controversial when the Glock was first introduced. However, it gained rapid acceptance and became the issue sidearm of many law enforcement agencies. This example is from the Metropolitan Washington, DC, Police Department.

3 Beretta Model 92 SB Texas Ranger-Issue Semi-Automatic Pistol - 9 mm - circa 1980-1985.

4 Smith & Wesson Chemical Co. Model 277 Tear Gas Pistol - 37 mm - circa 1980 - S&W revolver N frame formed the platform for this single-shot police arm for teargas and non-lethal rounds.

5 Smith & Wesson 1st Model Ladysmith Revolver -- .22 rimfire – ca.1905. The tiny seven-shot Ladysmith was significantly smaller than any traditional double-action revolver made today. This one was carried as a back-up gun by a law enforcement officer in Freedom, NH; replaced oversize grips.

6 Dwight Van Horn's Presentation Colt Gold Cup Pistol 1993 - .45 ACP - circa 1993 - Dwight Van Horn received this engraved and cased pistol as the winner of the Harry Reeves Trophy, awarded to the champion of the NRA Police Semi-Automatice Service Pistol Match at the NRA National Police Shooting Championships.

TO SERVE AND PROTECT

Greater love hath no man than this, that a man lay down his life for his friends.
– John 15:13

❶

1. Officer Weaver's
Smith &Wesson Model 640 Revolver - .38 Special – ca. 1993

This stainless steel revolver was recovered from the World Trade Center ruins at Ground Zero. It was carried by New York Police Officer Walter Weaver on September 11, 2001. Walter Weaver, shield #2784, became an officer with the New York City Police Department (NYPD) in 1992. He was first assigned to the 47th Precinct, and in February 1998, Weaver fulfilled his dream of becoming a member of the NYPD Emergency Services Unit (ESU). He was an avid hunter and shooter.

On September 11 he was last seen rushing to the scene of the disaster with three other members of Truck 3.

Weaver was posthumously awarded the NYPD Medal of Honor during the Annual Medal Day ceremony on December 4, 2001. The New York City Police Department Medal of Honor is the highest award that may be bestowed upon a member of the service.

Officer Weaver's S&W was identified by its serial number and traced back to him and then donated to the National Firearms Museum by his parents.

2. Officer Garbarino's SIG Sauer Model P266 Semi-Automatic Pistol – 9 mm – ca. 2006

This Sig P226 semi-automatic pistol was owned by Fairfax County Police Officer Michael E. Garbarino. Officer Garbarino was 53 years old in 2006 when he died in the line of duty. He had served 23 years on the force.

On May 17, 2006, Officer Garbarino, passed away due to complications from his injuries received on May 8, 2006. Officer Garbarino was known for his infectious energy and friendly personality. He grew up in Wanaque, NJ, and became a police officer at William Paterson College in 1981. Fairfax County later hired him in 1983.

During his years in the department, he was a two-time recipient of the Officer of the Year award. He received two meritorious service awards in 1986 and was a field training instructor for newly assigned officers. On May 8, at approximately 3:30 P.M., during a shift change, an 18-year-old male drove a van that he had just stolen into the rear parking lot of the Sully District Station, exited the vehicle, and opened fire with a rifle on Officer Garbarino, who was sitting in his patrol car, striking him five times. The suspect also opened fire on Detective Vicky Armel, fatally wounding her as well.

Master Police Officer Michael Garbarino was a devoted Christian, loving husband and father, and a member of the National Rifle Association.

❷

William B. Ruger

Born in Brooklyn, New York, William B. Ruger developed an early interest in firearms by shooting on his high school rifle team. Studying gun books and patents, he developed a strong interest in firearms design. Just prior to World War II, Ruger took a job at the Springfield Armory, where he designed a machine gun and obtained a patent. In 1948, he and a partner, Alex Sturm, developed a .22 caliber self-loading pistol, and began Sturm, Ruger & Company. The .22 caliber Standard semi-automatic pistol was the first firearm they produced. The success of the design set Ruger to work developing a high-quality revolver. These products were followed by a long line of firearms including the Blackhawk series of single-action revolvers, black-powder revolvers, police revolvers, self-loading carbines, falling-block single-shot rifles, bolt-action rifles, semi-automatic rifles and pistols, and Red Label shotguns. Today, Ruger guns are made for every interest from plinking to big game hunting. The genius and marketability of Ruger's designs have made Sturm, Ruger & Company an American success story.

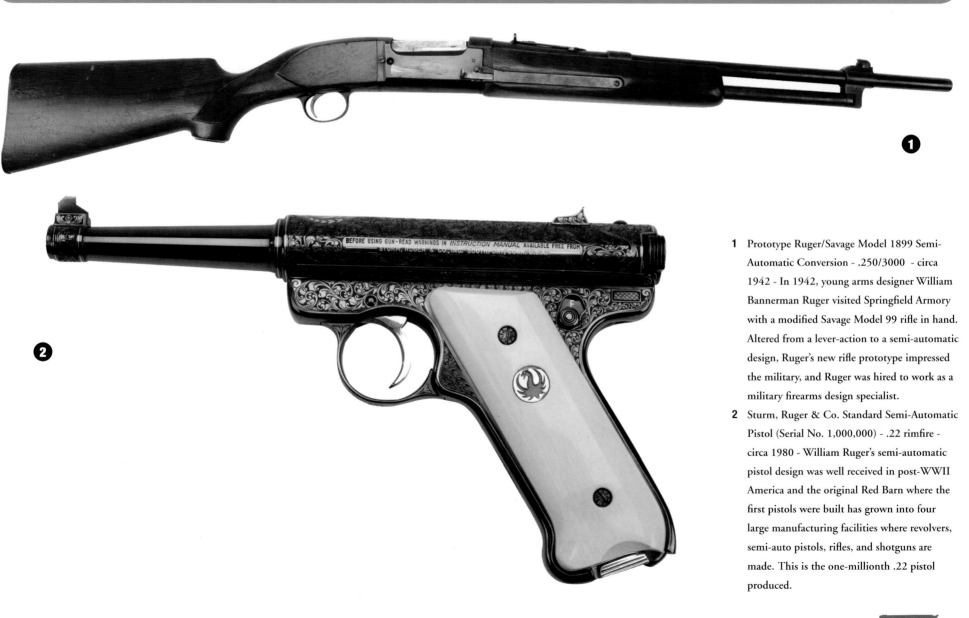

1 Prototype Ruger/Savage Model 1899 Semi-Automatic Conversion - .250/3000 - circa 1942 - In 1942, young arms designer William Bannerman Ruger visited Springfield Armory with a modified Savage Model 99 rifle in hand. Altered from a lever-action to a semi-automatic design, Ruger's new rifle prototype impressed the military, and Ruger was hired to work as a military firearms design specialist.

2 Sturm, Ruger & Co. Standard Semi-Automatic Pistol (Serial No. 1,000,000) - .22 rimfire - circa 1980 - William Ruger's semi-automatic pistol design was well received in post-WWII America and the original Red Barn where the first pistols were built has grown into four large manufacturing facilities where revolvers, semi-auto pistols, rifles, and shotguns are made. This is the one-millionth .22 pistol produced.

INNOVATIONS & ODDITIES

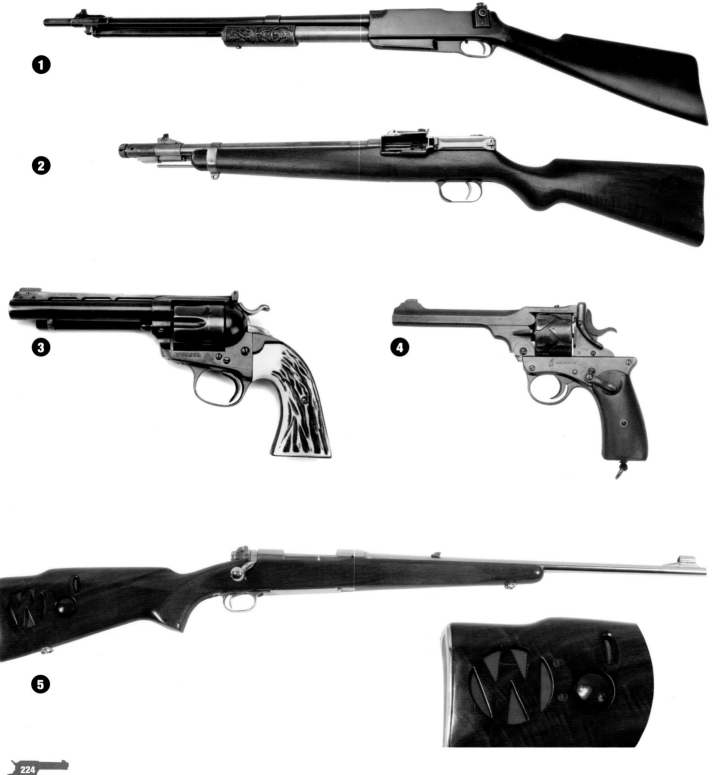

1 Standard Arms Model G Semi-Automatic Rifle - .35 Remington - circa 1910-1912 - While produced for less than four years (1910-1914), Standard Arms rifles were the first gas-operated longarms produced in America and offered the capability of shifting from slide-action to semi-automatic functioning; nearly 5,000 were made.

2 Heineman Experimental Prototype Semi-Automatic Carbine - 8mm Heineman - circa 1925 - Experimental 1920s' semi-auto design with sideways toggle-link action like a Luger pistol.

3 Elmer Keith's Colt Bisley Single Action Army Revolver (altered) -- .357 Magnum – Converted from .45 Colt and extensively modified by legendary shooter and firearms innovator Elmer Keith, who pushed handgun performance to new power levels, leading to the introduction of the .357 Magnum and .44 Magnum cartridges.

4 Webley-Fosbery Model 1902 Automatic Revolver - .455 Brit - circa 1920 - Combining the semi-automatic cycling of a pistol with the cylinder of a revolver, the Webley Fosbery was manufactured in both .38 (eight-shot) and .455 (six-shot) variants in calibers; less than 5,000 were made.

5 Winchester Model 70 Bolt-Action Rifle with Radio Stock - .30-06 - circa 1955 - Made in 1955, this plated Model 70 rifle features the first American-made transistor radio installed in its buttstock. According to the donor of this rifle, it was a custom project of the Winchester that was only shown at one trade show before the concept was abandoned.

1 Savage Albree Prototype Model 7 Semi-Automatic Rifle with telescopic sight - .22 rimfire - circa 1939 - Experimental slam-fire design.

2 Experimental/Prototype Mauser Semi-Automatic Pistol Carbine - 7.63 Mauser - circa 1900 - Combining the semi-automatic action of the Mauser M1896 pistol with a well-balanced carbine profile, this rifle never saw commercial production.

3 Winchester Model 52C Bolt-Action Rifle - .22 long rifle - circa 1955 - Toolroom prototype.

4 Armalite Golden Gun Semi-Automatic Shotgun - circa 1964-1965 - The glowing golden anodizing of the aluminum barrel and receiver gave the Golden Gun its name. Armalite produced only 2,000 examples of its AR-17 semi-automatic shotgun, with innovative ultra-lightweight construction and plastic stock ahead of its time, from 1964 to 1965.

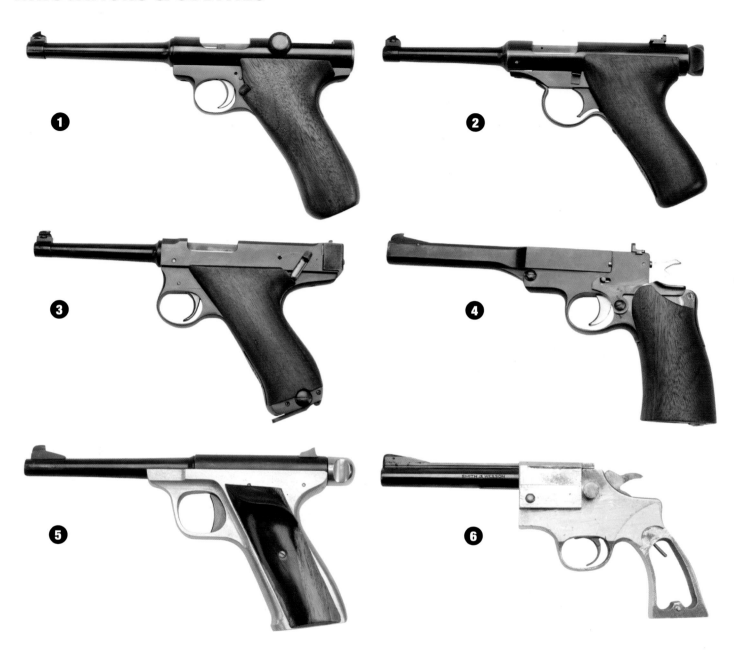

1 W.H.B. Smith WSP-50 Prototype Single-Shot Pistol - .22 rimfire - circa 1955 - Toggle-activated single-shot.

2 Smith Prototype WSP-90 Pistol - .22 rimfire - circa 1955 - Locked-cam single-shot.

3 W.H.B. Smith Prototype Straight-Pull Semi-Automatic Pistol - .22 rimfire - circa 1955 - Straight-pull semi-automatic.

4 Smith Prototype WSP-70 Single-Shot Pistol - .22 rimfire - circa 1955 - Break-open.

5 W.H.B. Smith Prototype WSP-75 Single-Shot Pistol - .22 rimfire - circa 1955 - Unfinished alloy frame.

6 W.H.B. Smith Prototype WSP-200A Single-Shot Pistol - .38 Special - circa 1955 - Break-open design made on alloy frame to test durability.

W.H.B. Smith

In the post-WWII era, W.H.B. Smith was a designer of firearms who incorporated expedient sintered-metal processes originally created by wartime German factories. Smith's prototypes included innovative toggle-link, break-open, and other handgun, rifle, and shotgun actions that were offered to companies including Winchester, Ithaca, and Marlin to serve as the foundation of new product lines. Smith authored the first editions of *Small Arms of the World*. The National Firearms Museum houses many of his design prototypes.

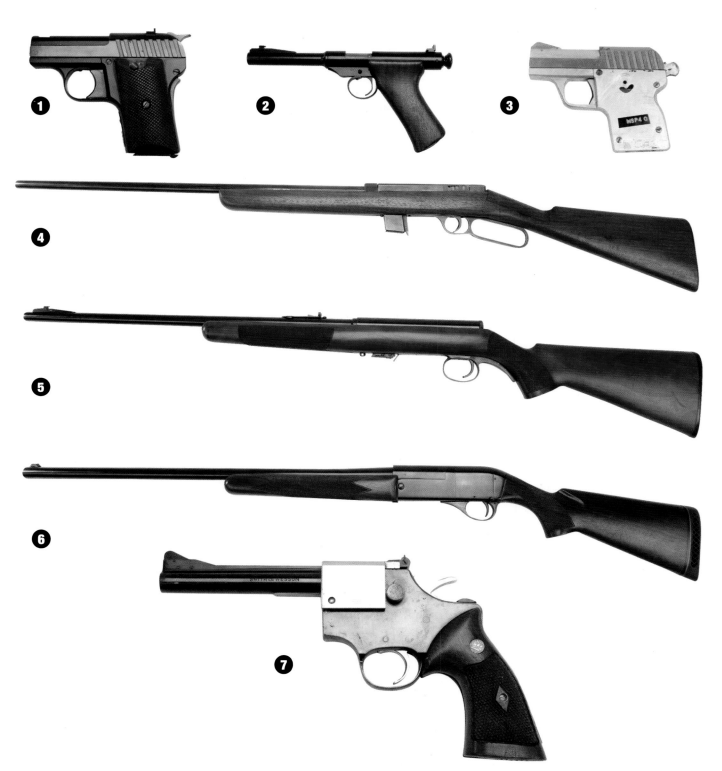

1 W.H.B. Smith Prototype WSP-20 Semi-Automatic Pistol - .22 rimfire - circa 1955 Sintered metal technology was used to create the receiver for this pistol.

2 W.H.B. Smith Prototype WSP-10 Single-Shot Pistol - .22 rimfire - circa 1955 - Manual-cocking single-shot.

3 W.H.B. Smith WSP-40 Second Model Prototype Semi-Automatic Pistol - .22 rimfire - circa 1955 - Unfinished toolroom sample.

4 Smith Prototype Lever-Action Rifle - circa 1955 - Intended for sale by Marlin as an inexpensive youth rifle.

5 Smith Prototype Semi-Automatic Rifle - .22 rimfire - circa 1955 - Demonstrator used in sales presentations.

6 W.H.B. Smith Prototype Single-Shot Shotgun - 12 gauge - circa 1955 - Fitted with interchangeable barrel assemblies.

7 W.H.B. Smith WSP-65 Prototype Single-Shot Pistol - .44 caliber - circa 1955 - Built as a test platform for .44 magnum ammunition then in production for the S&W Model 29 revolver; this pistol never made it past prototype status.

INNOVATIONS & ODDITIES

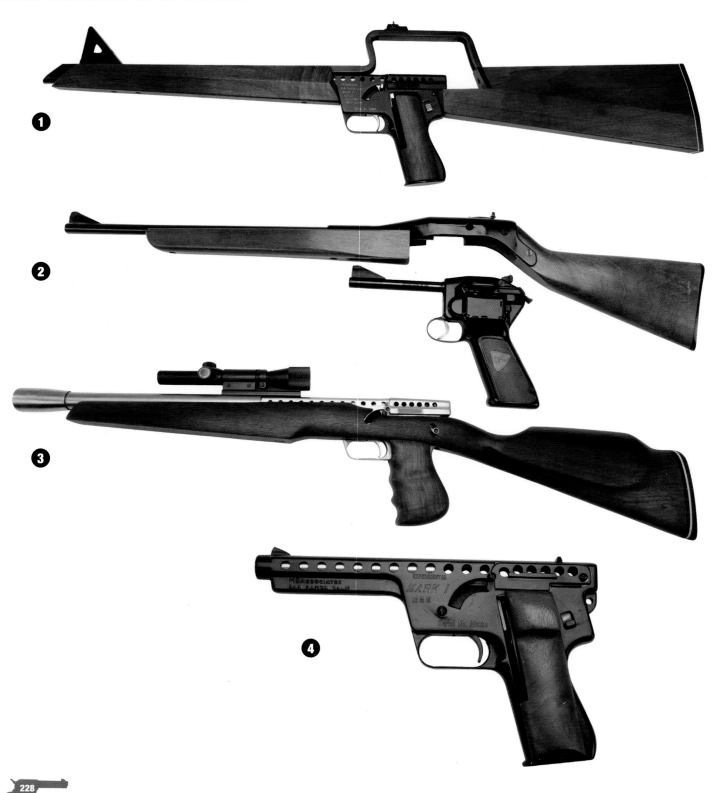

1. MB Associates Gyrojet Semi-Automatic Carbine - 13mm Gyrojet - circa 1966-1967 - Gyrojet rocket-ball projectiles started at low velocity inside the barrel, then accelerated to maximum velocity with 25 feet.

2. Dardick Series 1500 Pistol (Double-Action, Magazine-Fed Revolver) - .38 Dardick Tround - circa 1958-1960 - Fired ammunition called trounds, with bullet and powder housed in triangular polymer casings instead of round brass cases.

3. MB Associates Gyrojet 007 Semi-Automatic Carbine - 13mm Gyrojet - circa 1966-1967 - Reportedly made for a James Bond movie with SN 007.

4. MB Associates Gyrojet Mark I Pistol - 13mm Gyrojet - circa 1966-1967 - The first rocket-ball firearm, the MBA Associates Gyrojet, was manufactured as both 12mm and 13mm handgun and carbine arms; all relied on spin-stabilized rocket projectiles that were launched at an initially very low velocity from a vented smoothbore barrel.

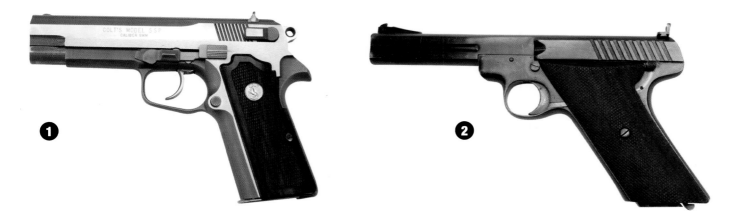

1 Colt Stainless Steel Pistol Prototype Semi-Automatic Pistol - 9mm Parabellum - circa 1972 - Less than 50 of the Stainless Steel Pistol (SSP) prototypes were manufactured by Colt after solicitation from the U.S. military to develop a double-action 9mm replacement for the Model 1911A1 pistol.

2 Colt Prototype WSP-60 Semi-Automatic Pistol - .22 rimfire - circa 1955 - Alternative pistol design for Colt Woodsman II.

3 Colt WSP-40 Prototype Semi-Automatic Pistol - .22 rimfire - circa 1955 - A variant of the Woodsman II design that had interchangeable barrels.

INNOVATIONS & ODDITIES

1 Chameleon Czechoslovakian Epoxy Revolver (non-firing model) - .44 Magnum - circa 1993 - Non-firing epoxy model built by Iron Curtain skating rink engineer with no firearms experience.

2 Danish Rifle Syndicate Schouboe Semi-Automatic Pistol - 11.35mm Schouboe - circa 1907 - Firing a lightweight wooden core bullet, the Schouboe was tested in U.S. Army trials in 1907.

3 Loosemore Prototype Open Bolt Rifle - .22 rimfire - circa 1988-1990 - Firing sample made for corporate presentations.

4 Loosemore Destroyer Semi-Automatic Pistol/Carbine Prototype - .30 Carbine - circa 1988-1990 - Handmade pistol blending Thompson and M1 carbine features.

1 Daisy-Heddon VL Single-Shot Caseless
   Cartridge Rifle - .22 VL - circa 1968-1969
   Daisy's VL system combined airgun and
   caseless ammunition technology. Designed to
   ignite a propellant charge moulded on the base
   of the projectile by compression, the Daisy was
   a hybrid airgun/firearm that met with little
   market acceptance.

2 Sommer & Ockenfuss GmbH German
   Marksman Tactical Rifle with Schmidt &
   Bender 3-12 x 50 Variable Scope - .308
   Winchester - circa 2001 - An unusually
   compact countersniper rifle, the Sommer &
   Ockenfuss utilizes a pump-action mechanism
   as part of its bullpup configuration.

INNOVATIONS & ODDITIES

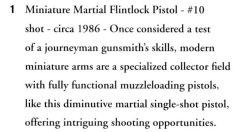

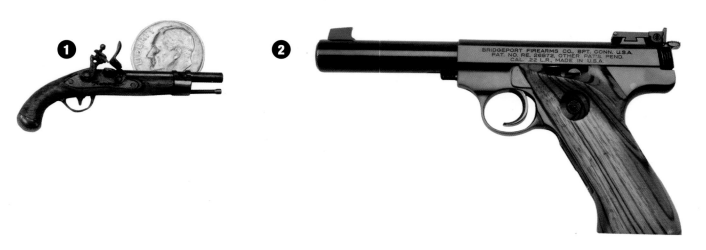

1 Miniature Martial Flintlock Pistol - #10 shot - circa 1986 - Once considered a test of a journeyman gunsmith's skills, modern miniature arms are a specialized collector field with fully functional muzzleloading pistols, like this diminutive martial single-shot pistol, offering intriguing shooting opportunities.

2 Bridgeport Firearms Co. Prototype P66 Pistol - .22 rimfire - circa 1966 - Semi-auto design made to compete with Colt/Ruger handguns: production ceased after Ruger lawsuit.

3 Dornaus and Dixon Bren Ten Semi-Automatic Pistol - 10 mm - circa 1983 - The first tactical semi-automatic pistol chambered for the 10mm cartridge, Dornhaus & Dixon's Bren Ten failed as a commercial success due to a lack of magazines available as the handguns were completed by the manufacturer.

4 Mikkenger Arms Grizzly Single-Action Revolver - .44 Magnum - circa 1976-1977 - Only American single-action revolver design to not utilize frame screws.

5 Smith & Wesson Model 66 Double-Action revolver (Blown up) - .357 Magnum - circa 1975 - Destroyed by handloaded ammunition.

1 Stevens Favorite Single-Shot Rifle - .32 rimfire - circa 1893-1939.

2 Noble Model 70 Slide-Action Shotgun - .410 gauge - circa 1953-1971.

3 Remington Model 6 Single-Shot Rifle - .22 rimfire - circa 1901-1933.

4 Quackenbush Convertible Air Rifle - circa 1884-1913 - An early BB gun popular at the turn of the century.

5 Harrington & Richardson 1920 Single-Shot Shotgun - .410 gauge - circa 1920 - This was a beginner shotgun for thousands of first-time gun owners who desired a solid and dependable, yet inexpensive shotgun.

6 Stevens No. 12 Marksman Single-Shot Rifle with Weaver B4 telescopic sight - .22 rimfire - circa 1912-1933.

Plinking

Since the turn of the century, the .22 caliber single-shot rifle has been the most popular first firearm for young boys and girls. Teaching the art and responsibility of safely handling a gun to a child or an adolescent is as old as firearms themselves. The craft and manufacture of specialized firearms for youth is nearly as old. By the late 19th century, well-known arms manufacturing companies regularly engaged in the design and sale of the boys' or ladies' rifles, as they were then termed. Many of America's youth came of age, as had their forefathers, learning to handle a gun safely and effectively. This instruction in safe gun handling, shared between parent and child, has become a traditional American rite of passage from childhood to adult responsibility.

FOR THE FUN OF IT

1 Thompson Center Classic semi-automatic rifle - .22 rimfire - circa 2000.

2 Remington Nylon 76 Lever-Action Rifle - .22 rimfire - circa 1972-1974 - This nylon stocked new-age rifle reflected the changing times and styles of the 1970s.

3 Savage Stevens Model 87 Semi-Automatic Rifle - .22 rimfire - circa 1938-1945.

4 Remington Model 512 Sportmaster Bolt-Action Rifle - .22 rimfire - circa 1940-1962.

5 Browning T-Bolt T-2 Straight-Pull Bolt-Action Rifle - .22 rimfire - circa 1965-1974 - Browning's T-Bolt .22 rifle offered a fast, straight-pull action that was built to move back and forth in one axis, unlike the turning motion needed with a traditional bolt-action rifle.

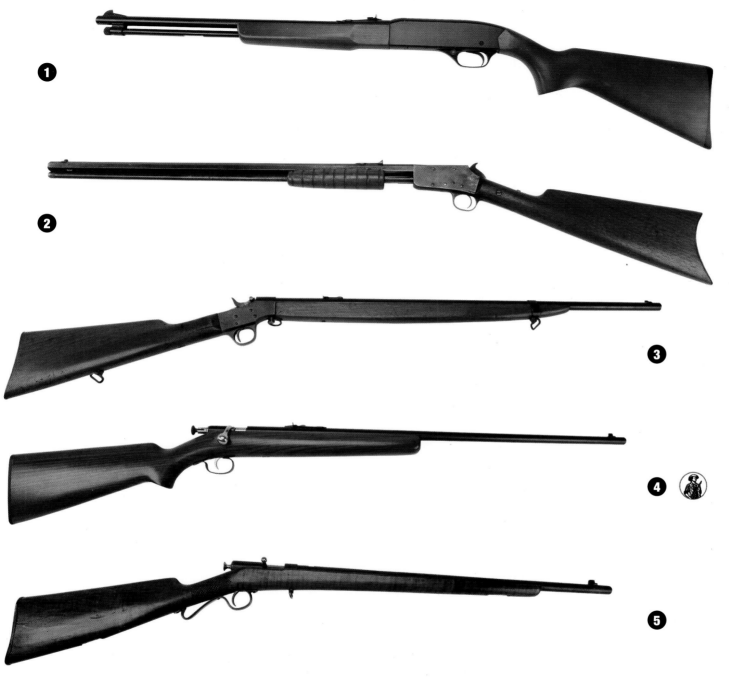

1 Winchester Model 190 Semi-Automatic Rifle - .22 rimfire - circa 1967-1980.

2 Marlin Model 20S Slide-Action Rifle - .22 rimfire - circa 1922-1927.

3 Meriden Arms Co. Single-Shot Rifle - .22 rimfire - circa 1913-1918.

4 Winchester Model 67 Bolt-Action Rifle - .22 rimfire - circa 1934.

5 Stevens No. 65 Little Krag Single-Shot Bolt-Action Rifle - .22 rimfire - circa 1903-1910.

FOR THE FUN OF IT

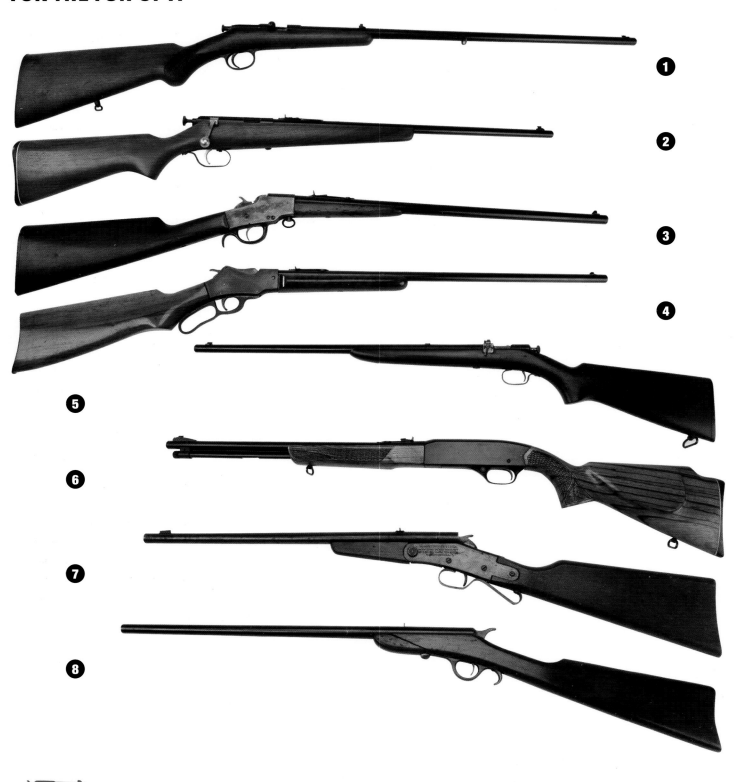

1 Simpson Bolt-Action Rifle - .22 rimfire - circa 1928-1941.

2 Marlin Model 101 Crown Prince Single-Shot Bolt-Action Rifle - .22 rimfire - circa 1959.

3 Hopkins & Allen Junior Falling-Block Single-Shot Rifle - .32 rimfire - circa 1905-1914.

4 Mossberg Model L Falling-Block Single-Shot Rifle - .22 rimfire - circa 1929-1932.

5 Winchester Model 59 Single-Shot Bolt-Action Rifle - .22 rimfire - circa 1930-1931.

6 Winchester Model 290 Deluxe Semi-Automatic Rifle - .22 rimfire - circa 1965-1973.

7 Hamilton No. 27 Single-Shot Rifle - .22 rimfire - circa 1907-1930.

8 Atlas Single-Shot Rifle - .22 rimfire - circa 1886-1890.

1 Hopkins & Allen Junior Repeater Rifle - .22 rimfire - circa 1902-1914.

2 Quackenbush Model 1886 Bicycle Pump Rifle - .22 rimfire/pellet - circa 1886-1890 Quackenbush's line of youth rifles were manufactured as rugged arms that could survive being tied to a bicycle for transport. Retractable wire stocks were offered on some models.

3 Anschutz Woodchucker Bolt-Action Rifle - .22 rimfire - circa 1960.

4 Winchester Model 36 Single-Shot Shotgun - 9mm rimfire shotshell - circa 1920-1927.

5 Browning BL-22 rifle - .22 long rifle - circa 1970-2003.

6 Daisy Model 2201 Bolt-Action Single-Shot Rifle - .22 rimfire - circa 1988-1991 - Daisy, traditionally a manufacturer of airguns, ventured into cartridge arms during the 1980s with their Legacy line of bolt-action rifles. While offered for less than four years, these single-shot or repeater .22 Daisy rifles were made with a choice of hardwood or plastic stocks.

7 Detroit Rifle Co. No. 11 Rifle - .22 rimfire - circa 1899-1905.

8 Armalite AR-7 Explorer Semi-Automatic Rifle - .22 rimfire - circa 1959-1960 - Designed to be broken down, with the collapsed parts stored in the water proof stock, this gun was designed to be used in wilderness and backpacking environments.

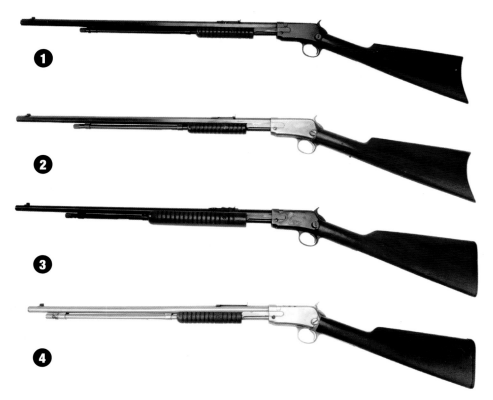

Original Coney Island Shooting Gallery, created in the first decade of the 20th century, on display at the National Firearms Museum.

Shooting Galleries

People have always been fascinated with testing their skill and marksmanship by shooting at a variety of objects. The development of the shooting gallery as a game at fairs, carnivals, and amusement parks is a distinctly American phenomenon. At the height of its popularity, amusement companies designed and produced elaborate galleries, which included still targets, knock downs, bells and chain-driven moving wheels, silhouettes, and bullseye targets. So popular was the pastime that all major firearms manufacturers produced lines of gallery rifles and pistols chambered for .22 rimfire ammunition, and ammunition makers turned out millions of .22 gallery cartridges.

1 Winchester Model 1890 Slide-Action Rifle - circa 1913.

2 Winchester Model 1890 Slide-Action Rifle - circa 1912.

3 Winchester Model 62A Slide-Action Rifle - .22 rimfire - circa 1936.

4 Winchester Model 1906 Slide-Action Rifle - .22 rimfire - circa 1926 - Almost 850,000 Model 1906 slide-action rifles were manufactured by Winchester from 1906 to 1932. It differed from the earlier Model 1890 in that it was only offered in a round barrel configuration.

5 Winchester Model 1906 Slide-Action Rifle - .22 rimfire - circa 1924.

6 Savage Model 29B Slide-Action Rifle - .22 rimfire - circa 1929-1950.

7 Remington Model 25 Slide-Action Rifle - .32-20 - circa 1886-1890.

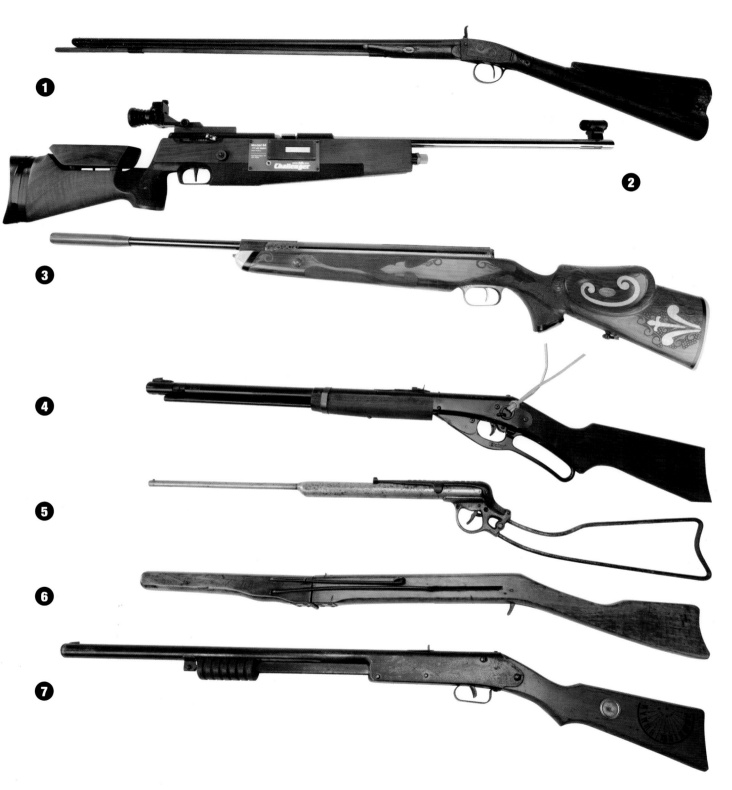

1 English Smoothbore Muzzleloading Air Rifle - .52 caliber - circa 1780-1800 - Air rifles go back as far as the 1600s in design and manufacture. Some were even uses as military arms during the Napoleonic Wars of the early 1800s.

2 Pres. George H.W. Bush's Crosman Challenger Air Rifle - .177 pellet - circa 1985 - Given to Vice President G.H.W. Bush during the 1984 Olympic Games in Los Angeles, CA. It has a unique metering register on the side that utilizes an LCD readout to report the amount of pressure available for shooting.

3 Prince Charles' Feinwerkbau Omega 124 Air Rifle - .177 pellet - circa 1988 - With detailed marquetry work on the buttstock featuring the symbol of the House of Windsor, this Feinwerkbau air rifle was presented to HRH Prince Charles, who donated the airgun to the National Firearms Museum in token of the NRA's assistance with providing firearms to Great Britain during WWII.

4 Daisy Red Ryder Commemorative Lever-Action Air Rifle - .177/BB - circa 1995 - Reproduced in 1984 as part of a movie promotion, the Daisy Red Ryder BB gun began manufacture in 1939. Many commemorative versions of this popular BB gun followed.

5 Markham Air Rifle Company Model 1886 Air Rifle - .177/BB - circa 1887-1910 - The Markham Air Rifle Company in Plymouth, MI, produced the first commercially successful BB guns in 1887. This example was presented to NRA President Harold Glassen in 1967 as a gift for the National Firearms Museum.

6 The first Daisy air gun - .177/BB - circa 1889-1900 This is the first Daisy air gun ever produced. It was donated in 1967 to NRA President Harold Galassen by the Daisy company as a gift for the NRA museum collection. It is a Model 1888 air rifle.

7 Daisy Buck Jones Special BB gun - .177 pellet - circa 1934-1942 - This slide-action BB gun manufactured by Daisy from 1934 to 1942 featured sundial markings on the stock as well as a small embedded compass.

FOR THE FUN OF IT

1. Crosman Model 130 Single-Shot Air Pistol (sectionalized) - .22 pellet - circa 1955-1970.
2. Daisy Model 177 Repeating Air Pistol - .177/BB - circa 1959-1978.
3. Daisy NRA Centennial Commemorative Peacemaker Repeating Air Pistol - .177/BB - circa 1971 - Part of an NRA centennial set with a Winchester-styled Daisy lever-action BB rifle, this single-action revolver-styled BB handgun was sold by the Daisy company in 1971 and 1972.
4. Daisy Model 118 Target Special Air Pistol - .118 pellet - circa 1937-1952.
5. Diana German Model No. 1 Air Pistol - .177/BB - circa 1924-1940.
6. Webley Junior Air Pistol - .177/BB - circa 1929-1938 - The last firearms produced by the venerable Webley firm, founded in 1790, were air guns.
7. Crosman Model 116 Air Pistol (sectionalized) - .177/BB - circa 1951-1954.
8. Crosman Hahn 45 Single-Action Air Pistol - .177/BB - circa 1959-1969.
9. Crosman Single-Action 6 CO2 Pistol - .22 rimfire - circa 1959-1969.
10. Healthways Model 175 Plainsman CO2 Pistol - .177/BB - circa 1969-1980.
11. Hahn Model 45 Single-Action CO2 Pistol - .177/BB - circa 1959-1969.
12. Hy-Score Model 800 Air Pistol - .22 pellet - circa 1948-1970.
13. Daisy Model 188 air pistol - .177 pellet / BB - circa 1980.
14. Crosman Marksman BB pistol - .177/BB - circa 1977.
15. Crosman Model 150 CO2 Pistol (sectionalized) - circa 1956-1967.
16. Webley Tempest Air Pistol - .177 pellet - circa 1979-1981.

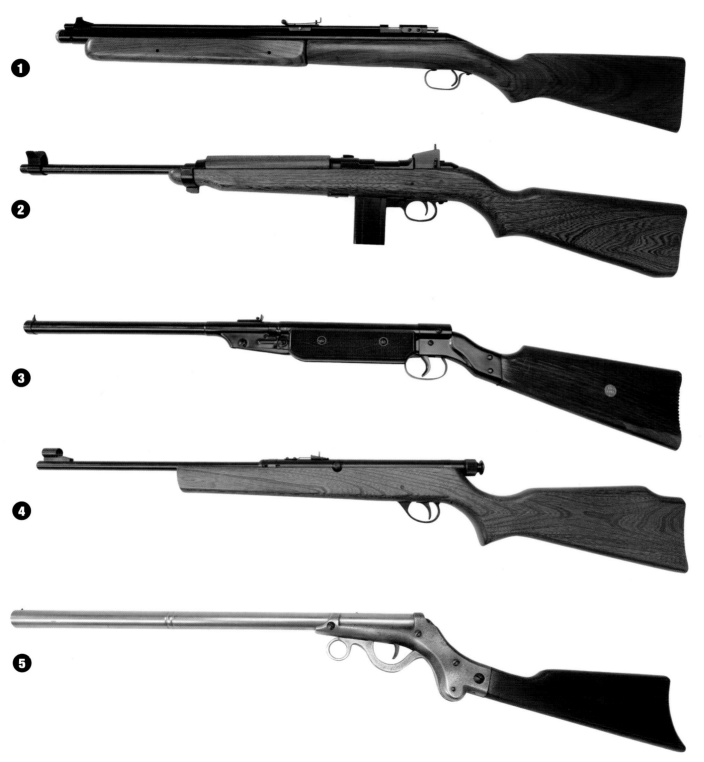

1   Sheridan Blue Streak Single-Shot Air Rifle -
    5mm pellet - circa 1952-1963.

2   Crosman M1 Carbine Air Rifle - .177/BB -
    circa 1968-1976 - This air rifle appealed to the
    post-war baby boomers who desired a realistic
    copy of the M1 Carbine.

3   Hy-Score Model 808 Single-Shot Air Rifle -
    .177 pellet - circa 1970-1980.

4   Crosman Model 700 Pellmaster Air Rifle - .22
    pellet - circa 1967-1971.

5   Atlas Single-Shot Air Rifle - .177/BB - circa
    1886-1890.

Air Guns

The firing of a projectile through the use of compressed air, gas, and spring-loaded guns has a long history of development and goes back as far as the 16th century. By the late 19th century, these guns developed into a popular toy for young boys and girls. While some are still used today for serious Olympic target and sporting purposes, the great majority of those manufactured are intended for recreational plinking by the youth of the world. In 1870, Henry M. Quackenbush patented an air gun that accepted both BBs and darts. In 1882, Clarence Hamilton of Plymouth, Michigan, developed an all-metal air gun. The Hamilton air gun was given the now-familiar name Daisy. The very first Daisy is on display at the National Firearms Museum, a gift of the present-day Daisy Manufacturing Company. In a child's world, the name Daisy has become as recognizable and familiar as Colt and Winchester. In 1890, Daisy was selling about 85,000 air guns per year. By 1960, annual production and sales were close to 1.5 million.

FOR THE FUN OF IT

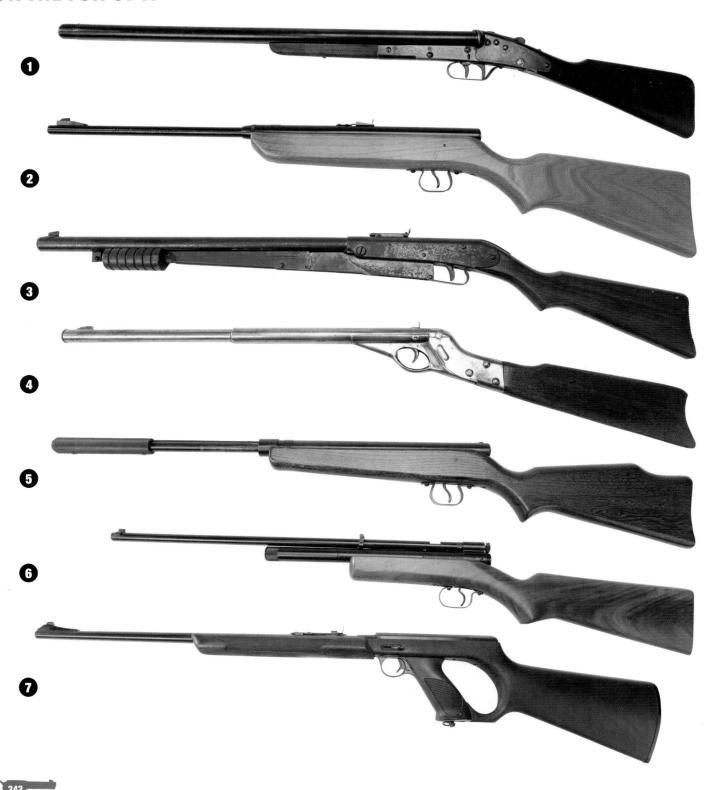

1. Daisy Model 104 Double-Barrel Air Gun - .177/BB - circa 1938-1940.

2. Crosman V-350 Air Rifle - .177/BB - circa 1961-1969.

3. Daisy Model 25 Slide-Action Air Rifle - .22 pellet - circa 1972.

4. Markham King Model D Air Rifle - .22 pellet - circa 1907-1909.

5. Crosman Experimental Air Rifle - .177/BB - circa 1960-1961.

6. Benjamin Model 362 CO2 Carbine - .22 pellet - circa 1956-1957.

7. Daisy Model 300 CO2 Rifle - BB - circa 1968-1975.

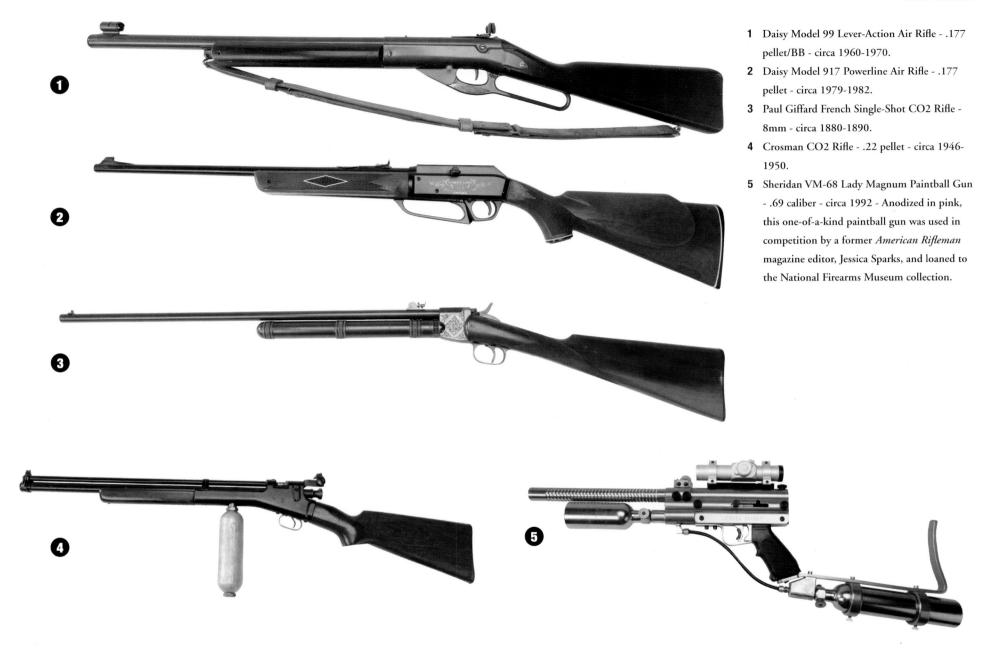

1 Daisy Model 99 Lever-Action Air Rifle - .177 pellet/BB - circa 1960-1970.

2 Daisy Model 917 Powerline Air Rifle - .177 pellet - circa 1979-1982.

3 Paul Giffard French Single-Shot CO2 Rifle - 8mm - circa 1880-1890.

4 Crosman CO2 Rifle - .22 pellet - circa 1946-1950.

5 Sheridan VM-68 Lady Magnum Paintball Gun - .69 caliber - circa 1992 - Anodized in pink, this one-of-a-kind paintball gun was used in competition by a former *American Rifleman* magazine editor, Jessica Sparks, and loaned to the National Firearms Museum collection.

FOR THE FUN OF IT

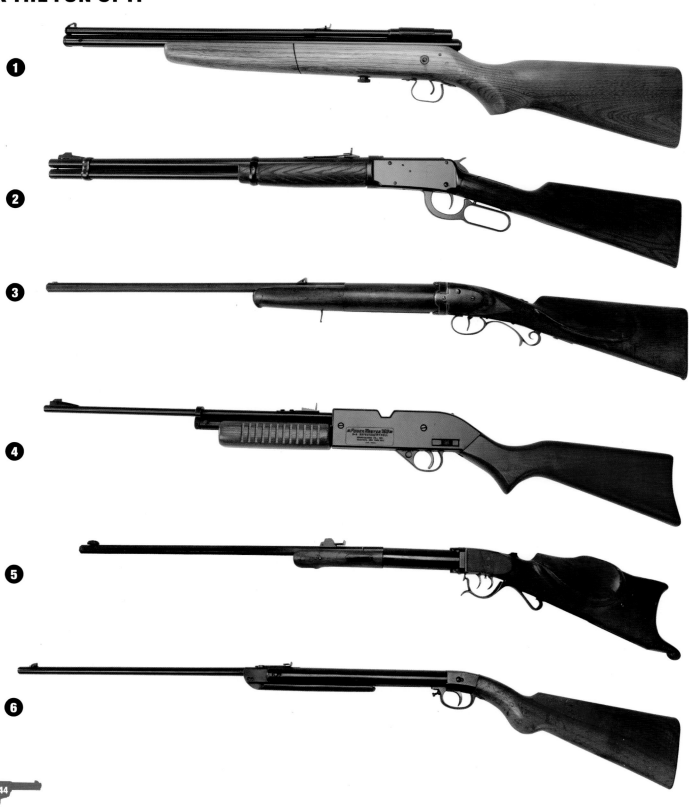

1 Crosman Model 140 Single-Shot Air Rifle - .22 pellet - circa 1956-1962.

2 Daisy Model 1894 Lever-Matic Repeating Air Rifle - .177/BB - circa 1970-1980.

3 German Crank-Action Air Rifle - 7 mm - circa 1870.

4 Crosman Powermaster 760 Air Rifle - .177 pellet - circa 1966-1970.

5 Mayer & Grammelspacher German Diana Model 27 Air Rifle - .177 pellet - circa 1910-1936.

6 German Lever-Action Single-Shot Air Rifle - 6.5mm - circa 1870.

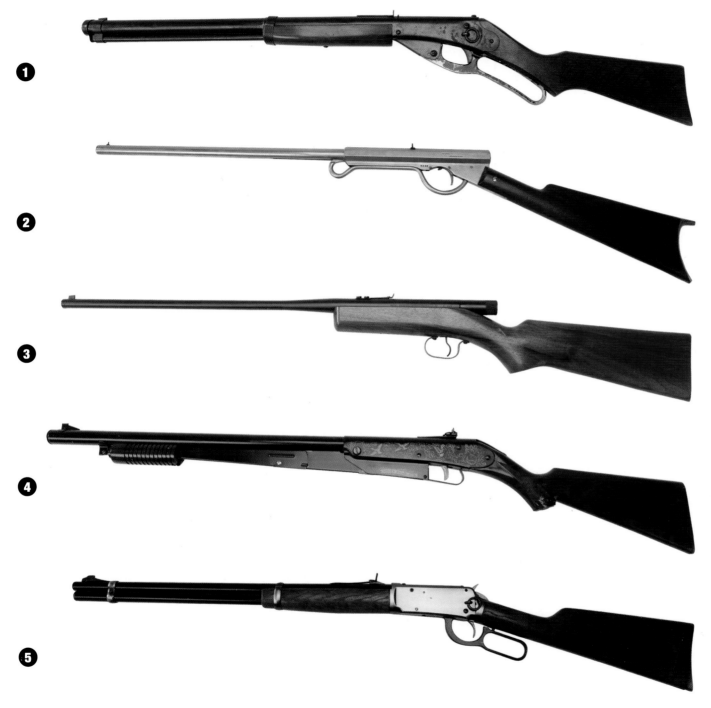

1 Daisy Red Ryder No. 111 Model 40 Lever-Action Air Rifle - .177/BB - circa 1947 - The Red Ryder is still in production, a favorite among youngsters.

2 Quackenbush Single-Shot Air Rifle - .21 pellet - circa 1881-1919.

3 Benjamin Model 30/30 Carbine - .177 pellet - circa 1972-1976.

4 Daisy Model 25 Slide-Action Air Rifle - .177 pellet - circa 1972.

5 Daisy Model 1894 NRA Centennial Commemorative Lever-Action Air Rifle - .177/BB - circa 1971 - Manufactured in 1971 and 1972, the Daisy BB gun made for the NRA centennial was based on a Winchester Model 1894 lever-action rifle. It was part of a set that also included a Daisy BB pistol based on a Colt single-action revolver.

FOR THE FUN OF IT

Thomas William Selleck

Actor, film producer, and member of the NRA Board of Directors, Tom Selleck is known for his interest in historical firearms. From the .45-110 Shiloh Sharps rifle that he wielded as Matthew Quigley in the 1990 film *Quigley Down Under,* to the Smith & Wesson Schofield revolver used in 2001's *Crossfire Trail,* Selleck chooses firearms that are eminently appropriate to the historical period depicted in the movie, using modern firing reproductions that are identical to the original arms of the period. For a film like *Last Stand at Saber River,* which made it to the silver screen in 1997, and was set on film as being just after the American Civil War, Selleck's armaments included an engraved Henry rifle and a Colt Open-Top revolver. For the 2004 film *Monte Walsh,* set as the western frontier is closing, Selleck's guns include a later Winchester Model 1886 carbine. Selleck's contracts with film producers have specified that any firearms that he uses onscreen become part of his compensation package. He has donated the guns shown here to the NRA.

1 Tom Selleck's Colt Open-Top Revolver - .44 caliber - Used by Tom Selleck in *Crossfire Trail* (2001).

2 Tom Selleck's Single-Action Army Revolver - .45 Colt - Used by Tom Selleck in *Last Stand at Saber River* (1997).

3 Tom Selleck's S&W Schofield Revolver - .45 Schofield - Used by Tom Selleck in *Crossfire Trail* (2001).

4 Tom Selleck's Reproduction Richards Conversion Revolver - Used by Tom Selleck in *Last Stand at Saber River* (1997).

5 Tom Selleck's Single-Action Army Revolver with ivory grips - .45 Colt - Used by Tom Selleck in *Monte Walsh* (2003).

6 Tom Selleck's Colt Single-Action Army Revolver with ivory grips - .45 Colt - Used by Tom Selleck in *Monte Walsh* (2003).

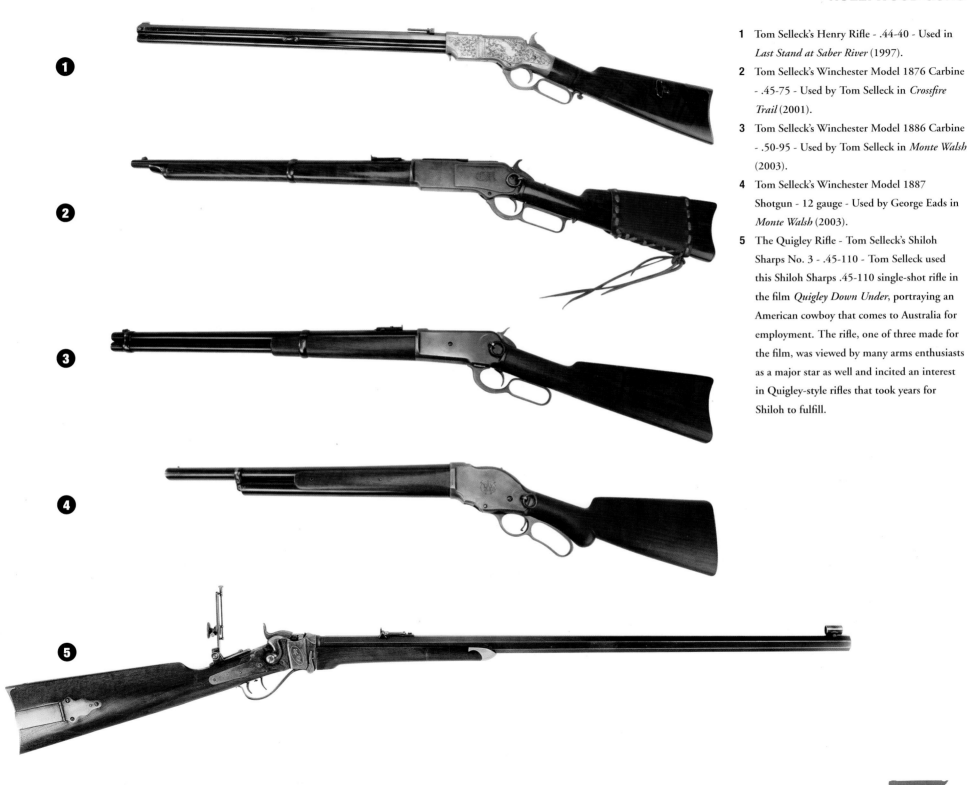

1 Tom Selleck's Henry Rifle - .44-40 - Used in *Last Stand at Saber River* (1997).

2 Tom Selleck's Winchester Model 1876 Carbine - .45-75 - Used by Tom Selleck in *Crossfire Trail* (2001).

3 Tom Selleck's Winchester Model 1886 Carbine - .50-95 - Used by Tom Selleck in *Monte Walsh* (2003).

4 Tom Selleck's Winchester Model 1887 Shotgun - 12 gauge - Used by George Eads in *Monte Walsh* (2003).

5 The Quigley Rifle - Tom Selleck's Shiloh Sharps No. 3 - .45-110 - Tom Selleck used this Shiloh Sharps .45-110 single-shot rifle in the film *Quigley Down Under*, portraying an American cowboy that comes to Australia for employment. The rifle, one of three made for the film, was viewed by many arms enthusiasts as a major star as well and incited an interest in Quigley-style rifles that took years for Shiloh to fulfill.

FOR THE FUN OF IT

1 Theatrical Trapdoor Pistol - .50-70 - circa 1875 - Large single-shot handguns like this trapdoor example were produced by theatrical companies seeking to have a firearm on hand that could be used for sound effect (shooting or thunder) for their productions.

2 Saco Defense Systems Division M60 E3 Light Machine Gun - 7.62mm NATO - circa 1971 - Originally serving with the U.S. military in Southeast Asia, this modified M60 light machine gun was purchased by a Hollywood prop house and used in several films including *Rambo II*, *Commando*, and *Predator*.

3 Dirty Harry's Smith & Wesson Model 29

Double-Action Revolver - .44 Magnum - circa 1960 - One of three Smith & Wesson Model 29 revolvers commissioned for the film *Dirty Harry*, this double-action .44 magnum revolver was presented to screenwriter John Milius, who coined its on-screen appellation of being the world's most powerful handgun (Inset, Clint Eastwood as Harry Callahan).

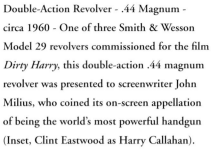

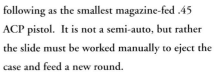

following as the smallest magazine-fed .45 ACP pistol. It is not a semi-auto, but rather the slide must be worked manually to eject the case and feed a new round.

8 Glock Model 17 Semi-Automatic Pistol (sectionalized) - 9 mm - circa 1987 - Featuring polymer construction, the Glock 17 was the invention of Austrian Gaston Glock. The Glock has been adopted by many law enforcement agencies to replace their revolvers. In addition to its large 17-round magazine capacity, a factor in its selection may have been the pistol's simple operation, which would ease the transition to the new gun. Like the double-action revolver, the Glock has no external safety devices to manipulate and requires only a single pull on the trigger for each shot.

9 Whitney Firearms Corp. Wolverine Semi-Automatic Pistol - .22 rimfire - circa 1955-1962.

1 Sturm, Ruger & Co. Redhawk Double-Action Revolver - .44 Magnum - circa 1985.

2 Sturm, Ruger & Co. Old Model Blackhawk Single-Action Revolver - .44 Magnum - circa 1971 - Ruger Blackhawk Models combined the classic Single-Action Army lines with modern design including coil springs, adjustable sights, and modern metallurgy. The .44 Magnum Blackhawk was only offered for a brief time before being replaced by the beefier Super Blackhawk.

3 Remington XP-100 Bolt-Action Pistol - .221 Fireball - circa 1963-1967 - One of the early specialty single-shot handgun designs made for high-power hunting and long-range target competition.

4 Thompson/Center Arms Contender Single-Shot Pistol - .45 Colt/.410 shotshell - circa 1967-1969 - Few firearms have the capability to fire as many cartridge types as the Thompson-Center Contender. Interchangeable barrels and selective firing pins allow this single-shot handgun design to fire rimfire or centerfire ammunition without disruption.

5 Arcadia Machine Tool AutoMag Semi-Automatic Pistol - .44 AMT/.357 AMT - circa 1971-1973 - Built as a semi-custom hot rod handgun, the stainless Automag pistol allowed owners to handload ammunition to meet metallic silhouette and hunting requirements. Interchangeable barrel assemblies allowed swapping from .357 to .41 or .44 Automag calibers.

6 Dan Wesson Model 12 Double-Action Revolver - .357 Magnum cartridge - circa 1971 - Dan Wesson revolvers featured interchangeable barrels, allowing users to go from snub nose concealment barrels to longer hunting barrels.

7 Semmerling LM Pistol - .45 ACP - circa 1978-1982 - The Semmerling enjoyed a cult

MODERN FIREARMS

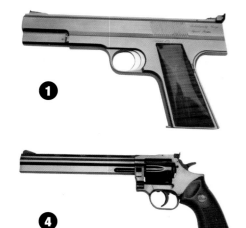

7 COP Four-Barrel Derringer - .357 Magnum - circa 1982 - COP is short for "Compact Off-Duty Police." Its small, heavy weight (28 oz.), and limited four-shot capacity restricted its popularity as a back-up.

8 Colt Agent Double-Action Revolver - .38 Special - circa 1956-1972 - This model featured a shortened grip frame for better concealment.

9 Colt Marshal Model Double-Action Revolver - .38 Special - circa 1955 - Round-butt variant of Official Police model. Only 2,500 were made.

10 Smith & Wesson Model 19 Combat Magnum Double-Action Revolver - .357 Magnum - circa 1958 - Classic mid-size K frame .357 Magnum. Widely popular police sidearm, made from 1955 to 1999.

11 Sturm, Ruger & Co. KSPNY-182 Double-Action-Only Revolver - .38 Special - circa 1990 - It has a factory-bobbed hammer and was made under a special law enforcement contract for State Police of New York.

12 Smith & Wesson Model 645 Double-Action Sem-Automatic Pistol - .45 ACP - circa 1988.

1 Sokolovsky .45 Automaster Semi-Automatic Pistols - .45 ACP - circa 1984-1985 - Handbuilt in Grass Valley, CA, about 20 of the Sokolovsky semi-automatic pistols were manufactured in versions that included a heavier target handgun. No screws were used in the Automaster design. The trigger had safety, magazine release, and firing functions.

2 MIL, Inc., Thunder Five Double-Action Revolver - .45 Colt / .410 shotshell - circa 1994-1998.

3 Thomas /AJ Ordnance Semi-Automatic Pistol - .45 ACP - circa 1971 - Short-lived design with unique features for the time, including blowback action, double-action only, and stainless steel barrel.

4 Dan Wesson Model 15 Double-Action Revolver with case - .357 Magnum - circa 2000 - Interchangeable barrels.

5 Israel Military Industries Desert Eagle Semi-Automatic Pistol - .357 Magnum - circa 2001 - Gas-operated semi-auto for high-power Magnum cartridges traditionally chambered in revolvers.

6 Freedom Arms Model 83 Premier-Grade Single-Action Revolver - .454 Casull - circa 1999 - Briefly eclipsed the .44 Magnum as the most powerful production revolver until the introduction of the .500 Magnum.

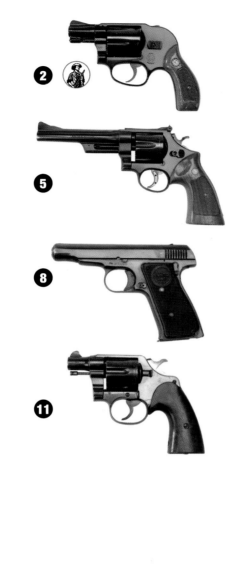

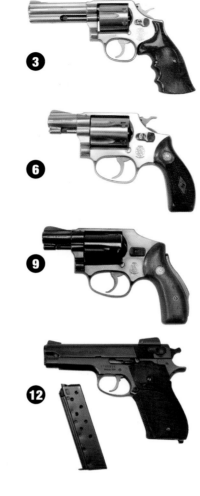

①

②

③

④

⑤

⑥

⑦

⑧

⑨

⑩

⑪

⑫

⑬

with a dull finish; it was made between 1954 and 1986.

6 Smith & Wesson Model 60 Chief's Special Double-Action Revolver - .38 Special - circa 1966-1967 - Stainless steel construction added corrosion resistance to five-shot compact concealment revolver; it has been made since 1965 to the present.

7 L. W. Seecamp LWS 32 Special Edition Semi-Automatic Pistol - .32 ACP - circa 2000-2001 - Ultracompact pocket pistol that got its start from Louis Seecamps's conversions of Colt M1911 pistols to double-action operation.

8 Remington Model 51 Semi-Automatic Pistol - .380 ACP - circa 1928-1930 - 65,000 made.

9 Smith & Wesson Centennial Model 40 Double-Action Revolver - .38 Special - circa 1960-1962 - Five-shot hammerless (concealed hammer) revolver with a grip safety.

10 SIG Sauer P220 NRA Semi-Automatic Pistol - circa 2010.

11 Colt New Service Model Double-Action Revolver - .45 Colt - circa 1915 - Colt's first large-frame swing-out cylinder revolver model; 365,000 were made from 1898 to 1944. This one has a bobbed barrel for concealment.

12 Smith & Wesson Model 539 Semi-Automatic Pistol - 9 mm - circa 1982 - Second-generation S&W semi-auto.

13 Coonan Arms, Inc. .357 Magnum Semi-Automatic Pistol - .357 Magnum - circa 1991 - Carried by a Vermont sheriff in the performance of his law enforcement duties.

1 Colt Trooper Double-Action Revolver - circa 1967.

2 Smith & Wesson Model 49 Bodyguard Double-Action Revolver - .38 Special - circa 1969-1970 - Frame extended to conceal hammer spur, which prevents snagging on clothing during concealed carry, but allows

hammer cocking for single-action firing if desired, made 1959-1996.

3 Smith & Wesson Model 681 Double-Action Revolver - circa 1981-1982 - Fixed-sight double-action stainless revolver model manufactured from 1980 to 1992.

4 Colt Police Positive Special Double-Action

Revolver - circa 1924 - Popular police revolver, a larger version of Police Positive; one million made from 1908 to 1978, most in .38 Special.

5 Smith & Wesson Model 28 Double-Action Revolver - .357 Magnum - circa 1973 - Also known as the "Highway Patrolman," a heavy N frame revolver similar to the Model 27, but

MODERN FIREARMS

①

②

③

④

⑤

⑥

⑦

⑧

⑨

system as Pre-Model (number).

7 High Standard Model D-100 Over/Under Derringer - .22 long rifle - circa 1967-1969 - Also offered in .22 Magnum, it enjoyed brief popularity as a backup gun.

8 Smith & Wesson Model 340PD Double-Action Revolver - .357 Magnum - circa 2004 Ultra-lightweight scandium alloy frame revolvers make for easy carry at the cost of heavy recoil when fired.

9 Kel-Tec Model P3AT Semi-Automatic pistol - .380 ACP - circa 2003-2006 - One of the first of a new wave of ultra-compact, ultra-lightweight .380 DAO pocket pistols. It is unsafe to carry a handgun in a pocket without an appropriate holster that covers the triggerguard.

1 Smith & Wesson Model 59 Semi-Automatic Pistol - 9 mm - circa 1980 - This was the first of the "wonder nine" pistols. The term is applied to traditional double-action 9 mm semi-autos with double-stack high-capacity magazines; it was introduced in 1971.

2 Heckler & Koch Model PSP Semi-Automatic Pistol - 9 mm - circa 1980 - With a unique squeeze-cocking action, the semi-automatic Heckler & Koch PSP and P7 pistols found little acceptance in the American law enforcement community and had only limited

issue in departments including the U.S. Capitol Police.

3 AMT Backup II Semi-Automatic Pistol - .380 ACP - circa 1996 - Original model introduced in the 1980s was one of the earlier stainless steel subcompact semi-auto pistols.

4 Colt Delta Elite Semi-Automatic Pistol - 10 mm - circa 1990 - Colt adapted its 1911 platform to many calibers after establishing it with the .45 ACP cartridge. The high-intensity 10mm cartridge in the Colt Delta Elite model pistol required slight modification

of the frame to prevent rail cracking under recoil stresses.

5 Charter Arms Undercover Double-Action Revolver - .38 Special - circa 1989 - Founded in 1964, Charter is best known for lightweight alloy frame concealable revolvers.

6 Smith & Wesson Pre-Model 27 Double-Action Revolver - .357 Magnum - circa 1956 - In the 1950s, S&W replaced model names with model numbers. The .357 Magnum became Model 27. Gun enthusiasts find it handy to refer to models made before the numbering

1 Valmet M-76W Semi-Automatic Rifle - 7.62mm x 39 - circa 1976-1986 - Finnish Kalashnikov offered in 5.56 and 7.62 NATO variants.

2 Steyr AUG Semi-Automatic Rifle - 5.56 mm NATO (.223) - circa 1989 - A bullpup design incorporating polymer components, the Steyr Armee Universal Gewehr (AUG) 5.56mm rifle was adopted by the Austrian army in 1977 and serves with several other military forces around the world.

3 Colt AR-15 Semi-Automatic Rifle - 5.56 mm - circa 1979 - Semi-auto version of military M16 rifle.

4 Springfield Armory M-1A Semi-Automatic Rifle - 7.62mm NATO - circa 1984 - Semi-auto version of military M14 rifle.

5 Marlin Model 88 Semi-Automatic Rifle (sectionalized) - .22 long rifle - circa 1948-1956.

MODERN FIREARMS

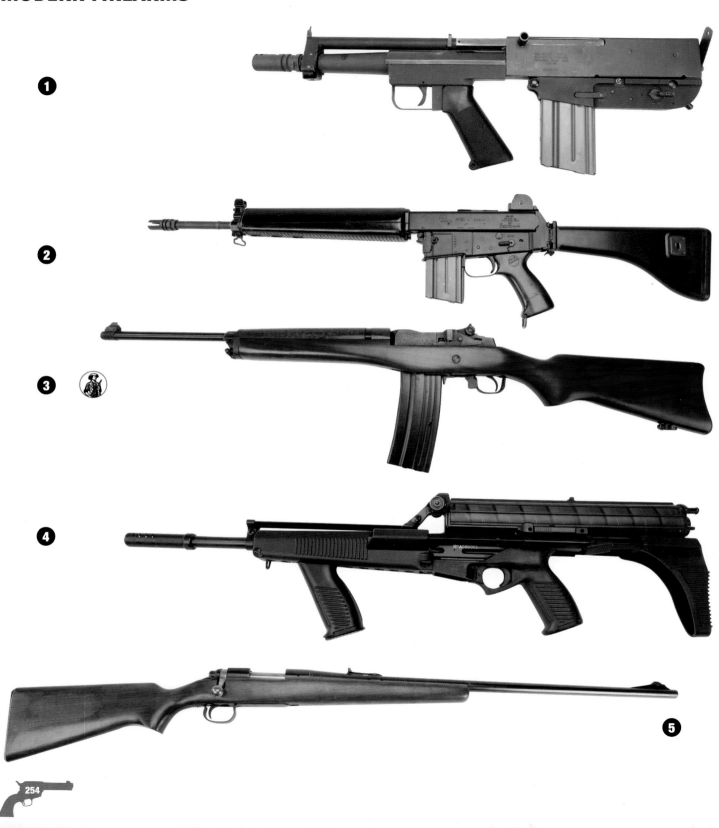

1 Bushmaster Semi-Automatic Pistol - .223
   Remington - circa 1986-1988 - Gwinn Arms
   blended AK-47 and AR-15 features into
   bullpup pistol.

2 Sterling Armament, Ltd. AR-180 Semi-
   Automatic Rifle - 5.56 mm - ca. 1980-1982
   Manufactured in California, Japan, and
   England, the Armalite AR-180 was a piston-
   driven rival to the Colt AR-15 design in the
   1960s and 1970s.

3 Sturm, Ruger & Co. Mini-14 Series 180
   Semi-Automatic Rifle - .223 Remington - circa
   1975 - Ruger offered both selective-fire and
   semi-auto versions.

4 Calico Systems M-951 Semi-Automatic
   Tactical Carbine - 9 mm - circa 1986 - Serial
   number NRA000001.

5 Remington Model 722(A) Bolt-Action
   Rifle - .244 Remington - circa 1948-1958 -
   Short-action model offered in choice of seven
   calibers.

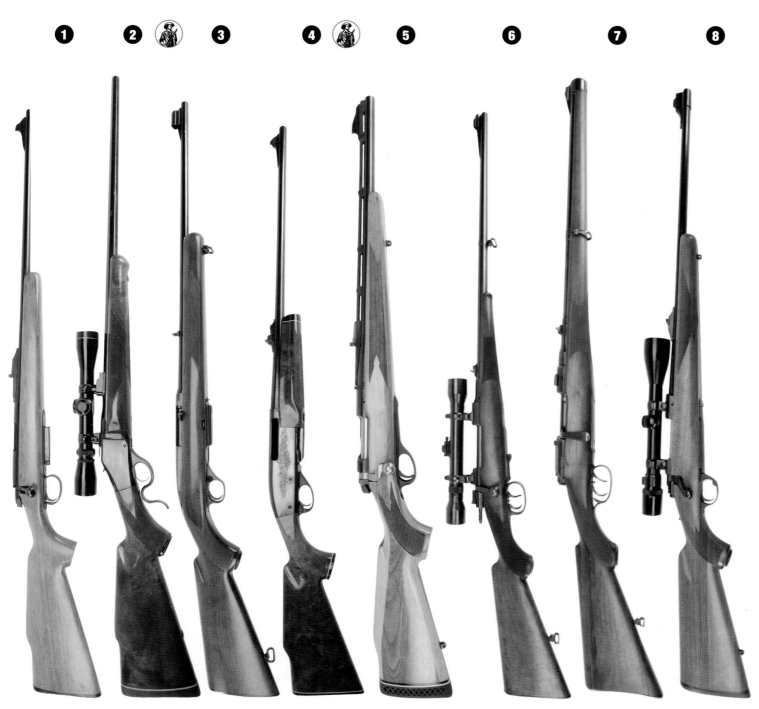

1. Remington Model 788 Bolt-Action Rifle - .222 Remington - circa 1967-1983 - Offered in nine calibers, but it has less features than Model 700 rifle.

2. Browning Model 78 Single-Shot Rifle with Leopold telescopic sight - .30-06 - circa 1973-1982 - Modern reintroduction of Winchester Hi-Wall.

3. Winchester Model 100 Semi-Automatic Rifle - .308 Winchester - circa 1961 - Over 262,000 produced.

4. Remington Model 6 Slide-Action Rifle - .308 Winchester – circa 1981-1987.

5. Remington Model 600 Magnum Bolt-Action Carbine - 6.5mm Remington Magnum - circa 1965-1968 - Laminated walnut/beech stock.

6. Mauser German Type B Bolt-Action Rifle with telescopic sight - 8 x 57 mm Mauser - circa 1920-1925 - Commercial scoped sporter.

7. Oester Waffenfabrik Ges. Steyr Austrian Sporter Bolt-Action Rifle - 9 x 56 mm Mannlicher/Schoenaue - circa 1968.

8. Sturm, Ruger & Co. Model 77 Bolt-Action Rifle with telescopic sight - .243 Winchester - circa 1968 - Refined Mauser-action sporter.

MODERN FIREARMS

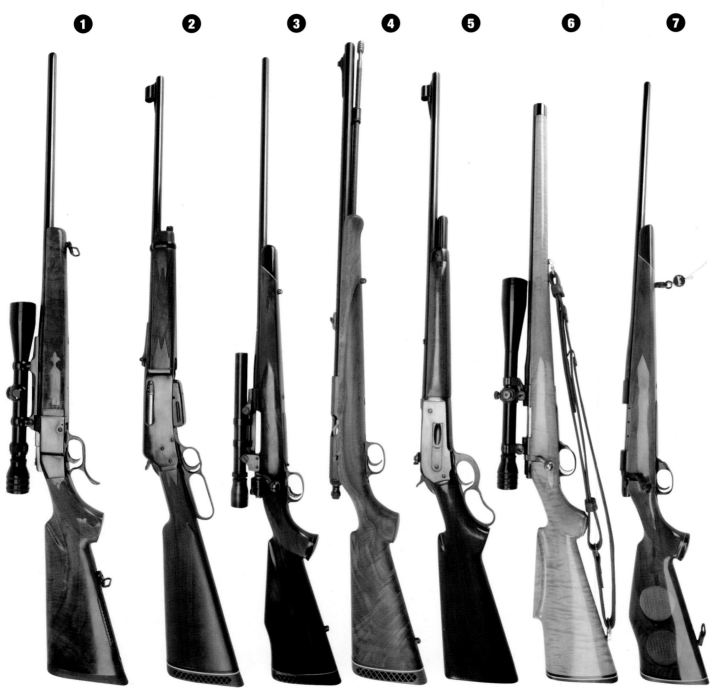

1. Colt/Sharps Falling Block Sporting Rifle with telescopic sight - .22-250 Remington - circa 1971 - About 500 made.

2. Browning Model 81 BLR Lever-Action Rifle - .308 Winchester - circa 1970-1980 - Modern box magazine levergun.

3. Weatherby FN Mauser Bolt-Action Rifle with telescopic sight - .300 Weatherby Magnum - circa 1971 - Author Erle Stanley Gardner, creator of Perry Mason, owned this early sporter.

4. Knight MK 85-1 Prototype In-line Percussion Muzzleloading Rifle - .50 caliber - circa 1985 In-line muzzleloaders like this prototype Knight rifle were among the first blackpowder arms to utilize regular centerfire primers for ignition. The hottest ignition provided allowed development of synthetic blackpowder materials like Pyrodex.

5. Winchester Model 71 Lever-Action Rifle - .348 Winchester - circa 1951 - About 47,000 made.

6. Sako Finnish L461 Bolt-Action Rifle with telescopic sight - .17/222 centerfire - circa 1971.

7. Weatherby Vanguard VGX Bolt-Action Rifle - .25-06 - circa 1989-1993 - Started in 1945, Weatherby is noted for development of proprietary high-velocity cartridges, strong accurate rifles, and the distinctive post-WWII modernistic aesthetics of their stock designs. This example has inlaid 1976 NRA Patriot Army medallions in the stock.

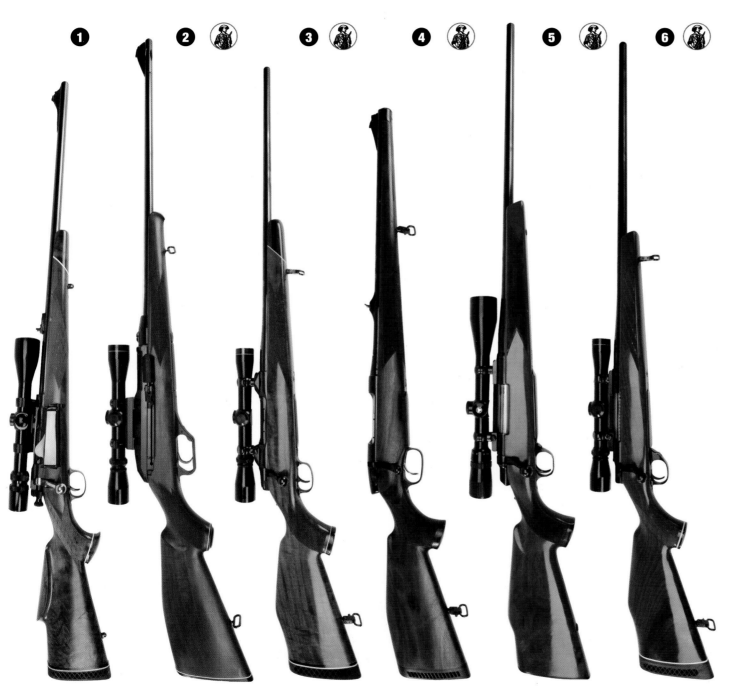

1 U.S. Springfield Krag-Jorgensen Model 1898 Bolt-Action Rifle (sporterized) - .30-40 Krag - circa 1940-1950 - Home-gunsmithed sporter.

2 Heckler & Koch Model 770 Semi-Automatic Rifle with Leopold telescopic sight - .308 Winchester - circa 1984.

3 Colt-Sauer Bolt-Action Rifle with Leopold telescopic sight - .30-06 - circa 1971.

4 Steyr-Mannlicher Austrian Model M-Luxus Bolt-Action Carbine - .270 Winchester - circa 1972.

5 Browning BBR Bolt-Action Rifle with Bausch & Lomb telescopic sight - .270 Winchester - circa 1978 - Mauser-style sporter built by Miroku in Japan. Earlier Brownings were built in Belgium.

6 Smith & Wesson Model 1500 Bolt-Action Rifle with Leopold telescopic sight - 7 mm Remington Magnum - circa 1983 - Made for only two years.

MODERN FIREARMS

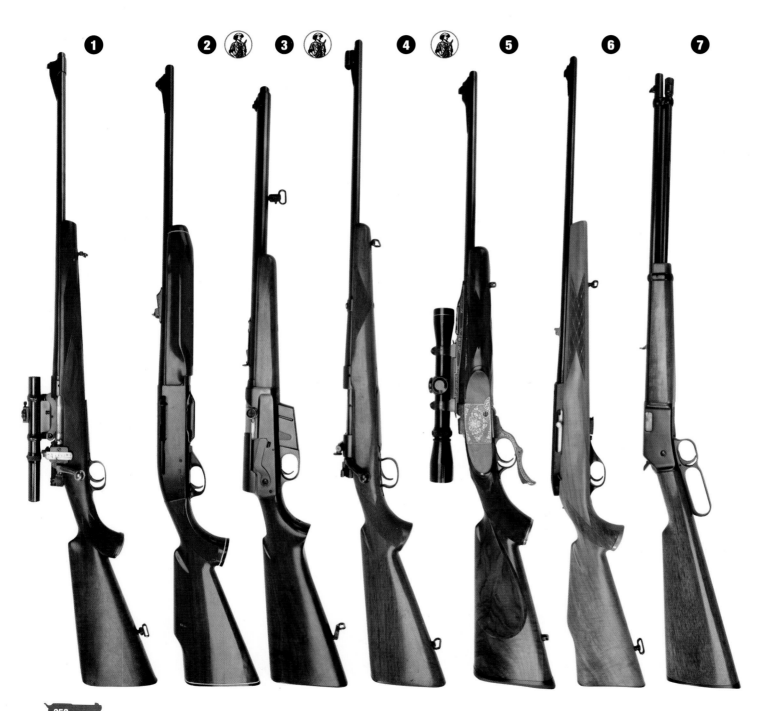

1. U.S. Springfield Model 1903 Bolt-Action Rifle (sporterized by Paul Jager) - .30-06 - circa 1946-1950 - Military rifles were popular as the starting point for custom sporters in the 1950s through 1970s.

2. Remington Model Four Semi-Automatic Rifle - .30-06 - circa 1982 - Made for only six years.

3. Remington Model 81 Woodmaster Semi-Automatic Rifle - .35 Remington - circa 1938-1940.

4. Winchester Model 54 Bolt-Action Rifle - .30-06 - circa 1934 - First high-velocity bolt gun the company made.

5. Paul Jaeger Custom Falling-Block Sporter Rifle with telescopic sight - .270 Winchester - circa 2000-2001 - Engraved by Claus Willig.

6. Weatherby Mark XXII Clip Mag Semi-Automatic Rifle - .22 rimfire - circa 1965-1970.

7. Browning BL-22 Grade I Lever-Action Rifle - .22 rimfire - circa 1969.

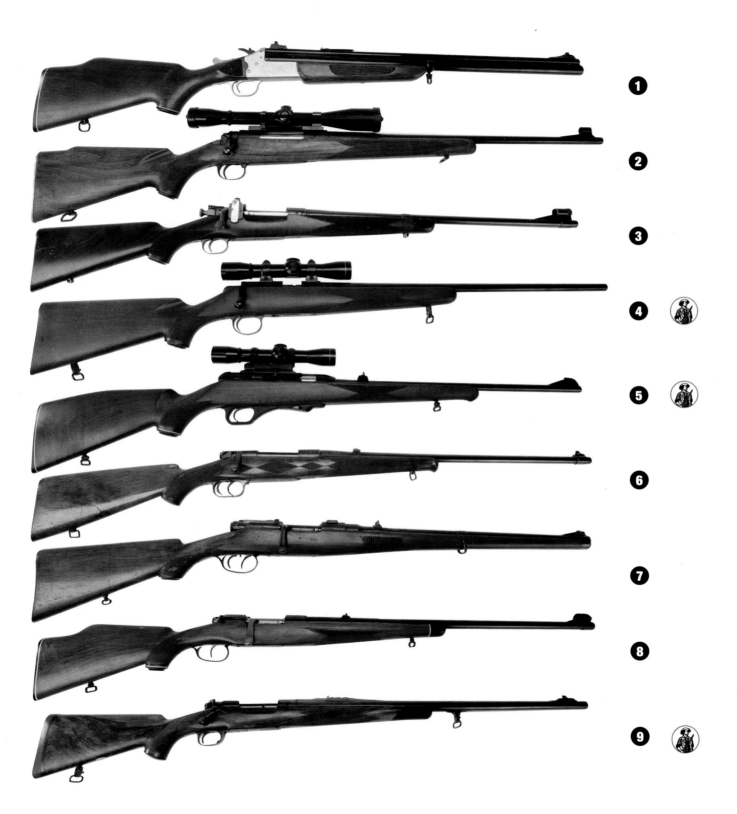

1. Savage Model 24J-SL Over/Under Combination Gun - .22 rimfire /20 gauge - circa 1974 - Versatile double-barrel rifle/shotgun.

2. Remington Model 725 Bolt-Action Rifle - .270 Winchester - circa 1959 - About 16,635 made.

3. Griffin & Howe Bolt-Action Sporter Rifle with Ziel Dialyt 2.5x telescopic sight - circa 1950.

4. Kimber Model 82 Custom Classic Bolt-Action Rifle with telescopic sight - .22 rimfire - circa 1982.

5. Heckler & Koch Model 300 Semi-Automatic Rifle with telescopic sight - .22 Winchester Magnum Rimfire - circa 1980.

6. Newton Arms Co. First-Type Standard Bolt-Action Rifle - .256 Newton - circa 1917 - Made in Buffalo, NY.

7. Waffenfabrik Steyr Austrian Mannlicher-Schoenauer Model 1905 Bolt-Action Sporting Rifle - 9 x 56 mm Mannlicher/Schoenaue - circa 1970.

8. Steyr-Mannlicher Mannlicher/Schoenauer Model 1961 MCA Bolt-Action Rifle - .338 Winchester Magnum - circa 1961 - Mannlichers Collectors Association edition.

9. Winchester Model 70 Super-Grade African Bolt-Action Rifle - .458 Winchester Magnum - circa 1960.

MODERN FIREARMS

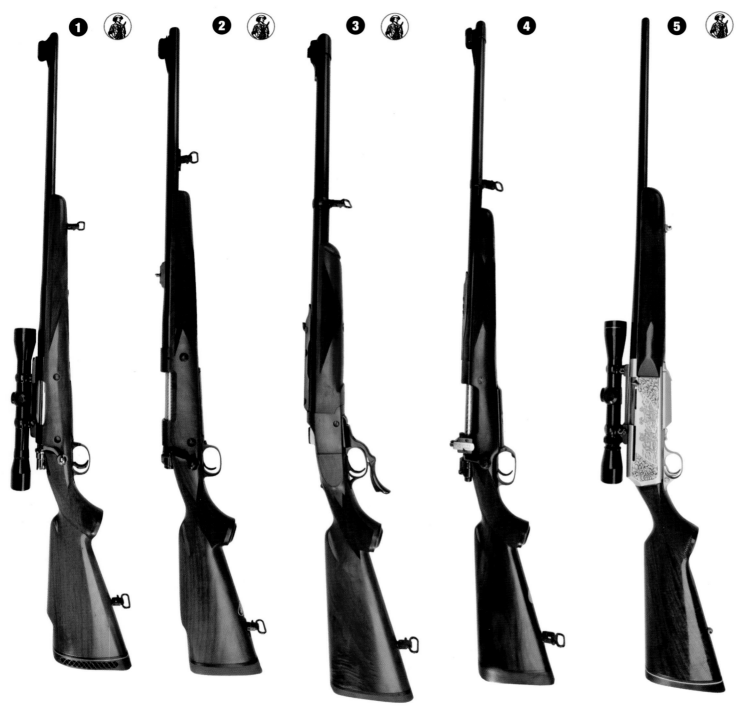

1. Browning FN High Power Bolt-Action Rifle with Browning telescopic sight - .458 Winchester Magnum - circa 1959 - Safari Grade.

2. Winchester Model 70 Super-Grade African Bolt-Action Rifle - .458 Winchester Magnum - circa 1960 - This customized pre-1964 Winchester rifle features a gold bas relief bull elephant on the floorplate. Manufacturing changes and redesign at Winchester in 1964 led to higher-priced collector's market for guns produced before that year in all models.

3. Sturm, Ruger & Co. No. 1-H Tropical Falling-Block Rifle - .458 Winchester Magnum - circa 1976.

4. Griffin & Howe Custom Bolt-Action Rifle - .416 Rigby - circa 1980.

5. Browning BAR Semi-Automatic Rifle with telescopic sight - 7 mm Remington Magnum - circa 1967.

1   Kleingunther K15 Bolt-Action Rifle with scope - .30-06 - circa 1999 - Built to offer extreme accuracy, this commerical rifle is sold with a guaranteed 100-yard accuracy level for the original purchaser.

2   Ludwig Borovnik Austrian Vierling Four-Barrel Combination Gun - 12 ga./12 ga./.22 Hornet/.308 - circa 1900-1920.

3   C. Sharps Arms Model 1875 Falling-Block Rifle - .38-55 - circa 1990 - Reproduction sidehammer Sharps made in Big Timber, MT.

4   Norinco Chinese MAK-90 Semi-Automatic Rifle - 7.62 mm x 39 - circa 1993 - Function is essentially the same as any semi-auto AK variant, but cosmetically redesigned to avoid federal ban during the so-called Clinton assault-weapon ban years.

5   Sturm, Ruger & Co. Model 10/22 International Semi-Automatic Rifle - .22 long rifle - circa 1968 - Full-length Mannlicher-style stock.

MODERN FIREARMS

1. Ross Rifle Co. Canadian Deer-Stalking-Pattern Bolt-Action Sporting Rifle - .280 Ross - circa 1901.

2. Michigan Arms (Clawson, MI) Wolverine In-Line Black Powder Rifle .50 caliber percussion.

3. CETME Spanish Model 58 Semi-Automatic Rifle - 7.62mm CETME - circa 1958.

4. Kleszczewski Excelsior Drilling - circa 1900 - Drillings are three-barrel guns, usually a rifle barrel with two shotgun barrels.

5. Shiloh Products Model 1874 Sharps Single-Shot Falling-Block Rifle - .45-70 - circa 1986 Reproduction sidehammer Sharps made in Farmingdale, NY.

6. Winchester Model 52-B Bolt-Action Rifle - .22 long rifle - circa 1948.

7. Savage Model 1895 Lever-Action Carbine - .303 British - circa 1898 - Cartridge counter magazine w/ cocked indicator. Rotary magazine allowed use of pointed spitzer bullets, which are unsafe in tube magazine lever actions.

8. Ranger Arms NRA Centennial Bolt-Action Rifle - circa 1971 - Ranger Arms in Gainesville, TX, was known as a manufacturer of fine-quality bolt-action rifles in the 1970s with this NRA centennial rifle being a sample produced in 1971 for advertising in the NRA *American Rifleman* magazine.

1   Uzi Israeli Model A Semi-Automatic Carbine
    with telescopic sight - 9 mm - circa 1982.

2   American Masters Series Custom Mauser Bolt-
    Action Rifle with Leupold telescopic sight,
    fitted leather case, and accessories - .30-06 -
    circa 1988 - Roberts American Masters Award
    rifle.

3   Beretta BM-59 Semi-Automatic Rifle -
    7.62mm NATO - circa 1960.

4   Savage Model 45 Bolt-Action Rifle with
    telescopic sight - .257 Roberts - circa 1935 -
    Bullpup configuration.

5   Marlin Camp Carbine Semi-Automatic Rifle -
    9mm - circa 1990.

MODERN FIREARMS

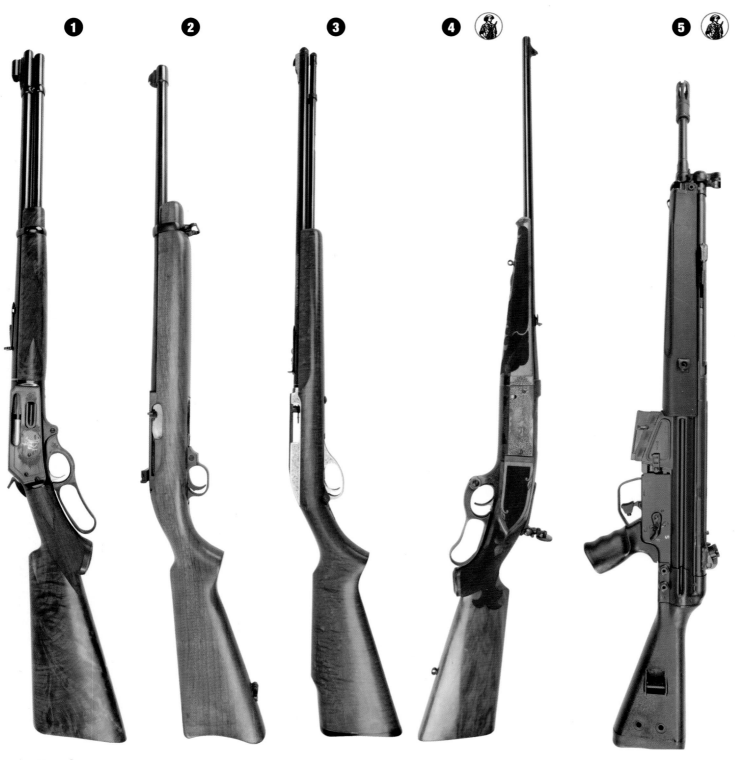

1 Marlin Model 336 Presentation-Grade Lever-Action Rifle - .30-30 - circa 1979 - Serial number 3,000,000.

2 Sturm, Ruger & Co. Model 44 Carbine - .44 Magnum - circa 1965.

3 Marlin Model 60 Glenfield Semi-Automatic Rifle - .22 rimfire - circa 1982 - Serial number 2,000,000.

4 Savage Model 99 Lever-Action Rifle - circa 1920.

5 Heckler & Koch Model 91 Semi-Automatic Rifle - .308 Winchester - circa 1988.

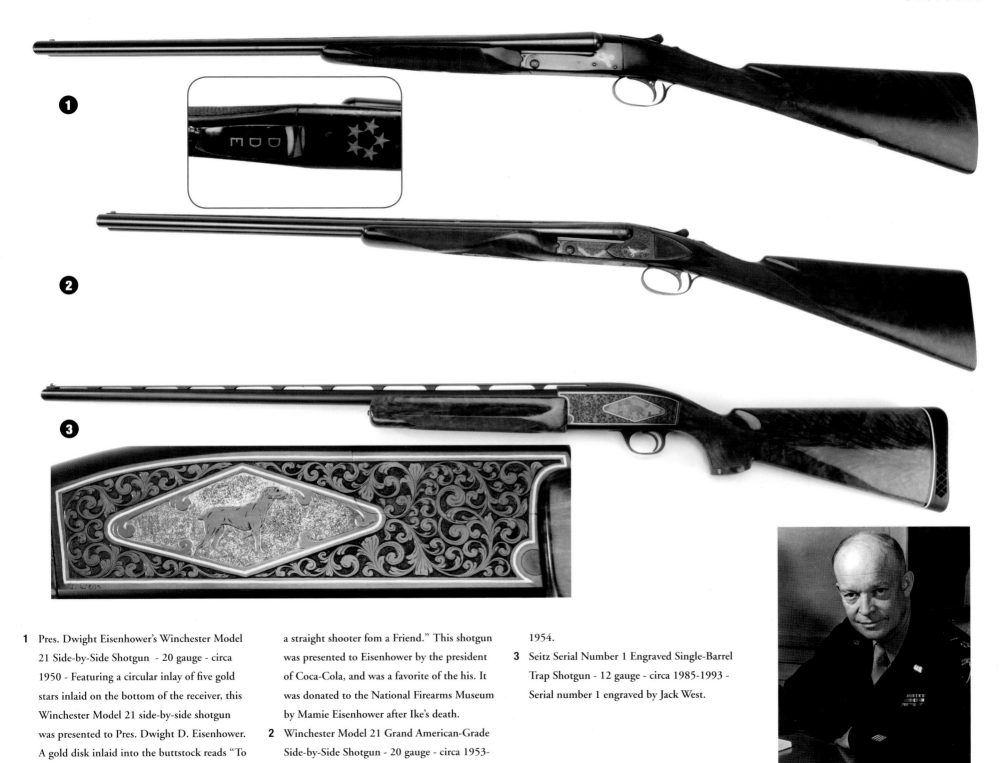

1 Pres. Dwight Eisenhower's Winchester Model 21 Side-by-Side Shotgun - 20 gauge - circa 1950 - Featuring a circular inlay of five gold stars inlaid on the bottom of the receiver, this Winchester Model 21 side-by-side shotgun was presented to Pres. Dwight D. Eisenhower. A gold disk inlaid into the buttstock reads "To a straight shooter fom a Friend." This shotgun was presented to Eisenhower by the president of Coca-Cola, and was a favorite of the his. It was donated to the National Firearms Museum by Mamie Eisenhower after Ike's death.

2 Winchester Model 21 Grand American-Grade Side-by-Side Shotgun - 20 gauge - circa 1953-1954.

3 Seitz Serial Number 1 Engraved Single-Barrel Trap Shotgun - 12 gauge - circa 1985-1993 - Serial number 1 engraved by Jack West.

MODERN FIREARMS

1 Winchester Model 21 Side-by-Side Shotgun - 12 gauge - circa 1931.

2 Winchester Model 42 Slide-Action Shotgun - .410 gauge - circa 1949.

3 Winchester Model 12 Skeet Slide-Action Shotgun - 12 gauge - circa 1960.

4 Parker VHE Grade Skeet Side-by-Side Shotgun - 20 gauge - circa 1937-1938.

5 Parker DHE Grade Side-by-Side Shotgun - 28 gauge - circa 1937-1938.

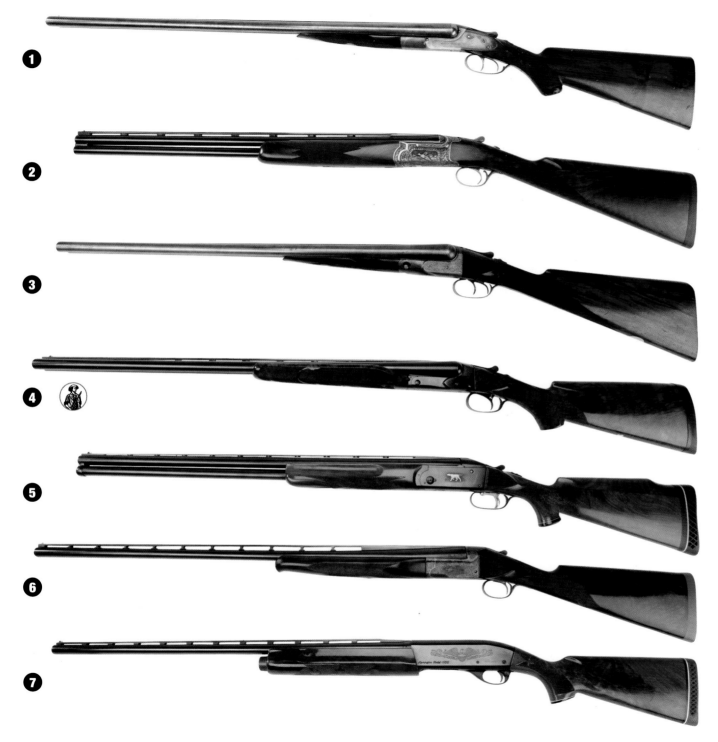

1 Lefever G Grade Side-by-Side Shotgun - 12 gauge - circa 1894.

2 Sturm, Ruger & Co. Stainless Red Label Skeet Over/Under Shotgun - 20 gauge - circa 1985 - Engraved by Neil Hartliep.

3 Parker Brothers BH Grade Side-by-Side Shotgun - 12 gauge - circa 1898.

4 Winchester Model 21 Side-by-Side Shotgun - 12 gauge - circa 1949 - Special-order factory engraving.

5 Remington Model 32 TC Over/Under Shotgun - 12 gauge - circa 1932-1942.

6 L.C. Smith Eagle-Grade Single-Barrel Trap Shotgun - 12 gauge - circa 1921.

7 Remington Model 1100 Trap Semi-Automatic Shotgun - 12 gauge - circa 1987-1999.

MODERN FIREARMS

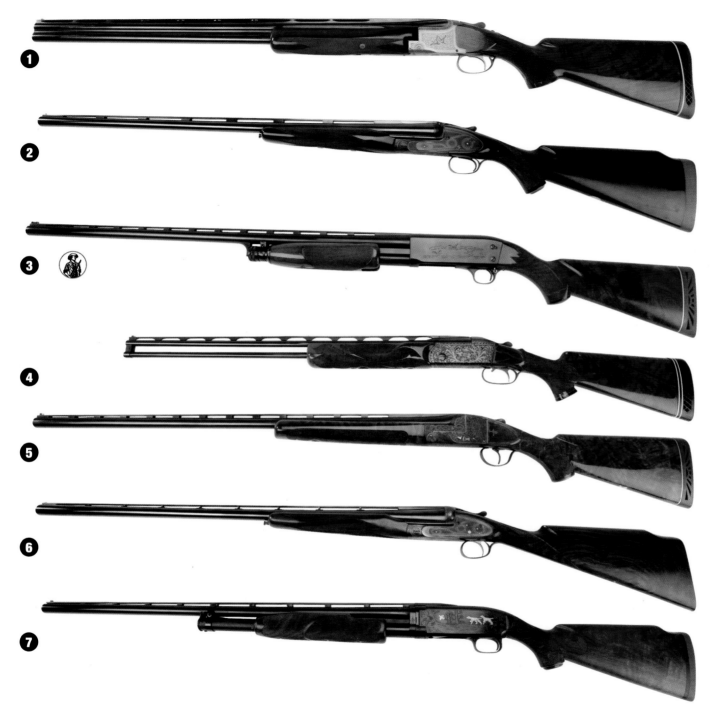

1 Browning Broadway Trap Presentation 3 Superposed Shotgun - 12 gauge - circa 1961-1976.

2 James Purdey Shotgun - 12 gauge - circa 1967 - Rose and scroll engraving.

3 Ithaca Model 37 Trap Slide-Action Shotgun - 12 gauge - circa 1937-1955.

4 Kreighoff Four-Barrel Shotgun Set - circa 1996.

5 Ithaca 7E Single-Barrel Trap Shotgun - 12 gauge - circa 1930 - Engraved by William McGraw.

6 James Purdy & Sons Single-Barrel Trap Shotgun - 12 gauge - circa 1924 - Restocked with Monte Carlo.

7 Winchester Model 12 Pigeon Grade Shotgun - 12 gauge - circa 1957.

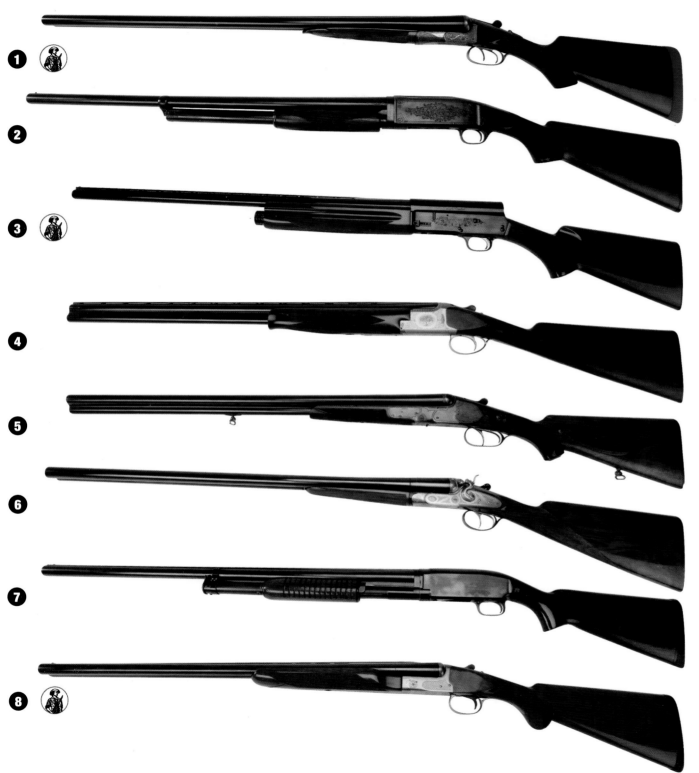

1. Charles Daly Side-by-Side Shotgun - 10 gauge - circa 1895.

2. Remington Model 10 Slide-Action Shotgun - 12 gauge - circa 1915-1925.

3. Browning Auto-5 Semi-Automatic Shotgun - 12 gauge - circa 1981.

4. Browning Euromarket Superposed Shotgun - 20 gauge - circa 1982.

5. Franz Jager Herold Three-Barrel Shotgun - 16 gauge - circa 1910-1920 - Built with three smoothbore barrels, this Franz Jager triple shotgun was created for an individual seeking the capability to utilize three different shot types while hunting.

6. Pietro Beretta Premium-Grade Side-by-Side Shotgun - 12 gauge - circa 1990 - Presentation given to Beretta VP.

7. Winchester Model 12 Black Diamond Trap Slide-Action Shotgun - 12 gauge - circa 1950.

8. Winchester Model 23 XTR Side-by-Side Shotgun - 20 gauge - circa 1979.

1 Winchester Model 21 Trap Grade Shotgun - 12 gauge - circa 1951.

2 Browning B-80 Semi-Automatic Shotgun - 20 gauge - circa 1980.

3 Savage Stevens 30-D Slide-Action Shotgun - 12 gauge - circa 1971.

4 James Purdey & Sons British Best-Grade Side-by-Side Shotgun with case - 10 gauge - circa 1908.

5 Katsenes Custom Side-by-Side Shotgun - .410 gauge - circa 1956.

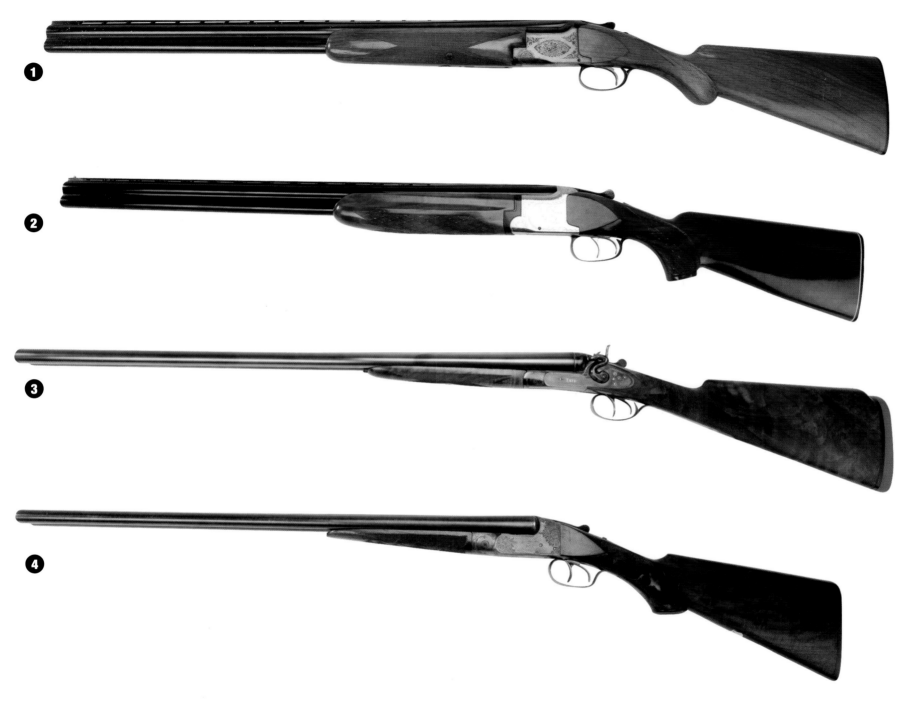

1 Tennessee Ernie Ford's Browning Superposed Shotgun - 12 gauge - circa 1954 - Owned by the popular singer and television host, known for songs such as *Sixteen Tons*.

2 Laurona Spanish Model 153 Over/Under Shotgun - 12 gauge - circa 1983.

3 Tate Vintager Side-by-Side Shotgun - 12 gauge - circa 2004.

4 Ithaca Engraved Hammerless Shotgun attributed to D.B. Wesson - 20 gauge - circa 1909.

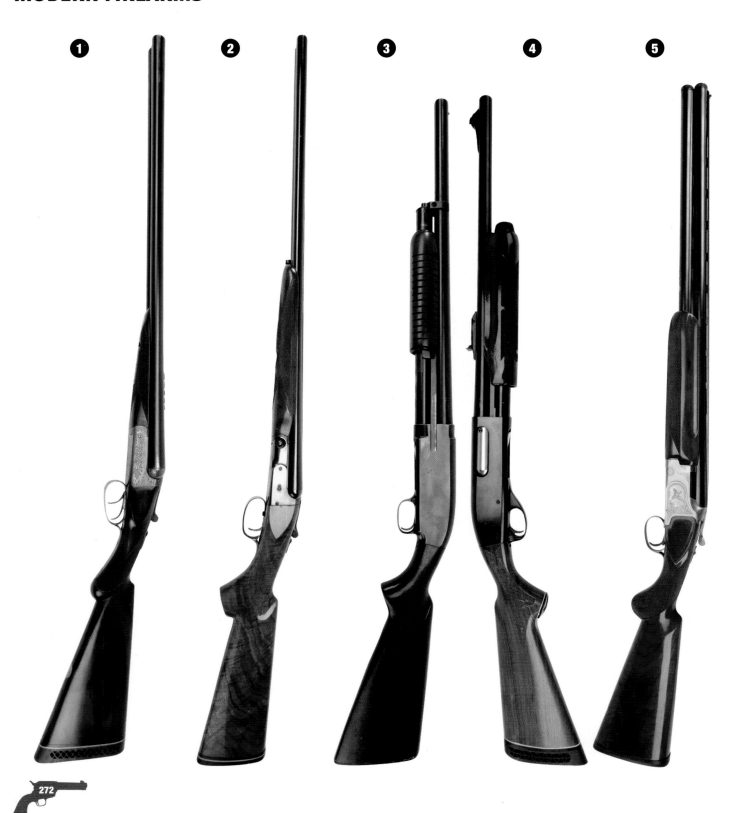

1 Westley Richards Super Magnum Paradox Side-by-Side Shotgun - 12 gauge - circa 1890-1900.

2 Remington Prototype Parker Shotgun - 20 gauge - circa 1987 - Original production of Remington's Parker shotguns ended in 1942. After a limited run of prototypes, including this example, a new line of Parker shotguns was announced in 2006. These new shotguns are manufactured at the Connecticut Shotgun Company.

3 Winchester Model 25 Slide-Action Shotgun - 12 gauge - circa 1951 - About 88,000 were made.

4 Remington Model 870 Slide-Action Shotgun - 12 gauge - circa 1980-1982.

5 Winchester Model 101 Over/Under Shotgun - 20 gauge - circa 1966.

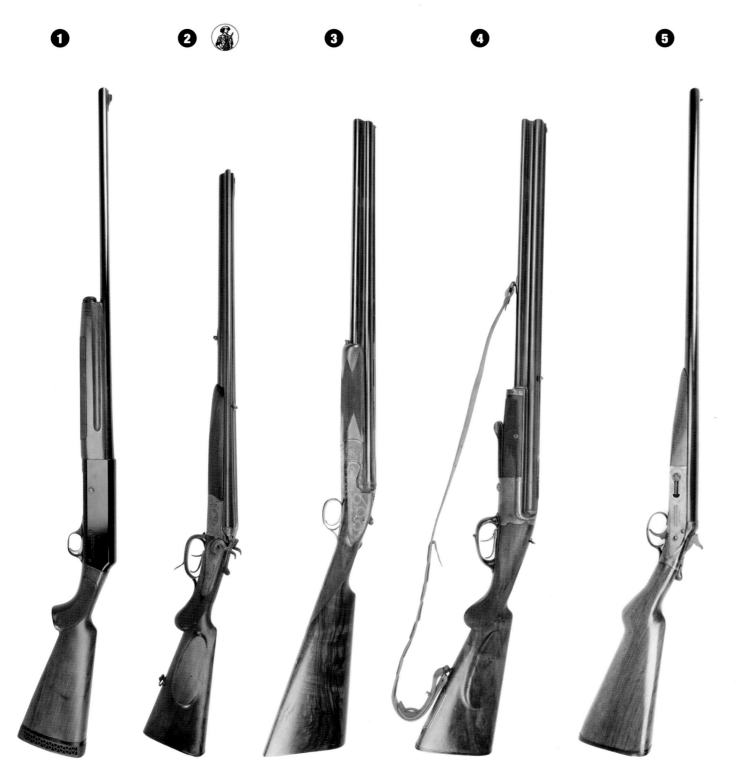

1 Luigi Franchi Semi-Automatic Shotgun - circa 1968.

2 Eduard Kettner Koln-Suhler German Gewehr-Fabrik Drilling - 16 gauge/.32 caliber - circa 1890.

3 James Purdey & Sons British Over/Under Shotgun - 12 gauge - circa 1953 - Presented to Thomas B. Walton by Purdey CEO Tom Purdey.

4 Wilhelm Collath German Over/Under Combination Gun - 12 gauge/9.3 x 65mmR - circa 1900.

5 Hopkins & Allen Forehand Single-Shot Shotgun - circa 1940.

MODERN FIREARMS

Beretta's "Set of Five" represents the finest of over/under shotguns manufactured by the world's oldest gunmaker. This premium-grade set includes two 12 gauge, two 20 gauge, and one 28 gauge shotguns. Receiver designs were executed by Master Engraver Angelo Galeazzi in the bulino, or bank note, technique in which designs are scribed using only a sharp tool and the pressure of the engraver's hand, rather than with the traditional hammer and graver method. The receivers of these guns depict aspects of the history and development of hunting from the Stone Age to the present. The English-style stocks, with straight wrists and checkered butts, are made from highly figured nut briar wood that had been held in reserve by Beretta for many years in anticipation of a special project such as this.

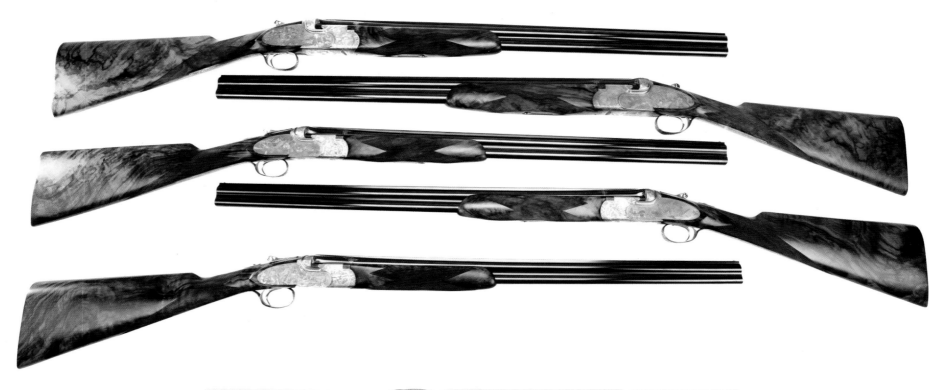

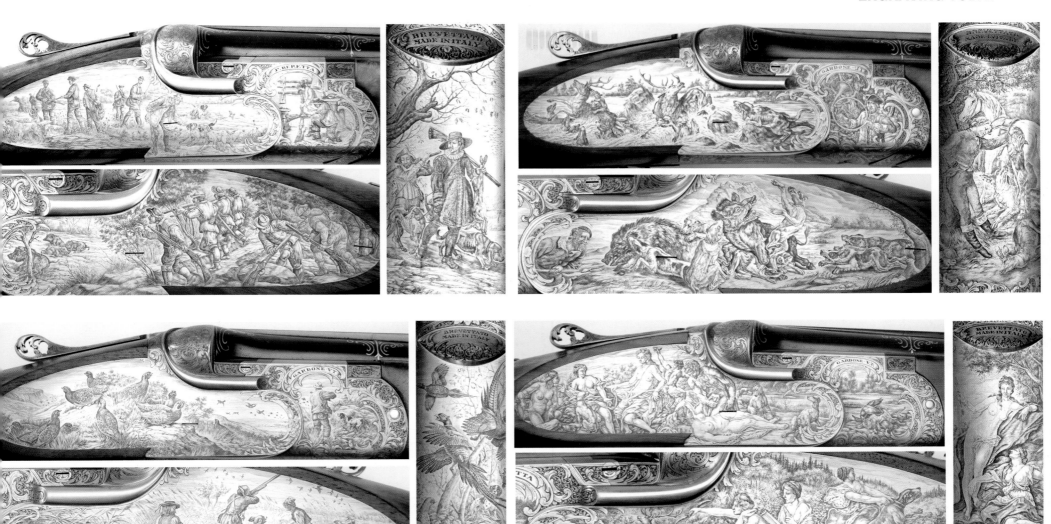

Despite the masterpieces of earlier eras, the most beautiful firearms engraving of all time is being done in the modern era. Master artisans still carve beautiful works by hand. The relatively new technique called "bulino" expanded the possibilities of engraving. Bulino uses hundreds of thousands, or even millions, of hand-punched dots of varying diameter and depth to create almost photo-realistic images on metal.

Machine or laser-cut engraving has made attractively decorated firearms accessible to the mass market, but the works made with a machine process can never compare to the handwork that created the pieces shown on these pages.

MODERN FIREARMS

The result of a unique collaboration between Ugo Beretta and fellow hunter Robert Jepson, the Beretta "Set of Four" is a spectacular group of double rifles, each engraved to depict the African big game species of the lion, cape buffalo, rhino, and elephant. Each rifle is chambered for an appropriate caliber, from .30-06 to 600 Nitro Express. The fine bulino engraving was executed by Master Engraver Angelo Galeazzi.

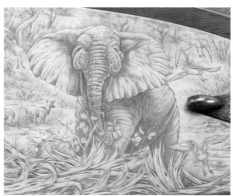

Artistry in Arms
The firearms illustrated here, many from the collection of Dr. William L. and Collette N. Roberts, are an assemblage of the finest examples that contemporary craftsmen have produced. From bold finishing to delicate inlay, each is a personal expression of an artist's skill, applied to one of mankind's most traditional media.

1 Colt Single-Action Army Revolver (Sheriff's Model) - .44-40 - circa 1980 - Ivory grips. Sheriff's Model Single-Action Army revolvers were offered by Colt on special order with shorter-than-standard barrels and no ejector rod.

2 Colt Python Double-Action Revolver - .357 Magnum - circa 1983.

3 Colt Engraved Single-Action Army Revolver - circa 1980 - Engraved by Robert Burt.

4 Colt Engraved Single-Action Army Revolver - circa 1980 - Engraved by Robert Burt.

1 Colt Diamondback Double-Action Revolver - .22 rimfire - circa 1987.

2 Colt Diamondback Double-Action Revolver - circa 1988.

3 Colt Trooper Double-Action Revolver - .357 Magnum - circa 1981.

4 Colt Detective Special Double-Action Revolver - .38 Special - circa 1980.

1 Smith & Wesson Model 36 Double-Action Revolver - circa 1980-1981.

2 Smith & Wesson Model 586 Double-Action Revolver - .357 Magnum - circa 1980.

3 Smith & Wesson Model 586 Double-Action Revolver - circa 1980.

4 Smith & Wesson Model 66 Double-Action Revolver - .357 Magnum - circa 1981.

1 Smith & Wesson Model 29 Double-Action
  Revolver - .44 Magnum - circa 1979-1980.

2 Smith & Wesson Model 57 Double-Action
  Revolver - .41 Magnum - circa 1979-1980.

3 Colt 2nd Generation Third Model Dragoon
  Percussion Revolver - .44 caliber - circa 1978 -
  Modern reproduction.

4 Colt (Hartford, CT) Model 1860 Army Single-
  Action Percussion Revolver .44 caliber.

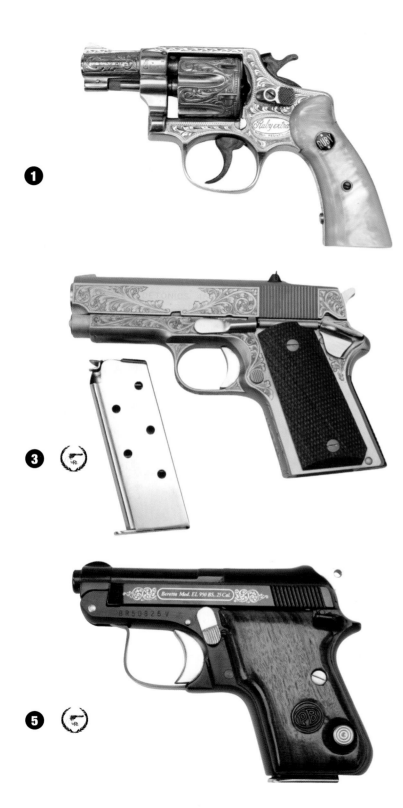

1 Gabilondo y Cia Ruby Extra Special Deluxe Double-Action Revolver - .22 rimfire - circa 1969-1976.

2 Mauser Model 1934 Semi-Automatic Pistol - circa 1938-1940.

3 Detonics Professional Semi-Automatic Pistol - .45 ACP - circa 1985-1988 - One of 250 factory-engraved Detonics.

4 Walther PPK/S Semi-Automatic Pistol - .380 ACP - circa 1992.

5 Beretta Model 950 Minx Semi-Automatic Pistol - .25 ACP - circa 1992.

❶

❷

❸

❹

1 Pietro Beretta Model 1951 Semi-Automatic Pistol - circa 1951-1960.

2 Browning Belgian Medalist Semi-Automatic Pistol - .22 rimfire - circa 1970-1975 - French gray finish.

3 Browning Renaissance Hi-Power Semi-Automatic Pistol - 9 mm - circa 1977.

4 Star, Bonifacio Echeverria S.A. Model PD Semi-Automatic Pistol - .45 ACP - circa 1990-1991.

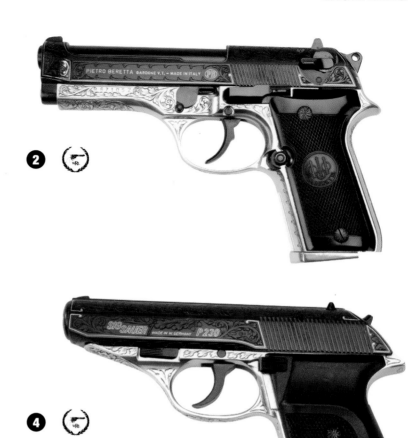

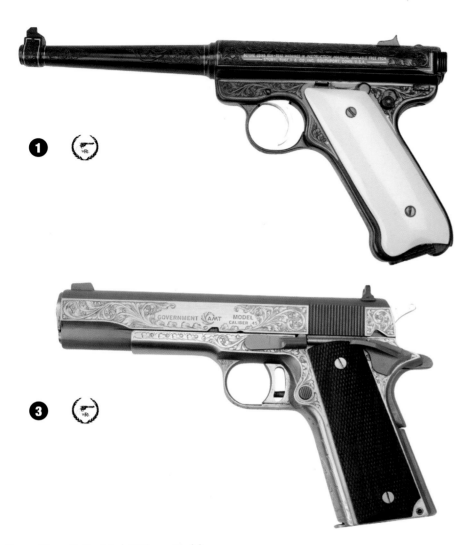

1 Sturm, Ruger & Co. Mark II Target Model
   Semi-Automatic Pistol - .22 rimfire - circa
   1982-1992.

2 Beretta Model 92SBC Semi-Automatic Pistol -
   9 mm - circa 1980-1985.

3 AMT Combat Skipper Semi-Automatic Pistol
   - .45 ACP - circa 1984.

4 SIG-Sauer Model P-230 Semi-Automatic
   Pistol - .380 ACP - circa 1976-1992 - Few SIG
   handguns have ever been factory engraved for
   the domestic market.

1 Dakota Arms Traveler Takedown Rifle - .30-06 - circa 1994 - The Dakota Arms Traveler rifle features a bolt-action design that has a threadless disassembly system for ease of takedown and reassembly. Offered in a variety of calibers, this model can also be procured with sets of interchangeable barrels for cartridges that share the same case-head dimensions.

2 Haskins Custom Presentation U.S. Bicenntennial Commemorative Bolt-Action Rifle - circa 1976.

3 Savage Model 99M Presentation-Grade Lever-Action Rifle - .300 Savage - circa 1967.

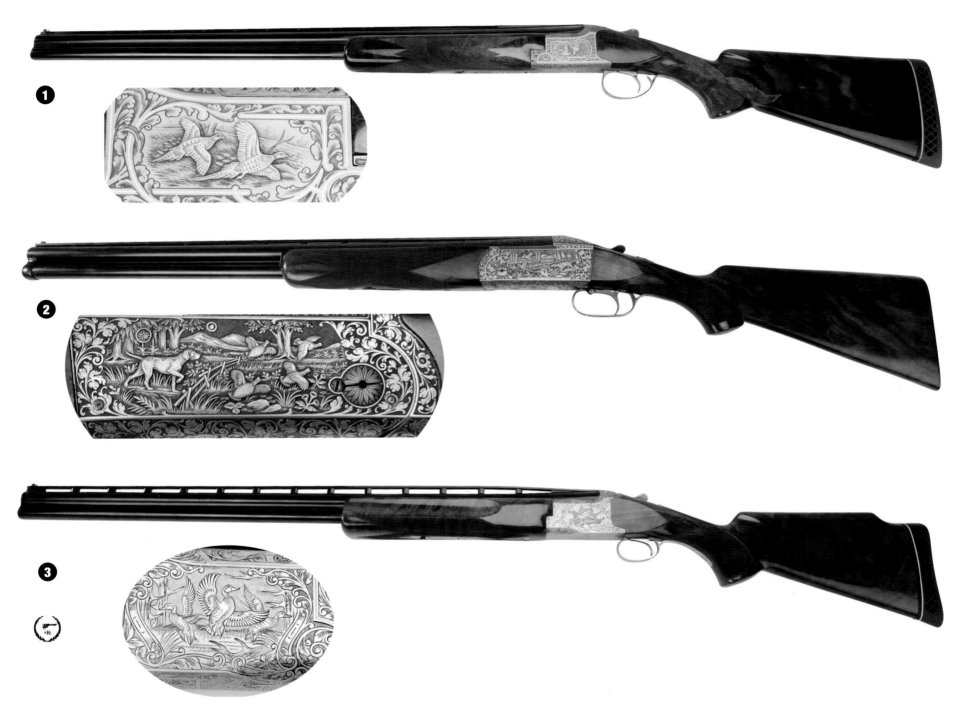

1 Browning Superposed Shotgun - circa 1936.

2 Remington Model 32 Over/Under Shotgun - circa 1936.

3 Browning Citori Over/Under Shotgun - circa 1980.

1 Remington Model 31 Slide-Action Shotgun - 20 gauge - circa 1949.

2 Ithaca Engraved Side-by Side Shotgun - 12 gauge - circa 1926 - Eagle grade.

1 Colt Pony Semi-Automatic Pistol - .380 ACP - circa 1991-1992 - By Master Engraver Leonard Francolini.

2 Colt Mark IV Series 70 Semi-Automatic Pistol - circa 1978.

3 Smith & Wesson Model 19 Double-Action Revolver - .357 Magnum - circa 1980.

4 Colt Single-Action Army Revolver - circa 1980 - Engraved by Robert Burt.

1   Suhler Jagd-und Sportwaffen GmbH German
    Exhibition-Grade Drilling - circa 1995.

2   Suhler Jagd-und Sportwaffen GmbH German
    Merkel Exhibition-Grade Double Rifle - 8 x
    57mm JR - circa 1995.

Firearms retain a unique place in American history and contemporary society because America is a unique democracy. It is unique because it is ultimately up to the people to decide who will govern. Nowhere else on earth has a constitutional government been established that guarantees the people a right to keep and bear arms as a balance against a tyrannical government or the invasion by a foreign foe.

Charlton Heston, in a speech before the National Press Club in September 1997, said:

" ...[the] doorway to freedom is framed by the muskets that stood between a vision of liberty and absolute anarchy at a place called Concord Bridge. ... go forth and tell the truth. There can be no free speech, no freedom of the press, no freedom to protest, no freedom to worship your god, no freedom to speak your mind, no freedom from fear, no freedom for your children and for theirs, for anybody, anywhere, without the Second Amendment freedom to fight for it."

These selected firearms represent parts of the myriad stories told within the National Firearms Museum

galleries that encompass the story of firearms, freedom, and the American experience. Each of these firearms represents a chapter or story in the history of the National Rifle Association of America. For over 140 years the members of the NRA have striven to keep America strong as a nation of marksmen, sportsmen, hunters, competitors, and above all, patriots, able to answer the call at a moment's notice, much like on the morning of April 19, 1775, when tyranny and oppression were faced with armed resistance so that all Americans could live free.

1 Remington Rolling Block Rifle - .45-70 caliber. This No. 1-sized action model of the rolling block was engraved by Louis D.

Nimschke and presented to D. Barclay of the NRA for winning one of the International Matches in 1876 at the Creedmoor range.

This gun is recorded as the first gun presented to the NRA for its collection, which eventually became the National Firearms Museum. The

No. 1-sized rolling-block action was one of Remington's most popular models with over one million produced between 1867 and 1888.

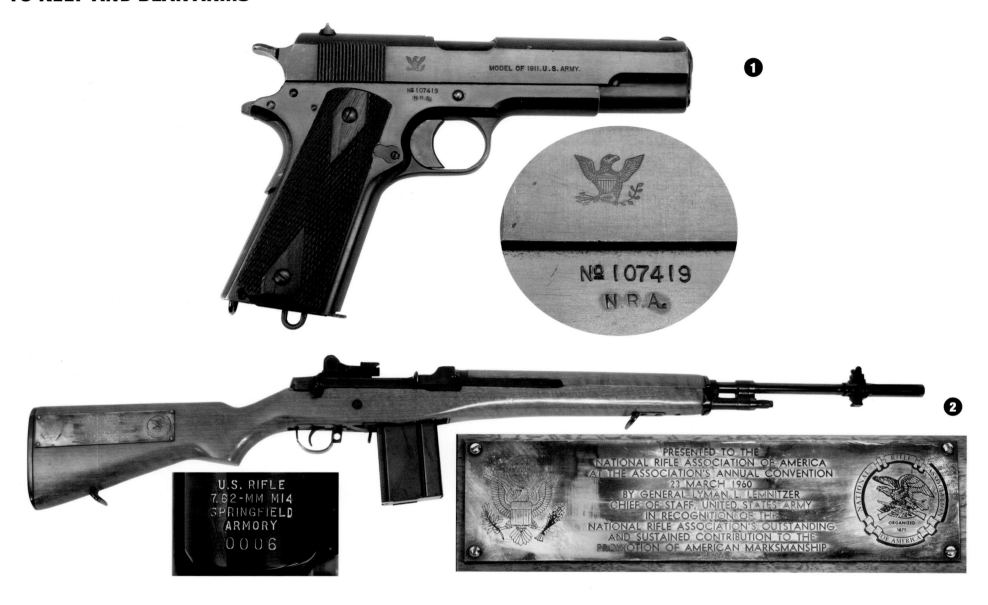

1 U.S. Springfield Model 1911 Semi-Automatic Pistol - .45 ACP - circa 1914-1915 - In 1915 and 1916, National Rifle Association life members and members of affiliated clubs could purchase a military Colt or Springfield Armory Model 1911 pistol for $16, nearly $6 cheaper than the commercial equivalent, the Colt Government pistol. Less than 300 of these pistols were sold through this program. They were marked "N.R.A." under the serial number of the pistol to distinguish it from other M1911 handguns still in military inventory. Today, the Civilian Marksmanship Program offers members of affiliated shooting clubs the oppurtunity to purhase surplus U.S. military rifles.

2 U.S. Springfield (Springfield, MA) Presentation-Grade M14 Semi-Automatic Rifle, serial number 6 (deactivated) - 7.62mm NATO - circa 1957 - The M14 selective-fire rifle, chosen to replace the semi-automatic M1 Garand rifle, was the U.S. Army's primary issue rifle from 1957 to 1958. Presented by CJCS General Lyman Lemnitzer at the NRA Annual Meetings in 1961, he related the significance of this gun's serial number 6. "Got your six" was Army radio code for "having someone's back," a tribute to the membership of the NRA who so generously support and participate in Army marksmanship programs.

1 Swinburn (Birmingham, England) Presentation-Grade Peabody/Martini-Henry Single-Shot Rifle - .577 caliber - circa 1874 - In 1874. Major Arthur Blennerhasset Leech, on behalf of the Irish Rifle Association, issued a challenge to the Riflemen of the World to compete in a long-range rifle match with the American team using American-made rifles. The Irish team used the finest Rigby muzzleloading target rifles. The American team won the match with a close score of 934 to 931. In token of the American victory, Major Leech presented this Martini-action single-shot rifle to the captain of the American team, Colonel George Wingate, later to become an NRA President. The presentation of this rifle symbolized the arrival of the National Rifle Association of America on the world stage of international competition. It was also the first rifle in the NRA's collection and would eventually come to be displayed in the National Firearms Museum.

2 Winchester Model 94 NRA Centennial Commemorative Lever-Action Rifle - .30-30 - circa 1971 - This Winchester NRA 100th anniversary rifle commemorative celebrates the NRA's century-long vigil of protection of Americans' Second Amendment rights. Presented to NRA President Woodson D. Scott on the 100th anniversary of the founding of the NRA.

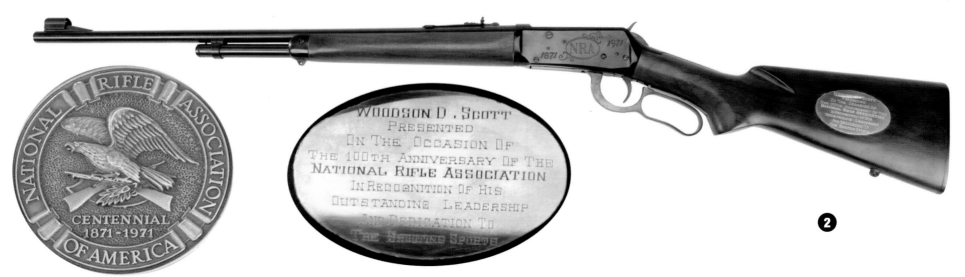

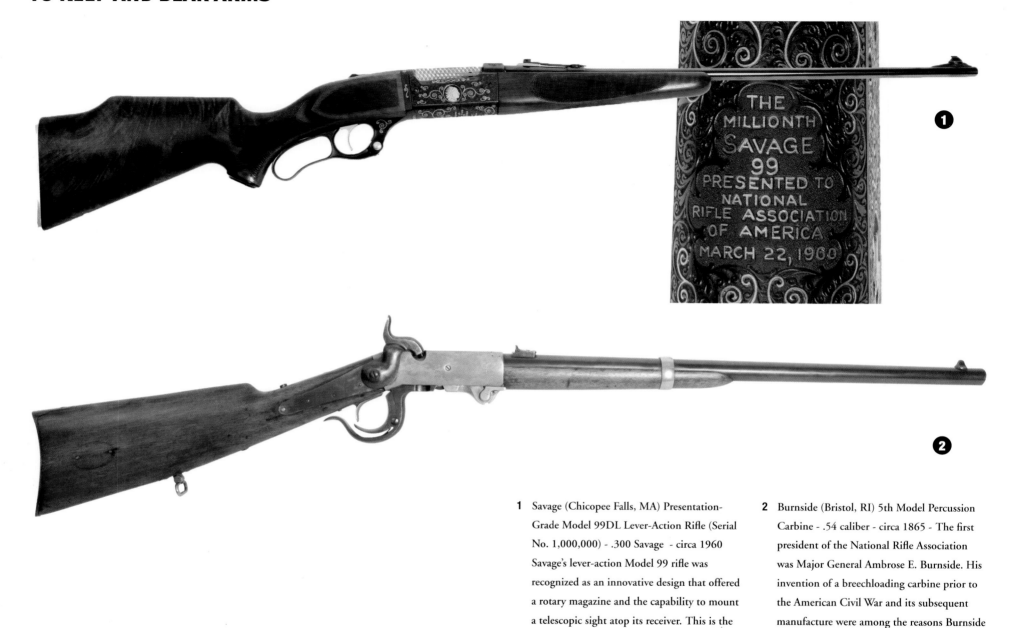

1 Savage (Chicopee Falls, MA) Presentation-Grade Model 99DL Lever-Action Rifle (Serial No. 1,000,000) - .300 Savage - circa 1960 Savage's lever-action Model 99 rifle was recognized as an innovative design that offered a rotary magazine and the capability to mount a telescopic sight atop its receiver. This is the one millionth Savage 99 rifle manufactured, fully engraved and inlaid with several types of gold. It was presented to the National Rifle Association.

2 Burnside (Bristol, RI) 5th Model Percussion Carbine - .54 caliber - circa 1865 - The first president of the National Rifle Association was Major General Ambrose E. Burnside. His invention of a breechloading carbine prior to the American Civil War and its subsequent manufacture were among the reasons Burnside was asked to serve as the Association's first chief officer. It is believed that this carbine may have been presented to the NRA by Burnside upon his retirement.

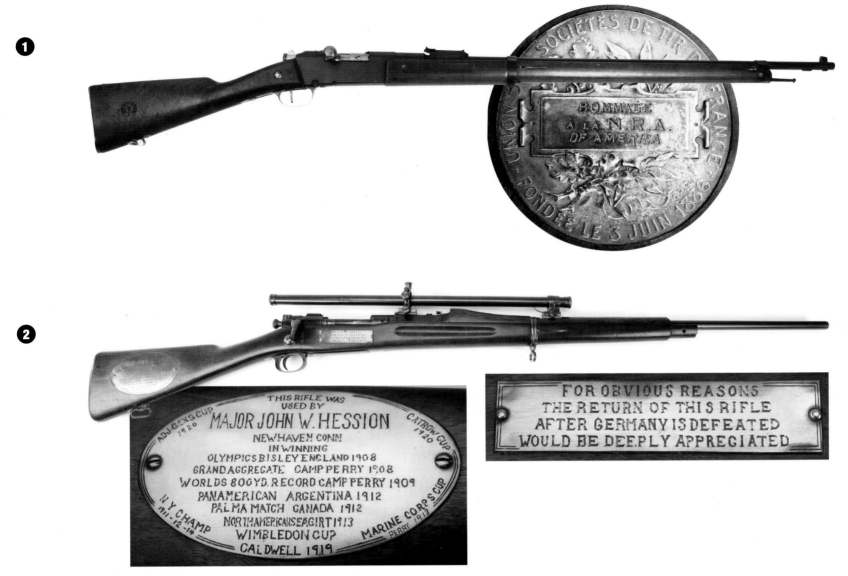

1 French (Culle) Model 1886/93 Presentation-Grade Rifle - 8mm Lebel - circa 1920
The National Rifle Association offered marksmanship training to military personnel of other countries. After World War I concluded, France presented this bolt-action Lebel rifle to the NRA in token of the assistance it rendered in training French soldiers.

2 U.S. Springfield Model 1903 Bolt-Action Rifle - .30-06 - circa 1907 - Originally issued in World War, I this Model 1903 Springfield rifle was purchased by Major John Hession, who modified it for competition and used it to set world records and win matches at Camp Perry, the Olympics, and elsewhere. A plaque on the buttplate records some of these honors. In the early dark days of World War II, it looked as if only the British Isles stood against the crushing might of Hitler's war machine. The English, with little tradition of civilian arms ownership, turned to America for the guns to defend their homeland. Individual Americans responded, sending their privately owned firearms across the Atlantic for the defense of England, including Hession, who sent his prize target rifle. He added a second plaque to the stock stating, "For obvious reasons, the return of this rifle after Germany is defeated would be deeply appreciated." Germany was defeated, and the prized rifle was returned to Hession, who donated it to the NRA. This rifle and its colorful past help us remember the words of George Santayana, "Those who cannot remember the past are condemned to repeat it."

ACKNOWLEDGEMENTS

ACKNOWLEDGEMENTS - DONORS and LENDERS

The collection of the NRA National Firearms Museum has been built over the past three-quarters of a century from donations by individuals, businesses, and organizations with the foresight to preserve America's firearms heritage and to ensure that future generations are educated on the history of Americans and their firearms.

Today, donors are supporting the NRA and the National Firearms Museum through gifts or bequests of guns to the Firearms for Freedom program, nrafff@nrahq.org or (877) NRA GIVE.

All the arms on display in the Museum can be seen at the NRAmuseum.com website.

The NRA and the National Firearms Museum would like to acknowledge those who donated or loaned firearms that appear in this book. In an effort of this scale, with additions, deletions, and changes, some donors and lenders may have been overlooked, and to them we offer our sincere apologies. While we do not list donors and lenders here whose guns are not pictured, we wish to extend our sincere gratitude to them as well.

THE ROBERT E. PETERSEN GALLERY

The 2010 opening of the Petersen Gallery marked the largest gift in NRA history. With over 400 guns donated by the Petersen Estate through Mrs. Margie Petersen, the museum is able to present an exceptional gallery of the finest engraved and historic firearms on display in the country. The Parker Invincible Shotguns are among the Petersen gifts displayed in this book, with more treasures from this famous collection to be included in future volumes.

THE AMERICAN LIBERTY COLLECTION

The minuteman symbol in this book indicates a gun that is part of the American Liberty Collection, donated by Dr. William L. Roberts and Mrs. Collette N. Roberts.

THE ARTISTRY IN ARMS COLLECTION

The circled revolver symbol indicates a gun that is part of the Artistry in Arms Collection, also donated by Dr. William L. Roberts and Mrs. Collette N. Roberts.

THANKS TO THE FOLLOWING WHO DONATED COLLECTIONS PICTURED IN THIS BOOK:

Dr. Harold Cottle

Mrs. Walter Groff

Tom Selleck

Rev. J.B.M. Frederick in memory of his father, Karl T. Frederick

Harmon Leonard

Estate of Max Shaefer

Eldon J. Owens

Maj. Gen. Julian S. Hatcher, U.S. Army

Leon C. Jackson

Lt. Gen. Milton A. Reckord, U.S. Army

Horace Greeley IV

Joel A. Gross

Ruth Strader

The Thomas W. Sefton Trust

Family of Bruce Stern

The Stanley Kellert Trust

Estate of Alan T. Schemm

THANKS TO THE FOLLOWING WHO DONATED ONE OR MORE FIREARMS PICTURED IN THIS BOOK:

Beretta U.S.A.

Sturm, Ruger & Co.

U.S. Army

E. Kiimalehto

Estate of Maj. Gordon Bess, U.S. Army

Joseph S. Kasaveach

Estate of Will Hoffeld

Michael Carrick

Lee L. Coleman

Harold G. Cheetham

C. Thomas Clagett, Jr.

National Park Service

Gary Fisher in memory of his father, Clay Fisher

Estate of Kenneth Tiny Miller

Family of Morgan Vance

Estate of Frank J. Woodworth

Hunter's Lodge

R. Alexander Montgomery

Dorothy A. Briggs in memory of her husband, Alfred Briggs

Estate of John F. Forsyth

Gen. Bryce Poe II, U.S.A.F.

William A. M. Burden IV

Earl Copeland

Val Forgett, Jr.

Colt

United States Department of State

Col. Nguyen Thanh Chuan, Special Forces, A.R.V.N

General P.X. Kelley, U.S.M.C., Ret.

Smith & Wesson

Estate of Lt. Col. William McMillan, U.S.M.C.

Estate of Clifford E. Bjornson

Dwight D. Van Horn

U.S. Post Office Department

Remington Arms

Savage Arms

Winchester-Western

Daisy

President George Herbert Walker Bush

His Royal Highness Charles, Prince of Wales

Crosman Arms Co.

Virginia Military Institute Museum

P.C. Dorsey

Karl Rankin

Robert Phelps

Alden Family in care of William Alden

Delmar Weigel

James E. Serven

Duncan Persons

Michael Zomber

Robert N. Luke in dedication to Ruth E. Dressel

Daisy Ligon

C.R. Gutermuth

Clifford Wetzel

Charlotte Gollobin in memory of Leonard P. Gollobin

Wilson I. Domer

Bertha Herrmann

John W. Johnston

Michael Davenport

Malcolm Colby

Anna McCleaft

G. W. Wilcox

L. R. Johnson

Richard Ellis

Melvin Gordon

Henry D. Palmer

John P. Sowle

Roger J. Muckerheide, Jr., in memory of his friend, Leon C. Red Jackson

Ernest Bell

Tom Bennett

Henry Blumberg in dedication to Glen B. Payne

Merrill W. Wright

Mrs. V.R. Mueller

Raymond E. Dirkin

Archie Walker

Albert C. Ross

George Martian

Max Sweet

Marv Adams

Vernon Berning

Garner D. Hook

Helen Hansen

Estate of Harvey M. Aungst, Jr.

Francis Parker, Jr.

Joseph Cervenka

Mary McDonough in memory of her husband,
    John P. McDonough

Dr. Pierce MacKenzie

Bruce Albert Gustafson

John H. Wesson

L.W.J. Reinger

Estate of Buford McCurry

Eugene A. Ferrand

Gerard Whitmore in memory of John J. McGurk

K. W. Warner, Sr.

Robert A. Yard

E. W. Griffin in memory of G. Carlyle Cooke

William Camp in memory of Mary Catherine Camp

Margaret Greeley

Island Gun Club

John Paty

William Payne

Eva C. (Kay) Tyler in memory of her husband,
    Maj. Donald J. Tyler, U.S.A.F.

Ned Choate

Frank Bulawa

William C. Thum

Estate of Charles F. Seitz, Jr.

Eugene Kjellander

Robert John Hart

Hildalgo Trading Company

James Adams

James Ritchie and Charles Taylor

John J. O'Hara

C. H. Olson

Harry Abernathy

James Murphy

John Macrae

Terry J. Popkin

Lt. Col. F.L. Greaves

Welton M. Modisette

F. Russek

Loma O'Allen

William Frayseth

Col. Townsend Whelen, U.S. Army

A. Mattson

Charles D. Brooks in memory of his father,
    Robert D. Brooks

Estate of Wayne B. McGinnis

Farrel Owen

Herbert Bishop

Robert Topham

Roland Scheffler

David Savadyga

Edson W. Hall

Winfield Arms Co.

Chauncey Williams

David Welch

Donald D. Carruth

Michael Scanlan

Raven E. Corn

Edward Raymond Clark

Franz Schager

Gene Taylor

George F. Steeg

Murray A. Popple

Richard E. Morrell

Robert A. Rolli

Wallace Walford

LCDR Robert D. Hatcher, U.S. Navy

Ronald A. Kosin

Gordon Baxter

Nelson Shultis

Robert Hall

George R. and N. Butonne Repaire Estate and Trust

Nelson Otto Klaner

A. F. Elwell

Alex Brown

Mrs. Calvin Goddard

Charles Stroudt

Charles W. Retz

Stephen W. Popple

Northwest Montana Arms Collectors

Don and Donna Norton

Kenneth E. Harte

Barbara C. Stoller

Edward J. Holba

Edward L. Gruber

Estate of Joseph W. Bell

Page Hufty

Rupert Andrews

J. H. DeFrees

Alan Osbourne
    in memory of his bird dog, Inky Dot

Fred T. Huntington

N.E. Thompson

Adrian Peters

Estate of Ralph Scott

Frank W. Jones

Otto J. Lindo and J.N. Perkins

Fred Rowan

William Salem

Cornelius V.S. Roosevelt

Owen Albert

R.C. Wright

J. Wagram

Clifford Ackerson

Harold E. Johnson

Edith Lauren

J. Cantor

M. Solimene

Willis Bledsoe

F. Bob Chow

J. R. Maxwell

Northwest Montana Arms Collectors Association

B. Beers

David Anderson

Dr. J.A. Smith, Jr.

Mrs. Donald Lewin

Commander Marvin O. Register, U.S. N avy, Ret.

Estate of Glen B. Payne

Mr. and Mrs. August Vander Ley

Thadeus L. Hartman
    with the assistance of Tris Barry

Century Arms Co.

Francis Meyer in dedication to Robert N. Newton

Col. Ralph V. Strauss, U.S. Army

Estate of Glen B. Payne

Titus Crow

Nevylle L. Smith

Winchester

Rueben Brown

Robert L. Baird

Springfield Armory, Inc.

Michael Marcus

Douglas Terrel and CWO4 Allen F. Manley, USN Ret.

John Reichwein

Robert Cox

Joseph L. O. Rubbio

William Boatman

C.E. Gregg

R.J. Buckwald

Estate of Glen B. Payne

Estate of Heer Dohrman

H.P. Abbott

Ida M. Younger

N. Ischkum

W. R. Warner

David Silk

ACKNOWLEDGEMENTS

Gordon Hill

John W. Lindberg

William C. Arthur, Jr.

Karl Funkhouser

Capt. Samuel G. Green, Jr., U.S. Navy

Robert Standish

Estate of Ruth E. Dressel

Dietrich Apel

Maurice A. Long

Ralph DeMarco

Raymond Landgren

Tom Hamon

James W. Davis

Robert Cornell Harriss

Capt. John T. Trussell,
   Metropolitan Police Dept., Washington, DC

Walter Bud Fisher

Charles S. Taylor
   in memory of his father, Charles L. Taylor

H. Dunkle

Paul Wahl

John H. Wesson

Mrs. Eric E. Anschutz

William A. Frederick

Jess C. Steinhauer

Golden State Arms Co.

Burton Brenner

Inter Ordnance

John Hayslip

Bruce Clark

Capt. Montgomery B. Graves

George Arbones

George B. Skidmore

Irv Benzion

J.H. Cosner

Ben Petree

James Beck Estate

B.Gen. Robert M. Gaynor, U.S. Army

James Brown

Malcolm J. MacCallum

Mrs. Francis A. Den Outer

Forest Brooks

Allan Cors

John Finn

Robert Joerg

Carl Hornberger

Lt. Gen. Willis D. Crittenberger, U.S. Army

Susan Nielsen in memory of Peter Nielsen

Frank D. Taylor

Jo Lynn Mohr in memory of her husband,
   Dr. Richard J. Mohr

Tom Caceci

Pacific Coast Stainless Steel German WWII U-Boat
   Flare Pistol Collectors

Edgar Rice Burroughs

Edward A. Baldwin

Estate of George H. Measley, Jr.

Fletcher Williams

Harris Johnson

Doris J. Kramer, with the assistance of Bill Pace

Gail Brophy Barry and William S. Brophy III

Ernestine Bellmore

Fairchild Engine and Airplane Co.

Charles E. Hunt

Colonel James C. Jewel, U.S. Army, Ret.

Estate of Terrence Hoffman

John Walter Moser

Gertrude B. Meyer

Phyllis Hall

John Fust in memory of
   Major General Donn R. Pepke

Jeannine M. Harvey

Arsenal, Inc.

Barrett Firearms Manufacturing Co.

Defense Procurement
   Manufacturing Services, Inc.

Bill J. Boyce

Bruce M. Wincentsen

Bernard Rieck

Donald Keefer

James Frisque

R. Hatcher

Rosco L. Slick

Otto Demplewolf

John Davis

NRA Technical Division

Jack Strader

John Pevear

Leo Manville

Raymond L. Sargent

Estate of Jane R. Taylor

Katherine Lee

Alan Aman

Dan W. Schlernitzauer

Francis Cason Estate

Merchantville Police Department on behalf of
   Glen Steely

Estate of Seymour R. Magee

Firearms International

Hammerli

Interarms

J. R. Cowman

Mr. Rogers

Edward Conrow

Eric R. England

Evelyn Baldwin in memory of Roy Ivan Baldwin

Francis W. Parker III

Thurman Randle

C. Suydam

David W. Arliss, Jr.

National Rifle Association of Great Britain

Wallace Beinfeld

Estate of Art Blatt

G. David Tubb

Richard Martin Ornburn

Anschutz

Jim Carmichel

Dieter Anschutz

Mrs. Frank C. Hoppe

Frank Lege III

Lt. Col. T.D. Smith, U.S.A.F.

Don Nissen

Drs. Lynn and Jerry Parson

Frank E. White

Norman George

Bill Jordan

Estate of David C. Ritchie

George A. Whitehead

Heckler & Koch, Inc.

W.O. Francis A. Higginson, U.S.M.C.

Bradley W. Taylor Collection

Richard Beckman

Family of Michael E. Garbarino

John DiStephano

Penguin Industries in memory of Frank A. Hoppe

W.T. Atkinson

Col. Theodore Shook, U.S. Army

Melvin Gordon

G. Norman Albree

John R. Lucas

Herbert T. Randall

Stockton Rush

Walther Howe

John W. Loosemore

Karel Michalek

Sommer & Ockenfuss

Halton Henderson

Harvey Leibowitz

Ralf E. Dieckmann

Robert Inness

Browning

Dr. William Saunders

James Keller

Noble

B. J. McCausey

H. W. Budd Schroeder

James Cassada, Jr.

Marlin

Armalite Corp.

Edward Hill

Gene's Sporting Center, Inc.

Kenneth L. Martin

Paul B. Miller

R.A. DeByle

W.T. Genetti

Allen Aman

Diamantis Demetriadis

E.P. Burlew

Estate of Harold W. Glassen

Louis F. Klusmeyer

Philip Y. Hahn, Sr.

Robert Hoelscher

Daniel Szatkowski

George H. McDaniel

Glen E. Liddy

Hy-Score

Merlin V. Fox

Sheridan Products, Inc.

Frank Wallace

Gen. Sydney Hinds, U.S. Army

Benjamin Air Rifle Co.

Elliott Jones

Thomas L. Stoughton

Ed Thompson

High Standard

John Kozina Estate

Leonard Cole

Milburn E. (Mel) Estes

Olan W. Christie

Sam Frank

Calico

Harry B. Andree, Jr.

Marlin Firearms Company

Constantine Vontsolos

Estate of Erle Stanley Gardner

Estate of Titus Crow

Gordon Treharne in dedication to Jesse C. Hartzell

Sharps Arms Company

William A. Knight

Sandy Cushman

Weatherby

A.D. Bissel in the name of Mrs. Charles Newton

Orvis C. Hoffman

Sam Friedman

Eileen Cumming

William L. Davies

Estate of Bertha A. Baier

Harold Christensen

Herbert Cox

Jeff Cooper

Gen. John S.D. Eisenhower

Josephine W. Snyder

Peter W. Duvall, Jr.

Robert L. Harper

Sheppard Kelly

Edward Finch

Mrs. Ernie Ford

Art Wheaton in honor of the efforts of
    Richard E. Heckert

Estate of Thomas Wang

Gabilondo y Cia

Joseph V. Falcon

George Whitehead

Robert E. Perry
    in memory of his mother, Elizabeth Jane Perry

Arthur B. Leech

James O. Adams

Mrs. John W. Hessian

Melissa Scott Smith

Savage Arms Company

Union of Shooting Societies of France

D. Phillips

Estate of Leslie P. Drew

THANKS TO THE FOLLOWING WHO HAVE LOANED FIREARMS PICTURED IN THIS BOOK:

The Smithsonian Institution, National Museum of
    American History

Beretta U.S.A.

Robert S. Jepson, Jr.

Michael Carrick

Robert Bonaventure

David Stefanye,
    loaned in his memory by his wife and children

John Milius

Norman Hall

H. Wayne Sheets

Robert H. Plimpton, Edith P. Reynolds Fleeman,
William P. Reynolds, and Katie P. Reynolds

Norman B. Tomlinson Collection
    through the courtesy of the Paterson Museum

Doug Wicklund

Dr. Frederick G. Novy

Valmore Forgett III

Woody Matthews

Micky Reilly Collection

Jacob Yost

Jim Supica

Logan Reed

Bill Miller

N. White

David W Bunn

Director of Civilian Marksmanship

Art Cook

Launi Meili

Norm White

Tom Bass

Philip Schreier

Jessica Sparks

Jason Hill

Doug Kelley

THANKS TO THE FOLLOWING FOR SPONSORSHIP OF MAJOR GALLERIES IN THE MUSEUM:

Estate of Robert E. Petersen

Eldon J. and Edith W. Owens

Beretta USA Corporation and
Benelli USA Corporation

Dr. William L. and Collette N. Roberts

Friends of Charlton Heston

William B. Ruger

INDEX

INDEX

INDEX

INDEX